Normandy & Brittany p95

Paris & Northeastern France p47

Loire Valley & Central France p135

Atlantic Coast p347

Alps, Jura & Rhône Valley p185

Pyrenees & Southwest France p307

Provence & Southeast France p233

Contents cont.

ROAD TRIP ESSENTIALS 412

Basque country Colourful houses in St-Jean de Luz

COVID-19

We have re-checked every business in this book before publication to ensure that it is still open after the COVID-19 outbreak. However, the economic and social impacts of COVID-19 will continue to be felt long after the outbreak has been contained, and many businesses, services and events referenced in this guide may experience ongoing restrictions. Some businesses may be temporarily closed, have changed their opening hours and services, or require bookings; some will unfortunately have closed their doors permanently. We suggest you check with venues before visiting for the latest information.

WELCOME TO
FRANCE

Iconic monuments, island abbeys, fabulous food, world-class wines — there are so many reasons to plan your very own French voyage.

Whether you're planning on cruising the corniches of the French Riviera, getting lost among the snowcapped Alps or tasting your way around Champagne's hallowed vineyards, this is a nation that's made for road trips and full of unforgettable routes that will plunge you straight into France's heart and soul.

There's a trip for everyone here: family travellers, history buffs, culinary connoisseurs, beach bums and outdoors adventurers. And if you've only got time for one trip, why not make it one of our eight Classic Trips, which take you to the very best France has to offer. Turn the page for more.

Buckle up, and bon voyage — you're in for quite a ride.

French Alps Annecy
ALEXANDER DEMYANENKO / SHUTTERSTOCK ©

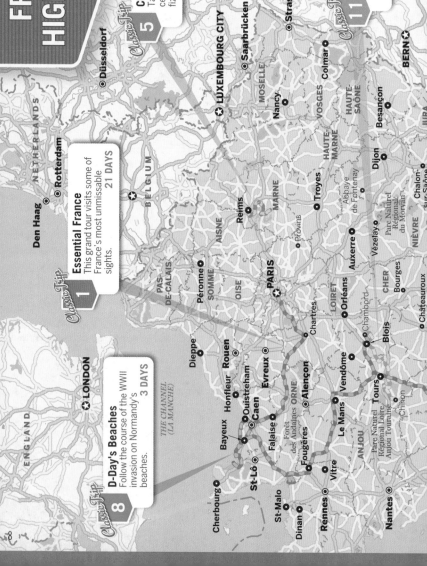

FRANCE HIGHLIGHTS

Classic Trip

5 Champagne Taster
Taste your way around the cellars of Champagne on this fizz-fuelled trip. **3 DAYS**

Classic Trip

11 Châteaux of the Loire
France's greatest châteaux, from medieval towers to royal palaces. **5 DAYS**

Classic Trip

1 Essential France
This grand tour visits some of France's most unmissable sights. **21 DAYS**

Classic Trip

8 D-Day's Beaches
Follow the course of the WWII invasion on Normandy's beaches. **3 DAYS**

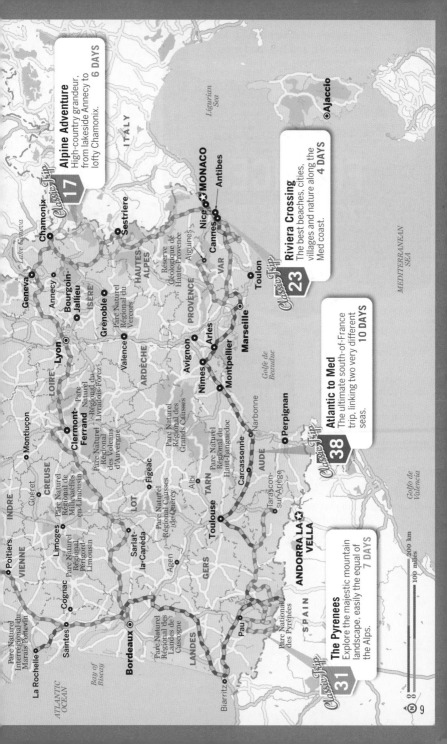

Classic Trip

17

Alpine Adventure
High-country grandeur, from lakeside Annecy to lofty Chamonix. **6 DAYS**

Classic Trip

23

Riviera Crossing
The best beaches, cities, villages and nature along the Med coast. **4 DAYS**

Classic Trip

38

Atlantic to Med
The ultimate south-of-France trip, linking two very different seas. **10 DAYS**

Classic Trip

31

The Pyrenees
Explore the majestic mountain landscape, easily the equal of the Alps. **7 DAYS**

ITALY

Ligurian Sea

○Ajaccio

MEDITERRANEAN SEA

MONACO
Antibes
Nice
Cannes

Sestriere

HAUTES-ALPES

Réserve Géologique de Haute-Provence

Aiguines

VAR

PROVENCE

Toulon

Marseille

Arles

Avignon

Golfe de Beauduc

Nîmes
Montpellier

Narbonne

Perpignan

Golfo de Valencia

Carcassonne

AUDE

Tarascon-sur-Ariège

ANDORRA LA VELLA

SPAIN

Parc National des Pyrénées

Biarritz○

Pau

GERS

Toulouse

Albi

TARN

Parc Naturel Régional du Haut-Languedoc

Parc Naturel Régional des Grands Causses

Agen

LOT

Parc Naturel Régional des Causses du Quercy

Figeac

Sarlat-la-Canéda

Parc Naturel Régional Périgord-Limousin

Bordeaux○

LANDES

Parc Naturel Régional des Landes de Gascogne

Cognac○

Saintes○

Bay of Biscay

ATLANTIC OCEAN

La Rochelle○

Parc Naturel Interrégional du Marais Poitevin

Poitiers○

VIENNE

Limoges

Parc Naturel Régional de Millevaches en Limousin

Guéret○

CREUSE

Montluçon○

INDRE

Clermont-Ferrand

Parc Naturel Régional des Volcans d'Auvergne

Parc Naturel Régional Livradois-Forez

LOIRE

Lyon○

Valence

ARDÈCHE

Parc Naturel Régional du Vercors

Grenoble

ISÈRE

Bourgoin-Jallieu○

Annecy

Geneva○

Lake Geneva

Chamonix○

100 miles
200 km

N

9

FRANCE
HIGHLIGHTS

Paris

What is there to say about the City of Light that hasn't been said a thousand times before? Quite simply, this is one of the world's essential cities: sexy, suave, sophisticated and more than a little snooty. There's a lifetime of experiences here, from the treasures of the Louvre to the cafes of Montmartre – but you'll need nerves of steel to brave the traffic.

Trip 1

Paris Cafe culture

HIGHLIGHTS ★

Pyrenees Vallée d'Ossau

Vézère Valley

Prehistoric people left an astonishing legacy of paintings and sculptures in the caves of the Vézère Valley. These artworks provide a glimpse into the lives of our ancient ancestors – but opinion is divided on what purpose they served. Were they sacred works imbued with magical significance or simply prehistoric posters? The truth is, no one knows. Decide for yourself on **Trip 35: Cave Art of the Vézère Valley**.

Trip 35

Mont St-Michel

Perched on an island and connected to the Norman coast by a causeway, this 11th-century abbey is one of France's most recognisable sights. Crowned by spires, ringed by ramparts and thronged by crowds, it looks like it's fallen from the pages of a fairy tale. It's a long climb to the top, but the views are worth every step. We've linked it with other unmissable sights in **Trip 1: Essential France**.

Trip 1

D-Day Beaches

On 6 June 1944 the largest invasion the world has ever seen stormed ashore the beaches of Normandy. Now known as D-Day, this audacious assault marked the turning point of WWII, and on **Trip 8: D-Day's Beaches**, you'll see many reminders of the fateful campaign – from the forbidding guns of Longues-sur-Mer to the moving cemetery above Omaha Beach.

Trip 8

Mont St-Michel Island abbey off the Norman coast

BEST ROADS FOR DRIVING

Riviera Crossing Cliff roads, sparkling seas, the drive of a lifetime. **Trip** 23

Gorges du Tarn Drive through a dramatic ravine in the Cévennes hills. **Trip** 28

Route des Vins d'Alsace Meander among vines with views of the Vosges. **Trip** 6

Col de l'Iseran Brave the Alps' highest road pass. **Trip** 17

The Lot Valley Cruise limestone cliffs beside the Lot River. **Trip** 37

Pyrenees

With their lofty passes and wide-open skies, the Pyrenees have the wow factor. Running along the Franco–Spanish border, they're home to some of the nation's wildest landscapes and some of its hairiest roads – although the closest you'll get to a traffic jam here is finding yourself stuck behind a herd of cows. Take **Trip 31: The Pyrenees** through quiet valleys, traditional villages and mountain-top observatories.

Trip 31

13

French Riviera Côte d'Azur

French Riviera

If it's a top-down, open-road, wind-in-your-hair drive you're after, there's only one corner of France that hits the mark and that's the flashy Riviera. Synonymous with glitz and glamour since the 19th century, it's still one of Europe's most fashionable spots. **Trip 23: Riviera Crossing** twists through hilltop towns and hairpin-bend roads – just remember to pack a camera and a pair of shades.

Trips 23 24

BEST TOWNS FOR WINE LOVERS

Beaune The heart and soul of Burgundy wine. **Trip** 15

St-Émilion Winemakers outnumber residents in this honey-stoned town. **Trip** 38

Bergerac Lesser-known vintages on the edge of the Dordogne. **Trip** 34

Épernay Tour the cellars of Champagne's classic brands. **Trip** 5

Colmar Sip Alsatian wines with a view of the canals. **Trip** 6

Provence The hilltop village of Gordes

Champagne Vineyards near Reims

Hilltop Villages

From red-roofed hamlets to hillside hideaways, France's *villages perchés* will be a highlight of your trip. Most are medieval and replete with flower-filled lanes, hidden courtyards and quiet squares. Life ticks along at a snail's pace, and there's nowhere better to settle in for a leisurely lunch. **Trip 22: Lavender Route** travels through some of Provence's prettiest villages.

Trips 6 19 22 36

Châteaux of the Loire

For sky's-the-limit extravagance, don't miss **Trip 11: Châteaux of the Loire**. Constructed by France's aristocratic elite between the 15th and 17th centuries, these lavish mansions were designed to show off their owners' wealth – something they managed to achieve in spectacular fashion. Chambord's the jewel in the crown, but there are many more to visit.

Trip 11

Champagne Vineyards

Let's face it – celebrations wouldn't be the same without a bottle of bubbly. The world's most exclusive tipple is produced from a handful of Champagne vineyards, many of which offer tours and the chance to taste the fruits of their labour. **Trip 5: Champagne Taster** takes in tiny family producers as well as big-name châteaux around Épernay and Reims.

Trip 5

17

The Camargue

Sprawling across the western edge of Provence, this huge natural wetland is a paradise for nature lovers, with its population of seabirds, wild horses and pink flamingos. **Trip 27: The Camargue** takes a leisurely wander along the back roads, with plenty of time factored in along the way to immerse yourself in the unique cowboy culture.

Trip 27

Brittany's Coastline

Golden beaches, surf-battered cliffs, quiet creeks, lonely lighthouses – **Trip 9: Breton Coast** is one long parade of postcard views. Some stretches of the coastline are busy, others feel wonderfully wild and empty – so plan your route, pack a decent map and just hit the Breton road.

Trip 9

(left) **Pont du Gard** Huge Roman aqueduct near Nimes

(below) **Camargue** Flamingos in Parc Ornithologique de Pont de Gau

Pont du Gard

The scale of this Roman aqueduct is astonishing: 35 arches straddle the 275m upper tier, and it once carried 20,000 cu metres of water per day. View it from beside the Gard River, clamber along the top deck, or arrive after dark to see it lit up in impressive fashion. It marks the start of **Trip 28: Pont du Gard to Viaduc de Millau**, which travels through the Cévennes to another amazing bridge.

Trip 28

BEST HILLTOP VILLAGES

Gordes The quintessential Provençal village. **Trip** 22

Vézelay Get spiritual in this ancient pilgrim village. **Trip** 14

St-Paul de Vence Dreamy Med vistas that drew countless artists. **Trip** 23

St-Jean Pied de Port Fortified town overlooking the Spanish border. **Trip** 32

IF YOU LIKE...

Camembert Cheese-trail marker

Art

Impressionist masterpieces, modernist marvels, landmark museums – France's astonishing artistic legacy is guaranteed to be one of the most memorable parts of your trip.

2 A Toast to Art

Inspiring architecture meets cutting-edge art on this trip via the new Louvre-Lens museum, the Centre Pompidou-Metz and Nancy's art nouveau architecture.

7 Monet's Normandy

Cruise through the countryside that inspired the impressionists, finishing with a walk around Monet's own lily garden.

21 Roman Provence

Experience Provence's fantastic Roman legacy, with exceptionally well-preserved ruins integrated into modern cities.

French Cuisine

French food might be synonymous with sophistication, but there's more to this foodie nation than fine dining – there's a whole culinary culture to experience, whether that's guzzling oysters, hunting for truffles, savouring cheeses or buying fresh baguettes from a village *boulangerie* (bakery).

10 Tour des Fromages

Taste your way around Normandy's world-famous cheeses – Camembert, Pont L'Évêque, Livarot and more.

34 Gourmet Dordogne

For rich French food, there's nowhere like the Dordogne, the spiritual home of foie gras and the black truffle.

20 Rhône Valley Fill up

on Lyonnaise cuisine in a cosy *bouchon* (small bistro), then head for Montélimar to indulge in nougat treats.

Nature

With seven national parks and a host of other protected areas, France's natural landscapes are ripe for outdoor adventure.

17 Alpine Adventure

Hike trails and spot wildlife among the peaks and ski resorts of France's highest mountain chain.

26 Corsican Coast

Cruiser Escape the French mainland for a cruise around the wild landscapes and coastline of Corsica, aptly named the Île de Beauté.

13 Volcanoes of the

Auvergne Discover this chain of extinct volcanoes that stretches across much of central France.

23 Riviera Crossing Keep

your eyes peeled for pink flamingos and wild horses in France's largest wetlands.

Versailles France's majestic palace

Wine Tasting

If there's one thing France knows about, it's wine. Viticulture has been a cornerstone of French culture for hundreds of years, and the merest mention of the nation's top vineyards makes even hardened sommeliers go weak at the knees.

5 Champagne Taster

Cellars echo to the sound of popping corks on this effervescent adventure through Champagne's hallowed brands.

15 Route des Grands Crus Few regions command more cachet in the wine world than Burgundy. Follow the trail along the Côte de Nuits and Côte d'Or.

6 Alsace Accents

Glossy vines and traditional villages form the backdrop to this meander along the Route des Vins d'Alsace.

Architecture

France has never been shy about showing off its taste for extravagant architecture. Castles and palaces, abbeys and cathedrals – France offers them all, and more.

11 Châteaux of the Loire

Resplendent châteaux line the banks of the Loire, each one more extravagant than the last.

1 Essential France

From Mont St-Michel to the palace of Versailles, this route explores France's unmissable sights.

30 Cheat's Compostela

Tick off churches and cathedrals along the old pilgrim route from Le Puy-en-Velay to St-Jean Pied de Port.

29 The Cathar Trail

Trek across the parched Languedoc plains, which feature crumbling fortresses and hilltop strongholds.

Historic Sites

With a history stretching back several millennia, it's little wonder that France is littered with reminders of its past – both ancient and recent.

21 Roman Provence

Travel back to the heyday of Gaul with an expedition around southern France's Roman ruins.

14 Medieval Burgundy

Once an independent duchy, Burgundy is home to marvellous medieval buildings and timeless villages.

4 In Flanders Fields

Take an emotional tour around the battlegrounds and cemeteries of the Great War.

8 D-Day's Beaches

The events of D-Day still resonate along the beaches of Normandy, while museums and memorials provide historical context.

NEED ^{TO} KNOW

CURRENCY
Euro (€)

LANGUAGE
French

VISAS
Visas are not required for stays of up to 90 days for travellers from 62 non-EU countries.

FUEL
Petrol stations are common around main towns and larger towns. Unleaded costs around €1.40 per litre; *gazole* (diesel) is usually at least €0.15 cheaper.

RENTAL CARS
Auto Europe (www. autoeurope.com)

Avis (www.avis.com)

Europcar (www.europcar. com)

Hertz (www.hertz.com)

IMPORTANT NUMBERS
Ambulance (SAMU; ☎15)

Police (☎17)

Fire (☎18)

Europe-wide emergency (☎112)

Climate

Brittany & Normandy ●
GO Apr–Sep

● **Paris**
GO May & Jun

● **French Alps**
GO late Dec–early Apr (skiing) or Jun & Jul (hiking)

French Riviera ●
GO Apr–Jun, Sep & Oct

Corsica ●
GO Apr–Jun, Sep & Oct

Warm to hot summers, mild winters
Warm to hot summers, cold winters
Mild year-round
Mild summers, cold winters
Alpine climate

When to Go

High Season (Jul & Aug)
» Queues at big sights and on roads.

» Christmas, New Year and Easter equally busy.

» Late December to March is high season in Alpine ski resorts.

» Book accommodation and restaurants in advance.

Shoulder (Apr–Jun & Sep)
» Accommodation rates drop in southern France and other hot spots.

» Spring brings warm weather, flowers and local produce.

» The *vendange* (grape harvest) is reason to visit in autumn.

Low Season (Oct–Mar)
» Prices up to 50% lower than high season.

» Sights, attractions and restaurants open fewer days and shorter hours.

» Hotels and restaurants in rural regions (like the Dordogne) close.

Your Daily Budget

Budget: Less than €130

» Dorm bed: €18–30

» Double room in a budget hotel: €60–90

» Admission to many attractions first Sunday of month: free

» Lunch *menus*: less than €20

Midrange: €130–220

» Double room in a midrange hotel: €90–190

» Lunch *menus* in gourmet restaurants: €20–40

Top end: More than €220

» Double room in a top-end hotel: €190–350

» Top restaurant dinner: *menu* €65, à la carte €100–150

Eating

Restaurants and bistros
Range from traditional to contemporary minimalist; urban dining is international, rural dining staunchly French.

Brasseries Open from dawn until late, these casual eateries are great for dining in between standard meal times.

Cafes Ideal for breakfast and light lunch; many morph into bars after dark.

Price ranges refer to the average cost of a two-course meal:

€	less than €20
€€	€20–40
€€€	more than €40

Sleeping

B&Bs Enchanting properties with maximum five rooms.

Hostels New-wave hostels are design-driven, lifestyle spaces

with single/double rooms as well as dorms.

Hotels Hotels embrace every budget and taste. Refuges and *gîtes d'étape* (walkers' lodges) for hikers on trails in mountainous areas.

Price ranges refer to a double room in high season, with private bathroom, excluding breakfast:

€	less than €90
€€	€90–190
€€€	more than €190

Arriving in France

Aéroport de Charles de Gaulle (Paris)
Trains, buses and RER suburban trains run to the city centre every 15 to 30 minutes between 5am and 11pm, after which night buses kick in (12.30am to 5.30am). Fares are €10.30 by RER and €2 to €13.70 by bus. Flat fare of €53/58 for 30-minute taxi journey to Right/Left Bank central Paris (15% higher between 5pm and 10am, and Sundays).

Aéroport d'Orly (Paris)
Linked to central Paris by Orlyval rail then RER (€12.10) or bus (€2 to €9.50) every 15 minutes between 5am and 11pm. Or T7 tram to Villejuif-Louis Aragon then metro to the centre (€3.80). The 25-minute journey by taxi costs €32/37 to Right/Left Bank central Paris (15% higher between 5pm and 10am, and Sundays).

Mobile Phones

European and Australian phones work, but only American cells with 900 and 1800 MHz networks are compatible. Use a French SIM card with a French number to make cheaper calls.

Internet Access

Wi-fi is available at major airports, in most hotels, and at many cafes, restaurants, museums and tourist offices.

Money

ATMs at every airport, most train stations and on every second street corner in towns and cities. Visa, MasterCard and Amex widely accepted.

Tipping

By law, restaurant and bar prices are *service compris* (ie include a 15% service charge), so there's no need to leave a *pourboire* (tip).

Useful Websites

French Government Tourist Office (www.france.fr) Sights, activities, transport and special-interest holidays.

Lonely Planet (www.lonelyplanet.com/france) Travel tips, accommodation and more.

Mappy (www.mappy.fr) Mapping and journey planning.

Opening Hours

Banks 9am–noon and 2–5pm Monday to Friday or Tuesday to Saturday

Restaurants noon–2.30pm and 7–11pm six days a week

Cafes 7am–11pm

Bars 7pm–1am

Clubs 10pm–3am, 4am or 5am Thursday to Saturday

Shops 10am–noon and 2–7pm Monday to Saturday

For more, see France Driving Guide (p413).

CITY GUIDE

PARIS

If ever a city needed no introduction, it's Paris – a trendsetter, fashion former and style icon for centuries and still very much at the cutting edge. Whether you're here to tick off the landmarks or seek out the secret corners, Paris fulfils all your expectations and leaves you wanting more.

Paris Musée d'Orsay

Getting Around

Driving in Paris is a nightmare. Happily, there's no need for a car. The metro is fast, frequent and efficient; tickets cost €1.90 (day passes €11.15) and are valid on the city's buses. Bikes can be hired from 1330 Vélib' (www.velib-metropole.fr) stations; insert a credit card, authorise a €300 deposit and pedal away. Day passes cost €5; first 30 minutes free, subsequent 30 minutes from €1.

Parking

Meters don't take coins; use a chip-enabled credit card. Municipal car parks cost €2 to €3.50 an hour, or €20 to €25 per 24 hours.

Where to Eat

Le Marais is one of the best areas for eating out, with its small restaurants and trendy bistros. Don't miss Paris' street markets: Marché Bastille, rue Montorgueil and rue Mouffetard are full of atmosphere.

Where to Stay

Base yourself in Montmartre for Parisian charm, if you don't mind crowds. Le Marais and Bastille provide style on a budget, while St-Germain is good for a splurge.

Useful Websites

Paris Info (www.parisinfo.com) Comprehensive tourist authority website.

Sortiraparis (www.sortiraparis.com) Up-to-date calendar listing what's on around town.

Secrets of Paris (www.secretsofparis.com) Online resources and more.

HiP Paris (www.hipparis.com) Vacation rentals, articles and reviews by expat locals.

Trips Through Paris

TOP EXPERIENCES

➡ Eiffel Tower at Twilight

Any time is a good time to take in the panorama from the top of the 'Metal Asparagus' (as Parisians snidely call it) – but the twilight view is extra special (www.toureiffel.fr).

➡ Musée du Louvre

France's greatest repository of art, sculpture and artefacts, the Louvre is a must-visit – but don't expect to see it all in a day (www.louvre.fr).

➡ Basilique du Sacré-Coeur

Climb inside the cupola of this Montmartre landmark for one of the best cross-city vistas (www.sacre-coeur-montmartre.com).

➡ Musée d'Orsay

Paris' second-most-essential museum, with a fabulous collection encompassing originals by Cézanne, Degas, Monet, Van Gogh and more (www.musee-orsay.fr).

➡ Cathédrale de Notre Dame

Peer over Paris from the north tower of this Gothic landmark, surrounded by gargoyles and flying buttresses (www.cathedraledeparis.com).

➡ Les Catacombes

Explore more than 2km of tunnels beneath the streets of Montparnasse, lined with the bones and skulls of millions of Parisians (www.catacombes.paris.fr).

➡ Cimetière Père-Lachaise

Oscar Wilde, Édith Piaf, Marcel Proust and Jim Morrison are just a few of the famous names buried in this wildly overgrown cemetery (www.pere-lachaise.com).

➡ Canal St-Martin

Join the locals for a walk or bike ride along the towpaths of this 4.5km canal, once derelict but now reborn as a haven from the city hustle.

Lyon Local *bouchon*

LYON

For centuries, Lyon has served as a crossroads between France's south and north, as well as a gateway to the nearby Alps. A commercial and industrial powerhouse for over 500 years, it's now a cosmopolitan and sophisticated city, with some outstanding museums and a notoriously lively nightlife.

Getting Around

Cars aren't much use for getting around Lyon itself. The same €1.90 tickets are valid on all the city's public transport, including buses, trams, the four-line metro and the two funiculars linking Vieux Lyon to Fourvière and St-Just. Day passes cost €6.20.

Parking

As always, parking is expensive, so pick a hotel with a private car park if you're planning on arriving with wheels.

Where to Eat

The classic place to eat in Lyon is a *bouchon* (literally, 'bottle stopper'), a small, cosy bistro that cooks up regional cuisine such as *boudin blanc* (veal sausage) and *quenelles de brochet* (pike dumplings in a creamy crayfish sauce). Afterwards, browse the stalls of the city's wonderful covered market, Les Halles de Lyon.

Where to Stay

Vieux Lyon and Presqu'Île both have a fantastic range of hotels and guesthouses that combine old Lyonnaise architecture with modern style. Croix Rousse is the handiest area for visiting the Roman remains around Fourvière.

Useful Websites

City of Lyon (www.lyon.fr)
My Little Lyon (www. mylittle.fr/mylittlelyon)
Petit Paume (www. petitpaume.com)

Trips Through Lyon

 1 **20**

Lille Place du General du Gaulle

LILLE

Lille may be France's most underrated major city. This once-tired industrial metropolis has transformed itself into a stylish, self-confident city with a strong Flemish accent. Three art museums, lots of fashionable shops and a lovely old town make it well worthy of investigation.

Getting Around

Driving into Lille is incredibly confusing, even with a good map; just suspend your sense of direction and blindly follow the 'Centre Ville' signs. Lille's buses and two speedy metro lines run until about 12.30am. Tickets cost €1.70; a Pass' Journée (all-day pass) costs €5.

Parking

If you're driving, the best idea is to leave your vehicle at the park-and-ride at Champ de Mars on bd de la Liberté (open from 10am to 6pm or 7pm, closed Saturdays and Sundays, September to March), 1.2km northwest of the centre. It costs €4 a day and includes return travel for five people to central Lille on bus 12.

Where to Eat

Lille's proximity to Belgium has influenced its cuisine. Cosy *estaminets* (Flemish eateries) serve Lillois specialities such as *carbonade* (braised beef stewed with beer, spiced bread and brown sugar) and *potjevleesch* (jellied chicken, pork, veal and rabbit).

Where to Stay

Most hotels are within striking distance of the city centre, but Lille's business focus means many are short on charm. On the plus side, rates drop at weekends.

Useful Websites

Lille Tourisme (www.lilletourism.com)

Trips Through Lille

NICE

The classic metropolis of the French Riviera, Nice has something to suit all moods: exceptional museums, atmospheric street markets, glittering Mediterranean beaches and a rabbit-warren old town, all bathed in radiant year-round sunshine. With its blend of city grit and old-world opulence, it deserves as much time as you can spare.

Getting Around

The complicated one-way system and heavy traffic can make driving in Nice stressful, especially in the heat of summer. Walking is the easiest way to get around. There's a handy tram line from the train station all the way to Vieux Nice and place Garibaldi; tickets cost €1.50 and are valid on buses.

Parking

Nearly all parking in Nice is *payant* (chargeable) – assuming you manage to find a space. Car parks are usually cheapest (around €2 to €3 per hour, or €17 to €30 per day). All parking meters take coins; car-park pay stations also accept credit cards.

Nice Promenade des Anglais

TOP EXPERIENCES

⇒ Strolling the Promenade des Anglais
Join sun worshippers, inline skaters and dog walkers on this magnificent boulevard, which runs right along Nice's shimmering seafront.

⇒ Musée Matisse
Just 2km north of the centre, this excellent art museum documents the life and work of Henri Matisse in painstaking detail. You'll need good French to get the most out of your visit (www.musee-matisse-nice.org).

⇒ Shopping on Cours Saleya
This massive market captures the essence of Niçois life. A chaotic assortment of stalls sells everything from fresh-cut flowers to fresh fish.

⇒ Parc du Château
Pack a picnic and head to this hilltop park for a panorama across Nice's red-tiled rooftops.

Where to Eat
Head for the alleyways of Vieux Nice (Old Nice) for the most authentic neighbourhood restaurants. Don't miss the local specialities of *socca* (chickpea-flour pancake), *petits farcis* (stuffed vegetables) and *pissaladière* (onion tart topped with black olives and anchovies).

Where to Stay
Old town equals atmosphere, but for the best views and classiest rooms you'll want to base yourself near the seafront – the Promenade des Anglais has several landmark hotels. The city's cheapest hotels are clustered around the train station.

Useful Websites
Nice Tourisme (http://en.nicetourisme. com)

Trips Through Nice 23 38

FRANCE
BY REGION

From rugged mountain roads to quiet country lanes, France is a driver's dream. Here's your guide to what each region has to offer, along with suggestions for our top road trips.

Normandy & Brittany

Welcome to two of France's most charming and varied regions. History buffs will make a beeline for the D-Day beaches; culture vultures will follow the steps of Monet in Giverny or marvel at Rouen's medieval old city; and food lovers will sample cheese, cider, seafood and crêpes. And if you're after dramatic landscapes, the Breton coast beckons.

Follow the Breton coast on Trip `9`

Loire Valley & Central France

The Loire is rightly famous for its châteaux, but there's more here than over-the-top architecture. A world of wine awaits in Burgundy, and the region's medieval heritage is a must for history buffs. Meanwhile, volcanic vistas unfold in the Auvergne, perhaps France's most undiscovered corner.

Taste grand cru wine on Trip `15`

Atlantic Coast

France's wonderfully varied west coast stretches from the vineyards of Bordeaux down to the busy beach towns of Arcachon and Biarritz. The southwest is a stronghold of French Basque culture, while the Dordogne and the Lot Valley offer a dreamy vision of the French countryside.

Hunt for truffles on Trip `34`

Paris & Northeastern France

No French trip would be complete without Paris, still one of the world's most vital cities. Beyond the capital, you could explore artistic connections in Nancy, home of art nouveau, tour Alsatian vineyards, visit prestigious Champagne cellars in Épernay or delve into the region's war-ravaged past in the fields of Flanders.

Quaff Champagne on Trip

Alps, Jura & Rhône Valley

Mountains spiral skywards and the roads get ever higher as you drive through the Alps and the Jura, both alive with outdoor possibilities. Brave the slopes and hike the trails, then head into the Rhône Valley for hearty food and postcard-pretty villages.

Enjoy sky-high views on Trip 17

Eat in bouchons on Trip 20

Provence & Southeast France

Sparkling beaches, glitzy towns, hilltop hamlets, lavender fields: Provence is the stuff of French-themed dreams. Cruise the corniches, head inland for Roman ruins and Provençal markets, and if you're feeling adventurous, the wild island of Corsica is only a boat ride away.

Follow the Riviera on Trip

Pyrenees & Southwest France

Straddling the Franco–Spanish border, the valleys and passes of the Pyrenees make for fantastic driving, but you'll need to keep your eyes on the road. Switch to the slow lane in the Languedoc, with its laid-back pace, Cathar castles and pilgrims' churches.

Head to the hills on Trip

FRANCE
Classic Trips

23

What is a Classic Trip?

All the trips in this book show you the best of France, but we've chosen eight as our all-time favourites. These are our Classic Trips – the ones that lead you to the best of the iconic sights, the top activities and uniquely French experiences.

Above: Nice
Left: Aiguille du Midi cable car, Chamonix

Classic Trip

Essential France

City to city, coast to coast, this grand tour visits some of France's most unmissable sights. There's some epic driving involved, but this is one trip you won't forget in a hurry.

1

TRIP HIGHLIGHTS

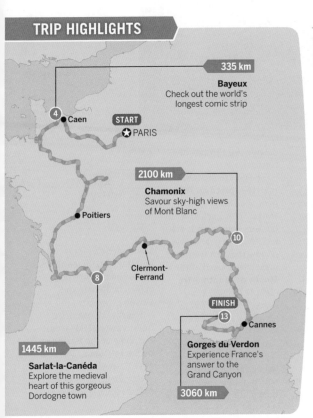

335 km
Bayeux
Check out the world's longest comic strip

4 ● Caen

START
⭐ PARIS

2100 km
Chamonix
Savour sky-high views of Mont Blanc

● Poitiers

10

Clermont-Ferrand

8

FINISH
13
● Cannes

1445 km

Sarlat-la-Canéda
Explore the medieval heart of this gorgeous Dordogne town

Gorges du Verdon
Experience France's answer to the Grand Canyon

3060 km

3 WEEKS
3060KM / 1902 MILES

GREAT FOR...

BEST TIME TO GO
April to June for sunny weather, longer days and flowers.

 ESSENTIAL PHOTO

Overlooking the Parisian panorama from the Basilique du Sacré-Coeur.

✓ **BEST FOR FAMILIES**

Braving the space-age rides and roller-coaster thrills of Futuroscope.

1 Essential France

This is the big one – an epic trek that travels all the way from the chilly waters of the English Channel to the gleaming blue Mediterranean. Along the way, you'll stop off at some of France's most iconic sights: the château of Versailles, the abbey of Mont St-Michel, the summit of Mont Blanc and the beaches of the French Riviera. *Allez-y!*

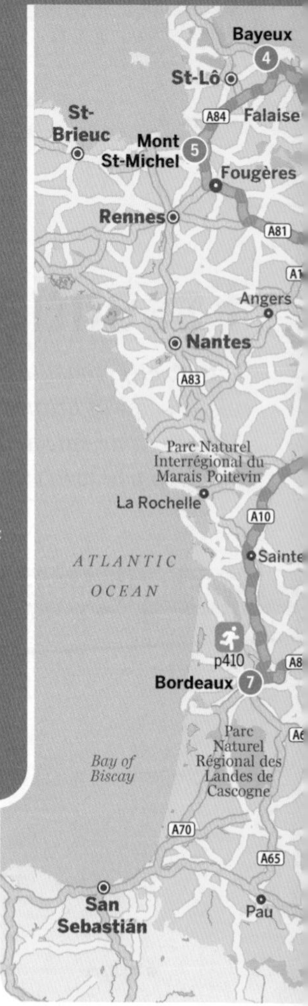

Bayeux ④
St-Lô
St-Brieuc
Mont St-Michel ⑤
Falaise
Fougères
Rennes
Angers
Nantes
Parc Naturel Interrégional du Marais Poitevin
La Rochelle
Sainte
ATLANTIC OCEAN
p410
Bordeaux ⑦
Parc Naturel Régional des Landes de Cascogne
Bay of Biscay
San Sebastián
Pau

① Paris

For that essentially Parisian experience, it's hard to beat Montmartre – the neighbourhood of cobbled lanes and cafe-lined squares beloved by writers and painters since the 19th century. This was once a notoriously ramshackle part of Paris, full of bordellos, brothels, dance halls and bars, as well as the city's first can-can clubs. Though its hedonistic heyday has long since passed, Montmartre still retains a villagey charm, despite the throngs of tourists.

The centre of Montmartre is **place du Tertre**, once the village's main square, now packed with buskers and portrait artists. You can get a sense of how the area would once have looked at the **Musée de Montmartre** (☎01 49 25 89 39; www.museedemontmartre.fr; 12 rue Cortot, 18e; adult/child €13/7, garden only €5; ☺11am-6pm Wed-Fri, to 7pm Sat & Sun Apr-Sep, to 6pm Wed-Sun Oct-Mar; Ⓜ Lamarck–Caulaincourt), which details the area's bohemian past. It's inside Montmartre's oldest building, a 17th-century manor house once occupied by Renoir and Utrillo.

Nearby, Montmartre's finest view unfolds from the dome of the **Basilique du Sacré-Coeur** (☎01 53 41 89 00; www.sacre-coeur-montmartre.com; Parvis du Sacré-Cœur, 18e; basilica

free, dome adult/child €6/4;
⏱ basilica 6am-10.30pm,
dome 10.30am-8.30pm;
Ⓜ Anvers, Abbesses). On a
clear day, you can see for
up to 30km.

✗ ⌂ p44

The Drive ››› From the centre
of Paris, follow the A13 west
from Porte d'Auteuil and take
the exit marked 'Versailles

LINK YOUR TRIP

17 Alpine Adventures

Chamonix features on
our Alps trip, so it's
easy to launch a cross-
mountain adventure
from there.

23 Riviera Crossing

Combine this
journey with our jaunt
down the French Riviera,
which begins in Cannes.

Château'. Versailles is 28km southwest of the city.

---

❷ Versailles

Louis XIV transformed his father's hunting lodge into the **Château de Versailles** (☎01 30 83 78 00; www.chateauversailles.fr; place d'Armes; adult/child passport ticket incl estate-wide access €20/free, with musical events €27/free, palace €18/free except during musical events; ⊙9am-6.30pm Tue-Sun Apr-Oct, to 5.30pm Tue-Sun Nov-Mar; ⓂRER Versailles-Château–Rive Gauche) in the mid-17th century, and it remains France's most majestic palace. The royal court was based here from 1682 until 1789, when revolutionaries massacred the palace

guard and dragged Louis XVI and Marie Antoinette back to Paris, where they were ingloriously guillotined.

The architecture is truly eye-popping. Highlights include the **Grands Appartements du Roi et de la Reine** (State Apartments) and the famous **Galerie des Glaces** (Hall of Mirrors), a 75m-long ballroom filled with chandeliers and floor-to-ceiling mirrors. Outside, the vast park incorporates terraces, flower beds, paths and fountains, as well as the **Grand and Petit Canals**.

Northwest of the main palace is the **Domaine de Trianon** (Trianon Estate; www.chateauversailles.fr; Château de Versailles; adult/child €12/free, with passport ticket free; ⊙noon-6.30pm Tue-Sun Apr-Oct, to 5.30pm Tue-Sat Nov-Mar), where the royal family would have

taken refuge from the intrigue and etiquette of court life.

The Drive 》 The N10 runs southwest from Versailles through pleasant countryside and forest to Rambouillet. You'll join the D906 to Chartres. All told, it's a journey of 76km.

---

❸ Chartres

You'll know you're nearing Chartres long before you reach it thanks to the twin spires of the **Cathédrale Notre Dame** (www.cathedrale-chartres.org; place de la Cathédrale; ⊙8.30am-7.30pm daily year-round, also to 10pm Tue, Fri & Sun Jul & Aug), considered to be one of the most important structures in Christendom.

The present cathedral was built during the late 12th century after the original was destroyed by fire. It's survived wars and revolutions remarkably intact, and the brilliant-blue stained-glass windows have even inspired their own shade of paint (Chartres blue). The cathedral also houses the Sainte Voile (Holy Veil), supposedly worn by the Virgin Mary while giving birth to Jesus.

The best views are from the 112m-high **Clocher Neuf** (North Tower; Cathédrale Notre Dame; adult/child €6/free; ⊙10am-12.30pm & 2-6pm Mon-Sat, 2-6pm Sun May-Aug, shorter hours Sep-Apr).

VISITING VERSAILLES

Versailles is one of the country's most popular destinations, so planning ahead will make your visit more enjoyable. Avoid the busiest days of Tuesday and Sunday, and remember that the château is closed on Monday. Save time by pre-purchasing tickets on the château's website, or arrive early if you're buying at the door – by noon queues spiral out of control.

You can also access off-limits areas (such as the Private Apartments of Louis XV and Louis XVI, the Opera House and the Royal Chapel) by taking a 90-minute **guided tour** (☎01 30 83 77 88; www.chateauversailles.fr; Château de Versailles; tours €10, plus palace entry).

✕ 🛏 p44

The Drive » Follow the D939 northwest for 58km to Verneuil-sur-Avre, then take the D926 west for 78km to Argentan – both great roads through typical Norman countryside. Just west of Argentan, the D158/N158 heads north to Caen, then turns northwest on the N13 to Bayeux, 94km further.

_ _ _ _ _ _ _ _ _ _ _ _ _ _ _

TRIP HIGHLIGHT

❹ Bayeux

The **Bayeux Tapestry** (La Tapisserie de Bayeux; 📞 02 31 51 25 50; www.bayeuxmuseum. com; 15bis rue de Nesmond; adult/child €9.50/7.50; ⌚ 9.30am-12.30pm & 2-6pm, closed Jan) is without doubt the world's most celebrated (and ambitious) piece of embroidery. Over 58 panels, the tapestry recounts the invasion of England in 1066 by William I, or William the Conqueror, as he's now known.

Commissioned in 1077 by Bishop Odo of Bayeux, William's half-brother, the tapestry retells the battle in fascinating detail: look out for Norman horses getting stuck in the quicksands around Mont St-Michel, and the famous appearance of Halley's Comet in scene 32. The final showdown at the Battle of Hastings is particularly graphic, complete with severed limbs, decapitated heads, and the English King Harold getting an arrow in the eye.

The Drive » Mont St-Michel is 125km southwest of Bayeux; the fastest route is along the D6 and then the A84 motorway.

_ _ _ _ _ _ _ _ _ _ _ _ _ _ _

❺ Mont St-Michel

You've already seen it on a million postcards, but nothing prepares you for the real **Mont St-Michel** (📞 02 33 89 80 00; www.abbaye-mont-saint-michel.fr/en; adult/child incl guided tour €11/free; ⌚ 9am-7pm May-Aug, 9.30am-6pm Sep-Apr, last entry 1hr before closing). It's one of France's architectural marvels, an 11th-century island abbey marooned in the middle of a vast bay.

When you arrive, you'll be steered into one of the Mont's huge car parks. You then walk along the causeway (or catch a free shuttle bus) to the island itself. Guided tours are included, or you can explore solo with an audioguide.

The **Église Abbatiale** (Abbey Church) is reached via a steep climb along the **Grande Rue**. Around the church, the cluster of buildings known as **La Merveille** (The Marvel) includes the cloister, refectory, guest hall, ambulatory and various chapels.

For a different perspective, take a guided walk across the sands with **Découverte de la Baie du Mont-Saint-Michel** (📞 02 33 70 83 49; www.decouvertebaie.com; 1 rue Montoise, Genêts; adult/child from

€10/5.50; ⌚ 9am-12.30pm & 1.30-6pm daily Apr-Oct, Mon-Fri Nov-Mar) or **Chemins de la Baie** (📞 02 33 89 80 88; www.cheminsdelabaie.com; 34 rue de l'Ortillon, Genêts; adult/child from €9/5), both based in Genêts. Don't be tempted to do it on your own – the bay's tides are notoriously treacherous.

🛏 p44

The Drive » Take the A84, N12 and A81 for 190km to Le Mans and the A28 for 102km to Tours, where you can follow a tour through the Loire Valley if you wish. Chambord is about 75km from Tours via the D952.

_ _ _ _ _ _ _ _ _ _ _ _ _ _ _

❻ Chambord

If you only have time to visit one château in the Loire, you might as well make it the grandest – and **Chambord** (📞 info 02 54 50 40 00, tour & show reservations 02 54 50 50 40; www.chambord. org; adult/child €14.50/free; parking distant/near €4/6; ⌚ 9am-6pm Apr-Oct, to 5pm Nov-Mar; 🅿) is the most lavish of them all. It's a showpiece of Renaissance architecture, from the double-helix staircase up to the turret-covered rooftop. With 426 rooms, the sheer scale of the place is mindboggling – and in the Loire, that's really saying something. If you have time, detour to the richly furnished and very elegant **Château de Chenonceau** (📞 02 47 23 90 07; www.chenonceau. com; adult/child €15/12, with

Classic Trip

WHY THIS IS A CLASSIC TRIP
OLIVER BERRY, WRITER

It's epic in every sense: in scale, views, time and geography. This once-in-a-lifetime journey covers France from every possible angle: top to bottom, east to west, city and village, old-fashioned and modern, coast and countryside. It links together many of the country's truly unmissable highlights, and by the end you'll genuinely be able to say you've seen the heart and soul of France.

Above: Mont St-Michel
Left: Gorges du Verdon
Right: Stained glass window, Cathédrale Notre Dame, Chartres

CLODIO/GETTY IMAGES ©

audio guide €19/15.50; ⊘9am or 10am-5pm or 6.30pm).

The Drive » It's 425km to Bordeaux via Blois and the A10 motorway. You could consider breaking the journey with stop-offs at Futuroscope and Poitiers, roughly halfway between the two.

7 Bordeaux

When Unesco decided to protect Bordeaux's medieval architecture in 2007, it simply listed half the city in one fell swoop. Covering 18 sq km, this is the world's largest urban World Heritage Site, with grand buildings and architectural treasures galore.

Top of the heap is the **Cathédrale St-André** (☎05 56 44 67 29; www.cathedrale-bordeaux.fr; place Pey Berland; treasury adult/child €2/free; ⊘2-7pm Mon, 10am-noon & 2-6pm Tue-Sat, 9.30am-noon & 2-6pm Sun, treasury 2.30-5.30pm Wed, Sat & Sun), known for its stone carvings and generously gargoyled belfry, the **Tour Pey Berland** (☎05 56 81 26 25; www.pey-berland.fr; place Pey Berland; adult/child €6/free; ⊘10am-6pm Jun-Sep, 10am-12.30pm & 2-5.30pm Oct-May). But the whole old city rewards wandering, especially around the **Jardin Public** (cours de Verdun; ⊘7am-8pm Jul & Aug, shorter hours rest of year), the pretty squares of **esplanade des Quinconces** and **place Gambetta**, and the city's 4km-long **riverfront esplanade**, with its playgrounds, paths and paddling pools. There's also the superb **La Cité du Vin** (📞05 56 16 20 20; www.laciteduvin.com; 134 quai de Bacalan; adult/child €20/9, priority access €25/14; 🕐10am-7pm May-Aug, shorter hours rest of year), **a must see for wine-lovers.**

🍴 🛏 p44, p366

The Drive ≫ It's a 194km drive to Sarlat-la-Canéda via the A89 motorway, or you can take a longer but more enjoyable route via the D936.

- - - - - - - - - - - - - - - -

TRIP HIGHLIGHT

8 Sarlat-la-Canéda

If you're looking for France's heart and soul, you'll find it among the forests and fields of the Dordogne. It's the stuff of French fantasies: riverbank châteaux, medieval villages, wooden-hulled *gabarres* (flat-bottomed barges) and market stalls groaning with truffles, walnuts and wines. The town of Sarlat-la-Canéda makes the perfect base, with a beautiful medieval centre and lots of lively markets.

It's also ideally placed for exploring the Vézère Valley, about 20km to the northwest, home to France's finest cave paintings. Most famous of all are the ones at the **Grotte de Lascaux**, although to prevent damage to the paintings, you now visit a replica of the cave's main sections in a nearby **grotto** (International Centre for Cave Art; 📞05 53 50 99 10; www.lascaux. fr; Montignac; adult/child €20/12.90; 🕐8.30am-6pm

Jul & Aug, 9am-5pm Apr-Jun, Sep & Oct, 10am-4pm Nov-Mar, closed Jan).

The Drive ≫ The drive east to Lyon is a long one, covering well over 400km and travelling across the spine of the Massif Central. A good route is to follow the A89 all the way to exit 6, then turn off onto the N89/D89 to Lyon. This route should cover between 420km and 430km.

- - - - - - - - - - - - - - - -

9 Lyon

Fired up by French food? Then you'll love Lyon, with its *bouchons* (small bistros), bustling markets and fascinating food culture. Start in **Vieux Lyon** and the picturesque quarter of **Presqu'île**, then catch the funicular to the top of **Fourvière** to explore the city's Roman ruins and enjoy crosstown views.

Film buffs will also want to make time for the **Musée Lumière** (📞04 78 78 18 95; www.institut-lumiere.org; 25 rue du Premier Film, 8e; adult/child €8.50/free; 🕐10am-6.30pm Tue-Sun; Ⓜ Monplaisir-Lumière), where the Lumière Brothers (Auguste and Louis) shot the first reels of the world's first motion picture, *La Sortie des Usines Lumières*, on 19 March 1895.

🍴 🛏 p45, p229

The Drive ≫ Take the A42 towards Lake Geneva, then the A40 towards St-Gervais-les-Bains. The motorway becomes the N205 as it nears Chamonix. It's a drive of at least 225km.

FUTUROSCOPE

Halfway between Chambord and Bordeaux on the A10, 10km north of Poitiers, **Futuroscope** (📞05 49 49 11 12; www.futuroscope.com; av René Monory, Chasseneuil-du-Poitou; day/evening ticket valid from 5pm €46/20; 🕐10am-11.15pm Jun–mid-Jul, 9.30am-11pm mid-Jul–early Aug, 8.30am-10.45pm Aug, shorter hours rest of year, closed Jan–mid-Feb; P 🚻) is one of France's top theme parks. It's a futuristic experience that takes you whizzing through space, diving into the ocean depths, racing around city streets and on a close encounter with creatures of the future. Note that many rides have a minimum height of 120cm.

You'll need at least five hours to check out the major attractions, or two days to see everything. The park is in the suburb of Jaunay-Clan; take exit 28 off the A10.

TRIP HIGHLIGHT

⑩ Chamonix

Snuggling among snow-clad mountains – including Europe's highest summit, Mont Blanc – adrenaline-fuelled Chamonix is an ideal springboard for the French Alps. In winter, it's a mecca for skiers and snowboarders, and in summer, once the snows thaw, the high-level trails become a trekkers' paradise.

There are two really essential Chamonix experiences. First, catch the dizzying cable car to the top of the **Aiguille du Midi** to snap a shot of Mont Blanc.

Then take the combination mountain train and cable car from the **Gare du Montenvers** (☎04 50 53 22 75; www.montblancnaturalresort.com; 35 place de la Mer de Glace; adult/child return €34/28.90; ☺10am-4pm late Dec–mid-Mar, to 5pm mid-Mar–Apr) to the **Mer de Glace** (Sea of Ice), France's largest glacier. Wrap up warmly if you want to visit the glacier's sculptures and ice caves.

The Drive » The drive to the Riviera is full of scenic thrills. An attractive route is via the D1212 to Albertville, and then via the A43, which travels over the Italian border and through the Tunnel de Fréjus. From here, the N94 runs through Briançon, and a combination of the A51, N85 and D6085 carries you south to Nice. You'll cover at least 430km.

⑪ French Riviera

If there's one coast road in France you simply have to drive, it's the French Riviera, with its rocky cliffs, maquis-scented air and dazzling Mediterranean views. Sun-seekers have been flocking here since the 19th century, and its scenery still never fails to seduce.

Lively **Nice** and cinematic **Cannes** make natural starts, but for the Riviera's loveliest scenery, you'll want to drive down the gorgeous **Corniche de l'Estérel** to **St-Tropez**, still a watch-word for seaside glamour. Crowds can make summer hellish, but come in spring or autumn and you'll have its winding lanes and fragrant hills practically to yourself. For maximum views, stick to the coast roads: the D6098 to Antibes and Cannes, the D559 around the Corniche de l'Estérel, and the D98A to St-Tropez. It's about 120km via this route.

The Drive » From St-Tropez, take the fast A8 for about 125km west to Aix-en-Provence.

⑫ Aix-en-Provence

Sleepy Provence sums up the essence of *la douce vie* (the sweet life). Cloaked in lavender and spotted with hilltop villages, it's a region that sums up everything that's good about France.

Cruising the back roads and browsing the markets are the best ways to get acquainted with the region. Artistic Aix-en-Provence encapsulates the classic Provençal vibe, with its pastel buildings and Cézanne connections, while **Mont Ste-Victoire**, to the east, makes for a superb outing.

✕ ⛏ p45

The Drive » The gorges are 140km northeast of Aix-en-Provence, via the A51 and D952.

TRIP HIGHLIGHT

⑬ Gorges du Verdon

Complete your cross-France adventure with an unforgettable expedition to the Gorges du Verdon – sometimes known as the Grand Canyon of Europe. This deep ravine slashes 25km through the plateaux of Haute-Provence; in places, its walls rise to a dizzying 700m, twice the height of the Eiffel Tower (321m).

The two main jumping-off points are the villages of **Moustiers Ste-Marie**, in the west, and **Castellane**, in the east. Drivers and bikers can take in the canyon panorama from two vertigo-inducing cliffside roads, but the base of the gorge is only accessible on foot or by raft.

Eating & Sleeping

Paris ❶

✕ Holybelly — International €

(www.holybellycafe.com; 5 & 19 rue Lucien Sampaix, 10e; dishes €6-16.50; ⏱9am-5pm; 🛜🍴; Ⓜ Jacques Bonsergent) Friendly vibes, sassy breakfast 'n' lunch dishes and specialist coffee define this duo. Holybelly at No 5 cooks all-day pancakes and eggs, while the Holybelly original at No 19 serves more creative, seasonal dishes to share. Last orders 4pm. No reservations.

🛏 Hôtel Amour — Design Hotel €€

(☎01 48 78 31 80; www.hotelamourparis.fr; 8 rue de Navarin, 9e; d from €165; 🛜; Ⓜ St-Georges, Pigalle) The inimitable black-clad Amour ('Love') in south Pigalle plays on its long-ago incarnation as a brothel, featuring a soft pink facade and nude artwork (some more explicit than others) in each of its 24 rooms. (No TVs, but that's not the point here.) The beloved ground-floor bistro–bar – open until 2am – has a leafy summer patio garden.

Chartres ❸

✕ Le Tripot — Bistro €€

(☎02 37 36 60 11; www.letripot.wixsite.com/chartres; 11 place Jean Moulin; 2-/3-course lunch menus €16/19, dinner menus €28-38, mains €22; ⏱noon-1.45pm & 7.30-9.15pm Wed-Sat, noon-1.45pm Sun) Tucked off the tourist trail and easy to miss even if you do chance down its narrow street, this atmospheric space with low-beamed ceilings is a treat for authentic and adventurous French fare like saddle of rabbit stuffed with snails or grilled turbot in truffled hollandaise sauce. Locals are on to it, so booking ahead is advised.

🛏 Le Grand Monarque — Hotel €€

(☎02 37 18 15 15; www.bw-grand-monarque.com; 22 place des Épars; d from €120; ❄🛜) With teal-blue shutters gracing its 1779 façade, a lovely stained-glass ceiling and a treasure trove of period furnishings, old B&W photos and knick-knacks, the epicentral Grand Monarque is a historical gem. Some rooms have air-conditioning; staff are charming. A host of hydrotherapy treatments are available at its spa. Its elegant restaurant, **Georges** (☎02 37 18 15 15; www.bw-grand-monarque.com; 22 place des Épars; menus €59-103; ⏱noon-1pm & 7.30-9.30pm Tue-Sat), has a Michelin star. Family rooms have sofa beds; cots and babysitting services are available.

Mont St-Michel ❺

🛏 Vent des Grèves — B&B €

(☎Estelle 02 33 48 28 89; www.ventdesgreves.com; 27 rte de la Côte, Ardevon; s/d from €50/60; 🛜) Offering outstanding value, this friendly, family-run B&B has five modern, simply furnished rooms with magical views of the Mont. It's located an easily walkable 1km east of the shuttle stop in La Caserne. Breakfast is included in rates.

Bordeaux ❼

✕ Au Bistrot — French €€

(☎06 63 54 21 14; www.facebook.com/aubistrotbordeaux; 61 place des Capucins; mains €16-26; ⏱noon-2.30pm & 7-11pm Wed-Sun) There's nothing flashy or fancy about this hardcore French bistro, an ode to traditional market cuisine with charismatic François front of house and talented French-Thai chef Jacques In'On in the kitchen. Marinated herrings, lentil salad topped with a poached egg, half a roast pigeon or a feisty *andouillette* (tripe sausage) roasted in the oven are some of the dishes on offer – 80% of produce is local or from the surrounding Aquitaine region.

🛏 Mama Shelter — Design Hotel €€

(☎05 57 30 45 45; www.mamashelter.com/en/bordeaux; 19 rue Poquelin Molière; d €89-199; ❄@🛜) With personalised iMacs, video booths and free movies in every room, Mama Shelter is up-to-the-minute. White rooms are small, medium or large; XL doubles have a sofa bed. The joyous ground-floor restaurant sports the same signature rubber rings strung above the bar as other Philippe Starck–designed hotels. Summertime drinks and dinner are served on the sensational rooftop terrace. Weekends usher concerts, gigs and other cultural happenings onto the small stage. Should you be wondering why on earth the strange tower is protruding from the hotel building, know that Mama Shelter squats inside the city's landmark Gas Tower building, designed by Modernist architects in 1927.

Lyon 9

✖ Le Poêlon d'Or   Bouchon €

(☎04 78 37 65 60; www.lepoelondor-restaurant. fr; 29 rue des Remparts d'Ainay, 2e; menus €18-35; ⏱noon-2pm & 7-9.30pm Mon-Fri; Ⓜ Ampère-Victor Hugo) This upmarket *bouchon*, around the corner from the Musée des Tissus, is well known among local foodies, who recommend its superb *andouillette* (sausages made from pigs' intestines) and pike dumplings. Save room for the delicious chocolate mousse.

🛏 Mob Hotel   Boutique Hotel €€

(☎04 58 55 55 88; www.mobhotel.com; 55 quai Rambaud, 2e; d from €75; ⓅⓇ; 🚊T1) The Mob Hotel is a magnet for designers and the creative set. Metal lacework encases the avant-garde building overlooking the Saône, while the inside is a playful mixture of polished concrete, pale blond woods, artful lighting and subtle pastels. Book a Master Mob room for a balcony and ample space.

The 1st-floor terrace is the place to be on warm days, and the restaurant serves excellent pizzas made from organic, locally sourced ingredients. Regular events include yoga and Pilates classes, as well as DJ-fuelled parties on weekends.

Aix-en-Provence 12

✖ Le Petit Verdot   Provencal €€

(☎04 42 27 30 12; www.lepetitverdot.fr; 7 rue d'Entrecasteaux; mains €20-25; ⏱7pm-midnight Mon-Sat) It's all about hearty, honest dining here, with tabletops made out of old wine crates, and a lively chef-patron who runs the place with huge enthusiasm, happily showing how good Provençal food and wine can be. Expect dishes such as *onglet* (skirt steak) in green-pepper sauce or Pata Negra pork with mustard and honey, accompanied by great wines and seasonal veggies.

🛏 Villa Gallici   Historic Hotel €€€

(☎04 42 23 29 23; www.villagallici.com; 18 av de la Violette; r from €315; Ⓟ❄Ⓡ🏊) Baroque and beautiful, this fabulous villa was built as a private residence in the 18th century and still feels marvellously opulent. Rooms are more like museum pieces, stuffed with gilded mirrors, toile de Jouy wallpaper and filigreed furniture. It has a lovely lavender-filled garden to breakfast in, plus a pool, a superb restaurant and a wine cellar.

Paris & Northeastern France

FROM THE BOULEVARDS OF PARIS TO THE LOFTY CHALK CLIFFS OF THE OPAL COAST, northern France is primed with possibilities – whether that means touring Champagne's vineyards, sampling Alsatian cuisine, admiring art in Metz or simply moseying around Strasbourg's attractive city centre. And with its abundance of coast and countryside, it's a pleasure to drive, too. It's a region whose long (and turbulent) history is plain to see. Two thousand years of royalty, renaissance and revolution have left their mark on the streets of Paris, while the scars of war can still be traced on the fields of Flanders. Elsewhere, cathedrals and châteaux hint at the splendour of a bygone age, and experimental art museums point to an equally flashy future.

Northern Coast Cap Gris-Nez

Paris & Northeastern France

2 **A Toast to Art 7 Days**
Visit art galleries in Lens and Metz, then get lost in old Strasbourg. (p51)

3 **Northern Coast 2–4 Days**
Discover a sublime stretch of coast along the English Channel. (p59)

4 **In Flanders Fields 3 Days**
The ghosts of the Great War still linger on the battlefields of northern France. (p67)

Classic Trip
5 **Champagne Taster 3 Days**
Taste your way around the cellars of Champagne on this fizz-fuelled trip. (p75)

6 **Alsace Accents 3 Days**
Alsace's rich cuisine and crisp wines combine on this eastern road trip. (p85)

 DON'T MISS

Centre Pompidou-Metz

It's hard to know here which is more avant-garde – the architecture or the art. Take in this groundbreaking gallery on Trip **2**

Vimy Ridge

Walk through one of the only surviving trench systems from WWI on Trip **4**

Musée Bartholdi

Visit the Colmar home of the man who made Lady Liberty – and see a life-sized model of the statue's ear – on Trip **6**

Amiens

Marvel at one of France's most spectacular cathedrals in this charming (and largely underrated) city on Trip **4**

Dunes de la Slack

Wander amid undulating, wind-sculpted sand dunes on Trip **3**

A Toast to Art

2

One for culture vultures: an artistic expedition across northeastern France, taking in art nouveau in Nancy, glorious glass in Baccarat and avant-garde experimentation in Metz and Strasbourg.

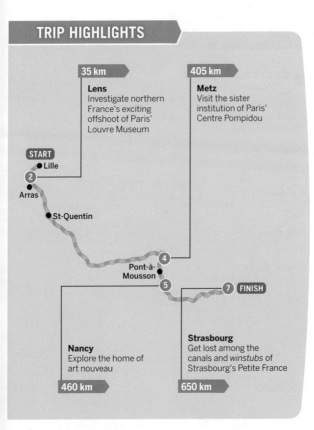

35 km

Lens
Investigate northern France's exciting offshoot of Paris' Louvre Museum

405 km

Metz
Visit the sister institution of Paris' Centre Pompidou

START
● Lille

②
●
Arras

● St-Quentin

④
Pont-à-Mousson
⑤

⑦ **FINISH**

Nancy
Explore the home of art nouveau
460 km

Strasbourg
Get lost among the canals and *winstubs* of Strasbourg's Petite France
650 km

7 DAYS
650KM / 404 MILES

GREAT FOR...

BEST TIME TO GO
April to July (avoid the school-holiday crowds).

ESSENTIAL PHOTO
Snap yourself sipping a coffee on Nancy's grand central square, place Stanislas.

BEST FOR SHOPPING
Strasbourg's old quarters for chocolate, glassware and other souvenirs.

2 A Toast to Art

France's northeast is one of the country's most artistic corners, thanks to the arrival of high-profile addresses like the Louvre-Lens and Metz's Centre Pompidou. But these glitzy contemporary museums are simply the continuation of a long artistic legacy. This high-culture tour takes in Gothic cathedrals, neoclassical squares, chic crystalware and art nouveau mansions — not to mention some of Europe's most experimental art.

1 Lille

Lille may be France's most underrated major city. In recent decades this once-grimy industrial metropolis has morphed into a glittering and self-confident cultural and commercial hub – and a key shopping, art and culture stop with an attractive old town and a trio of renowned art museums.

Classic works find a home at the **Palais des Beaux Arts** (Fine Arts Museum; ☏03 20 06 78 00; www.pba-lille.fr; place de la

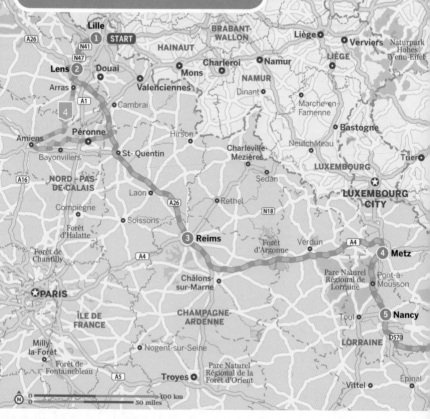

République; adult/child €7/4; ⊘2-6pm Mon, 10am-6pm Wed-Sun; Ⓜ République-Beaux-Arts), an illustrious fine-arts museum with a first-rate collection of 15th- to 20th-century paintings, including works by Rubens, Van Dyck and Manet.

Contrast these with the playful – and sometimes just plain weird – works on show at the **Musée d'Art Moderne** (⌨03 20 19 68 68; www.musee-lam.fr; 1 allée du Musée, Villeneuve-d'Ascq; adult/child €7/5; ⊘museum 10am-6pm Tue-Sun, sculpture park 9am-6pm Tue-Sun). Big names including Braque, Calder, Léger, Miró, Modigliani and Picasso are the main draws. It's in Villeneuve-d'Ascq, 9km east of Gare Lille-Europe.

A few miles north at **La Piscine Musée d'Art et d'Industrie** (⌨03 20 69 23 60; www.roubaix-lapiscine.com; 23 rue de l'Espérance, Roubaix; adult/child €9/6; ⊘11am-6pm Tue-Thu, 11am-8pm Fri, 1-6pm Sat & Sun; Ⓜ Gare Jean Lebas), the building is almost as intriguing as the art: a glorious art deco swimming pool has been beautifully converted into a cutting-edge gallery, showing contemporary paintings and sculptures.

 p73

The Drive » The quickest route to Lens is via the A1, but a less hectic route takes the N41 and N47. It's a 37km drive from the outskirts of Lille.

TRIP HIGHLIGHT

② Lens

A coal-mining town might not seem like the most obvious place to continue your investigation of French art, but *au contraire*. The jewel in the crown of industrial Lens is the **Louvre-Lens** (⌨03 21 18 62 62; www.louvrelens.fr; 99 rue Paul Bert; ; ⊘10am-6pm Wed-Mon). An offshoot of the Paris original, this innovative gallery showcases hundreds of treasures from Paris' venerable Musée du Louvre in state-of-the-art exhibition spaces. The centrepiece, the 120m-long Galerie du Temps, displays a semi-permanent collection of judiciously chosen objects – some of them true masterpieces – from the dawn of civilisation to the mid-1800s.

The Drive » Follow the N17 south of town and join the A26 toll road for 178km to Reims, about a two- to 2½-hour drive away.

----

③ Reims

Along with its towering Gothic cathedral and Champagne connections,

Koblenz

[A1]

Wiesbaden
Mainz

RHINELAND - PALATINATE

Kaiserslautern

SAARLAND

Saarbrücken

Wissembourg

Wingen-sur-Moder

Parc Naturel Régional de Lorraine p56

Strasbourg ⑦

Baccarat

FINISH

ALSACE

Raon-l'Étape ⑥

Parc Naturel Régional des Ballons des Vosges

[A5]

Freiburg im Breisgau

Colmar

LINK YOUR TRIP

④ In Flanders Fields
WWI French battlefields are covered in this emotional tour; loop back at the end to Lille, and it makes an ideal combo with this trip.

⑥ Alsace Accents
To extend your journey, pick up the Route des Vins d'Alsace after ending this trip in Strasbourg.

Reims is also worth visiting for its splendid **Musée des Beaux-Arts** (☏03 26 35 36 00; http://musees-reims.fr; 8 rue Chanzy; adult/child €5/free; 🚉A or B), located inside an 18th-century abbey. Highlights include 27 works by Camille Corot (only the Louvre has more), 13 portraits by German Renaissance painters Cranach the Elder and the Younger, lots of Barbizon School landscapes, and two works each by Monet, Gauguin and Pissarro. But its most celebrated possession is probably Jacques-Louis David's world-famous *The Death of Marat,* depicting the Revolutionary leader's bloody, just-murdered corpse in the bathtub. It's one of only four known versions of the painting in the world. At the time of research, the museum is being renovated and is scheduled to reopen in 2023.

✗ 🛏 p57, 83

The Drive » Metz is 192km east of Reims via the A4 toll road, another two-hour drive.

TRIP HIGHLIGHT

❹ Metz

The swoopy, spaceship façade of the **Centre Pompidou-Metz** (☏03 87 15 39 39; www.centrepompidou-metz.fr; 1 parvis des Droits de l'Homme; adult €7-12, child free; ⏰10am-6pm Mon, Wed & Thu, to 7pm Fri-Sun) fronts one of France's boldest galleries. Drawing on the Pompidou's fantastic modern art collection, it's gained a reputation for ambitious exhibitions, such as the one spotlighting the graphic works of American conceptual artist Sol LeWitt.

While you're in town, don't miss Metz's amazing **Cathédrale St-Étienne** (www.cathedrale-metz.fr; place St-Étienne; combined ticket treasury & crypt adult/child €4/2, audioguide €7; ⏰8am-6pm, treasury & crypt 9.30am-12.30pm & 1.30-5.30pm Mon-Sat, 2-6pm Sun), a lacy wonder lit by kaleidoscopic curtains of stained glass. It's known as 'God's lantern' for good reason – look out for the technicolour windows created by the visionary artist Marc Chagall.

🛏 p57

The Drive » The most scenic option to Nancy is the D657, which tracks the banks of the Moselle River. Head southwest on the A31 toll road, then take exit 30a (signed to Jouy les Arches). Follow the road through rolling Alsatian countryside as far as Pont-à-Mousson, then continue through town on the D657 all the way to Nancy. It's a point-to-point drive of about 65km.

TOP TIP:
STRASBOURG CENT SAVERS

The Strasbourg Pass Musées (one/three-day pass €12/18; www.musees.strasbourg.eu) covers admission to all of Strasbourg's museums; buy it at museums. Alternatively, the three-day Strasbourg Pass (adult €22, child €10-15) includes one museum, a trip up to the 66m-high viewing platform at the city's cathedral platform and a boat tour.

HUANG ZHENG / SHUTTERSTOCK ©

Nancy Stained glass at Musée de l'École de Nancy

TRIP HIGHLIGHT

5 Nancy

Home of the art nouveau movement, Nancy has an air of grace and refinement that's all its own. Start your art appreciation at the **Musée de l'École de Nancy** (School of Nancy Museum; ☎03 83 85 30 01; https://musee-ecole-de-nancy.nancy.fr; 36-38 rue du Sergent Blandan; adult/child €6/4; ⏰10am-6pm Wed-Sun), an art nouveau showpiece of dreamy interiors and curvy glass, housed in a 19th-century villa 2km southwest of the centre.

Next, head into the city's heart, magnificent **place Stanislas**, a vast neoclassical square that's now a Unesco World Heritage Site. Designed by Emmanuel Héré in the 1750s, it's encircled by glorious buildings, including the **hôtel de ville** and the **Opéra National de Lorraine**, and contains a treasure trove of statues, rococo fountains and wrought-iron gateways.

On one side of the square is the city's **Musée des Beaux-Arts** (☎03 83 85 30 01; https://musee-des-beaux-arts.nancy.fr; 3 place Stanislas; adult/child €7/4.50; ⏰10am-6pm Wed-Mon), where Caravaggio, Rubens, Picasso and Monet hang alongside works by Lorraine-born artists, including the dreamlike landscapes of Claude Lorrain and the pared-down designs of Nancy-born architect Jean Prouvé (1901–84).

On nearby Grand Rue, the regal Renaissance Palais Ducal was once home to the dukes of Lorraine. It's now the **Musée Lorrain** (www.musee-lorrain.nancy.fr; 64 & 66 Grande Rue; ⏰10am-12.30pm & 2-6pm Tue-Sun), with a rich fine-art and history collection, including medieval statuary

DETOUR:
MUSEE LALIQUE

Start: ❼ Strasbourg

René Lalique was one of the great figures of the art nouveau movement, and the **Musée Lalique** (📞03 88 89 08 14; www.musee-lalique.com; rue du Hochberg, Wingen-sur-Moder; adult/child €6/3; ⏰10am-7pm, closed Mon Oct-Mar) provides a fitting tribute to his talents. At home on the site of the old Hochberg glassworks, this museum investigates Lalique's fascination with naturalistic forms (especially flowers, insects and foliage) and the curves of the female body. The collection illustrates his astonishing breadth of work, from gem-encrusted jewellery to perfume bottles and sculpture.

The museum is 60km northwest of Strasbourg in Wingen-sur-Moder.

and faience (glazed pottery) – unfortunately the museum is closed for renovation till 2023, though the church inside remains open.

✖ p57

The Drive ❯❯ Head south from Nancy on the main A330 toll road. Take exit 7, signed to Flavigny-sur-Moselle, which will take you onto the rural riverside D570. Stay on this road all the way to Bayon, then cross the river through town, following the D22 east through quiet countryside to Baccarat. It's a drive of 78km.

- - - - - - - - - - - - - - - - - -

❻ Baccarat

The glitzy glassware of Baccarat was considered the height of sophisti-cation in 18th-century France, and its exquisite crystal could be found gracing mansions and châteaux all over Europe. The **Musée Baccarat** (www.baccarat.fr; cours des Cristalleries; adult/child €5/free; ⏰10am-noon & 2-6pm Tue-Sun) displays 1100 pieces, and the boutique out front is almost as dazzling as the museum. Nearby crystal shops sell lesser, and less expensive, brands.

Glass aficionados will also want to stroll across the River Meurthe to the 1950s-built **Église St-Rémy** (1 av de Lachapelle; ⏰8am-5pm), whose austere façade conceals a blindingly bright interior

containing 20,000 Baccarat panels.

The Drive ❯❯ Take the D590 southeast to Raon-l'Étape, then turn northeast on the D392A, a lovely back road that winds up through woodland and mountains, offering great views of the Vosges en route. Eventually you'll link up with the D1420, which will take you on to Strasbourg. It's a good two-hour drive of about 100km.

- - - - - - - - - - - - - - - - - -

TRIP HIGHLIGHT

❼ Strasbourg

Finish with a couple of days exploring the architectural splendour of Strasbourg and visiting the **Musée d'Art Moderne et Contemporain** (MAMCS; www.musees.strasbourg.eu; 1 place Hans Jean Arp; adult/child €7/free; ⏰10am-6pm Tue-Sun; 🚇Musée d'Art Moderne), a striking glass-and-steel cube showcasing fine art, graphics and photography. The art's defiantly modern: Kandinsky, Picasso, Magritte and Monet canvases can all be found here, alongside curvaceous works by Strasbourg-born abstract artist Jean Arp.

Afterwards, have a good wander around **Grande Île**, Strasbourg's historic and Unesco-listed old quarter, as well as **Petite France**, the canal district.

✖ 🛏 p57

Eating & Sleeping

Reims ❸

✗ Brasserie Le Boulingrin Brasserie €€

(☎03 26 40 96 22; www.boulingrin.fr; 29-31 rue de Mars; menus €25-45; ⏰noon-2.30pm daily & 7-11pm Mon-Sat) A genuine, old-time brasserie – the decor and zinc bar date back to 1925 – whose ambience and cuisine make it an enduring favourite. From September to June, the culinary focus is on *fruits de mer* (seafood) such as Breton oysters.

🛏 Les Telliers B&B €€

(☎09 53 79 80 74; https://telliers.fr; 18 rue des Telliers; s €68-85, d €80-121, tr €117-142, q €133-163; P 🖤) Enticingly positioned down a quiet alley near the cathedral, this bijou B&B extends one of Reims' warmest *bienvenues*. The high-ceilinged rooms are big on art deco character, and handsomely decorated with ornamental fireplaces, polished oak floors and the odd antique. Breakfast costs an extra €9 and is a generous spread of pastries, fruit, fresh-pressed juice and coffee.

Metz ❹

🛏 Hôtel de la Cathédrale Historic Hotel €€

(☎03 87 75 00 02; www.hotelcathedrale-metz. fr; 25 place de Chambre; d €82-122; 🖤) You can expect a friendly welcome at this classy little hotel, occupying a 17th-century townhouse in a prime spot right opposite the cathedral. Climb the wrought-iron staircase to your classically elegant room, with high ceilings, hardwood floors and antique trappings. Book well ahead for a cathedral view. Breakfast will set you back €11.

Nancy ❺

✗ La Gentilhommiere French €€

(☎03 83 32 26 44; www.lagentilhommierenancy. fr; 29 rue des Maréchaux; menus €26-40; ⏰noon-1.30pm & 7-9.30pm Mon-Fri, 7-9.30pm Sat) Warm-hued, subtly lit Le Gentilhommiere stands head and shoulders above most of the restaurants on rue des Maréchaux. Expect stylishly presented French dishes, including beef fillet and veal stew.

Strasbourg ❼

✗ Winstub S'Kaechele French €

(☎03 88 22 62 36; www.skaechele.fr; 8 rue de l'Argile; mains €17-19; ⏰11.45am-1.30pm & 7-9.30pm Tue-Sat; 🚊Langstross/Grand Rue) Traditional French and Alsatian grub doesn't come more authentic than at this snug, amiable *winstub* (wine tavern), run with love by couple Karine and Daniel. Cue wonderfully cosy evenings spent in stone-walled, lamp-lit, wood-beamed surrounds, huddled over dishes such as escargots oozing Roquefort, fat pork knuckles braised in pinot noir, and *choucroute garnie* (sauerkraut garnished with meats).

🛏 Cour du Corbeau Boutique Hotel €€

(☎03 90 00 26 26; www.cour-corbeau.com; 6-8 rue des Couples; r €160-260; ❄🖤; 🚊Porte de l'Hôpital) A 16th-century inn lovingly converted into a boutique hotel, Cour du Corbeau wins you over with its half-timbered charm and its location, just steps from the river. Gathered around a courtyard, rooms blend original touches such as oak parquet and Louis XV furnishings with mod cons including flat-screen TVs.

Northern Coast

3

Stretching for 140km along the English Channel, the sublime Opal Coast enchants visitors with lofty chalk cliffs, rolling green hills, sandy beaches, scrub-dotted sand dunes and charming seaside villages.

TRIP HIGHLIGHTS

11 km

Cap Blanc-Nez
Breathtaking views across the English Channel

● Calais
START

② ④

Boulogne-sur-Mer ●

Cap Griz-Nez
Just 28km from the White Cliffs of Dover

29km

Le Touquet-Paris-Plage ●

148 km

St-Valery-sur-Somme
A charming old port with a pint-sized walled city

122 km

Parc du Marquenterre Bird Sanctuary
Home to an astonishing 300 species of bird

⑩

St-Valery-sur-Somme ● Le Crotoy

⑫

FINISH

2–4 DAYS
148KM / 92 MILES

GREAT FOR...

BEST TIME TO GO

May to August for long days and warm weather.

ESSENTIAL PHOTO

The Channel panorama from atop Cap Blanc-Nez.

BEST FOR HISTORY

A colossal German bunker, part of Nazi Germany's Atlantic Wall, houses the WWII museum Musée du Mur de l'Atlantique.

3 Northern Coast

Named for the ever-changing interplay of greys and blues in the sea and sky, the Côte d'Opale (Opal Coast) is on spectacular display between Calais and Boulogne-sur-Mer. Further south, the relatively flat coastline is broken by the estuaries, wetlands and tidal marshes created by the Rivers Canche, Authie and Somme. The area has several attractive beach resorts and excellent spots for bird-watching and seal spotting.

Channel Tunnel

English Channel (La Manche)

Sangatte

Cap Blanc-Nez ②

Cap Gris-Nez ④ ③ **Wissant**
D940   A16
D191
⑤ **Audinghen**

Audresselles

⑥ **Ambleteuse**

Dunes de la Slack ⑦

Wimereux

Boulogne-sur-Mer
⑧

D940

A16

D901

Le Touquet-Paris-Plage
⑨   Les Étaples

D939

Berck-sur-Mer

A16

St-Quentin-en-Tourmont   D940
Parc du Marquenterre Bird Sanctuary
⑩   Rue

Pointe du Hourdel   D4

Cayeux-sur-Mer   Baie de Somme   ⑪ **Le Crotoy**

⑫   Noyelles-sur-Mer

FINISH   **St-Valery-sur-Somme**   Somme

7

154km

① Calais

France's premier trans-Channel port is a short hop from England by car ferry, Eurotunnel rail shuttle or fast Eurostar train. Begin the itinerary at Rodin's famous 1895 sculpture the **Burghers of Calais** (Les Bourgeois de Calais; place du Soldat Inconnu), in front of Calais' Flemish- and Renaissance-style **Hôtel de Ville** (town hall). Then head to the city's sandy, cabin-lined **beach**, whose singularly riveting attraction is watching huge car ferries as they sail majestically to and from Dover. The sand continues westward along 8km-long, dune-lined **Blériot**

Plage, broad and gently sloping. It's named for the pioneer aviator Louis Blériot, who began the first ever trans-Channel flight from here – it lasted 27 minutes – in 1909.

✗ ⊨ p65

The Drive ›› Take the D940 west, past Blériot Plage in the commune of Sangatte, and a further 5km southwest to reach Cap Blanc-Nez.

TRIP HIGHLIGHT

② Cap Blanc-Nez

Just past Sangatte, the coastal dunes give way to cliffs that culminate in windswept, 134m-high Cap Blanc-Nez, which affords breathtaking views of the Bay of Wissant, the

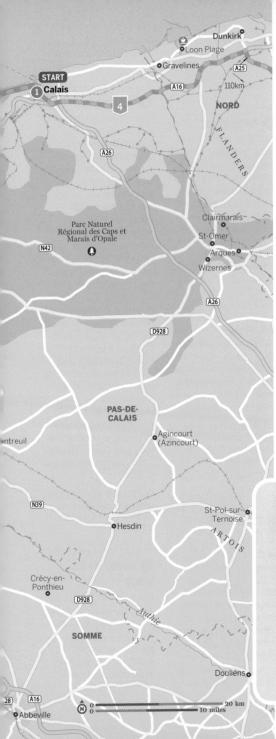

port of Calais, the Flemish countryside (pockmarked by Allied bomb craters, eg on the slopes of Mont d'Hubert) and the distant chalk cliffs of Kent. A grey stone obelisk honours the WWI Dover Patrol. Paths lead to a number of massive WWII German bunkers.

The Drive » It's an 8km descent on the D940 from Cap Blanc-Nez to Wissant.

3 Wissant

The attractive seaside village of Wissant, long home to both fishers and farmers, is centered around a 15th-century church. It's a good base for exploring the area between Cap Blanc-Nez and Cap Gris-Nez, including a wide-at-low-tide beach that's long, flat and clean – perfect for young children and kitesurfers.

The Drive » From Wissant, take the D940 southwestward for 6km. About 700m past the

LINK YOUR TRIP

4 In Flanders Fields

From Calais, drive 110km to the southeast, on the A16 and A25, to start this trip in Lille.

7 Monet's Normandy

From St-Valery-sur-Somme, it's a 170km drive south to Giverny.

centre of Audinghen, turn right onto the D191 and continue northwest for 3.5km.

TRIP HIGHLIGHT

④ Cap Gris-Nez

Topped by a lighthouse and a radar station that keeps track of the more than 500 ships that pass by here each day, the 45m-high cliffs of **Cap Gris-Nez** (off D191) are only 28km from the white cliffs of the English coast. The name, which means 'grey nose' in French, is a corruption of the archaic English 'craig ness', meaning 'rocky promontory'. The area is a stopping-off point for millions of migrating birds. The parking lot is a good starting point for hikes, such as along the **GR120 du Littoral** coastal trail (marked with red and white blazes).

The Drive » From Cap Gris-Nez, take the D191 3.5km southeast back to the D940 and turn right. After about 100m, at the Maison du Site des Deux Caps tourist office, turn right again and continue for 400m for the Musée du Mur de l'Atlantique.

----

⑤ Audinghen

Oodles of WWII hardware, including a massive, rail-borne 283mm German artillery piece with a range of 86km (more than enough to hit the English coast), are on display at Audinghen's well-organised **Musée du Mur de l'Atlantique** (Atlantic Wall Museum; ☎03 21 32 97 33; www.batterietodt.com; rte du Musée, Hameau de Haringzelle, Audinghen; adult/child €9/6; ⏰10am-6.30pm Jul & Aug, 2-6pm Mon, 10am-6pm Tue-Sun Apr-Jun, Sep & Oct, 2-5.30pm mid-Feb–Mar & to early Nov). It is housed in Batterie Todt, a colossal, round German pillbox.

The Drive » From Audinghen it's 5.5km south along the D940 to Ambleteuse. On the way you'll pass the colourful village of Audresselles, still active as a fishing port. It's a great place to dine on super-fresh seafood.

----

⑥ Ambleteuse

The seaside village of Ambleteuse is home to **Fort Mahon** (Fort d'Ambleteuse), a small fortress built by Louis XIV in the 1680s, and a pebbly beach. At the modern **Musée 39–45** (☎03 21 87 33 01; www.musee3945.com; 2 rue des Garennes, Ambleteuse; adult/child €9/6; ⏰10am-6.30pm Jul & Aug, to 6pm Apr-Jun & Sep, to 4pm Oct, 10am-6pm Sat & Sun Mar, 10am-4pm Sat & Sun Nov), popular period songs accompany visitors as they stroll past dozens of life-size tableaux of WWII military and civilian life. The museum screens archival films. The dashing but wildly impractical French officers' dress uniforms of 1931 hint at possible reasons why France fared so poorly on the battlefields of 1940.

The Drive » From Ambleteuse drive 1.5km southeast along the D940 to reach the Dunes de la Slack.

----

⑦ Dunes de la Slack

Just south of Ambleteuse along the estuary of the tiny River Slack, wind-sculpted sand dunes are covered with – and stabilised by – clumps of marram grass and

---

✓ **TOP TIP:**
TWO CAPES TOURIST INFORMATION

The **Maison du Site des Deux Caps** (☎03 21 21 62 22; www.lesdeuxcaps.fr; Ferme d'Haringzelle, Audinghen; ⏰9.30am-6pm Jul & Aug, 10am-12.30pm & 2-6pm Apr-Jun, Sep & Oct, 10am-12.30pm & 2-5.30pm Tue-Sat Feb, Mar, Nov & Dec) serves as a visitors information centre for the 'two capes', ie the area around and between Cap Blanc-Nez and Cap Gris-Nez. Staff have English brochures, rent out bicycles – both regular (per half-/ whole day €10/15) and electric (€15/20) – and sell hiking maps.

Le Touquet-Paris-Plage Beach huts

brambles such as privet and wild rose. The best way to appreciate the undulating landscape of Dunes de la Slack is to follow the marked walking paths that criss-cross the area.

The Drive ›› From the Dunes de la Slack head south on the D940 for 10km to reach Boulogne-sur-Mer.

- - - - - - - - - - - - - -

⑧ Boulogne-sur-Mer

France's most important fishing port, Boulogne-sur-Mer is home to **Nausicaá** (📞03 21 30 99 99; www.nausicaa.fr; bd Ste-Beuve; adult/child €26/19; ⏰9.30am-6.30pm, closed 3 weeks Jan), one of Europe's premier aquariums. Boulogne-sur-Mer's **Basse-Ville** (Lower City) is a bustling but uninspiring assemblage of postwar structures, but the attractive **Haute-Ville** (Upper City), perched

high above the rest of town and girded by a 13th-century wall, is an island of centuries-old buildings and cobblestone streets. You can walk all the way around this 'Fortified City' (Ville Fortifiée) atop the ancient stone walls – look for signs for the **Promenade des Remparts**.

✖ 🛏 p65

The Drive ›› From Boulogne-sur-Mer, take the D940 south for 28km. At Les Étaples, turn west onto the D939 and continue for 4km.

- - - - - - - - - - - - - -

⑨ Le Touquet-Paris-Plage

This leafy beach resort was hugely fashionable in the interwar period, when the British upper

---

BRASSERIE ARTISANALE DES 2 CAPS

Historic farm buildings deep in the countryside house the **Brasserie Artisanale des 2 Caps** (📞03 21 10 56 53; www.2caps.fr; Ferme de Belle Dalle, Tardinghen; ⏰brewery 10am-7pm Tue-Sat, 3-7pm Sun Jul & Aug, 10am-7pm Fri & Sat Sep-Jun), one of northern France's best microbreweries. Sample and buy here, or look for 2 Caps, Blanche de Wissant and Noire de Slack in area pubs. Brewmaster Christophe Noyon offers occasional 90-minute tours. Situated 1.5km along the D249 from the church in the village of Tardinghen, which is midway between Wissant and Audinghen.

TOP TIP:
NATURE WALKS

Non-profit **Eden 62** (📞03 21 32 13 74; www.eden62.
fr; ⏰mid-Feb–Oct) organises two-hour nature walks
several times a week. They're in French but tourists,
including families, are welcome. No need to reserve –
just show up at the meeting point.

crust found it positively
smashing. The town
was a favourite of Noël
Coward, and in 1940 a
politically oblivious PG
Wodehouse was taken
prisoner here by the
Germans. These days it
remains no less posh and
no less British, though
it also attracts plenty of
chic Parisians.

🛏 p65

The Drive » From Les Étaples,
take the D940 south for 34km.
Just past the village of Rue, turn
right onto the D4, continuing
westward on the D204, for a
total of 6km.

TRIP HIGHLIGHT

⑩ Parc du Marquenterre Bird Sanctuary

An astonishing 300
species of bird have been
sighted at the 2-sq-km
Parc du Marquenterre
(📞03 22 25 68 99; www.
parcdumarquenterre.fr; 25bis
chemin des Garennes, St-
Quentin-en-Tourmont; adult/
child €10.50/7.90, binoculars
€4/2; ⏰10am-7pm Apr-Sep,

to 6pm early Feb-Mar & Oct,
to 5pm Nov-early Feb), an
important migratory
stopover between the UK,
Iceland, Scandinavia and
Siberia and the warmer
climes of West Africa.
Marked **walking circuits**
(2km to 6km) take you to
marshes, dunes, mead-
ows, freshwater ponds, a
brackish lagoon and 13
observation posts. Year
round, the park's friendly
guides – they're the ones
carrying around tel-
escopes on tripods – are
happy to help visitors,
especially kids, spot and
identify birds.

The Drive » From the Parc
du Marquenterre, take the D204
east for 4km to the D4 and turn
right. After 4.5km continue
onto the D104 for the 2km to
Le Crotoy.

⑪ Le Crotoy

Occupying a wonderfully
picturesque spot on the
northern bank of the
Baie de Somme (Somme
estuary), laid-back Le
Crotoy is a lovely place to
relax. Attractions include

scenic walks around the
Somme estuary – vast
expanses are exposed at
low tide – and the only
sandy beach in northern
France that faces south;
restaurants and cafes
can be found nearby.
Jules Verne wrote *Twenty
Thousand Leagues Un-
der the Sea* (1870) while
living here.

The Drive » St-Valery-sur-
Somme is 16km around the
Somme estuary from Le Crotoy.
Take the D104 to the D940,
follow it for 11km and then turn
right onto the D3.

TRIP HIGHLIGHT

⑫ St-Valery-sur-Somme

This old port town has
a charming maritime
quarter, a pocket-sized
walled city and an
attractive seaside prom-
enade. The colours of
St-Valery-sur-Somme are
the colours of maritime
Picardy: the deep brick
reds of the houses and
the sea hues that range
from a sparkling blue
to overcast grey are ac-
cented by dashes of red,
white and blue from flap-
ping French flags, just
like in an impression-
ist seascape. Grey and
harbour seals can often
be spotted off **Pointe du
Hourdel**, 8km northwest
of town.

🍴🛏 p65

Eating & Sleeping

Calais

🍴 Histoire Ancienne   Bistro €€

(☎03 21 34 11 20; www.histoire-ancienne.com;
20 rue Royale; 2- & 3-course menus €21-34;
🕑 noon-2pm Mon, noon-2pm & 6.45-9.30pm
Tue-Sat; 🛜) Bistro-style French dishes, such
as grilled pig's trotters with *Béarnaise* sauce,
sea bass with *beurre blanc* (emulsified butter
sauce) and chocolate-drenched profiteroles, are
served in a classic dining room with a zinc bar.

🛏 Le Cercle de Malines   B&B €

(☎03 21 96 80 65; www.lecercledemalines.fr;
12 rue de Malines; s/d/f from €75/85/150; 🛜)
Built in 1884, this stately town house has been
elegantly furnished in a modern spirit, with
generous public areas and a wisteria-draped
walled garden. Among its five spacious rooms,
top choices are La Leavers, with its claw-footed
Victorian bathtub, and Guipure, with a private
sauna; family room Chantilly sleeps four. Rooms
are on the 1st and 2nd floors (no lift).

Boulogne-sur-Mer 🔟

🍴 Le Châtillon   Seafood €

(☎03 21 31 43 95; www.le-chatillon.com; 6 rue
Charles Tellier; 3-course lunch menu €25, mains
€15-25, seafood platters €36; 🕑 restaurant
11.30am-3.30pm Mon-Fri, bar 5am-4.30pm Mon,
Tue & Thu, 4am-4.30pm Wed & Fri, 4-11am Sat;
🛜) With its red banquettes and brass maritime
lanterns, this bar-restaurant has long been a
favourite of fishers after spending the night
at sea. Its house-speciality seafood platters –
piled with crab claws, scampi, whelks, winkles,
oysters and langoustines – must be reserved
24 hours in advance. Book ahead for lunch.
It's in an industrial area dominated by fish
warehouses.

🛏 Les Terrasses de l'Enclos   B&B €€

(☎03 91 90 05 90; www.enclosdeleveche.
com; L'enclos de l'Évêché, 6 rue de Pressy; r/f
from €90/150; 🛜) An imposing 19th-century
mansion next to the basilica has been turned
into an elegant B&B with a cobbled courtyard.

The five spacious rooms have hardwood floors
and contemporary furnishings, along with some
antique pieces; the family room sleeps four (one
double bed and two singles). Check-in is strictly
from 5pm. The breakfast is excellent.

Le Touquet-Paris-Plage 9️⃣

🛏 Hôtel Bristol   Hotel €€

(☎03 21 05 49 95; www.hotelbristol.fr; 17 rue
Jean Monnet; r/ste from €95/160; 🅿 @ 🛜)
Opened in 1927, this 47-room hotel is just 200m
from the beachfront promenade. Some rooms
have balconies; family rooms come with a
double and two single beds. Public areas retain
something of a pre-war vibe, while the rooms
are contemporary.

St-Valéry-sur-Somme 1️⃣2️⃣

🍴 Le Bistrot des Pilotes   Bistro €€

(☎03 22 60 80 39; www.lespilotes.fr; 62 rue
de la Ferté; mains €15-35; 🕑 noon-2.30pm &
7-9.30pm Jul & Aug, noon-2.30pm & 7-9.30pm
Wed-Sat, noon-2.30pm Sun Feb-Jun & Sep-Dec)
Outdoor tables on the waterfront, creative
seafood dishes on a menu that changes daily,
Baie de Somme specialities such as *agneau
de pré-salé* (salt-marsh lamb), and a great
mousse au chocolat make this bistro a perennial
favourite. It's downstairs from the stylish **hotel**
(s/d/f from €65/80/105; 🛜) of the same name.

🛏 Au Vélocipède   B&B €€

(☎03 22 60 57 42; http://auvelocipede.fr;
1 rue du Puits Salé; r from €107; 🅿 🛜) Two
town houses facing the church have been
transformed into this swish B&B. The nine
comfortable rooms are huge, with stripped-
back wooden floors, hip furnishings and modern
slate-and-cream bathrooms. Those up in the
attic (Vélo 3 and Vélo 4) are especially romantic,
with sloped ceilings and exposed timber beams.
Check-in is 6pm to 7pm. There's a rustic-chic
restaurant (mains €9-20; 🕑 noon-6pm
Wed-Mon Apr-Sep, shorter hours Oct-Mar; 🅿 🛜)
on-site.

In Flanders Fields

4

WWI history comes to life on this tour of Western Front battlefields, where Allied and German troops endured four years of trench warfare. Lille, Arras and Amiens offer an urban counterpoint.

TRIP HIGHLIGHTS

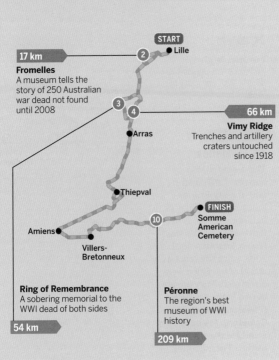

17 km

Fromelles
A museum tells the story of 250 Australian war dead not found until 2008

START
● Lille

66 km

Vimy Ridge
Trenches and artillery craters untouched since 1918

●Arras

●Thiepval

FINISH
● Somme American Cemetery

Amiens●

Villers-Bretonneux

Ring of Remembrance
A sobering memorial to the WWI dead of both sides

54 km

Péronne
The region's best museum of WWI history

209 km

3 DAYS
235KM / 146 MILES

GREAT FOR...

BEST TIME TO GO

March to November; a few sites close in December and January.

ESSENTIAL PHOTO

The staggering list of missing soldiers' names at Thiepval.

BEST FOR HISTORY

Historial de la Grande Guerre, Péronne's first-rate WWI museum.

4 In Flanders Fields

Shortly after WWI broke out in 1914, Allied troops established a line of resistance against further German advances in the northern French countryside near Arras, initiating one of the longest and bloodiest standoffs in military history. This tour of Flanders and Picardy takes in some of France's most important WWI battle sites and memorials, along with the charming cities of Lille, Arras and Amiens.

❶ Lille

A convenient gateway to northern France's WWI battlefields, cosmopolitan Lille offers an engaging mix of grand architecture and Flemish culture. Stop in for dinner at an *estaminet* (traditional Flemish restaurant) and stroll around the bustling pedestrianised centre, whose highlights include the **Vieille Bourse** (place du Général de Gaulle), a 17th-century Flemish Renaissance extravaganza decorated with caryatids and cornucopia, and the neighbourhood of **Vieux Lille** (Old Lille), where restored 17th- and 18th-century brick houses are home to chic boutiques.

✕ 🛏 p73

The Drive » Take the westbound A25, the southbound N41, the D207 and finally the D141B to Fromelles, a distance of 17km.

TRIP HIGHLIGHT

❷ Fromelles

The death toll was horrific – 1917 Australians and 519 Britons killed in just one day of fighting – yet the 1916 Battle of Fromelles was largely forgotten until 2008, when the remains of 250 of the fallen were discovered. They are now buried in the **Fromelles (Pheasant Wood) Cemetery**; 144 have been identified thanks to DNA testing. The adjoining

and excellent **Musée de la Bataille de Fromelles** (☏03 59 61 15 14; www.musee-bataille-fromelles.fr; 2 rue de la Basse Ville; cemetery free, museum adult/child €6.50/4; ⊙cemetery 24hr, museum 9.30am-5.30pm Wed-Mon early Mar–mid-Jan) evokes life in the trenches with reconstructed bunkers, photos and biographies.

The Drive ≫ Take the D22 4km south to the N41, turn southwest and after 3km turn south onto the N47; continue for 12km before turning west onto the A21. Get off at the D937, drive southeast for 5km and then follow the signs to Notre-Dame de Lorette. Total distance: 37km.

TRIP HIGHLIGHT

3 Ring of Remembrance

It's hard not to be overwhelmed by the folly and waste of the Western Front at the **Ring of Remembrance** (L'Anneau

LINK YOUR TRIP

2 A Toast to Art
From Vimy, detour 9km to Lens for this tour of northern France's arts scene.

3 Northern Coast
From Bony, head northwest to Calais (200km) to begin this spectacular drive along the Channel coast.

de la Mémoire; 📞03 21 74 83 15; www.memorial1418.com; chemin du Mont de Lorette, Ablain-St-Nazaire; ⊗Ring of Remembrance 8.30am-11pm Apr-Nov, to 8pm Dec-Mar, Notre-Dame de Lorette 10am-1pm & 2-6pm Tue-Sun Apr-Sep, to 5pm Oct-Mar) as you walk past panel after panel engraved with almost 580,000 names: WWI dead from both sides who are listed in strict alphabetical order, without reference to nationality, rank or religion.

The Drive » Return to the D937 and drive south for 6km. Then take the D49 east for 3km, the D917 north for 1km and finally the D55E2 northwest. Total distance: 12.5km

TRIP HIGHLIGHT

❹ Vimy Ridge

Right after the war, the French attempted to erase all signs of battle and return northern France to agriculture and normalcy. The Canadians took a different approach, deciding that the most evocative way to remember their fallen was to preserve part of the crater-pocked battlefield exactly the way it looked when the guns fell silent. As a result, the best place to get some sense of the hell known as the Western Front is the chilling, eerie moonscape of **Vimy Ridge** (📞03 21 50 68 68; www.cheminsde memoire.gouv.fr; chemins des Canadiens, Vimy; ⊗memorial site 24hr, visitor centre 10am-6pm May-Oct, 9am-5pm Nov-

Apr). During visitor centre opening hours, bilingual Canadian students lead free guided tours of re-constructed tunnels and trenches.

The Drive » Follow the D55E2, N17 and D917 12km into Arras.

❺ Arras

Contemplating the picture-perfect Flemish-style façades of Arras' two gorgeous market squares, the **Grand' Place** and the **Petite Place** (Place des Héros), it's hard to believe that almost the entire city centre was reduced to rubble during WWI (it was reconstructed in the 1920s). To get a sense of life in wartime Arras, head 1.5km south to **Carrière Wellington** (Wellington Quarry; 📞03 21 51 26 95; www.carrierewellington. com; rue Arthur Delétoille; private tours per person from €26; ⊗9.30am-12.30pm & 2-6pm Tue-Sun, closed Jan, longer hours summer), a subterranean quarry that served as a staging area for the Allies' 1917 spring offensive. Prior to the attack, 500 New Zealand soldiers worked round the clock for five months expanding medieval quarries to accommodate kitchens, a hospital and several thousand Commonwealth troops. Reminders of these events are everywhere, from Maori-language graffiti to candle burn marks from the Easter Mass celebrat-

ed underground the day before the troops stormed German front lines.

🍴 🛏 p73

The Drive » Take the D919, D174 and D73 31km southwest to the Newfoundland Memorial, detouring briefly at kilometre 15 to the Ayette Indian and Chinese Cemetery, a Commonwealth cemetery where Hindi, Arabic and Chinese inscriptions mark the graves of Indian soldiers and Chinese labourers recruited by the British government.

❻ Newfoundland Memorial

On 1 July 1916 the volunteer Royal Newfoundland Regiment stormed entrenched German positions and was nearly wiped out. The evocative **Beaumont-Hamel Newfoundland Memorial** (📞03 22 76 70 86; www. veterans.gc.ca; rue de l'Église, Beaumont-Hamel; ⊗10am-6pm Apr-Sep, 9am-5pm Oct-Mar) preserves the battlefield much as it was at fighting's end. Climb to the bronze caribou statue, on a hillside surrounded by native Newfoundland plants, for views of the shell craters, barbed-wire barriers and zigzag trenches that still fill with mud in winter. The on-site welcome centre offers guided tours.

The Drive » Head 5km east-southeast on the D73 through tiny Beaumont-Hamel, across a pretty valley, past the 36th (Ulster) Division Memorial (site of a Northern Irish war monument and a homey tearoom) and on to the easy-to-spot arches of the Thiepval Memorial.

---

❼ Thiepval

On a lonely, windswept hilltop, the towering **Thiepval Memorial** (📞03 22 74 60 47; www.historial. org; rue de l'Ancre; memorial free, museum adult/child €6/3; ⏰9.30am-6pm Mar-Oct, to 5pm Nov-Feb) to 'the Missing of the Somme' marks the site of a German stronghold that was stormed on 1 July 1916 with unimaginable casualties. Thiepval catches visitors off guard, both with its monumentality and its staggering simplicity: inscribed below the enormous arch, which is visible from miles around, are the names of over 72,000 British and South African soldiers whose remains were never recovered or identified. The **Museum at Thiepval**, run by Péronne's outstanding Historial de la Grande Guerre (p72), has good large-scale displays.

The Drive ›› A 44km ride on the D73 and the D929 brings you to Amiens.

---

❽ Amiens

Amiens' attractive, pedestrianised city centre offers a relaxing break from the battlefields. Climb the north tower of breathtaking, 13th-century **Cathédrale Notre Dame** (📞03 22 92 03 32; www.

Vimy Ridge Memorial to Canadian soldiers

cathedrale-amiens.fr; 30 place Notre Dame; cathedral free, north tower adult/child €6/free, treasury €4/free; ⏰ cathedral 8.30am-5.15pm daily, north tower to mid-afternoon Wed-Mon), a Unesco World Heritage Site, for stupendous views of town; a free, 45-minute **light show** bathes the cathedral's façade in vivid medieval colours nightly in summer.

Across the Somme River, gondola-like boats offer tours of Amiens' vast market gardens, the **Hortillonnages** (📞03 22 92 12 18; www.hortillonnages-amiens.fr; 54 bd Beauvillé; adult/child from €18/5; ⏰9am-noon & 1.30-6pm Apr-Oct), which have supplied the city with vegetables and flowers since the Middle Ages.

Literature buffs will love the **Maison de Jules Verne** (Maisons des Illustres; 📞03 22 45 45 75; www.amiens .fr; 2 rue Charles Dubois; adult/

child €7.50/4, audioguide €2; ⏰10am-12.30pm & 2-6pm Mon & Wed-Fri, 2-6pm Sat & Sun), the turreted home where Jules Verne wrote some of his best-known works of science fiction.

✕ 🛏 p73

The Drive ›› Take the D1029 19km east to Villers-Bretonneux.

---

❾ Villers-Bretonneux

During WWI, 46,000 of Australia's 313,000 volunteer soldiers met their deaths on the Western Front (14,000 others perished elsewhere). In the village of Villers-Bretonneux, the **Musée Franco-Australien** (Franco-Australian Museum; 📞03 22 96 80 79; www.museeaus tralien.com; 9 rue Victoria; adult/child €6/3; ⏰9.30am-6pm) displays a collection of highly personal WWI Australiana, including

71

DETOUR: CLAIRIERE DE L'ARMISTICE

Start: ⑪ **Somme American Cemetery**

On the 11th hour of the 11th day of the 11th month of 1918, WWI officially ended at **Clairière de l'Armistice** (Armistice Clearing), 7km northeast of the city of Compiègne, with the signing of an armistice inside the railway carriage of Allied supreme commander Maréchal Ferdinand Foch. In the same forest clearing, in an almost identical railroad car, the **Mémorial de l'Armistice** (☏ 03 44 85 14 18; www.musee-armistice-14-18. fr; rte de Soissons; adult/child €7/5; ⊙10am-6pm daily Apr-Sep, to 5.30pm Wed-Mon Oct-Mar) commemorates these events with memorabilia, newspaper clippings and stereoscopic photos that capture – in 3D – all the mud, muck and misery of WWI; some of the furnishings, hidden away during WWII, were the ones actually used in 1918.

From the Somme American Cemetery, take the D1044, D1 and D1032 94km southwest towards Compiègne, then follow signs 8km east along the N1031 and D546 to Clairière de l'Armistice.

ings by Otto Dix, capture the aesthetic sensibilities, enthusiasm, naive patriotism and unimaginable violence of the time.

For excellent English-language brochures about the battlefields, visit Péronne's **tourist office** (Office of Haute Somme Tourism; ☏ 03 22 84 42 38; www.hautesomme-tourisme. com; 1 rue Louis XI; ⊙9.30am-12.30pm & 1.30-6.30pm Mon-Sat, 10am-noon & 2-5pm Sun Jul & Aug, 9am-noon & 2-5pm Mon-Sat Apr-Jun, Sep & Oct, shorter hours Nov-Mar), opposite the museum.

🛏 p73

The Drive » The American cemetery is 24km east-northeast of Péronne via the D6, D406 and D57.

---

letters and photographs that evoke life on the front. The names of 10,722 Australian soldiers whose remains were never found are engraved on the base of the 32m-high **Australian National War Memorial** (☏ 03 60 62 01 40; https://sjmc.gov.au; rte de Villers-Bretonneux, Fouilloy; ⊙memorial 24hr, museum 9.30am-6pm mid-Apr–Oct, to 5pm Nov–mid-Apr), **2km north of town.**

The Drive » From the Australian National War Memorial, take the D23 briefly north, then meander east through pretty rolling country, roughly paralleling the Somme River, along the D71 and D1 via La Neuville-lès-Bray for 41km into Péronne.

TRIP HIGHLIGHT

⑩ Péronne

Housed in a fortified medieval château, Péronne's **Historial de la Grande Guerre** (Museum of the Great War; ☏ 03 22 83 14 18; www.historial.org; Château de Péronne, place André Audinot; adult/child €10/5; ⊙9.30am-6pm Apr-Oct, to 5pm Thu-Tue Nov-Mar), provides a superb overview of WWI's historical and cultural context, telling the story of the war chronologically, with equal space given to the French, British and German perspectives. Visually engaging exhibits, including period films and bone-chilling engrav-

⑪ Somme American Cemetery

In late September 1918, six weeks before the end of WWI, American units – flanked by their Commonwealth allies – launched an assault on the Germans' heavily fortified Hindenburg Line. Some of the fiercest fighting took place near the village of Bony, on the sloping site now occupied by the 1844 Latin crosses and Stars of David of the **Somme American Cemetery** (☏ 03 23 66 87 20; www.abmc.gov; rue de la Libération; ⊙9am-5pm); the names of 333 other men whose remains were never recovered are inscribed on the walls of the **Memorial Chapel**.

Eating & Sleeping

Lille ❶

✕ Estaminet Au Vieux de la Vieille
Flemish €

(📞 03 20 13 81 64; www.estaminetlille.fr; 2-4 rue des Vieux Murs; mains €12-20; 🕑 noon-2pm & 7-10.30pm Sun-Thu, to 11pm Fri & Sat; 🛜; 🅼 Gare Lille-Flandres) Hops hang from the rafters at this *estaminet* (Flemish-style restaurant), where specialities include *carbonade flamande* (braised beef slow-cooked with beer, onions, brown sugar and ginger bread) and *Welsh au Maroilles* (toast and ham smothered with Maroilles cheese melted in beer). In warm weather, there's outdoor seating on picturesque place aux Oignons.

🛏 Grand Hôtel Bellevue
Historic Hotel €€

(📞 03 20 57 45 64; www.grandhotelbellevue. com; 5 rue Jean Roisin; r from €102; 🕷 @ 🛜; 🅼 Rihour) Opened in 1913, this venerable establishment has 64 spacious rooms with high ceilings, all-marble bathrooms, gilded picture frames and a mix of inlaid-wood antiques and ultramodern furnishings. Higher-priced rooms have sweeping views of place du Général de Gaulle.

Arras ❺

✕ Café Georget
Bistro €

(📞 03 21 71 13 07; http://le-georget.metro.bar; 42 place des Héros; mains €6-15; 🕑 9am-10pm Tue-Sun) Madame Delforge has been preparing dishes such as *bavette* (flank steak) and cod with mustard sauce at this unpretentious old-time cafe *comme à la maison* (as she would at home) since 1985. Drop by for a quick trip back to the France of François Mitterrand.

🛏 Hôtel Les 3 Luppars
Hotel €€

(📞 03 21 60 02 03; www.hotel-les3luppars.com; 49 Grand' Place; r from €85; @ 🛜) Occupying the Grand' Place's only non-Flemish-style building (it's Gothic and dates from the 1400s), Les 3 Luppars (derived from 'Leopards') has a private courtyard and 42 rooms, 10 with fine views of the square. The decor is basic, but the location is great and the atmosphere is welcoming. Amenities include a sauna.

Amiens ❽

✕ Le T'chiot Zinc
Bistro €€

(📞 03 22 91 43 79; www.facebook.com/ letchiotzinc; 18 rue de Noyon; lunch menu from €16, mains €12-25; 🕑 noon-2.30pm & 7-10.30pm Mon-Sat; 🛜) Inviting, bistro-style decor reminiscent of the Belle Époque provides an atmospheric backdrop for home-style French and Picard cuisine, including fish dishes and *caqhuse* (pork in a cream, wine vinegar and onion sauce).

🛏 Hôtel Marotte
Boutique Hotel €€

(📞 03 60 12 50 00; www.hotel-marotte.com; 3 rue Marotte; r from €175; 🅿 🕷 🛜) Modern French luxury is at its most romantic at this boutique hotel. All 12 light-drenched rooms are huge (at least 35 sq metres), but the two sauna suites (100 sq metres), sporting free-standing stone bathtubs weighing 1.5 tonnes, are really luxury apartments; one opens to a rooftop terrace. Some (but not all) rooms have air-conditioning. Parking spaces are limited, so book well ahead.

Péronne ❿

🛏 Hôtel Le Saint-Claude
Hotel €€

(📞 03 22 79 49 49; www.hotelsaintclaude. com; 42 place du Commandant Louis Daudré, Péronne; r from €90; 🛜) Originally a *relais de poste* (coaching inn), the Saint-Claude is in the centre of Péronne just 200m from the medieval château housing the Historial de la Grande Guerre. The 40 contemporary rooms are decorated in chic greys and creams and are spread over three floors; some have château views. The table-strewn walled courtyard is hot and sunny in summer.

Classic Trip

Champagne Taster

From musty cellars to vine-striped hillsides, this Champagne adventure whisks you through the heart of this Unesco World Heritage region and explores the world's favourite celebratory tipple.

5

TRIP HIGHLIGHTS

0 km

Reims
Descend into the cellars of Mumm and Taittinger

① START

● Vrigny

25 km

Verzenay
Climb to the top of a lighthouse for Champagne views

Rilly-la-Montagne ●

Mailly-Champagne ●

②

Cumières ● ● Dizy

65 km

⑤

Épernay
Tick off the prestigious names along the av de Champagne

⑦

FINISH

85 km

Le Mesnil-sur-Oger
View vintage Champagne-making equipment at the village museum

---

3 DAYS
85KM / 53 MILES

GREAT FOR...

BEST TIME TO GO

April to June for spring sunshine or September and October to see the harvest in Champagne.

ESSENTIAL PHOTO

Overlooking glossy vineyards from the Phare de Verzenay.

☑ BEST FOR CULTURE

Sip Champagne in the cellars of Moët & Chandon.

Biscuits roses (pink biscuits) and Champagne

75

Classic Trip

5 Champagne Taster

'My only regret in life is that I didn't drink enough Champagne,' wrote the economist John Maynard Keynes, but by the end of this tour, you'll have drunk enough bubbly to last several lifetimes. Starting at the prestigious Champagne centre of Reims, passing through Épernay and ending in Le Mesnil-sur-Oger, this fizz-fuelled trip includes stops at some of the world's most famous producers – with ample time for tasting en route.

TRIP HIGHLIGHT

① Reims

There's nowhere better to start your Champagne tour than the regal city of **Reims**. Several big names have their *caves* (wine cellars) nearby. **Mumm** (☏03 26 49 59 70; www.mumm.com; 34 rue du Champ de Mars; tours incl tasting €23-42), pronounced 'moom', is the only *maison* in central Reims. Founded in 1827, it's the world's third- or fourth-largest Champagne producer, depending on the year.

One-hour tours explore its enormous cellars, filled with 25 million bottles of bubbly, and include tastings of several vintages.

North of town, **Taittinger** (☏03 26 85 45 35; https://cellars-booking.taittinger.fr; 9 place St-Niçaise; tours €25-77; ⊙tours 9.30am-5.30pm) provides an informative overview of how Champagne is actually made – you'll leave with a good understanding of the production process, from grape to bottle. Parts of the cellars occupy Roman stone

quarries dug in the 4th century.

Before you leave town, don't forget to drop by **Waïda** (5 place Drouet d'Erlon; ⏱7.30am-7.30pm Tue-Fri, 8am-8pm Sat, 8am-2pm & 3.30-7.30pm Sun), an old-fashioned confectioner which sells Reims' famous *biscuits roses* (pink biscuits), a sweet treat traditionally nibbled with a glass of Champagne.

✗ 🛏 p57, p83

The Drive » The countryside between Reims and Épernay is carpeted with vineyards, fields and back roads that are a dream to drive through. From Reims, head south along the D951 for 13km. Near Mont Chenot, turn onto the D26, signposted to Rilly and the 'Route Touristique du Champagne'. The next 12km takes you through the pretty villages of Rilly-la-Montagne and Mailly-Champagne en route to Verzenay.

🔗 LINK YOUR TRIP

Essential France
1 Lying 150km west of Épernay, Paris marks the beginning of our epic journey around France's most essential sights.

A Toast to Art
2 Pick up our art-themed tour in Reims, where it takes in the city's renowned Musée des Beaux-Arts.

Classic Trip

TRIP HIGHLIGHT

② Verzenay

Reims marks the start of the 70km **Montagne de Reims Champagne Route**, the prettiest (and most prestigious) of the three signposted road routes which wind their way through the Champagne vineyards. Of the 17 *grand cru* villages in Champagne, nine lie on and around the Montagne, a hilly area whose sheltered slopes and chalky soils provide the perfect environment for viticulture (grape growing).

Most of the area's vineyards are devoted to the pinot noir grape. You'll pass plenty of producers offering *dégustation* (tasting) en route. It's up to you how many you visit – but don't miss the panorama of the vineyards of Verzenay from the top of the **Phare de Verzenay** (Verzenay Lighthouse; www. lepharedeverzenay.com; D26;

CHAMPAGNE KNOW-HOW

Types of Champagne

Blanc de Blancs Champagne made using only chardonnay grapes. Fresh and elegant, with very small bubbles and a bouquet reminiscent of 'yellow fruits' such as pear and plum.

Blanc de Noirs A full-bodied, deep golden Champagne made solely with black grapes (despite the colour). Often rich and refined, with great complexity and a long finish.

Rosé Pink Champagne (mostly served as an aperitif) with a fresh character and summer-fruit flavours. Made by adding a small percentage of red pinot noir to white Champagne.

Prestige Cuvée The crème de la crème of Champagne. Usually made with grapes from *grand cru* vineyards and priced and bottled accordingly.

Millésimé Vintage Champagne produced from a single crop during an exceptional year. Most Champagne is nonvintage.

Sweetness

Brut Dry; most common style; pairs well with food.

Extra Sec Fairly dry but sweeter than Brut; nice as an aperitif.

Demi Sec Medium sweet; goes well with fruit and dessert.

Doux Very sweet; a dessert Champagne.

Serving & Tasting

Chilling Chill Champagne in a bucket of ice for 30 minutes before serving. The ideal serving temperature is 7°C to 9°C.

Opening Grip the bottle securely and tilt it at a 45-degree angle facing away from you. Rotate the bottle slowly to ease out the cork – it should sigh, not pop.

Pouring Hold the flute by the stem at an angle and let the Champagne trickle gently into the glass – less foam, more bubbles.

Tasting Admire the colour and bubbles. Swirl your glass to release the aroma and inhale slowly before tasting the Champagne.

lighthouse adult/child €3/2, museum €8/4, combined ticket €9/5; ☉10.30am-5pm Tue-Sun, closed Jan), a lighthouse constructed as a publicity gimmick in 1909.

The Drive » Continue south along the D26 for 3km.

----

❸ Verzy

This village is home to several small vineyards that provide an interesting contrast to the big producers. **Étienne and Anne-Laure Lefevre** (☎03 26 97 96 99; www.champagne-etienne-lefevre.com; 30 rue de Villers; ☉10am-noon & 2-6pm Mon-Fri, to 5pm Sat) run group tours of their family-owned vineyards and cellars – if you're on your own, ring ahead to see if you can join a pre-arranged tour. There are no flashy videos or multimedia shows – the emphasis is firmly on the nitty-gritty of Champagne production.

For a glass of fizz high above the treetops, seek out the sleek **Perching Bar** (www.facebook.com/perchingbar; Forêt de Brise-Charrette, Verzy; ☉noon-8pm Wed-Sun mid-Apr–mid-Dec) deep in the forest.

The Drive » Stay on the D26 south of Verzy, and enjoy wide-open countryside views as you spin south to Ambonnay. Detour west onto the D19, signed to Bouzy, and bear right onto the D1 along the northern bank of the Marne River. When you reach the village of Dizy, follow signs onto the D386 to Hautvillers.

Reims Champagne cave (cellar)

It's a total drive of 32km or 45 minutes.

----

❹ Hautvillers

Next stop is the hilltop village of Hautvillers, a hallowed name among Champagne aficionados: it's where a Benedictine monk by the name of Dom Pierre Pérignon is popularly believed to have created Champagne in the late 16th century. The great man's tomb lies in front of the altar of the **Église Abbatiale** (rue de l'Abbaye; ☉9am-6.30pm Mon-Fri, from 10am Sat & Sun).

The village itself is well worth a stroll, with a jumble of lanes, timbered houses and stone-walled vineyards. On place de la République, the **tourist office** (☎03 26 57 06 35; www.tourisme-hautvillers.com; place de la République; ☉9.30am-1pm & 1.30-5.30pm Mon-Sat, 10am-4pm Sun,

shorter hours Nov–mid-Apr) hands out free maps detailing local vineyard walks; one-hour guided tours cost €7 (€9 with a tasting).

Steps away is **Au 36** (www.au36.net; 36 rue Dom Pérignon; ☉10.30am-6pm Apr-Oct, to 4pm Fri-Tue Nov-Dec & Mar), a wine boutique with a 'wall' of Champagne quirkily arranged by aroma. There's a tasting room upstairs; a two-/three-glass session costs €13/17.

The Drive » From the centre of the village, take the rte de Cumières for grand views across the vine-cloaked slopes. Follow the road all the way to the D1, turn left and follow signs to Épernay's centre-ville, 6km to the south.

TRIP HIGHLIGHT

❺ Épernay

The prosperous town of Épernay is the self-proclaimed *capitale du*

SYLVAIN SONNET/GETTY IMAGES ©

BARNALIN/GETTY IMAGES ©

WHY THIS IS A CLASSIC TRIP
KERRY CHRISTIANI, WRITER

You can sip Champagne anywhere, but a road trip really slips under the skin of these Unesco-listed vineyards. Begin with an eye-opening, palate-awakening tour and tasting at *grande maison* cellars in Épernay and Reims. I love the far-reaching view from Phare de Verzenay and touring the back roads in search of small producers, especially when the aroma of new wine hangs in the air and the vines are golden in autumn.

Above: Phare de Verzenay, Verzenay
Left: Champagne tasting
Right: Chardonnay grapes, Le Mesnil-sur-Oger

EDOVAG/SHUTTERSTOCK ©

Champagne and is home to many of the most illustrious Champagne houses. Beneath the streets are an astonishing 110km of subterranean cellars, containing an estimated 200 million bottles of vintage bubbly.

Most of the big names are arranged along the grand av de Champagne. **Moët & Chandon** (📞03 26 51 20 20; www.moet.com; 20 av de Champagne; 1½hr tour with tasting €25-47, 10-17yr €10; ⏱ tours 9.30-11.30am & 2-4.30pm) offers frequent and fascinating one-hour tours of its prestigious cellars, while at nearby **Mercier** (📞03 26 51 22 22; www.champagnemercier.fr; 68-70 av de Champagne; adult incl 1/2/3 glasses €18/25/28, 10-17yr €8; ⏱ tours 9.30-11.30am & 2-4.30pm, closed mid-Dec–mid-Feb) tours take place aboard a laser-guided underground train.

Finish with a climb up the 237-step tower at **De Castellane** (📞03 26 51 19 19; www.castellane.com; 57 rue de Verdun; adult incl 1 glass €14, under 12yr free; ⏱ tours 10-noon & 2-6pm Wed-Sun, closed Christmas–mid-Mar), which offers knockout views over the town's rooftops and vine-clad hills.

✕ 🛏 p83

The Drive » Head south of town along av Maréchal Foch or av du 8 Mai 1945, following 'Autres Directions' signs across the roundabouts until you see signs for Cramant. The village is 10km southeast of Épernay via the D10.

THE SCIENCE OF CHAMPAGNE

Champagne is made from the red pinot noir (38%), the black pinot meunier (35%) or the white chardonnay (27%) grape. Each vine is vigorously pruned and trained to produce a small quantity of high-quality grapes. Indeed, to maintain exclusivity (and price), the designated areas where grapes used for Champagne can be grown and the amount of wine produced each year are limited.

Making Champagne according to the *méthode champenoise* (traditional method) is a complex procedure. There are two fermentation processes, the first in casks and the second after the wine has been bottled and had sugar and yeast added. Bottles are then aged in cellars for two to five years, depending on the *cuvée* (vintage).

For two months in early spring the bottles are aged in cellars kept at 12°C and the wine turns effervescent. The sediment that forms in the bottle is removed by *remuage*, a painstakingly slow process in which each bottle, stored horizontally, is rotated slightly every day for weeks until the sludge works its way to the cork. Next comes *dégorgement:* the neck of the bottle is frozen, creating a blob of solidified Champagne and sediment, which is then removed.

---

⑥ Cramant

You'll find it hard to miss this quaint village, as the northern entrance is heralded by a two-storey-high Champagne bottle. From the ridge above the village, views stretch out in all directions across the Champagne countryside, taking in a patchwork of fields, farmhouses and rows upon rows of endless vines. Pack a picnic and your own bottle of bubbly for the perfect Champagne country lunch.

The Drive » Continue southeast along the D10 for 7km, and follow signs to Le-Mesnil-sur-Oger.

TRIP HIGHLIGHT

⑦ Le Mesnil-sur-Oger

Finish with a visit to the excellent **Musée de la Vigne et du Vin** (☎03 26 57 50 15; www.champagne-lau nois.fr; 2 av Eugène Guillaume, cnr D10; adult incl 3 flutes €15; ⊙ tours 10am & 2.30pm Mon-Fri, 10.30am Sat & Sun), where a local wine-growing family has assembled a collection of century-old Champagne-making equipment. Among the highlights is a massive 16-tonne oak-beam grape press from 1630. Reservations must be made by phone or online; ask about the availability of English tours when you book.

Round off your trip with lunch at **La Gare** (☎03 26 51 59 55; www. lagarelemesnil.com; 3 place de la Gare; menus €18-26; ⊙ noon-1.30pm Mon-Wed, noon-1.30pm & 7-9pm Thu-Sat; ⊕), which prides itself on serving bistro-style grub prepared with seasonal produce, simple as pork tenderloin with cider and potatoes. There's a €9 menu for *les petits*.

Eating & Sleeping

Reims ❶

🍴 Brasserie Le Boulingrin
Brasserie €€

(📞03 26 40 96 22; www.boulingrin.fr; 29-31 rue de Mars; menus €25-45; 🕐noon-2.30pm daily & 7-11pm Mon-Sat) A genuine, old-time brasserie – the decor and zinc bar date back to 1925 – whose ambience and cuisine make it an enduring favourite. From September to June, the culinary focus is on *fruits de mer* (seafood) such as Breton oysters.

🍴 L'Assiette Champenoise
Gastronomy €€€

(📞03 26 84 64 64; www.assiettechampenoise. com; 40 av Paul-Vaillant-Couturier, Tinqueux; menus €125-325; 🕐noon-2pm & 7.30-10pm Thu-Mon) Heralded far and wide as one of Champagne's finest tables and crowned with the holy grail of three Michelin stars, L'Assiette Champenoise is headed up by chef Arnaud Lallemen. Listed by ingredients, his intricate, creative dishes rely on outstanding produce and play up integral flavours – be they Breton scallops or milk-fed lamb with preserved vegetables. One for special occasions.

🛏 Les Telliers
B&B €€

(📞09 53 79 80 74; https://telliers.fr; 18 rue des Telliers; s €68-85, d €80-121, tr €117-142, q €133-163; P📶) Enticingly positioned down a quiet alley near the cathedral, this bijou B&B extends one of Reims' warmest *bienvenues* (welcomes). The high-ceilinged rooms are big on art-deco character, and handsomely decorated with ornamental fireplaces, polished oak floors and the odd antique. Breakfast costs an extra €9 and is a generous spread of pastries, fruit, fresh-pressed juice and coffee.

Épernay ❺

🍴 La Cave à Champagne
French €€

(📞03 26 55 50 70; https://cave-champagne. fr; 16 rue Gambetta; menus €25-40; 🕐noon-2pm & 7-10pm Thu-Mon; 🚗) 'The Champagne Cellar' is well regarded by locals for its humble *champenoise* cuisine (snail-and-pig's-trotter casserole, fillet of beef in pinot noir), served in a warm, traditional, bourgeois atmosphere. Pair these dishes with inexpensive regional Champagnes and wines.

🍴 La Grillade Gourmande
French €€

(📞03 26 55 44 22; www.lagrilladegourmande. com; 16 rue de Reims; lunch menus €22, dinner menus €33-59; 🕐noon-1.45pm & 7.30-9.30pm Tue-Sat) This chic, art-slung bistro is an inviting spot to try chargrilled meats and dishes rich in texture and flavour, such as crayfish pan-fried in Champagne, and lamb cooked in rosemary and honey until meltingly tender. Diners spill out onto the covered terrace in the warm months. Both the presentation and service are flawless.

🛏 La Villa Eugène
Boutique Hotel €€€

(📞03 26 32 44 76; www.villa-eugene.com; 84 av de Champagne; d €175-315, ste from €354; P❄📶🚗) Sitting handsomely astride the Avenue de Champagne, with an outdoor pool, La Villa Eugène is a class act. It's in a beautiful 19th-century town mansion that once belonged to the Mercier family. The roomy doubles exude understated elegance, with soft, muted hues and the odd antique. Splash out more for a private terrace or four-poster bed.

Alsace Accents

French and German cultures come together in Alsace, renowned for cosy winstubs (traditional taverns) and centuries-old wine culture. Enjoy castles, vineyards, pastel-shaded towns and the canals of Colmar.

6

TRIP HIGHLIGHTS

START

1

30 km

Obernai
Wander the alleys of this colourful Alsatian town

65 km

3

Dambach-la-Ville
Visit one of Alsace's most striking châteaux

● Bergheim

5

80 km

Hunawihr
See Alsatian storks at Hunawihr's bird park

105 km

9

FINISH

Colmar
Cruise the canals of this chocolate-box town

3 DAYS
105KM / 66 MILES

GREAT FOR...

BEST TIME TO GO
May to October for the best chance of sunshine.

ESSENTIAL PHOTO
As you're punting along the flower-decked canals of Colmar in a romantic rowboat.

BEST FOR FAMILIES
Watching the storks at the Centre de Réintroduction Cigognes & Loutres.

Colmar River boat

85

6 Alsace Accents

Gloriously green and reassuringly rustic, the Route des Vins d'Alsace is one of France's most evocative drives. Vines march up the hillsides to castle-topped crags and the mist-shrouded Vosges, and every mile or so a roadside cellar or half-timbered village invites you to stop and raise a toast. The official route runs between Marlenheim and Thann, but we've factored in a stop at Colmar, too.

TRIP HIGHLIGHT

❶ Obernai

Sitting 31km south of Strasbourg (take the A35 and turn off at exit 11) is the typically Alsatian village of Obernai. Life still revolves around the **Place du Marché**, the market square where you'll find the 16th-century town hall, the Renaissance **Puits aux Six Seaux** (Six Bucket Well) and the bell-topped **Halle aux Blés** (Corn Exchange). Visit on Thursday mornings for the weekly market.

There are lots of flower-decked alleyways to explore – don't miss **ruelle des Juifs** – and

you can access the town's 13th-century **ramparts** in front of the **Église St-Pierre et St-Paul**.

✕ 🛏 p91

The Drive ❯❯ Follow the D422 and D1422 for 9km south of Obernai, then turn off onto the D62. Mittelbergheim is another 1.5km west, among dreamy vine-covered countryside.

---

❷ Mittelbergheim

Serene and untouristy, hillside Mittelbergheim sits amid a sea of grape-vines and wild tulips, its streets lined with red-roofed houses.

Like most Alsatian towns, it's home to numerous wineries, each marked by a wrought-

iron sign. **Domaine Gilg** (www.domaine-gilg.com; 2 rue Rotland; ⏰8am-noon & 1.30-6pm Mon-Fri, to 5pm Sat, 9.30-11.30am Sun) is a family-run winery that's won many awards for its *grand cru* sylvaners, pinots and rieslings.

From the car park on the D362 next to the cemetery, a vineyard trail, the **Sentier Viticole**, winds towards the twin-towered **Château du Haut Andlau** and the forested Vosges.

The Drive » Follow rue Principale onto the D425, signed to Eichhoffen. The road winds through lush Alsatian countryside and becomes the D35 as it travels to Dambach-la-Ville, 12km south.

TRIP HIGHLIGHT

❸ Dambach-la-Ville

Dambach is another chocolate-box village, with lots of pre-1500 houses painted in

LINK YOUR TRIP

2 A Toast to Art

Our art tour ends in Strasbourg, so it's a natural addition to this trip along the Route des Vins d'Alsace.

16 The Jura

Travel 170km southwest to Besançon to take a jaunt through the mountains and plateaux of the Jura.

ice-cream shades of pistachio, caramel and raspberry. To the southwest is the **Château du Haut Kœnigsbourg** (www.haut-koenigsbourg.fr; Orschwiller; adult/child €9/5; ⏰9.15am-6pm, shorter hours winter), a turreted castle hovering above vineyards and hills. The castle dates back nine centuries, but it was rebuilt (with typical grandiosity) by Kaiser Wilhelm II in 1908. The wraparound panorama from its pink-granite ramparts alone is worth the admission fee.

The Drive » Stay on the D35, which becomes the D1B as it nears Ribeauvillé, 22km south. It's a truly lovely drive, travelling through carpets of vines and quiet villages. You'll see the turn-off to the château about halfway to Ribeauvillé.

- - - - - - - - - - - - - - - - - -

❹ Ribeauvillé

Nestled snugly in a valley and presided over by a castle, medieval Ribeauvillé is a Route des Vins must – so you'll definitely

share it with crowds during the busy season. Along the main street, keep an eye out for the 17th-century **Pfifferhüs** (Fifers' House; 14 Grand'Rue), which once housed the town's fife-playing minstrels; the **Hôtel de Ville** and its Renaissance fountain; and the nearby clock-topped **Tour des Bouchers** (Butchers' Bell Tower).

It's also worth stopping in at the **Cave de Ribeauvillé** (📞03 89 73 20 35; www.vins-ribeauville.com; 2 rte de Colmar; ⏰8am-noon & 2-6pm Mon-Fri, 9.30am-12.30pm & 2.30-6.30pm Sat & Sun), France's oldest winegrowers' cooperative, founded in 1895. It has an interesting viniculture museum and offers free tastings of its excellent wines. It's two roundabouts north from the tourist office.

 p91

The Drive » Hunawihr is 2.5km south of Ribeauvillé.

PAWEL KAZMIERCZAK / SHUTTERSTOCK ©

DRIVING THE ROUTE DES VINS

The Route des Vins is signposted, but local tourist offices have maps, which come in handy. Among these are free English-language maps – *The Alsace Wine Route* and *Alsace Grand Cru Wines* – detailing Alsace's prestigious AOC regions. There is info online at www.routedesvins.alsace.

Parking can be a nightmare in the high season, especially in Ribeauvillé and Riquewihr; your best bet is to park outside the town centre and walk for a few minutes.

TRIP HIGHLIGHT

❺ Hunawihr

Cigognes (white storks) are Alsace's most emblematic birds. They feature in many folk tales and are believed to bring good luck (as well as newborn babies). They've been roosting on rooftops here for centuries, but their numbers fell

Kaysersberg Vineyards and village

dramatically during the 20th century as a result of environmental damage and habitat loss.

Thankfully, conservation programs have helped revive the birds' fortunes. **NaturOparC** (www.centredereintroduction. fr; rte de Ribeauvillé; adult/ child €11/9.50; ☺10am-6.30pm, closed early Nov-late Mar; 👪) houses more than 200 storks, plus cormo-

rants, penguins, otters and sea lions.

The Drive » Backtrack to the D1B and travel 4km south, following signs to Riquewihr. Distant hills unfold to the south as you drive.

----

6 Riquewihr

Competition is stiff, but Riquewihr just may be *the* most enchanting town on the Route des

Vins. Medieval ramparts enclose a maze of twisting lanes and halftimbered houses, each brighter and lovelier than the next.

The **Tour des Voleurs** (Thieves' Tower; www.museeriquewihr.fr; €5, incl Dolder €7; ☺10.30am-1pm & 2-6pm Easter-Oct) houses a gruesome torture chamber that's guaranteed to enthral the kids.

The late-13th-century, half-timbered **Dolder** (www.musee-riquewihr.fr; €3; ⏱2-6pm Sat & Sun Apr-Nov, daily Jul–mid-Aug), topped by a 25m bell tower, is worth a look for its panoramic views and small local-history museum.

The Drive » A scenic minor road winds 7km south from av Méquillet in Riquewihr to Kientzheim, then joins the D28 for another 1km to Kaysersberg.

7 Kaysersberg

Just 10km northwest of Colmar, Kaysersberg is another instant heartstealer with its backdrop of vines, castle and 16th-century bridge. An old-town saunter through the **Vieille Ville** brings you to the Renaissance **hôtel de ville** and the red-sandstone **Église Ste-Croix** (41 rue du Général de Gaulle; ⏱9am-4pm), whose altar has 18 painted panels of the Passion and the Resurrection.

Kaysersberg was also the birthplace of Albert Schweitzer (1875–1965), a musicologist, doctor and winner of the Nobel Peace Prize.

The Drive » Take the N415 southeast of Kaysersberg for 7km, passing through Ammerschwihr and then following signs to Katzenthal.

8 Katzenthal

Katzenthal is great for tiptoeing off the tourist trail. *Grand cru* vines ensnare the hillside, topped by the medieval ruins of **Château du Wineck**, where walks through forest and vineyard begin.

It's also a great place for some wine tasting thanks to **Vignoble Klur** (☎03 89 80 94 29; www.klur.net; 105 rue des Trois Épis; apt from €110), an organic, family-run winery that also offers cookery classes, vineyard walks and back-to-nature holidays.

The Drive » Rejoin the D415. Colmar is another 8km south and is clearly signed.

TRIP HIGHLIGHT

9 Colmar

At times the Route des Vins d'Alsace fools you into thinking it's 1454, but in Colmar the illusion is complete.

Mosey around the canal quarter of **Petite Venise** (Little Venice; rowboats per 30min €6), then head along **rue des Tanneurs**, with its rooftop verandahs for drying hides, and **quai de la Poissonnerie**, the former fishermen's quarter. Afterwards, hire a **rowing boat** (€6 per 30 minutes) beside the rue de Turenne bridge for that Venetian vibe.

The town also has some intriguing museums. The star attraction at the **Musée d'Unterlinden** (www.musee-unterlinden.com; 1 rue d'Unterlinden; adult/child €13/8; ⏱10am-6pm Wed & Fri-Mon, to 8pm Thu) is the Rétable d'Issenheim (Issenheim Altarpiece), a medieval masterpiece that depicts scenes from the New Testament.

Meanwhile, the **Musée Bartholdi** (☎03 89 41 90 60; www.musee-bartholdi.fr; 30 rue des Marchands; adult/child €6.70/free; ⏱10am-noon & 2-6pm Tue-Sun Mar-Dec) is the birthplace of sculptor Frédéric Auguste Bartholdi, architect of the Statue of Liberty. Highlights include a full-sized model of Lady Liberty's left ear (the lobe is watermelon-sized!) and the family's sparklingly bourgeois apartment.

Look out for the miniature version of the statue on the rte du Strasbourg (N83), erected to mark the centenary of Bartholdi's death.

✕ ⛌ p91

Eating & Sleeping

Obernai ❶

✕ La Fourchette des Ducs   Gastronomy €€€

(☎03 88 48 33 38; www.lafourchettedesducs.com; 6 rue de la Gare; menus €140-175; ⊙7-9.30pm Tue-Sat, noon-1.30pm Sun) A great believer in fastidious sourcing, chef Nicolas Stamm serves regional cuisine with gourmet panache and a signature use of herbs to a food-literate crowd at this two-Michelin-starred restaurant. The tasting *menus* go with the seasons, featuring specialities such as Alsatian pigeon with *baerewecke* (spiced fruit cake) and sweetbreads of veal with onions and caramelised potatoes – simple but sublime.

🛏 Le Gouverneur   Historic Hotel €

(☎03 88 95 63 72; www.hotellegouverneur.com; 13 rue de Sélestat; d €65-125; [P] [📶]) Overlooking a courtyard, this old-town hotel strikes a perfect balance between half-timbered rusticity and contemporary comfort. Its petite rooms have a boutiquey feel, with bursts of vivid colour and art-slung walls.

Ribeauvillé ❹

✕ Winstub Zum Pfifferhüs   French €€

(☎03 89 73 62 28; 14 Grand'Rue; menus €26-52; ⊙noon-1.30pm & 6.30-8.30pm Fri-Tue) If it's good old-fashioned Alsatian grub you're after, look no further than this snug wine tavern, which positively radiates rustic warmth with its beams, dark wood and checked tablecloths. Snag a table for copious dishes including *choucroute garnie* (sauerkraut with smoked meats), pork knuckles and *coq au riesling* (chicken braised in riesling and herbs).

🛏 Le Clos Saint Vincent   Boutique Hotel €€€

(☎03 89 73 67 65; www.leclossaintvincent.com; Osterbergweg; s/d from €175/195; [P] [📶] [🏊]) Gasp you might as you crest the hill and gaze out across the vines and the wooded peaks of the Vosges near this elegant guesthouse. The sound is silence and the smart, light-drenched rooms capitalise on those incredible views, as does the restaurant, serving French cuisine inspired by the seasons. An indoor pool and a little spa area invite relaxation. It's 1km north of Ribeauvillé.

Colmar ❾

✕ L'Atelier du Peintre   Gastronomy €€€

(☎03 89 29 51 57; www.atelier-peintre.fr; 1 rue Schongauer; menus €38-80, mains €21-42; ⊙noon-1.30pm & 7-9.30pm Wed-Sat, 7-9.30pm Tue) With its art-filled walls and carefully composed cuisine, this Michelin-starred bistro lives up to its 'Painter's Studio' name. Seasonal masterpieces such as roasted veal with chorizo and citrus or char lakefish with mushrooms and quince are cooked with verve and served with panache.

🛏 Hôtel les Têtes   Historic Hotel €€€

(☎03 89 24 43 43; www.maisondestetes.com; 19 rue des Têtes; d from €225; [❄] [📶]) Luxurious but never precious, this hotel occupies the magnificent Maison des Têtes. Each of its 21 rooms has rich wooden panelling, an elegant sitting area, a marble bathroom and romantic views. With its wrought ironwork and stained glass, the brasserie provides a sumptuously historic backdrop for French-Alsatian specialities (mains €26 to €42).

STRETCH YOUR LEGS
PARIS

Start Place de la Concorde

Finish Place du Panthéon

Distance 4.5km

Duration Three hours

Paris is one of the world's most strollable cities, whether that means window-shopping on the boulevards or getting lost among the lanes of Montmartre. This walk starts by the Seine, crosses to the Île de la Cité and finishes in the Latin Quarter, with monuments and museums aplenty en route.

Take this walk on Trip

Place de la Concorde

If it's Parisian vistas you're after, the place de la Concorde makes a fine start. From here you can see the Arc de Triomphe, the Assemblée Nationale (the lower house of parliament), the Jardin des Tuileries and the Seine. Laid out in 1755, the square was where many aristocrats lost their heads during the Revolution, including Louis XVI and Marie Antoinette. The obelisk in the centre originally stood in the Temple of Ramses at Thebes (now Luxor).

The Walk » Walk east through Jardin des Tuileries.

Jardin des Tuileries

This 28-hectare landscaped **garden** (rue de Rivoli, 1er; ⊙7am-11pm Jun-Aug, 7am-9pm Apr, May & Sep, 7.30am-7.30pm Oct-Mar; Ⓜ Tuileries, Concorde) was laid out in 1664 by André Le Nôtre, who also created Versailles' gardens. Filled with fountains, ponds and sculptures, the gardens are part of the Banks of the Seine World Heritage Site.

The Walk » Walk across place du Carrousel onto the Cour Napoléon.

Musée du Louvre

Overlooking the Cour Napoléon is the mighty **Louvre**, with its controversial 21m-high glass **Grande Pyramide**, designed by IM Pei in 1989. Nearby is the **Pyramide Inversée** (Upside-Down Pyramid), which acts as a skylight for the underground Carrousel du Louvre shopping centre.

The Walk » Continue southeast along riverside Quai du Louvre to Pont Neuf metro station.

Pont Neuf

As you cross the Seine, you'll walk over Paris' oldest bridge – ironically known as the 'New Bridge', or Pont Neuf. Henri IV inaugurated the bridge in 1607 by crossing it on a white stallion.

The Walk » Cross the Pont Neuf onto the Île de la Cité. Walk southeast along Quai des Horloges, and then turn right onto bd du Palais.

Conciergerie

On bd du Palais, the elegant **Conciergerie** (☏01 53 40 60 80; www.paris-conciergerie.

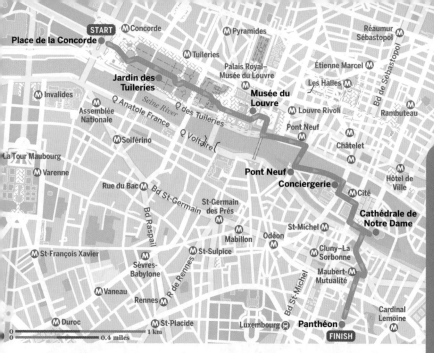

START Concorde
Place de la Concorde
Pyramides
Réaumur
Sébastopol

Tuileries
Palais Royal–
Musée du Louvre
Étienne Marcel

**Jardin des
Tuileries**
Les Halles

Invalides
Q Anatole France
Seine River
Q des Tuileries
**Musée du
Louvre**
Louvre Rivoli
Rambuteau

Assemblée
Nationale
Q Voltaire
Pont Neuf

Solférino
Châtelet

La Tour Maubourg
Varenne

Pont Neuf
Hôtel de
Ville

Rue du Bac
Bd St-Germain
Bd Raspail
Conciergerie
Cité

St-Germain
des Prés
**Cathédrale de
Notre Dame**

St-Michel

St-François Xavier
Mabillon
Odéon
Cluny–La
Sorbonne

Sèvres-
Babylone
St-Sulpice
Maubert-
Mutualité

R de Rennes
Bd St-Michel

Vaneau
Rennes

Cardinal
Lemoine

Duroc
St-Placide
Luxembourg
Panthéon

FINISH

1 km
0.4 miles

fr; 2 bd du Palais, 1er; adult/child €9.50/free, combined ticket with Sainte-Chapelle €17/free; ⊙10.30am-6.30pm; MCité) is a royal palace that became a prison and torture chamber for enemies of the Revolution. The 14th-century Salle des Gens d'Armes (Cavalrymen's Hall) is Europe's largest surviving medieval hall. The nearby church of **Sainte-Chapelle** (joint ticket with Conciergerie €17) has stunning stained glass.

The Walk » Continue east along rue de Lutèce, then cross place du Parvis Notre Dame and walk towards the cathedral.

Cathédrale de Notre Dame

Built on a site occupied by earlier churches and, a millennium prior, a Gallo-Roman temple, **Notre Dame** (www.notredamedeparis.fr; 6 Parvis Notre Dame – place Jean-Paul-II, 4e) was begun in 1163 and largely completed by the early 14th century. While its interior is closed following the devastating fire of April 2019, this French Gothic masterpiece remains the city's geographic and spiritual heart. Its grand exterior, with its two enduring towers and flying buttresses, is a definitive Parisian landmark and symbol of hope during its restoration to its former glory.

The Walk » Cross the river on Pont au Double and follow rue Lagrange to bd St-Germain. Then take rue des Carmes and rue Valette south to the place du Panthéon.

Panthéon

Once you reach the left bank you'll be in the Latin Quarter, the centre of Parisian higher education since the Middle Ages, and still home to the city's top university, the Sorbonne. It's also where you'll find the **Panthéon** (☎01 44 32 18 00; www.paris-pantheon.fr; place du Panthéon, 5e; adult/child €11.50/free; ⊙10am-6.30pm Apr-Sep, to 6pm Oct-Mar; MMaubert-Mutualité or RER Luxembourg), the neoclassical mausoleum where some of France's greatest thinkers are entombed, including Voltaire, Rousseau and Marie Curie.

The Walk » It's a long walk back, so catch the metro. Walk east to place Monge, take line 7 to Palais Royal Musée du Louvre, then line 1 west to Concorde.

Normandy & Brittany

NORMANDY OFFERS SOME OF FRANCE'S MOST ICONIC SIGHTS, including the spectacular island monastery of Mont St-Michel, the poignant memorials along the D-Day beaches and the picture-postcard village of Giverny, intrinsically linked with impressionism. It also enjoys coastal landscapes, pastoral villages and architectural gems ranging from Rouen's medieval old city to the maritime charms of Honfleur and the striking postwar modernism of Le Havre.

Further west, Brittany has a wonderfully undiscovered feel once you go beyond famous sights like stunning St-Malo, charming Dinan and delightful Pont-Aven. Unexpected gems – including the towns of Quimper and Vannes, the megaliths of Carnac and the Presqu'île de Crozon – demonstrate there's more to Brittany than crêpes and cider.

Breton Coast Golfe du Morbihan
BORIS STROUJKO / SHUTTERSTOCK ©

Normandy & Brittany

English Channel (La Manche)

Alderney

Guernsey

Sark

Jersey

Les Minquiers

Cherbourg

Île Tatihou

Arromanche

Parc Naturel Régional des Marais du Cotentin et du Bessin

Baye

St-Lô

Perros-Guirec

Roscoff

Île de Bréhat

St-Quay-Portrieux

Île de Cézembre

Île des Landes

Lesneven

D786

St-Malo

Morlaix

St-Brieuc

Parc Natur Région Normandie-Mai

Brest

N176

Dinan

Parc Naturel Régional d'Armorique

Crozon

BRITTANY

Fougères

Châteaulin

Île de Sein

Quimper

Rennes

Lava

Concarneau

Ploërmel

Pont-Aven

9

Lorient

Rivière d'Etel

Bay of Biscay

Île de Groix

Vannes

Carnac

Île aux Moines

Belle-Île-en-Mer

Île d'Houat

A11

Île d'Hoëdic

Parc Naturel Régional de Brière

Nantes

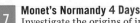

0 ——— 100 km
0 ——— 50 miles

DON'T MISS

Distillerie Christian Drouin

Taste two of Normandy's top tipples – calvados and cider – at this traditional distillery. Refresh yourself on Trip 1

Musée d'Art Moderne André Malraux

This museum in Le Havre contains the best impressionist collection outside Paris. Take it all in on Trip 7

Dinan

Explore this beautiful medieval town replete with narrow cobblestone streets and squares lined with half-timbered houses. Discover it on Trip 9

Longues-sur-Mer

See where parts of the famous D-Day movie, *The Longest Day* (1962), were filmed on Trip 8

Île de Batz

Find brilliant sand beaches on this tiny speck of paradise. Get away from it all on Trip 9

Monet's Normandy

This eclectic trip takes art lovers on a fascinating spin around eastern Normandy. En route you'll hit the key landscapes and cities that inspired Monet, the father of impressionism.

7

TRIP HIGHLIGHTS

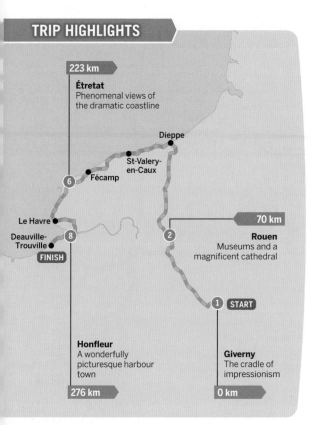

223 km

Étretat
Phenomenal views of the dramatic coastline

Dieppe

St-Valery-en-Caux

6 **Fécamp**

Le Havre

Deauville-Trouville

8

FINISH

70 km

2

Rouen
Museums and a magnificent cathedral

1 **START**

Honfleur
A wonderfully picturesque harbour town

276 km

Giverny
The cradle of impressionism

0 km

4 DAYS
290KM / 180 MILES

GREAT FOR...

BEST TIME TO GO

Any time from September to June for perfectly nuanced light.

ESSENTIAL PHOTO

Snap the truly extraordinary coastal vista from the clifftop in Étretat.

BEST FOR CULTURE

Rouen has plenty of top-quality museums and historic buildings.

Giverny Maison et Jardins de Claude Monet

7 Monet's Normandy

Be prepared for a visual feast on this three-day trip around the eastern part of Normandy – the cradle of impressionism. Starting from Giverny, location of the most celebrated garden in France, you'll follow in the footsteps of Monet and other impressionist megastars, taking in medieval Rouen, the dramatic Côte d'Albâtre, Le Havre, Honfleur and Trouville-sur-Mer. This is your chance to see first-hand why so many painters were attracted to this place.

TRIP HIGHLIGHT

❶ Giverny

The tiny country village of Giverny is a place of pilgrimage for devotees of impressionism. Monet lived here from 1883 until his death in 1926, in a rambling house – surrounded by flower-filled gardens – that's now the immensely popular **Maison et Jardins de Claude Monet** (📞02 32 51 28 21; www.fondation-monet.com; 84 rue Claude Monet; adult/child €10.50/6.50; ⏰9.30am-6pm Apr-Oct). His pastel-pink

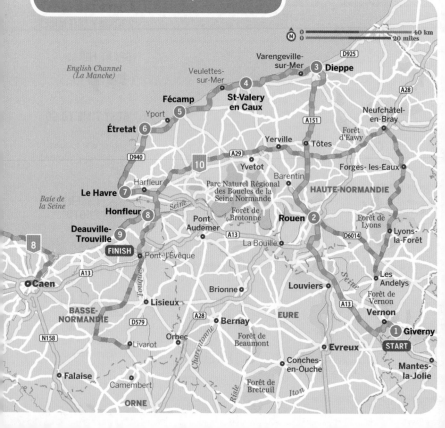

house and Water Lily studio stand on the periphery of the garden (called 'Clos Normand'), with its symmetrically laid-out gardens bursting with flowers.

The Drive >> It's a 71km trip (one hour) to Rouen. Head to Vernon and follow signs to Rouen along the A13. A more scenic (but slower) route is the D313 via Les Andelys, along the east bank of the Seine.

TRIP HIGHLIGHT

② Rouen

With its elegant spires and atmospheric medieval quarter complete with narrow lanes and wonky half-timbered houses, it's no wonder that Rouen has inspired numerous painters, including Monet. Some of his works, including one

LINK YOUR TRIP

Tour des Fromages

From Honfleur or Rouen you can embark on a gastronomic drive, and taste and learn about some of the best cheese in France at various cheese museums.

D-Day's Beaches

From Trouville, it's an easy 50km drive west to Caen, the obvious starting point for the D-Day beaches.

of his studies of the stunning Gothic **Cathédrale Notre Dame** (☎02 35 71 85 65; www.cathedrale-rouen.net; place de la Cathédrale; ⏰2-7pm Mon, 9am-7pm Tue-Sat, 8am-6pm Sun Apr-Oct, shorter hours Nov-Mar), are displayed at the splendid **Musée des Beaux-Arts** (☎02 35 71 28 40; www.mbarouen.fr; esplanade Marcel Duchamp; ⏰10am-6pm Wed-Mon). Feeling inspired? Sign up for an art class with the **tourist office** (☎02 32 08 32 40; www.rouentourisme.com; 25 place de la Cathédrale; ⏰9am-7pm Mon-Sat, 9.30am-12.30pm & 2-6pm Sun May-Sep, 9.30am-12.30pm & 1.30-6pm Mon-Sat Oct-Apr) and create your own Rouen Cathedral canvas from the very room in which Monet painted his series of that building.

If you're at all interested in architectural glories, the 14th-century **Abbatiale St-Ouen** (https://rouen.fr/abbatiale-saint-ouen; place du Général de Gaulle; ⏰10am-noon & 2-6pm Tue-Thu, Sat & Sun, to 5pm Nov-Mar), which is a marvellous example of the Rayonnant Gothic style, is a must-see abbey. There's also much Joan of Arc lore in Rouen (she was executed here in 1431). For the story of her life don't miss the spectacular audio-visual displays in the **Historial Jeanne d'Arc** (☎02 35 52 48 00; www.historial-jeannedarc.fr; 7 rue St-Romain; adult/

child €10.50/7.50; ⏰10am-6pm Tue-Sun).

✗ 🏠 p105, p131

The Drive >> Follow signs to Dieppe. Count on 45 minutes for the 64km trip via the A151 and N27.

③ Dieppe

Sandwiched between limestone cliffs, Dieppe is a small-scale fishing port with a pleasant seafront promenade. Still used by fishing vessels but dominated by pleasure craft, the **port** makes for a bracing sea-air stroll. High above the city on the western cliff, the 15th-century **Musée de Dieppe** (☎02 35 06 61 99; www.dieppe.fr; rue de Chastes; adult/child €4.50/free; ⏰10am-noon & 2-5pm Wed-Sun Oct-May, 10am-6pm Wed-Sun Jun-Sep) is the town's most imposing landmark. Monet immortalised **Pourville**, a seaside village on the western outskirts of Dieppe.

The Drive >> Take the scenic coastal roads (D75 and D68), rather than the inland D925, via the resort towns of Pourville, Varengeville-sur-Mer, Quiberville, St-Aubin-sur-Mer, Sotteville-sur-Mer and Veules-les-Roses (35km, 45 minutes).

④ St-Valery en Caux

You're now in the heart of the scenic Côte d'Albâtre (Alabaster Coast), which stretches from Dieppe southwest to Étretat. With its lofty bone-white cliffs, this wedge of coast is a geological wonderworld that charmed a generation of impressionists, including Monet. Once you get a glimpse of sweet little St-Valery en Caux, with its delightful port, lovely stretch of stony beach and majestic cliffs, you'll see why.

The Drive >> Take the coastal road (D79) via Veulettes-sur-Mer. Count on an hour for the 36km trip.

⑤ Fécamp

After all that driving along the Côte d'Albâtre, it's time to stop for a glass of Bénédictine at the **Palais de la Bénédictine** (📞02 35 10 26 10; www.benedictinedom.com; 110 rue Alexandre Le Grand; adult €18; ⊙ bar & shop 10.30am-12.30pm & 2.30-6.30pm daily, longer hours summer). Opened in 1900, this unusually ornate factory is where all the Bénédictine liqueur in the world is made.

Be sure to drive up north to **Cap Fagnet** (110m), which offers gobsmacking views of the town and the coastline.

The Drive >> Follow signs to Étretat (17km, along the D940). You could also start on the D940 and turn off onto the more scenic D11 (via Yport).

TRIP HIGHLIGHT

⑥ Étretat

Is Étretat the most enticing town in Normandy?

SERGIYN / SHUTTERSTOCK ©

It's picture-postcard everywhere you look. The dramatic white cliffs that bookend the town, the **Falaise d'Aval** to the southwest and the **Falaise d'Amont** to the northeast, will stick in your memory. Once at the top, you'll pinch yourself to see if it's real – the views are sensational. Such irresistible scenery made Étretat a favourite of painters, especially Monet, who produced more than 80 canvases of the scenery here.

The Drive >> Follow signs to Le Havre (28km, along the D940 and the D147). Count on about half an hour for the journey.

⑦ Le Havre

It was in Le Havre that Monet painted the defining impressionist view. His 1873 canvas of the harbour at dawn was entitled *Impression: Sunrise*. Monet wouldn't recognise present-day Le Havre: all but obliterated in September 1944 by Allied bombing raids, the city centre was totally redesigned after the war by Belgian architect Auguste Perret. Make sure you visit the **Musée d'Art Moderne André Malraux** (MuMa; 📞02 35 19 62 62; www.muma-lehavre.fr; 2 bd Clemenceau; adult/child

Honfleur Vieux Bassin

€10/6; ☉10am-6pm Tue-Fri, 11am-7pm Sat & Sun), which houses a truly fabulous collection of impressionist works, with canvases by Claude Monet, Eugène Boudin, Camille Corot and many more. Then take in the **Église St-Joseph** (www.uneteauhavre.fr/fr/eglise-saint-joseph; 130 bd François 1er; ☉10am-6pm), a modern church whose interior is a luminous work of art – thanks to 13,000 panels of coloured glass on its walls and tower. For doses of Baroque ecclesiastical architecture, stop by **Cathédrale Notre-Dame** (rue de Paris; ☉hours vary).

✕ ⊨ p105

The Drive ⟫ Follow the A131 and A29 for 25km, which link Le Havre to Honfleur.

- - - - - - - - - - - - - - - - - -

TRIP HIGHLIGHT

8 Honfleur

Honfleur is exquisite to look at. (No, you're not dreaming!) Its heart is the highly picturesque **Vieux Bassin** (Old Harbour), from where explorers once set sail for the New World. Marvel at the extraordinary 15th-century wooden **Église Ste-Catherine** (✆02 31 89 23 30; place Ste-Catherine; ☉9am-7pm), complete with a roof that from the inside resembles an upturned boat, then wander the warren of flower-filled cobbled streets lined with wooden and stone buildings.

Honfleur's graceful beauty has inspired numerous painters, including Eugène Boudin, an early impressionist painter born here in 1824, and Monet. Their works are displayed at the **Musée Eugène Boudin** (✆02 31 89 54 00; www.musees-honfleur.fr; 50 rue de l'Homme de Bois; adult/child Jun-Oct €8/free, Nov-May €6/free; ☉10am-6pm Wed-Mon Jul & Aug, 10am-noon & 2-6pm

CLAUDE MONET

The undisputed leader of the impressionists, Claude Monet was born in Paris in 1840 and grew up in Le Havre, where he found an early affinity with the outdoors.

From 1867 Monet's distinctive style began to emerge, focusing on the effects of light and colour and using the quick, undisguised broken brushstrokes that would characterise the impressionist period. His contemporaries were Pissarro, Renoir, Sisley, Cézanne and Degas. The young painters left the studio to work outdoors, experimenting with the shades and hues of nature, and arguing and sharing ideas. Their work was far from welcomed by critics; one of them condemned it as 'impressionism', in reference to Monet's *Impression: Sunrise* when exhibited in 1874.

From the late 1870s Monet concentrated on painting in series, seeking to recreate a landscape by showing its transformation under different conditions of light and atmosphere. In 1883 Monet moved to Giverny, planting his property with a variety of flowers around an artificial pond, the Jardin d'Eau, in order to paint the subtle effects of sunlight on natural forms. It was here that he painted the *Nymphéas* (Water Lilies) series.

For more info on Monet and his work, visit www.claude-monet.com.

Wed-Mon Apr-Jun & Sep, shorter hours Oct-Mar).

Honfleur was also the birthplace of composer Erik Satie. The fascinating **Les Maisons Satie** (☏02 31 89 11 11; www.musees-honfleur.fr/maison-satie.html; 67 bd Charles V & 90 rue Haute; adult/child €6.30/free; ☉10am-7pm Wed-Mon May-Sep, 11am-6pm Wed-Mon Oct-Apr) is packed with surrealist surprises, all set to his ethereal compositions.

✕ 🛏 p105 , p131

The Drive ⟫ From Honfleur it's a 14km trip to Trouville-sur-Mer along the D513 (about 20 minutes).

---

9 Deauville-Trouville

Finish your impressionist road trip in style by heading southwest to the twin seaside resorts of Deauville and Trouville-sur-Mer, which are only separated by a river bridge but maintain distinctly different personalities. Exclusive, expensive and brash, **Deauville** is packed with designer boutiques, deluxe hotels and public gardens of impossible neatness and is home to two racetracks and a high-profile American film festival (www.festival-deauville.com).

Trouville-sur-Mer, another veteran beach resort, is more down to earth. During the 19th century the town was frequented by writers and painters, including Monet, who spent his honeymoon here in 1870. No doubt he was lured by the picturesque port, the 2km-long sandy beach lined with opulent villas, and the laid-back seaside ambience.

Eating & Sleeping

Rouen ②

✕ Comptoir des Halles Seafood €

(☎02 32 10 64 79; place du Vieux Marché; mains €10-20; ☺11am-3pm Tue-Sat) Rouen's covered market bursts with the region's bounty. Among several excellent eateries, casual yet polished **Bar à Huîtres** stands out for its fresh seafood. Sit at the horseshoe-shaped bar and choose from specials that change daily based on what's fresh, from giant shrimp to dorado and fillet of sole. Naturally, there are also several varieties of *huîtres* (oysters) on offer.

⊨ La Boulangerie B&B €

(☎06 12 94 53 15; www.laboulangerie.fr; 59 rue St-Nicaise; s/d from €67/77; 🛜) Tucked away in a quiet side street 1.2km northeast of the cathedral, this adorable B&B sits above a historic (and very good) bakery and has three bright, pleasingly decorated rooms that feature artwork and exposed-beam ceilings. Charming host Aminata is a mine of local information. Parking available nearby for €5; breakfast included.

Le Havre ⑦

✕ La Taverne Paillette Brasserie €€

(☎02 35 41 31 50; www.taverne-paillette.com; 22 rue Georges Braque; lunch menus €16-32, mains €15-28; ☺noon-midnight) Solid brasserie food is served up at this Le Havre institution whose origins go back to the late 16th century. Expect bowls overflowing with mussels, generous salads, gargantuan seafood platters and, in the Alsatian tradition, eight types of *choucroute* (sauerkraut). Diners leave contentedly well fed, and many are here for its famous beer too. It's five blocks north of Église St-Joseph, at the northeastern corner of a park called Le Square St-Roch.

⊨ Vent d'Ouest Hotel Boutique Hotel €€

(☎02 35 42 50 69; www.ventdouest.fr; 4 rue de Caligny; r from €125, ste from €140, apt from €175; 🛜) This terrific and stylish luxe establishment is all nautical downstairs and has cheerfully painted rooms upstairs arranged with sisal flooring and attractive furnishings; ask for one with a balcony. There are lovely common areas where you can while away the hours with a book if the weather sours, including an enticing cafe-bar with leather armchairs. There's also a good restaurant and a sparkling spa on-site; breakfast costs €15/8 per adult/child. The hotel is across the street from Église St-Joseph.

Honfleur ⑧

✕ La Fleur de Sel Gastronomy €€€

(☎02 31 89 01 92; www.lafleurdesel-honfleur. com; 17 rue Haute; menus from €34; ☺12.15-1.30pm & 7.15-9.30pm Wed-Sun) Honfleur-raised Vincent Guyon cooked in some of Paris' top kitchens before returning to his hometown to make good and open his own (now celebrated) restaurant. Guyon uses the highest-quality locally sourced ingredients and plenty of invention (with roast meats and wild-caught seafood featuring ginger and kaffir-lime vinaigrettes, Camembert foams and hazelnut tempura) in his beautifully crafted dishes. Reserve ahead.

⊨ La Maison de Lucie Boutique Hotel €€€

(☎02 31 14 40 40; www.lamaisondelucie.com; 44 rue des Capucins; r from €180; P 🛜) This marvellous and intimate nine-room, three-suite hideaway is a gem. Some bedrooms, panelled in oak, have Moroccan-tile bathrooms and fantastic views across the harbour to the Pont de Normandie. The shady terrace is a glorious place for a summer breakfast (from €14). A chic Jacuzzi-spa (€40 for two people, 45 minutes) in the brick-vaulted cellar rounds things off. No lift. Parking is €15 per day.

Classic Trip

D-Day's Beaches

Explore the events of D-Day, when Allied troops stormed ashore to liberate Europe from Nazi occupation. From war museums to landing beaches, it's a fascinating and sobering experience.

8

TRIP HIGHLIGHTS

88 km
Omaha Beach
Pay your respects at the American Cemetery & Memorial

Utah Beach
FINISH

Carentan

Isigny-sur-Mer

8

7

Sully

1

START

Pointe du Hoc
Wander amongst shell craters that haven't changed since D-Day
98 km

Caen
Visit an award-winning multimedia D-Day museum
0 km

3 DAYS
142KM / 88 MILES

GREAT FOR...

BEST TIME TO GO

April to July, to avoid summer-holiday traffic around the beaches.

ESSENTIAL PHOTO

The forest of white marble crosses at the Normandy American Cemetery & Memorial.

BEST FOR HISTORY

The Caen-Normandie Mémorial provides you with a comprehensive D-Day overview.

8 D-Day's Beaches

The beaches and bluffs are quiet today, but on 6 June 1944 the Normandy shoreline witnessed the arrival of the largest armada the world has ever seen. This patch of the French coast will forever be synonymous with D-Day (known to the French as Jour-J), and the coastline is strewn with memorials, museums and cemeteries – reminders that though victory was won on the Longest Day, it came at a high price.

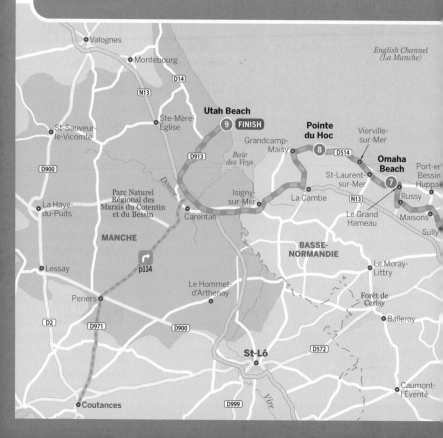

TRIP HIGHLIGHT

1 Caen

Situated 3km north-west of Caen, the award-winning **Caen-Normandie Mémorial** (📞02 31 06 06 44; www.memorial-caen.fr; esplanade Général Eisenhower; adult/child pass €14.50/free; ⏰9am-7pm daily Apr-Sep, 9.30am-6pm daily Oct, 9.30am-5pm Sat & Sun Nov-Mar) is a brilliant place to begin with some background on the historic events of D-Day and the wider context of WWII. Housed in a purpose-designed building covering 14,000 sq metres, the memorial offers an immersive experience, using sound, lighting, film, animation and audio testimony to evoke the grim realities of war, the trials of occupation and the joy of liberation.

The visit begins with a whistle-stop overview of Europe's descent into total war, tracing events from the end of WWI through to the rise of fascism in Europe, the German occupation of France and the Battle of Normandy. A second section focuses on the Cold War. There's also the well-preserved original bunker used by German command in 1944.

On your way around, look out for a Hawker Typhoon fighter plane and a full-size Sherman tank.

🍴 🛏 p115

The Drive ▶ From the museum, head northeast along Esplanade Brillaud de Laujardière, and follow signs to Ouistreham. You'll join the E46 ring road; follow it to exit 3a (Porte d'Angleterre), and merge onto the D515 and D84 to Ouistreham. Park on the seafront on bd Aristide Briand. In all it's a trip of 18km.

2 Ouistreham

On D-Day, the sandy sea-front around Ouistreham was code-named **Sword Beach** and was the focus of attack for the British 3rd Infantry Division.

Baie de la Seine

0 ——————— 20 km
0 ——————— 10 miles

Longues-sur-Mer
5
4 (D514)
Arromanches
Juno & Gold Beaches
3
Courseulles-sur-Mer
●Crepon
6 **Bayeux**
Beny-sur-Mer
(D79)
Rade de Caen
●Douvres
Ouistreham 2
(D514)
●Ranville
1
(N13)
START
1
Caen p132
(A13)
(D6)
●Fortenay-le-Pesnel
30 km to
7
(A84)
CALVADOS
(N158)
●Villers-Bocage
Amayé-sur-Ome

LINK YOUR TRIP

1 Essential France
The island abbey of Mont St-Michel is about 140km from the Normandy coastline, about two hours' drive via the A84 motorway.

7 Monet's Normandy
From the end of our Monet-themed trip at Fécamp, drive southwest on the A29 and A13 to Caen, a journey of just over 130km.

There are precious few reminders of the battle now, but on D-Day the scene was very different: most of the surrounding buildings had been levelled by artillery fire, and German bunkers and artillery positions were strung out along the seafront. Sword Beach was the site of some of the most famous images of D-Day – including the infamous ones of British troops landing with bicycles, and bagpiper Bill Millin piping troops ashore while under heavy fire.

The Drive ≫ Follow the seafront west onto rue de Lion, following signs for 'Overlord – L'Assaut' onto the D514 towards Courseulles-sur-Mer, 18km west. Drive through town onto rue de Ver, and follow signs to 'Centre Juno Beach'.

---

③ Juno & Gold Beaches

On D-Day, Courseulles-sur-Mer was known as Juno Beach, and was stormed mainly by Canadian troops. It was here that the exiled French General Charles de Gaulle came ashore after the landings – the first 'official' French soldier to set foot in mainland Europe since 1940. He was followed by Winston Churchill on 12 June and King George VI on 16 June. A Cross of Lorraine marks the historic spot.

The area's only Canadian museum, the **Juno Beach Centre** (☎02 31 37 32 17; www.junobeach.org; voie des Français Libres, Courseulles-sur-Mer; museum adult/child €7/6, incl park €12/10; ☺9.30am-7pm Jul & Aug, 10am-6pm Apr-Jun, Sep & Oct, 10am-5pm Nov, Dec, Feb & Mar, closed Jan) has exhibits on Canada's role in the war effort and the landings, and offers guided tours of Juno Beach, including the bunker there, from April to October.

A short way west is Gold Beach, attacked by the British 50th Infantry on D-Day.

The Drive ≫ Drive west along the D514 for 14km to Arromanches. You'll pass a car park and viewpoint marked with a statue of the Virgin Mary, which overlooks Port Winston and Gold Beach. Follow the road into town and signs to Musée du Débarquement.

---

④ Arromanches

This seaside town was the site of one of the great logistical achievements of D-Day. In order to unload the vast quantities of cargo needed by the invasion forces without capturing one of the heavily defended Channel ports, the Allies

---

D-DAY IN FIGURES

Code named 'Operation Overlord', the D-Day landings were the largest military operation in history. On the morning of 6 June 1944, swarms of landing craft – part of an armada of over 6000 ships and 13,000 aeroplanes – hit the northern Normandy beaches, and tens of thousands of soldiers from the USA, the UK, Canada and elsewhere began pouring onto French soil. The initial landing force involved some 45,000 troops; 15 more divisions were to follow once successful beachheads had been established.

The majority of the 135,000 Allied troops stormed ashore along 80km of beaches north of Bayeux code named (from west to east) Utah, Omaha, Gold, Juno and Sword. The landings were followed by the 76-day Battle of Normandy, during which the Allies suffered 210,000 casualties, including 37,000 troops killed. German casualties are believed to have been around 200,000; another 200,000 German soldiers were taken prisoner. About 14,000 French civilians also died.

For more background and statistics, see www.normandie44lamemoire.com, www.dday.org and www.6juin1944.com.

set up prefabricated marinas off two landing beaches, code named **Mulberry Harbour**. These consisted of 146 massive cement caissons towed over from England and sunk to form a semi-circular breakwater in which floating bridge spans were moored. In the three months after D-Day, the Mulberries facilitated the unloading of a mind-boggling 2.5 million men, four million tonnes of equipment and 500,000 vehicles.

At low tide, the stanchions of one of these artificial quays, **Port Winston** (named after Winston Churchill), can still be seen on the sands at Arromanches.

Beside the beach, the **Musée du Débarquement** (Landing Museum; 📞02 31 22 34 31; www.musee-arromanches.fr; place du 6 Juin; adult/child €8/6; 🕘9am-7pm Jul & Aug, 10am-12.30pm & 1.30-5pm Sep-Nov & Feb-Jun) explains the logistics and importance of Port Winston; the museum was expanded and renovated for the 75th anniversary of D-Day in 2019.

The Drive ≫ Continue west along the D514 for 6km to the village of Longues-sur-Mer. You'll see the sign for the Batterie de Longues on your right.

- - - - - - - - - - - - - - - -

⑤ Longues-sur-Mer

At Longues-sur-Mer you can get a glimpse of the awesome firepower

D-DAY DRIVING ROUTES

There are several signposted driving routes around the main battle sites – look for signs for 'D-Day-Le Choc' in the American sectors and 'Overlord – L'Assaut' in the British and Canadian sectors. A free booklet called *The D-Day Landings and the Battle of Normandy,* available from tourist offices, has details on the main routes.

Maps of the D-Day beaches are widely available in the region.

available to the German defenders in the shape of a row of 150mm artillery guns, still housed in their concrete casements. On D-Day they were capable of hitting targets over 20km away – including Gold Beach (to the east) and Omaha Beach (to the west). Parts of the classic D-Day film *The Longest Day* (1962) were filmed here.

The Drive ≫ Backtrack to the crossroads and head straight over onto the D104, signed to Vaux-sur-Aure/Bayeux, for 8km. When you reach town, turn right onto the D613, and follow signs to the 'Musée de la Bataille de Normandie'.

- - - - - - - - - - - - - - - -

⑥ Bayeux

Though best known for its medieval tapestry, Bayeux has another claim to fame: it was the first town to be liberated after D-Day (on the morning of 7 June 1944).

It's also home to the largest of Normandy's 18 Commonwealth military cemeteries – the **Bayeux War Cemetery** (www.cwgc.

org; 1945 bd Fabien Ware; 🕘24hr), situated on bd Fabien Ware. It contains 4848 graves of soldiers from the UK and 10 other countries – including Germany. Across the road is a memorial for 1807 Commonwealth soldiers whose remains were never found. The Latin inscription reads: 'We, whom William once conquered, have now set free the conqueror's native land'.

Nearby, the **Musée Mémorial de la Bataille de Normandie** (Battle of Normandy Memorial Museum; 📞02 31 51 46 90; www.bayeuxmuseum.com; bd Fabien Ware; adult/child €7.50/5; 🕘9.30am-12.30pm & 2-6pm, closed Jan) explores the battle through photos, personal accounts, dioramas and film.

✖ ⌂ p115

The Drive ≫ After overnighting in Bayeux, head northwest of town on the D6 towards Port-en-Bessin-Huppain. You'll reach a supermarket after about 10km. Go round the roundabout and turn onto the D514 for another

Classic Trip

WHY THIS IS A CLASSIC TRIP
OLIVER BERRY, WRITER

You'll have heard the D-Day story many times before, but there's nothing quite like standing on the beaches where this epic struggle played out. D-Day marked the turning point of WWII and heralded the end for Nazism in Europe. Paying your respects to the soldiers who laid down their lives in the name of freedom is an experience that will stay with you forever.

Above: Utah Beach
Left: Juno Beach
Right: Pointe du Hoc

LIONEL LOUREL/GETTY IMAGES ©

8km. You'll see signs to the 'Cimetière Americian' near the hamlet of Le Bray. Omaha Beach is another 4km further on, near Vierville-sur-Mer.

TRIP HIGHLIGHT

7 Omaha Beach

If anywhere symbolises the courage and sacrifice of D-Day, it's Omaha – still known as 'Bloody Omaha' to US veterans. It was here, on the 7km stretch of coastline between Vierville-sur-Mer, St-Laurent-sur-Mer and Colleville-sur-Mer, that the most brutal fighting on D-Day took place. US troops had to fight their way across the beach towards the heavily defended cliffs, exposed to underwater obstacles, hidden minefields and withering crossfire. The toll was heavy: of the 2500 casualties at Omaha on D-Day, more than 1000 were killed, most within the first hour of the landings.

High on the bluffs above Omaha, the **Normandy American Cemetery & Memorial** (☎02 31 51 62 00; www. abmc.gov; Colleville-sur-Mer; ◷9am-6pm Apr-Sep, to 5pm Oct-Mar) provides a sobering reminder of the human cost of the battle. Featured in the opening scenes of *Saving Private Ryan,* this is the largest American cemetery in Europe, containing the graves of 9387 American soldiers, and a memorial

NORMANDY & BRITTANY **8** D-DAY'S BEACHES

113

NORMANDY & BRITTANY **8** D-DAY'S BEACHES

to 1557 comrades 'known only unto God'.

Start off in the very thoughtfully designed visitor centre, which has moving portrayals of some of the soldiers buried here. Afterwards, take in the expanse of white marble crosses and Stars of David that stretch off in seemingly endless rows, surrounded by an immaculately tended expanse of lawn.

The Drive » From the Vierville-sur-Mer seafront, follow the rural D514 through quiet countryside towards Grandcamp-Maisy. After about 10km you'll see signs to 'Pointe du Hoc'.

TRIP HIGHLIGHT

8 Pointe du Hoc

West of Omaha, this craggy promontory was the site of D-Day's most audacious military exploit. At 7.10am, 225 US Army Rangers command-ed by Lt Col James Earl Rudder scaled the sheer 30m cliffs, where the Germans had stationed a battery of artillery guns trained onto the beaches of Utah and Omaha. Un-fortunately, the guns had already been moved in-land, and Rudder and his men spent the next two days repelling counter-

attacks. By the time they were finally relieved on 8 June, 81 of the rangers had been killed and 58 more had been wounded.

Today the **Pointe du Hoc Ranger Memorial** (☎02 31 51 62 00; www.abmc. gov; ☺9am-6pm Apr-Sep, to 5pm Oct-Mar), which France turned over to the US government in 1979, looks much as it did on D-Day, complete with shell craters and crumbling gun emplace-ments.

The Drive » Stay on the D514 to Grandcamp-Maisy, then continue south onto the D13. Stay on the road till you reach the turn-off for the D913, signed to St-Marie-du-Mont/Utah Beach. It's a drive of 44km.

9 Utah Beach

The D-Day tour ends at Ste-Marie-du-Mont, aka

DETOUR: COUANCES

Start: 9 Utah Beach

The lovely old Norman town of Coutances makes a good detour when travelling between the D-Day beaches and Mont St-Michel. At the town's heart is its Gothic **Cathédrale Notre-Dame de Coutances** (☎02 33 45 00 41; http://cathedralecoutances.free.fr; parvis Notre-Dame; ☺8am-7pm Nov-Mar, to 6pm Apr-Oct). Interior highlights include several 13th-century windows, a 14th-century fresco of St Michael skewering the dragon, and an organ and high altar from the mid-1700s. You can climb the lantern tower on a tour (adult/child €8/4).

Coutances is 50km south of Utah Beach by the most direct route via the D913 and D971.

Utah Beach, assaulted by soldiers of the US 4th and 8th Infantry Divisions. The beach was relatively lightly defended, and by midday the landing force had linked with para-troopers from the 101st Airborne. By nightfall, some 20,000 men and 1700 vehicles had arrived on French soil, and the road to European libera-tion had begun.

Today the site is marked by military me-morials and the **Musée du Débarquement** (Utah Beach Landing Museum; ☎02 33 71 53 35; www.utah-beach. com; Plage de la Madeleine, Ste-Marie-du-Mont; adult/ child €8/5; ☺9.30am-7pm Jun-Sep, 10am-6pm Oct-May, closed Jan), a modern and impressive museum just inland from the beach.

Eating & Sleeping

Caen ❶

✗ À Contre Sens
French €€

(☎02 31 97 44 48; www.acontresens.fr; 8-10 rue des Croisiers; mains €21-44, menus from €44; ☺7.30-9.15pm Tue, noon-1.15pm & 7.30-9.15pm Wed-Sat) À Contre Sens' stylish interior and serene atmosphere belie the hotbed of creativity to be found in the kitchen. Under the direction of chef Anthony Caillot, meals are thoughtfully crafted and superbly presented. Expect dishes such as seaweed risotto with apple and coriander or veal rubbed with herbs, endive and ham.

✗ Café Mancel
French €€

(☎02 31 86 63 64; www.cafemancel.com; Château de Caen; menus €18-25; ☺9am-9.30pm Tue-Sat, to 2pm Sun) In the same building as the **Musée des Beaux-Arts** within the Château de Caen, this stylish place serves up delicious, traditional French cuisine – everything from pan-fried Norman-style beefsteak to hearty Caen-style *tripes,* delivered by attentive staff. There's a lovely sun terrace, which also makes a fine spot for a drink outside of busy meal times. After your meal, enjoy a walk along the ramparts of the castle.

☷ Hôtel des Quatrans
Hotel €

(☎02 31 86 25 57; www.hotel-des-quatrans.com; 17 rue Gémare; r from €80; ☎) This typically modern hotel has an excellent central location, with 47 comfy, unfussy rooms in white and chocolate. The breakfast buffet can be enjoyed in the brightly coloured cafe or you can retreat to your room.

Bayeux ❻

✗ L'Alchimie
French €€

(☎02 14 08 03 97; 49 rue St-Jean; menus €13-25; ☺noon-1.30pm & 7-9pm Mon-Wed, Fri & Sat) On a street lined with restaurants, L'Alchimie

has a simple but elegant design, with beautifully presented dishes. Choose from the day's specials listed on a chalkboard menu, which might include hits such as *brandade de morue* (baked codfish pie) or *pastilla de poulet au gingembre et cumin* (chicken pastilla with ginger and cumin). Book ahead.

✗ Au Ptit Bistrot
French €€

(☎02 31 92 30 08; www.facebook.com/auptitbistrot; 31 rue Larcher; lunch menus €18-21, dinner menus €32-36, mains €19-28; ☺noon-1.30pm & 7-9pm Tue-Sat) Near the cathedral, this friendly, welcoming eatery whips up creative dishes that highlight the Norman bounty without pretension. Recent popular dishes include braised beef cheek with red wine, polenta, grapefruit tapenade and vegetables, or roast pigeon with mushrooms and mashed parsnip. The kids' menu is €12. Reservations essential.

☷ Logis Les Remparts
B&B €

(☎02 31 92 50 40; www.lecornu.fr; 4 rue Bourbesneur; r from €75; ☎) The three rooms of this delightful and well-managed *maison de famille* ooze old-fashioned cosiness. Our favourite, the Bajocasse, has parquet flooring, a canopy bed and Toile de Jouy wallpaper. The largest room is the Bourbesneur suite at 430 sq ft. The large shop downstairs is the perfect place to stock up on top-quality, homemade cider and *calvados* (apple brandy).

☷ Villa Lara
Boutique Hotel €€€

(☎02 31 92 00 55; www.hotel-villalara.com; 6 place du Québec; r from €200; P ❄ ☎) This modern and luxurious 28-room hotel combines an appealing blend of minimalist colour schemes, top-quality fabrics and decor juxtaposing 18th- and 21st-century tastes. Amenities include a bar, a gym and a comfortable library-lounge with a fireplace. Most rooms have cathedral views and are well equipped and tastefully decorated, with attractive bathrooms.

Breton Coast

On this sea-salty drive, you'll experience serene coastal towns, dramatic storm-lashed headlands and the world's greatest concentration of megalithic sites.

9

TRIP HIGHLIGHTS

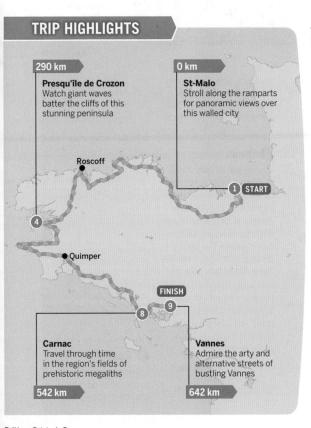

290 km

Presqu'île de Crozon
Watch giant waves batter the cliffs of this stunning peninsula

0 km

St-Malo
Stroll along the ramparts for panoramic views over this walled city

Roscoff

4

Quimper

1 START

FINISH

8

9

Carnac
Travel through time in the region's fields of prehistoric megaliths

542 km

Vannes
Admire the arty and alternative streets of bustling Vannes

642 km

---

8 DAYS
642KM / 399 MILES

GREAT FOR...

BEST TIME TO GO

April and May can see fine, sunny weather and no crowds.

 ESSENTIAL PHOTO

Standing on the precipice of the cliffs of the Pointe du Raz.

 BEST FOR HISTORY

Walking through the embarrassment of prehistoric megalithic sites at Carnac.

---

9 Breton Coast

This is a trip for explorers who want to experience a very different slice of French life; instead of the Eiffel Tower, fine wines and haute couture, you'll take in a dramatic coastline, excellent seafood, medieval towns, prehistoric mysticism and Celtic pride.

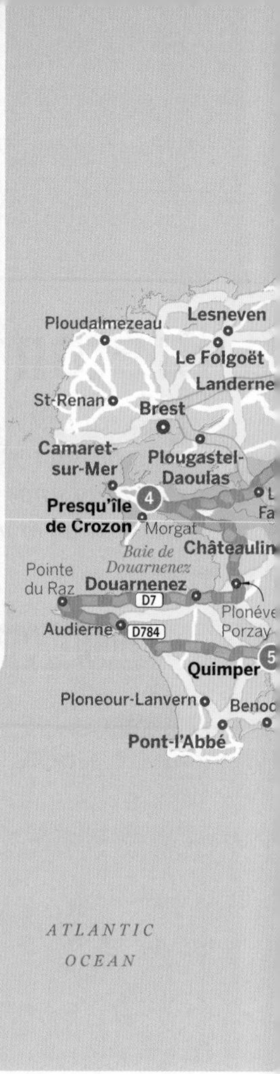

Ploudalmezeau Lesneven
Le Folgoët
St-Renan Landerne
Brest
Camaret- Plougastel-
sur-Mer Daoulas
Presqu'île ④ L
de Crozon Morgat Fa
Baie de Châteaulin
Pointe *Douarnenez*
du Raz Douarnenez
D7
Plonéve
Audierne D784 Porzay
Quimper ⑤
Ploneour-Lanvern Benod
Pont-l'Abbé

ATLANTIC
OCEAN

TRIP HIGHLIGHT

① St-Malo

Once a haven for pirates and adventurers, the impressive walled town of St-Malo is today a genteel mast-filled port hemmed by pretty beaches and guarded by an array of offshore islands. The walled quarter of **Intra-Muros** is arguably the most interesting urban centre in Brittany, but it's not as old as it appears. Most of the town was flattened in WWII and has since been painstakingly rebuilt.

🍴 🛏 p123

The Drive » The 35km, half-hour drive along the D137 between St-Malo and Dinan is through a largely built-up area and offers little of interest. Expect heavy traffic and delays.

② Dinan

Set high above the fast-flowing Rance River, the narrow – and sometimes plunging – cobblestone streets of Dinan are lined with crooked, creaking half-timbered houses straight out of the Middle Ages. All of this guarantees a tourist bonanza in the warmer months, of course, but choose anything slightly off-season and you may find the place deserted.

The Drive » Take the wiggly and very slow (count on a 3½-hour drive) coastal D786 between Dinan and Roscoff. Highlights include the pretty port of Paimpol and the breathtaking Côte de Granit Rose, which extends west of the town of Perros-Guirec. This leg is 220km.

③ Roscoff

Set around an arcing harbour studded with granite cottages and

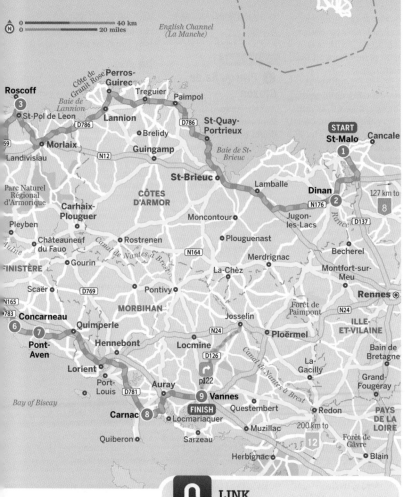

English Channel (La Manche)

40 km
20 miles

Roscoff
3
Côte de Granit Rose
Perros-Guirec
Baie de Lannion
St-Pol de Leon
Treguier
Paimpol
St-Quay-Portrieux
Lannion
D786
D786
Brelidy
Baie de St-Brieuc
Morlaix
59
Landivisiau
N12
Guingamp
START
St-Malo
Cancale
1
St-Brieuc
Lamballe
Dinan
2
N176
127 km to
8
Parc Naturel Régional d'Armorique
Carhaix-Plouguer
CÔTES D'ARMOR
Moncontour
Jugon-les-Lacs
D137
Pleyben
Châteauneuf du Faou
Rostrenen
Plouguenast
Becherel
FINISTÈRE
Gourin
Canal de Nantes à Brest
N164
Merdrignac
Montfort-sur-Meu
Scaër
D769
La-Chèz
Pontivy
Rennes
N165
MORBIHAN
Josselin
Forêt de Paimpont
N24
ILLE-ET-VILAINE
783
Concarneau
6
Quimperle
7
Pont-Aven
Hennebont
N24
Locmine
Ploërmel
Bain de Bretagne
Lorient
D126
La-Gacilly
Grand-Fougeray
Port-Louis
D781
Auray
p122
Canal de Nantes à Brest
Bay of Biscay
Carnac
8
9 Vannes
FINISH
Questembert
Redon
PAYS DE LA LOIRE
Locmariaquer
200 km to
12
Quiberon
Sarzeau
Muzillac
Forêt de Gâvre
Herbignac
Blain

seafront villas, Roscoff is one of the more captivating cross-channel ferry ports.

After you've explored the town, set sail for the peaceful **Île de Batz**, which sits a short way offshore. The mild island climate supports the luxuriant **Jardins Georges Delaselle** (☎02 98 61 75 65;

LINK YOUR TRIP

8 D-Day's Beaches
Combining a drive around the Breton coast with the war memorials of Normandy is easy. Caen is 170km along the A84 from St-Malo.

12 Caves & Cellars of the Loire
From Vannes it's 268km to Montsoreau, where you can pick up our tour of the Western Loire's cave dwellings and wine cellars.

www.jardin-georgesdelaselle.fr; adult/child €5/2.50; ☺11am-6pm Apr-Oct), with over 1500 plants from all five continents.

Ferries (adult/child return €9/6, child under four €2, bike €9, 15 minutes each way) run every 30 minutes in July and August; less frequently the rest of the year.

 p123

The Drive ≫ Taking the D69, D30 and D791, drive the 88km between Roscoff and Crozon, the main town on the Presqu'île de Crozon. You'll follow the western edge of the Parc Naturel Régional d'Armorique. Visit famous Breton parish closes (enclosed churches with special architecture) at

St-Thégonnec, Guimiliau and/or Sizun.

TRIP HIGHLIGHT

④ Presqu'île de Crozon

Anchor-shaped Crozon Peninsula is without doubt one of the most scenic spots in Brittany.

At the western extremity of the peninsula, **Camaret-sur-Mer** is a classic fishing village that lures artists. Three kilometres south of the village is the spectacular **Pointe de Pen-Hir** headland.

Nearby **Morgat** is one of the prettier resorts in this part of Brittany,

with colourful houses clustered at one end of a long sandy beach.

🛏 p123

The Drive ≫ Using the D63 it's just over 50km from Crozon town to Quimper. But if you turn off onto the D7 at Plonévez-Porzay after 30km and head west for another 46km, you'll reach Pointe du Raz, one of Brittany's most spectacular rocky points. Then you can swing back east on the D784 via Audierne for the 53km to Quimper.

----

⑤ Quimper

At the centre of the Finistère region's thriving capital is the **Cathédrale St-Corentin** (☎02 98 92 00

MIGHTY MEGALITHS

This entire region is rich in neolithic menhirs, dolmens, cromlechs, tumuli and cairns. Just north of Carnac there is a vast array of monoliths set up in several distinct alignments, all visible from the road, though fenced for controlled admission. The main information point for the Carnac alignments is the **Maison des Mégalithes** (☎02 97 52 29 81; www.menhirs-carnac.fr; rte des Alignements (D196); tour adult/child €9/5; ☺9.30am-7pm Jul & Aug, to 6pm Sep, Apr & Jun, 10am-1pm & 2-5pm Oct-Mar), which explores the history of the site and has a rooftop viewpoint overlooking the alignments. The Maison organises one-hour guided visits several times daily in French and weekly in English during the summer.

Across the road from the Maison des Mégalithes, the largest menhir field – with 1170 stones – is the **Alignements du Ménec**, 1km north of Carnac-Ville. From here, the D196 heads northeast for about 1.5km to the equally impressive **Alignements de Kermario**, parts of which are open year-round. Climb the stone **observation tower** midway along the site to see the alignment from above.

The **Tumulus de Kercado** lies just east of Kermario and 500m to the south of the D196. It's the massive burial mound of a neolithic chieftain dating from 3800 BCE. Deposit your fee (€1) in an honour box at the entry gate. The easternmost of the major groups is the **Alignements de Kerlescan**.

Be sure to visit the **Musée de Préhistoire** (☎02 97 52 22 04; www.museedecarnac.fr; 10 place de la Chapelle, Carnac-Ville; adult/child €7/3; ☺10am-6.30pm Jul & Aug, 10am-12.30pm & 2-6pm Wed-Mon Apr-Jun & Sep, shorter hours Oct-Mar) in Carnac-Ville to see incredible neolithic artefacts found throughout the region.

Presqu'île de Crozon Rock climber

50; https://diocese-quimper.
fr/fr/diocese/paroisses/
quimper-saint-corentin; place
St-Corentin; ☻8.30am-noon
& 1.30-6.30pm Mon-Sat,
8.30am-noon & 2-6.30pm
Sun), with its distinctive
dip, said to symbolise
Christ's inclined head
as he was dying on the
cross. Next door the
**Musée Départemental
Breton** (☎02 98 95 21 60;
http://musee-breton.finistere.
fr; 1 rue du Roi Gradlon; adult/
child €5/free; ☻10am-7pm Jul
& Aug, 9.30am-5.30pm Tue-Fri,
2-5.30pm Sat & Sun Sep–Jun)
showcases Breton his-
tory, furniture, costumes,
crafts and archaeology.

The Drive » Rather than
taking the faster N165 between
Quimper and Concarneau,
meander along the more scenic
D783. Even on this slower road
you only need 30 minutes to
travel the 23km.

⑥ Concarneau

The sheltered harbour of
Concarneau is one of the
busiest fishing ports in
Brittany and is a hugely
popular summer holiday
destination with numer-
ous attractive **beaches**
and coves. In the middle
of the harbour is the old
quarter of the **Ville Close**,
encircled by medieval
walls and crammed with

121

DETOUR:
JOSSELIN

Start: ⑨ Vannes

In the shadow of an enormous, cone-turreted 14th-century castle, the storybook village of Josselin lies on the banks of the Oust River, 45km northeast of Vannes. Place Notre Dame, a beautiful square of 16th-century half-timbered houses, is the little town's heart, but it's to visit the magnificent **Château de Josselin** (🗷02 97 22 36 45; www.chateaudejosselin.com; place de la Congrégation; adult/child €10.50/5.50; ⏰1.30-6pm mid-Jul–Aug, 2-6pm Apr–mid-Jul & Sep, 2-5.30pm Sat & Sun only Oct) that you'd really make this detour. From Vannes it's an easy one-hour drive along the D126 through an increasingly green and rural landscape of cows and forests.

enchanting old stone houses.

The Drive » Cross the picturesque Moros River on the D783 and trundle on for 17km (30 minutes) through rural scenery to Pont-Aven.

-----

❼ Pont-Aven

Long ago discovered by artists like Paul Gauguin (1848–1903), the tiny village of Pont-Aven is brimming with galleries. For an insight into the town's place in art history, stop by the excellent **Musée de Pont-Aven** (🗷02 98 06 14 43; www.museepontaven.fr; place Julia; adult/child €5/free, with special exhibit €8/free; ⏰10am-7pm Jul & Aug, to 6pm Tue-Sun Apr-Jun, Sep & Oct,

2-5.30pm Tue-Sun Mar, Nov & Dec, closed most of Jan). The town also has excellent eateries, so it's perfect for a pit-stop.

🍴 p123

The Drive » From Pont-Aven to Carnac it's a fast but dull one-hour (81km) drive down the N165 dual carriageway past the large industrial city of Lorient.

TRIP HIGHLIGHT

❽ Carnac

With enticing beaches and a pretty town centre, Carnac would be a popular tourist town even without its collection of magnificent megalithic sites (p120). The area surrounding the town has 3000 of these upright stones – the world's largest concentration – erected between 5000 and 3500 BCE.

The Drive » Rather than taking the N165 to Vannes (31km), opt for the beautiful coastal route. From Carnac head south to Carnac Plage and then east to pretty La Trinité-sur-Mer. Join the D781 and then the D28 inland to Auray. From here join the D101, which leads into Vannes. This 40km route takes just over an hour.

TRIP HIGHLIGHT

❾ Vannes

Street art, sculptures and intriguing galleries pop up unexpectedly through the half-timbered, lively cobbled city of Vannes. Surrounding the pretty walled old town is a broad moat; within the ramparts explore the web of narrow alleys ranged around the 13th-century Gothic **Cathédrale St-Pierre**.

The nearby **Golfe du Morbihan** is one of France's most attractive stretches of coastline. From April to September, **Navix** (🗷02 97 46 60 00; www.navix.fr; 9 allée Loïc Caradec, Gare Maritime, Vannes; ⏰Apr-Sep) and other companies run a range of cruises.

🛏 p123

Eating & Sleeping

① St-Malo

✕ Le Comptoir Breizh Café — Crêpes €

(📞02 99 56 96 08; www.breizhcafe.com; 6 rue de l'Orme; crêpes €14.50-19.50; ⊗noon-2pm & 7-10.30pm Wed-Sun) This will be one of your most memorable meals in Brittany, from the delicious menu to the excellent service. The creative chef combines traditional Breton ingredients and *galette* and crêpe styles with Japanese flavours, textures and presentation, where seaweed meets local ham, organic eggs and roast duck. It's all about *les crêpes autremont* ('crêpes as they used to be'), as they say here.

🛏 La Maison des Armateurs — Hotel €€

(📞02 99 40 87 70; www.maisondesarmateurs. com; 6 Grand' Rue; d €99-295, f/ste €180/430; ⊗closed Dec; ❄🛜) Enthusiastically run by a helpful French-American couple, this sassy 45-room four-star hotel is all sexy minimalism: stylish furniture throughout, gleaming bathrooms with power showers and cool chocolate, pale orange and neutral grey tones. Families can plump for the super-sized suites. Buffet breakfast (adult/child €16/10).

Roscoff ③

✕ Le Surcouf — Brasserie €€

(📞02 98 69 71 89; www.surcoufroscoff.fr; 14 rue de l'Amiral Réveillère; mains €16-30; ⊗noon-2pm & 6.30-9.30pm Sun-Fri, to 10pm Sat) Bang in the heart of Roscoff, this brasserie serves excellent seafood. You can choose your own crab and lobster from the window tank, tuck into the classic fish soup or opt for a heaped platter of fresh shellfish.

🛏 Hôtel aux Tamaris — Hotel €€

(📞02 98 61 22 99; www.hotel-aux-tamaris.com; 49 rue Édouard Corbière; d €60-100, sea view €80-120; 🛜) This smart, family-run place in an old granite building overlooking the water at the western end of town is an excellent choice, with 25 well-equipped, light, seabreeze-filled rooms, all with a pleasant maritime aura and yacht sails for ceilings. Half the rooms have sea views. Expect locally sourced goodies at breakfast (€7 to €11).

Presqu'île de Crozon ④

🛏 Hôtel de la Baie — Hotel €

(📞02 98 27 07 51; www.hoteldelabaiecrozon morgat.com; 46 bd de la Plage, Morgat; d €68-91, studio €97-150; 🛜) One of the *very* few places to remain open year-round and one of the best deals about, this friendly, family-run spot on Morgat's promenade has 19 clean and pleasant rooms; pricier rooms have views over the sea, while studio apartments with kitchenette are also available.

Pont-Aven ⑦

✕ Sur Le Pont — Modern French €€

(📞02 98 06 16 16; www.surlepont-pontaven. fr; 11 place Paul Gauguin; lunch/dinner menu €27/34, mains €17-25; ⊗12.30-2pm & 7.30-9pm Wed-Sun) You couldn't wish for a more perfect setting, lodged in a stylishly renovated building by the Pont-Aven bridge. A just-so palette of cool greys, beiges, blacks and whites creates the feel of an elegant bistro. Dishes are refined takes on Breton cooking, with an emphasis on seafood.

Vannes ⑨

🛏 La Villa Garenne — B&B €€

(📞06 76 01 80 83; www.chambresdhotes-vannes.fr; 3 rue Monseigneur Tréhiou; d €80-125, 3-/4-person apt from €120/160; 🛜) A stone's throw from the imposing ramparts, this very attractive option has five charmingly and uniquely decorated rooms in a handsome stone building as well as two apartments. They're light, airy and furnished with great taste, and breakfasts come in for warm praise.

Tour des Fromages

10

On this gastronomic drive you'll savour some of the best cheese in France and see where the seaside inspired artists, where Joan of Arc was executed and where Richard the Lionheart prowled.

TRIP HIGHLIGHTS

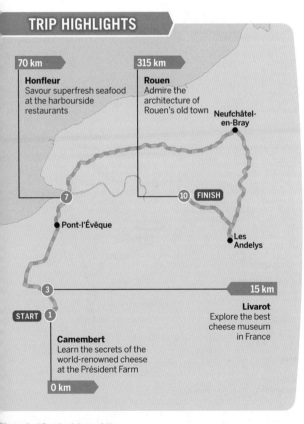

70 km

Honfleur
Savour superfresh seafood at the harbourside restaurants

315 km

Rouen
Admire the architecture of Rouen's old town

Neufchâtel-en-Bray

7

10 FINISH

● **Pont-l'Évêque**

● **Les Andelys**

15 km

Livarot
Explore the best cheese museum in France

3

START 1

Camembert
Learn the secrets of the world-renowned cheese at the Président Farm

0 km

---

5 DAYS
315KM / 196 MILES

GREAT FOR...

BEST TIME TO GO

In May Pont L'Évêque celebrates all that is cheese during the Fête du Fromage.

 ESSENTIAL PHOTO

Snap a shot of the Seine through the ruined windows of Château Gaillard.

 BEST FOR HISTORY

Pay your respects to the memory of Joan of Arc in Rouen.

Camembert Bread and cheese platter

10 Tour des Fromages

More cheese, please! It's said that in France there is a different variety of cheese for every day of the year. On this driving culinary extravaganza, you'll taste – and learn about – some of the very finest of French cheeses. Cheese cravings sated, explore the backstreets of Rouen, build castles made of sand on the seashore and clamber up to castles made of stone in the interior.

TRIP HIGHLIGHT

❶ Camembert

The delicious soft cheese Camembert is known the world over. Therefore, it can come as a surprise to learn that Camembert is also a small, but very picturesque, classic Norman village of half-timbered buildings. The big attraction here is, of course, its cheese, and you can learn all about it during a guided tour of the **Maison de Camembert** (02 33 12 10 37; www.maisonducamembert.com;

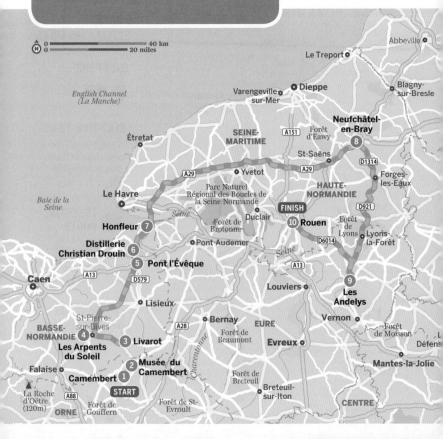

adult/child €4/2; ⏰10am-noon & 2-5pm Apr-Sep, closed Mon & Tue Mar & Oct, closed Nov-Feb), an early-19th-century farm restored by Président, one of the region's largest Camembert producers.

The Drive » It's a 5km, 10-minute drive along the D246 and then the D16 from Camembert village to the Musée du Camembert in Vimoutiers.

❷ Musée du Camembert

Make a stop in the in the tiny village of Vimoutiers to visit the small **Musée du Camembert** (☎02 33 39 30 29; www.museeducam embert.fr; 10 Avenue du Général de Gaulle; ⏰10am-6pm Jul & Aug, 2-6pm Sep-Jun; adult/child €3/free), which gives you the lowdown on the history and culture of the smelly stuff. Needless to say, you'll get to do plenty of sampling of a variety of regional cheeses and ciders.

The Drive » It's another 10-minute drive north to stop 3, Livarot, along the D579.

TRIP HIGHLIGHT

❸ Livarot

Although not as famous internationally as Camembert, Livarot is a big deal in France, where this traditional soft cheese is beloved for its nutty flavour. The town where the namesake cheese originated is home to probably the best cheese tour in Normandy. **Le Village Fromager** (L'Atelier Fromager; ☎02 31 48 20 10; www.graindorge.fr; 42 rue du Général Leclerc; ⏰9.30am-5pm Mon-Sat, from 10.30am Sun Jul & Aug, 9.30am-1pm & 2-5.30pm Mon-Sat Apr-Jun, Sep & Oct, shorter hours rest of year) offers free tours and tastings at the Graindorge factory. A self-guided walk accompanied by multimedia displays leads through a series of aromatic viewing rooms where you can watch Livarot, Camembert and Pont l'Évêque being made.

After you've deepened your fromage knowledge on the tour, work up an appetite for more on a walk around the town. Its wobbly-wiggly half-timbered buildings make it a real charmer.

The Drive » Head west along the D4 from Livarot to the village of St-Pierre-sur-Dives. The D271 leads to Les Arpents du Soleil winery a little south of the village en route to Grisy.

❹ Les Arpents du Soleil

From Livarot, we're detouring a little further

SOMME

Somme

Amiens

D929

Longueau

A16

NORD - PAS-DE-CALAIS

OISE

auvais

Forêt d'Halatte   Bray

A16

Forêt d'Ermenonville

Forêt de Chantilly

110km to

PARIS ✪

ÎLE DE FRANCE

Versailles

LINK YOUR TRIP

4 In Flanders Fields
The war memorials of northern France are a powerful symbol of the wastefulness of war. Amiens, on our Flanders Fields drive, is 120km from Rouen.

5 Champagne Taster
From Rouen it's 284km to Reims and the start of another culinary adventure – this one fuelled by the bubbly stuff.

west. Just outside the village of St-Pierre-sur-Dives is something of a surprise for Normandy – not a cider farm, but a renowned vineyard, **Les Arpents du Soleil** (📞02 31 40 71 82; www.arpents-du-soleil.com; Chemin des Vignes, Grisy; guided tour adult/child €9/free; 🕐 shop 2-6pm Mon-Tue & Thu-Sat, tour 2.30pm Thu Apr–mid-Nov), a winemaker since medieval times. The current crop includes three dry whites and a fruity, oaky pinot noir. The shop is open year-round and offers the chance to try the estate's wines, but guided tours only run on certain days, so phone ahead.

The Drive » A gentle countryside cruise of about 45 minutes (42km) up the D16 via St-Pierre-sur-Dives will see you easing into Pont l'Évêque.

KIRK FISHER / SHUTTERSTOCK ©

⑤ Pont l'Evêque

Since the 13th century this unpretentious little town with rivers meandering through its centre has been known for its eponymous cheese. Although two-thirds of the town was destroyed in WWII, careful reconstruction has brought much of it back to life. Half-timbered buildings line the main street, and 1960s stained glass bathes the 15th-century Église St-Michel in coloured light.

There is no shortage of **cheese shops** in town.

If you're passing through over the second weekend in May, don't miss the **Fête du Fromage**, when the townsfolk throw a little party for cheese.

The Drive » To get to the Distillerie Christian Drouin, your next stop, head out of Pont l'Évêque in a northeasterly direction on the D675. At the roundabout on the edge of the town, take the third exit (rue St-Mélaine/D677) and continue for about 2.5km until you see the farm on your left.

⑥ Distillerie Christian Drouin

In case you were starting to wonder if Normandy was merely a one-cheese pony, pay a visit to the **Distillerie Christian Drouin** (📞02 31 64 30 05; www.calvados-drouin.com;

Honfleur Market outside Église Ste-Catherine

rte de Trouville, Coudray-Rabut; ⊘9am-noon & 2-6pm Mon-Sat), which will let you in on the delights of Norman cider and *calvados* (apple-flavoured brandy; that other classic Norman tipple). Entrance is free.

The Drive » It's a simple 17km drive along the D579 to Honfleur and your first sea views (yes, the sun will be out by the time you get there...).

TRIP HIGHLIGHT

⑦ Honfleur

Long a favourite with painters, Honfleur is arguably Normandy's most charming seaside town.

On the west side of the **Vieux Bassin**, with its many pleasure boats, **quai Ste-Catherine** is lined with tall, taper-thin houses – many protected

from the elements by slate tiles – dating from the 16th to the 18th centuries. The **Lieutenance**, at the mouth of the old harbour, was once the residence of the town's royal governor.

Initially intended as a temporary structure, the **Église Ste-Catherine** (☎02 31 89 23 30; place Ste-Catherine; ⊘9am-7pm) has been standing in the

129

square for more than 500 years. The church is particularly notable for its double-vaulted roof and twin naves, which from the inside resemble a couple of overturned ships' hulls.

 p105, p131

The Drive » Switching from nice, mellow country lanes, hit the gas for the 111km run down the A29 to Neufchâtel-en-Bray.

⑧ Neufchâtel-en-Bray

The small market town of Neufchâtel-en-Bray is renowned for its heart-shaped cheese called, imaginatively, Neufchâtel. To buy it in the most authentic way, try to time your arrival to coincide with the Saturday-morning **market**.

Appetite satisfied, it's now time for some culture. Check out the **Musée Mathon-Durand** (☏02 35 93 06 55; 53 Grande Rue Saint-Pierre; adult/child €4/2; ⊙2-6pm Tue-Sun mid-June–mid-Sep, 2-6pm Sat & Sun Apr–mid-June & mid-Sep–Oct), inside a 16th-century half-timbered building that once belonged to a knight. He's long since gone off to fight dragons in the sky, and today the house contains a small museum of local culture.

The Drive » The most obvious route between Neufchâtel-en-Bray and stop 9, Les Andelys, is along the A28, but that means skirting around Rouen – time it badly and you'll be stuck in noxious traffic. Instead, take the more serene D921 country road. Going this way should take you about 80 minutes to cover the 75km.

⑨ Les Andelys

On a hairpin curve in the Seine lies Les Andelys (the 's' is silent), the old part of which is crowned by the noble ruin of Château Gaillard, the 12th-century hilltop fastness of Richard the Lionheart.

Built from 1196 to 1197, **Château Gaillard** (☏02 32 21 31 29; www.cape-tourisme. fr/chateau-gaillard-2020; adult/child €3.50/3; ⊙10am-1pm & 2-6pm Wed-Mon late Mar-Oct) once secured the western border of English territory along the Seine until Henry IV ordered its destruction in 1603. Fantastic views of the Seine's white cliffs can be enjoyed from the platform a few hundred metres up the one-lane road from the castle.

🛏 p131

The Drive » It's a 45km, 50-minute jaunt (assuming you don't hit rush-hour traffic) down the D6014 to your final stop, Rouen.

TRIP HIGHLIGHT

⑩ Rouen

With its elegant spires, beautifully restored medieval quarter and soaring Gothic cathedral, the ancient city of Rouen is one of Normandy's highlights. It was here that the young French heroine Joan of Arc (Jeanne d'Arc) was tried for heresy.

Rouen's stunning **Cathédrale Notre Dame** (☏02 35 71 85 65; www. cathedrale-rouen.net; place de la Cathédrale; ⊙2-7pm Mon, 9am-7pm Tue-Sat, 8am-6pm Sun Apr-Oct, shorter hours Nov-Mar) is the famous subject of a series of paintings by Monet.

Rue du Gros Horloge runs from the cathedral west to **Place du Vieux Marché**, where you'll find the arresting **Église Ste-Jeanne-d'Arc** (☏03 32 32 08 32 40; ⊙10am-noon & 2-6pm Mon-Thu, 2-6pm Fri-Sun), with its fish-scale exterior and vast, sublime wall of stained glass. It sits on the spot where the 19-year-old Joan was burned at the stake.

🍴🛏 p105, p131

Eating & Sleeping

Honfleur ⑦

🍴 La Fleur de Sel — Gastronomy €€€

(📞02 31 89 01 92; www.lafleurdesel-honfleur.com; 17 rue Haute; menus from €34; ⏱12.15-1.30pm & 7.15-9.30pm Wed-Sun) Honfleur-raised Vincent Guyon cooked in some of Paris' top kitchens before returning to his hometown to make good and open his own (now celebrated) restaurant. Guyon uses the highest-quality locally sourced ingredients and plenty of invention (with roast meats and wild-caught seafood featuring ginger and kaffir-lime vinaigrettes, Camembert foams and hazelnut tempura) in his beautifully crafted dishes. Reserve ahead.

🛏 La Petite Folie — B&B €€

(📞06 43 29 95 09; www.lapetitefolie-honfleur.com; 44 rue Haute; r from €125, apt from €175; 🛜) Penny Vincent, an American, and her French husband, Thierry, are the gracious hosts at this elegant home, built in 1830 and still adorned by the original stained glass and tile floors. Each room has a different design, with original artwork, and the best are filled with vintage furnishings and overlook the pretty garden. The lovely apartments have kitchenettes. The appealing common areas make a fine spot for the sumptuous breakfast (€15) or an evening glass of wine.

Les Andelys ⑨

🛏 Hôtel de la Chaîne d'Or — Hotel €€

(📞02 32 54 00 31; www.hotel-lachainedor.com; 27 rue Grande, Petit Andely; r €100-200; 🅿🛜) Packed with character and a measure of grandeur, this hideaway is a gem: rustically stylish without being twee. The 12 rooms are spacious, elegant, tasteful and romantic, with antique wood furnishings and plush rugs, and some are so close to the Seine you could almost fish out the window (if you don't catch anything, the atmospheric ceiling-timbered restaurant serves fine fare).

Rouen ⑩

🍴 La Rose des Vents — Modern French €

(📞02 35 70 29 78; 33 Place de la Basse Vieille Tour; mains from €16; ⏱noon-4pm Tue-Sat) This charming and fun establishment is hugely popular with foodies and hipsters. Patrons rave about the lunches, which change weekly according to what's available in the market. They usually whip up something for vegetarians as well. Reservations are recommended.

🛏 La Boulangerie — B&B €

(📞06 12 94 53 15; www.laboulangerie.fr; 59 rue St-Nicaise; s/d from €67/77; 🛜) Tucked away in a quiet side street 1.2km northeast of the cathedral, this adorable B&B sits above a historic (and very good) bakery and has three bright, pleasingly decorated rooms that feature artwork and exposed-beam ceilings. Charming host Aminata is a mine of local information. Parking available nearby for €5; breakfast included.

🛏 Hôtel de Bourgtheroulde — Luxury Hotel €€€

(📞02 35 14 50 50; www.hotelsparouen.com; 15 place de la Pucelle; r from €200; 🅿❄🛜♨) Rouen's finest hostelry (it's part of the Marriott empire) serves up a sumptuous mix of early-16th-century architecture – Flamboyant Gothic, to be precise – and sleek, modern luxury. The 78 rooms are spacious and gorgeously appointed. Amenities include a pool (18m), sauna and spa in the basement; the Atrium Bar has live piano music on Saturday evening.

STRETCH YOUR LEGS
CAEN

Start/Finish Château de Caen

Distance 4.5km

Duration 3 hours

Soaring Romanesque churches, picturesque medieval plazas and a mighty castle are all features of this stroll around Caen's historic centre. Although much of Caen was destroyed during WWII, there are still some extraordinary remnants from the past — along with vibrant streets sprinkled with outdoor cafes, colourful shops and new-wave Norman eateries.

Take this walk on Trip

Château de Caen

Caen's mighty **Château de Caen** (www.musee-de-normandie.caen.fr; ☺ grounds 8am-10pm; P) looms high above the centre, and must have inspired fear in William the Conqueror's enemies when he established the fortress back in 1060. There's much to see inside the castle walls, including the tiny 12th-century Église St-Georges, with fine stained glass windows, and the Échiquier, the oldest building in Normandy. Don't miss the views from the ramparts.

The Walk » Exiting the castle grounds, turn right on rue de Geôle and then left onto rue Calibourg. Follow this as it turns into rue des Croisiers and rue St-Sauveur. You'll pass Église St-Sauveur (on your right) just before reaching the plaza.

Place St-Sauveur

This lovely plaza is the oldest square in Caen, and it survived the bombing raids of WWII relatively unscathed. Lined with elegant 18th-century mansions, it was once home to a medieval market (come on Friday to browse modern market vendors) and once served as a site of public execution. Cafes with outdoor tables facing the plaza make fine vantage points for contemplating the past.

The Walk » Continue walking southwest along rue St-Sauveur. Take the second left at the roundabout. After 50m you'll see Hôtel de Ville (City Hall) on your right, and the church towers of the abbey on the far right.

Abbaye-aux-Hommes

Known as the 'men's abbey', this former Benedictine **monastery** (Abbaye-St-Étienne; ☏ 02 31 30 42 81; esplanade Jean-Marie-Louvel; church free, cloisters €3; ☺ church 9.30am-1pm & 2-7pm Mon-Sat, 2-6.30pm Sun, cloister 8.30am-5pm Mon-Fri, 9.30am-1pm & 2-5.30pm Sat & most Sun) is the most impressive Romanesque building in Normandy, with soaring spires that seem to pierce the sky. When approaching the building, head right to visit the imposing church, where you can see William the Conqueror's tomb. To view the medieval cloister head straight into Hôtel de Ville, which occupies much of the former monastery.

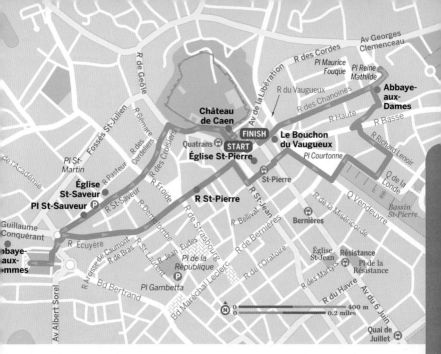

The Walk >> Leaving the Abbaye-aux-Hommes, walk back to the roundabout, and take the first right along rue Écuyère, which joins rue St-Pierre after a few blocks.

Rue St-Pierre

Branching off rue Écuyère, a bar-lined street that a draws festive young crowd by night, is one of Caen's most elegant streets, the narrow, cobblestone lane of rue St-Pierre. It is lined with boutiques and cafes, with the medieval **Église St-Pierre** (🖉02 31 86 13 11; ⏰8.30am-5pm Mon-Sat, 9.30am-1pm Sun) anchoring its eastern end.

The Walk >> Although not the most direct route, it's worth heading onto busy av de la Libération and following this past the pleasure boats docked on Bassin St-Pierre. Turn left on rue Michel Cabieu, left again on rue Richard Lenoir and dogleg onto rue Manissier.

Abbaye-aux-Dames

After having a look at the men's abbey, it would be unseemly not to visit the 'women's abbey', another 11th-century stunner once used as a Benedictine nunnery. William the Conqueror and his wife Matilda founded this **church complex** (Abbaye-de-la-Trinité; 🖉02 31 06 98 75; www.abbayes-normandie.com; place Reine Mathilde; ⏰8am-1.30pm & 2.30-6pm Mon-Fri), which has a magnificent interior. Don't miss the columns topped with 900-year-old carvings near the choir.

The Walk >> It's an easy downhill walk along rue des Chanoines heading west. After taking a very slight left onto rue Montoir Poissonnerie, look for the restaurant on your left.

Le Bouchon du Vaugueux

End the day's wanders with a meal of creative Norman cooking. The giant wine cork marks the spot at this tiny **bistrot gourmand** (🖉02 31 44 26 26; www.bouchonduvaugueux.com; 12 rue Graindorge; lunch menus €16-25, dinner menus €23-38; ⏰noon-1.45pm & 7-9.45pm Tue-Sat; 👶), which has a first-rate wine selection. Staff are happy to translate the chalkboard menu and there's a kids menu. Reservations recommended.

The Walk >> From the restaurant it's a two-minute saunter back to the castle, completing the day's loop.

133

Loire Valley & Central France

WORLD-RENOWNED CHÂTEAUX AND MAGNIFICENT WINES are two obvious reasons to visit central regions of France, but they're only the headline acts. The area is also home to Europe's grandest volcanoes, its largest concentration of cave dwellings and some of the continent's finest medieval architecture. When you've had your fill of châteaux hopping and vineyard sampling, make some time for roads less travelled: wind through the Auvergne's magnificent landscape of green pastures and vestigial cinder cones; go underground to discover the Loire's ancient troglodyte culture; or spend some time exploring Burgundy's medieval abbeys, churches and walled towns.

Central France is also prime walking and cycling country; look for trails wherever you go.

Burgundy Vineyards
TICHR / SHUTTERSTOCK ©

Loire Valley & Central France

Classic Trip
11 Châteaux of the Loire 5 Days
Tour France's greatest châteaux, from austere 11th-century donjons to exuberant Renaissance pleasure palaces. (p139)

12 Caves & Cellars of the Loire 3 Days
Discover the Loire's subterranean world: cave dwellings, wine cellars and mushroom farms. (p149)

13 Volcanoes of the Auvergne 4 Days
Green pastures, volcanic scenery, fabulous hiking and some of France's tastiest cheeses. (p159)

14 Medieval Burgundy 6 Days
Search for medieval gems in Burgundy's churches, monasteries and walled villages. (p167)

15 Route des Grands Crus 2 Days
Sample France's most renowned vintages on this wine lover's tour of Burgundy. (p175)

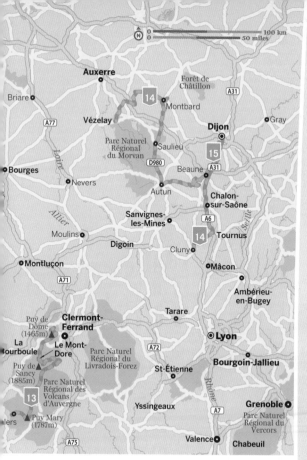

DON'T
MISS

Château de Chambord

The Loire Valley's grandest castle is famed for its double-helix staircase. Discover it on Trip 11

Ancient Volcanoes, Auvergne

The Auvergne's three dormant volcanoes are a hiker's paradise. Climb them on Trip 13

Polyptych of the Last Judgement, Hôtel-Dieu des Hospices de Beaune, Beaune

Heaven and hell are presented in vividly literal detail. See it on Trip 14

Caveau de Puligny-Montrachet

Sample some of Burgundy's extraordinary white wines without breaking the bank. Enjoy them on Trip 15

Château de La Rochepot

Enjoy superb views of the Burgundian countryside from this medieval castle. Visit it on Trip 15

Classic Trip

Châteaux
of the Loire

*France's longest river has been the backdrop
for royal intrigue and extravagant castles for
centuries. This trip weaves together nine of the
Loire Valley's most spectacular châteaux.*

11

TRIP HIGHLIGHTS

189 km

Chambord
France's château
superstar, a royal hunting
lodge on steroids

120 km

Amboise
Charles VIII's Loire-side
birthplace and Da
Vinci's last home

Blois **9** **FINISH**

6

● Villandry

5

4

Chinon
START

Azay-le-Rideau
A Renaissance
jewel on a lovely
island

52 km

Chenonceaux
Wander a fairy-tale
landscape of reflected
arches and riverside
gardens

107 km

5 DAYS
189KM / 118 MILES

GREAT FOR...

BEST TIME TO GO

May and June for
good cycling weather;
July for gardens and
special events.

**ESSENTIAL
PHOTO**

Château de Chenon-
ceau's graceful arches
reflected in the Cher
River.

**BEST TWO
DAYS**

The stretch between
Chenonceau and
Chambord takes in the
true classics.

Classic Trip

11 Châteaux of the Loire

From warring medieval warlords to the kings and queens of Renaissance France, a parade of powerful men and women have left their mark on the Loire Valley. The result is France's most magnificent collection of castles. This itinerary visits nine of the Loire's most evocative châteaux, ranging from austere medieval fortresses to ostentatious royal pleasure palaces. Midway through, a side trip leads off the beaten track to four lesser-known châteaux.

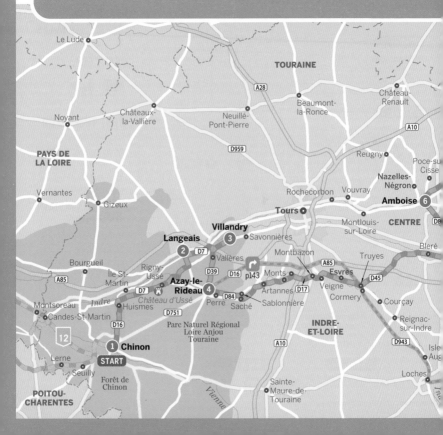

① Chinon

Tucked between the medieval **Forteresse Royale de Chinon** (☎02 47 93 13 45; www.forteressechinon.fr; adult/child €10.50/8.50; ☺9.30am-7pm May-Aug, to 5pm or 6pm Sep-Apr) – a magnificent hilltop castle – and the Vienne River, Chinon is known to French schoolchildren as the venue of Joan of Arc's first meeting with Charles VII, future king of France, in 1429. Highlights include superb panoramas from the castle's ramparts and, down in the medieval part of town (along rue Voltaire), several fine buildings dating from the 15th to 17th centuries.

✗ 📖 p147, 157

The Drive » Follow the D16 north of Chinon for 10km, then head 15km east on the riverside D7 past the fairy-tale Château d'Ussé (the inspiration for the fairy tale Sleeping Beauty) to Lignières, where you catch the D57 3km north into Langeais.

② Langeais

The most medieval of the Loire châteaux, the **Château de Langeais** (☎02 47 96 72 60; www. chateau-de-langeais.com; adult/child €10.50/5.20; ☺9.30am-6.30pm or 7pm daily Apr–mid-Nov, 10am-5pm or 5.30pm mid-Nov–Mar) – built in the 1460s – is superbly preserved inside and out, looking much as it did at the tail end of the Middle Ages, with crenellated ramparts and massive towers dominating the surrounding village. Original 15th-century furniture and Flemish tapestries fill its flagstoned chambers. In one room, a life-size wax-figure tableau portrays the marriage of Charles VIII and Anne of Brittany, held here on 6 December 1491, which brought about the historic union of France and Brittany.

Langeais presents two faces to the world. From the town you see a fortified castle, nearly windowless, with machicolated

🔗 LINK YOUR TRIP

12 **Caves & Cellars of the Loire**

Tour wineries and centuries-old cave dwellings between Chinon and Saumur.

14 **Medieval Burgundy**

Three hours east of Blois, steep yourself in the world of Burgundy's medieval churches and abbeys.

walls rising forbiddingly from the drawbridge. But the newer sections facing the courtyard have large windows, ornate dormers and decorative stonework designed for more refined living.

Behind the château stands a ruined stone **keep** constructed in 994 by the warlord Foulques Nerra, France's first great château builder. It is the oldest such structure in France.

The Drive » Backtrack south across the Loire River on the D57, then follow the riverbank east 10km on the D16 to Villandry.

❸ Villandry

The six glorious land-scaped gardens at the **Château de Villandry** (📞02 47 50 02 09; www. chateauvillandry.com; 3 rue Principale; chateau & gardens adult/child €12/7.50, gardens only €7.50/5, cheaper Dec-Feb, audio guide €4; ☺9am-5pm or 6.30pm year-round, château interior closed mid-Nov–early Dec & early Jan-early Feb) are among the finest in France, with over 6 hec-tares of cascading flowers, ornamental vines, mani-cured lime trees, razor-sharp box hedges and tinkling fountains. Try to visit when the gardens are blooming, between April and October; midsummer is most spectacular.

Wandering the pebbled walkways, you'll see the classical **Jardin d'Eau** (Water Garden), the **Laby-rinthe** (Maze) and the **Jardin d'Ornement** (Or-namental Garden), which depicts various kinds of love (fickle, passionate, tender and tragic). But the highlight is the 16th-century-style **Potager Décoratif** (Decorative Kitchen Garden), where cabbages, leeks and car-rots are laid out to create nine geometrical, colour-coordinated squares.

For bird's-eye views across the gardens and the nearby Loire and Cher Rivers, climb to the top of the **donjon** (keep), the only medieval remnant in this otherwise Renaissance-style château.

The Drive » Go southwest 4km on the D7, then turn south 7km on the D39 into Azay-le-Rideau.

TRIP HIGHLIGHT

❹ Azay-le-Rideau

Romantic, moat-ringed **Azay-le-Rideau** (📞02 47 45 42 04; www.azay-le-rideau. fr; adult/child €11.50/free, audioguide €3; ☺9.30am-7pm Jul & Aug, to 6pm Apr-Jun & Sep, 10am-5.15pm Oct-Mar), built in the early 1500s on a natural island in the middle of the Indre River, is wonderfully adorned with elegant turrets, Renaissance-style dormer windows, delicate stonework and steep slate roofs. Its most famous feature is an Italian-style **loggia staircase** overlook-

ing the central courtyard, decorated with the royal salamanders and ermines of François I and Queen Claude. The interior furnishings are mostly 19th century. Outside, the lovely English-style gardens are great for a stroll. A sound-and-light spectacular, **Les Nuits Fantastiques**, is usually projected on the chateau's walls in July and August.

The Drive » Follow the D84 east 6km through the tranquil Indre valley, then cross the river south into Saché, home to an attractive château and Balzac museum. From Saché continue 26km east on the D17, 11km northeast on the D45 and 9km east on the D976. Cross north over the Cher River and follow the D40 east 1.5km to Chenonceaux village and the Château de Chenonceau.

TRIP HIGHLIGHT

❺ Chenonceaux

Spanning the languid Cher River atop a su-premely graceful arched bridge, the **Château de Chenonceau** (📞02 47 23 90 07; www.chenonceau.com; adult/child €15/12, with audio guide €19/15.50; ☺9am or 10am-5pm or 6.30pm) is one of France's most elegant castles. It's hard not to be moved and exhilarated by the glorious setting, the formal gardens, the magic of the architecture and the château's fascinating history. The interior is decorated with rare fur-nishings and a fabulous art collection.

DETOUR:
SOUTH OF
THE LOIRE RIVER

Start: ④ Azay-le-Rideau

Escape the crowds by detouring to four less-visited châteaux between Azay-le-Rideau and Chenonceaux. First stop: **Loches**, where Joan of Arc, fresh from her victory at Orléans in 1429, famously persuaded Charles VII to march to Reims and claim the French crown. The undisputed highlight here is the walled **Cité Royale** (☎02 47 19 18 08; www.citeroyaleloches.fr; ⊗24hr), a vast citadel that spans 500 years of French château architecture in a single site, from Foulques Nerra's early 11th-century **donjon** to the Flamboyant Gothic and Renaissance styles of the **Logis Royal**. To get here from Azay-le-Rideau, head 55km east and then southeast along the D751, A85 and D943.

Next comes the quirky **Château de Montrésor** (☎02 47 92 60 04; www.chateaude montresor.fr; D760, Montrésor; adult/child €9/5; ⊗10am-6pm or 7pm Mar–mid-Nov), 19km east of Loches on the D760, still furnished much as it was 160 years ago, when it belonged to Polish-born count, financier and railroad magnate Xavier Branicki. The eclectic Second Empire decor includes a Cuban mahogany spiral staircase, a piano once played by Chopin and a sumptuous library. Next, head 20km north on the D10 and D764 to the turreted **Château de Montpoupon** (☎02 47 94 21 15; www.montpoupon. com; D764; adult/child €10/5; ⊗10am-6pm or 7pm Jul-Oct, shorter hours May & Jun, also open Sat, Sun & school holidays early Feb-Mar), idyllically situated in rolling countryside. Furnished in the late 19th and early 20th centuries by the family that still resides there, it has an intimate, lived-in feel. Continue 12km north on the D764 to the ruins of the hilltop **Château de Montrichard**, another massive fortress constructed in the 11th century by Foulques Nerra. You can picnic in the park by the Cher River or taste sparkling wines at **Caves Monmousseau** (☎02 54 32 35 15; www.monmousseau.com; 71 rue de Vierzon, Montrichard; €5; ⊗10am-noon & 2-5.30pm Mon-Sat Nov-Mar, 10am-12.30pm & 1.30-6pm Apr-Jun & Sep-Oct, 10am-6pm Jul & Aug). From Montrichard, head 10km west on the D176 and D40 to rejoin the main route at Chenonceaux.

This extraordinary complex is largely the work of several remarkable women (hence its nickname, Le Château des Dames). The distinctive arches and the eastern formal garden were added by Diane de Poitiers, mistress of King Henri II. Following Henri's death, Catherine de Médicis, the king's scheming widow, forced Diane (her 2nd cousin) to exchange Chenonceau for the rather less grand Château de Chaumont. Catherine completed the château's construction and added the yew-tree maze and the western rose garden. Chenonceau had an 18th-century heyday under the aristocratic Madame Dupin, who made it a centre of fashionable society; guests included Voltaire and Rousseau.

The château's pièce de résistance is the 60m-long, chequerboard-floored **Grande Gallerie** over the Cher. From 1940 to 1942 it served as an escape route for Jews and other refugees fleeing from German-occupied France (north of the Cher) to the Vichy-controlled south.

The Drive » Follow the D81 north 13km into Amboise; 2km south of town, you'll pass the Mini-Châteaux theme park (www.parcminichateaux.com), whose intricate scale models of 41 Loire Valley châteaux are great fun for kids!

TRIP HIGHLIGHT

⑥ Amboise

Towering above town, the **Château Royal d'Amboise** (☎02 47 57 00 98; www. chateau-amboise.com; place Michel Debré; adult/child

Classic Trip

STEVANZZ/SHUTTERSTOCK ©

YURI TURKOV/SHUTTERSTOCK ©

WHY THIS IS A CLASSIC TRIP
DANIEL ROBINSON, WRITER

Travel doesn't get more splendidly French – or elegantly sumptuous – than this tour of the most famous Loire Valley châteaux, which bring together so many of the things I love most about France: supremely refined architecture, dramatic history, exquisite cuisine and delectable wines. My kids especially enjoy the forbidding medieval fortresses of Langeais and Loches, which conjure up a long-lost world of knights, counts and court intrigue.

Above: Château de Chambord, Chambord
Left: Château Royal de Blois, Blois
Right: Château de Villandry, Villandry

€13.10/9; ⊙9am-12.30pm & 1.30pm-5.30pm mid-Nov–Feb, 9am-6.15pm or 7.45pm Mar–mid-Nov) was a favoured retreat for all of France's Valois and Bourbon kings. The ramparts afford thrilling views of the town and river, and you can visit the furnished **Logis** (Lodge) and the Flamboyant Gothic **Chapelle St-Hubert** (1493), where Leonardo da Vinci's presumed remains have been buried since 1863.

Amboise's other main sight is **Le Clos Lucé** (📞02 47 57 00 73; www.vinci -closluce.com; 2 rue du Clos Lucé; adult/child €17/12, mid-Nov–Mar €14/11; ⊙9am-7pm or 8pm Feb-Oct, 9am or 10am-6pm Nov-Jan; 👶), the grand manor house where Leonardo da Vinci (1452–1519) took up residence in 1516 and spent the final years of his life at the invitation of François I.

The most exciting Loire château to open to visitors in years, the **Château Gaillard** (📞02 47 30 33 29; www.chateau-gaillard-amboise. fr; 99 av Léonard de Vinci & 29 allée du Pont Moulin; adult/child €13/11; ⊙11am-7pm, shorter hours Jan-early Feb) is the earliest expression of the Italian Renaissance in France.

✕ 🛏 p147

The Drive ≫ Follow the D952 northeast along the Loire's northern bank, enjoying 35km of beautiful river views en route to Blois. The Château de Chaumont-sur-Loire, renowned for its world-class contemporary art and magnificent international garden

festival (April to early November), makes a wonderful stop.

----

7 Blois

Seven French kings lived in the **Château Royal de Blois** (📞02 54 90 33 33; www. chateaudeblois.fr; place du Château; adult/child €12/6.50, audioguide €3; ⏰9am-6.30pm or 7pm Apr-early Nov, 10am-5pm early Nov-Mar), whose four grand wings were built during four distinct periods in French architecture: Gothic (13th century), Flamboyant Gothic (1498–1501), early Renaissance (1515–20) and classical (1630s). You can easily spend a half-day immersing yourself in the château's dramatic and bloody history and its extraordinary architecture.

In the Renaissance wing, the most remarkable feature is the spiral **loggia staircase**, decorated with fierce salamanders and curly Fs, heraldic symbols of François I. The **King's Chamber** was the setting for one of the bloodiest episodes in the château's history. In 1588 Henri III had his arch-rival, Duke Henri I de Guise, murdered by royal bodyguards. Dramatic and very graphic oil paintings illustrate these gruesome events next door in the **Council Chamber**.

✕ 🛏 p147

The Drive » Cross the Loire and continue 16km southeast into Cheverny via the D765 and, for the final 1km, the D102.

----

8 Cheverny

Perhaps the Loire's most elegantly proportioned château, **Cheverny** (📞02 54 79 96 29; www.chateau-cheverny.fr; av du Château, Cheverny; château & gardens adult/child €12.50/9; ⏰9.15am-6.30pm Apr-Sep, 10am-5pm Oct-Mar) represents the zenith of French classical architecture: the perfect blend of symmetry, geometry and aesthetic order. Inside are some of the most elegantly furnished rooms in the Loire Valley. Highlights include the **dining room**, with panels depicting the story of Don Quixote; the **king's bedchamber**, with murals and tapestries illustrating Greek myths; and a children's **playroom** complete with toys from the time of Napoléon III.

Cheverny's **kennels** house about 100 pedigreed hunting dogs. Feeding time, known as the **Soupe des Chiens**, takes place on Monday, Wednesday, Thursday and Friday at 11.30am (daily from April to mid-September). Behind the château, the 18th-century **orangerie**, which sheltered priceless artworks – including (apparently) the *Mona Lisa* – during WWII, is now a tearoom (open April to mid-November).

Fans of Tintin may recognise the château's façade as the model for Captain Haddock's ancestral home, Marlinspike Hall. **Les Secrets de Moulinsart** (Château de Cheverny; adult/child €4.50/4; 🚶) has interactive exhibits about the comics hero.

🛏 p147

The Drive » Take the D102 10km northeast into Bracieux, then turn north on the D112 for the final 8km run through the forested Domaine National de Chambord, the largest walled park in Europe. Catch your first dramatic glimpse of France's most famous château on the right as you arrive in Chambord.

TRIP HIGHLIGHT

9 Chambord

One of the crowning achievements of French Renaissance architecture, **Château de Chambord** (📞info 02 54 50 40 00, tour & show reservations 02 54 50 50 40; www.chambord.org; adult/child €14.50/free, parking distant/near €4/6; ⏰9am-6pm Apr-Oct, to 5pm Nov-Mar; 🚶) – with 426 rooms, 282 fireplaces and 77 staircases – is the largest, grandest and most visited château in the Loire Valley.

Rising through the centre, the world-famous **double-helix staircase** – very possibly designed by the king's chum Leonardo da Vinci – ascends to the great **lantern tower** and the rooftop, where you can marvel at a veritable skyline of cupolas, domes, turrets, chimneys and lightning rods and gaze out across the vast grounds.

Eating & Sleeping

Chinon ❶

🛏 Hôtel Diderot Historic Hotel €

(📞02 47 93 18 87; www.hoteldiderot.com; 4 rue de Buffon; d €70-110, q €160; 🅿 🛜) This gorgeous town house is tucked amid luscious rose-filled gardens and crammed with polished antiques. The owners – Jean-Pierre, who's French, and Jamie, who hails from Florida – impart the sort of charm you'd expect for twice the price. The 26 cheerful rooms are all individually styled, some with 18th-century-style *jouy* wallpaper. No lift. Situated 250m north of place Jeanne d'Arc. Rates drop 30% from November to April.

Amboise ❻

🍴 Sunday Food Market Market €

(quai du Général de Gaulle; ⏰7.30am-1.30pm Sun, small market 7.30am-1pm Fri) Voted France's *marché préféré* (favourite market) a few years back, this riverfront extravaganza, 400m southwest of the château, hosts 200 to 300 open-air stalls selling everything you need for a scrumptious picnic. So delicious it's worth timing your visit around.

🛏 Le Clos d'Amboise Historic Hotel €€€

(📞02 47 30 10 20; www.leclosamboise.com; 27 rue Rabelais; d €89-229, 6-person ste €209-369; 🅿 ❄ @ 🛜 🏊) Overlooking a lovely garden with a 200-year-old cedar and a heated pool, this posh pad – most of it built in the 17th century – offers exquisite country living in the heart of town. Stylish features abound, from luxurious fabrics to antique furnishings. Half of the 20 rooms still have their original, now non-functioning, marble fireplaces. The restaurant serves traditional French cuisine.

Blois ❼

🍴 L'Orangerie du Château Gastronomy €€€

(📞02 54 78 05 36; www.orangerie-du-chateau. fr; 1 av du Dr Jean Laigret; menus €40-88; ⏰noon-1.45pm & 7-9.15pm Tue-Sat; 🅿) Serves *cuisine gastronomique inventive* inspired by French tradition and seasonal local products, including Sologne-raised caviar and black truffles. For dessert try the house speciality, soufflé, in versions that change with the seasons.

🛏 Hôtel Anne de Bretagne Hotel €

(📞02 54 78 05 38; www.hotelannedebretagne. com; 31 av du Dr Jean Laigret; d €54-89, q €79-119; ⏰reception 7am-11pm; 🅿 🛜) This ivy-covered hotel, in a great location midway between the train station and the château, has friendly staff, a cosy piano-equipped *salon* and 29 rooms with snow-white quilts. A three-course packed picnic lunch costs €11.50. Rents out bicycles (€16) and has free enclosed bike parking.

Cheverny ❽

🛏 La Levraudière B&B €

(📞02 54 79 81 99; www.lalevraudiere.fr; 1 chemin de la Levraudière, Cheverny; d with breakfast €85-95, 4-person ste €150; 🛜 🏊) In a peaceful 1892 farmhouse, amid 3.5 hectares of grassland, La Levraudière's four spacious rooms are comfortable and homey, with colorful pillows and furry bedspreads. Sonia Maurice, the friendly owner, speaks English and is happy to arrange bike rental. Situated 1.5km south of the Château de Cheverny, just west of the D102. The 10m heated swimming pool is open from April or May to September. A homemade, Sologne-style dinner that includes four courses, an aperitif, wine and coffee costs €30.

Caves & Cellars of the Loire

12

This tour of caves, wine cellars and châteaux explores the best of the western Loire Valley, home to habitations troglodytiques (cave dwellings) and some of France's finest food and wine.

TRIP HIGHLIGHTS

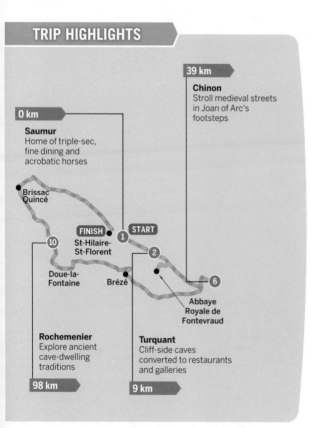

39 km

Chinon
Stroll medieval streets in Joan of Arc's footsteps

0 km

Saumur
Home of triple-sec, fine dining and acrobatic horses

Brissac Quincé

FINISH ① **START**
St-Hilaire-St-Florent ②

⑩

Doue-la-Fontaine   Brézé

⑥

Abbaye Royale de Fontevraud

Rochemenier
Explore ancient cave-dwelling traditions

98 km

Turquant
Cliff-side caves converted to restaurants and galleries

9 km

**3 DAYS
160KM / 100 MILES**

GREAT FOR...

BEST TIME TO GO

May for greenery; September and October for grape harvest.

ESSENTIAL PHOTO

Turquant's cliff face, with converted cave dwellings and a windmill.

BEST FOR WINE-TASTING

The 15km stretch between St-Hilaire-St-Florent and Montsoreau.

12 Caves & Cellars of the Loire

The Loire Valley's easily excavated tuffeau (soft limestone) has been central to the area's culture for millennia. From Merovingian quarries that did a booming long-distance trade in Christian sarcophagi, to medieval and Renaissance châteaux, to modern restaurants and wine cellars ensconced in one-time cave dwellings, this tour offers an introduction to local troglodyte culture and opportunities to savour the region's renowned gastronomy and wines.

TRIP HIGHLIGHT

1 Saumur

Start your tour in sophisticated Saumur, one of the Loire Valley's great gastronomic and viticultural centres.

For an overview of the region's wine producers, along with tastings (for a small fee), head to the **Maison des Vins d'Anjou et de Saumur** (02 41 38 45 83; mdvins.anjousaumur@ gmail.com; 7 quai Carnot; 11am-1pm & 3-7.30pm Tue-Sat, plus Mon Jul-late Sep), right next to the

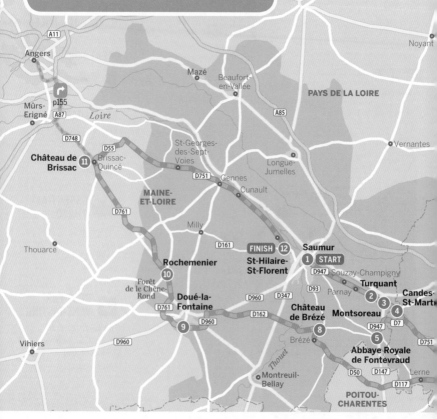

tourist office (www.ot-saumur.fr). Next, explore Saumur's other claim to fermented fame at **Distill-erie Combier** (📞 02 41 40 23 02; www.combier.fr; 48 rue Beaurepaire; tours adult/child €5/free; ☺ tours 10.30am, 2.30pm & 4pm or 4.30pm Tue-Sun Apr-Oct, plus Mon Jun-Sep; shop 10am-12.30pm & 2-7pm Tue-Sat year-round, Sun & Mon hours vary), where triple sec liqueur was invented in 1834; one-hour tours offer an engaging, behind-the-scenes look at vintage architecture by Eiffel, gleaming century-old copper stills

and fragrant vats full of Haitian bitter oranges. Combier also produces absinthe, legal in France since 2011 – you can taste it for no charge in the shop. Around town, make sure to try Saumur's iconic aperitif, *soupe saumuroise* – made with triple sec, lemon juice and sparkling wine.

The **École Nationale d'Équitation** (📞 02 41 53 50 60; www.ifce.fr/cadre-noir; av de l'École Nationale d'Équitation, St-Hilaire-St-Florent; tours adult/child €8/6; ☺ tours 2.30pm & 4pm Mon, 10am, 11am, 2.30pm & 4pm Tue-Fri, 10am & 11am Sat early Feb-Oct, more frequently early Apr–mid-Sep) is a renowned equestrian academy that trains France's Olympic teams and the Cadre Noir, an elite group of riding instructors. Take a one-hour guided visit, or book ahead for one of the not-to-be-missed **Cadre Noir performances** (📞 02 41 53 50 80; www.ifce.fr/cadre-noir; l'École Nationale d'Équitation; Matinale adult/child €19/13, Gala from €35/15; ☺ specific dates Mar-Oct), 'horse ballets' that show

off the equines' astonishing acrobatic capabilities and discipline.

Saumur also has several excellent museums, including the **Musée des Blindés** (📞 02 41 83 69 95; www.museedesblindes. fr; 1043 rte de Fontevraud; adult/child €10/6; ☺ 10am or 11am-5pm or 6pm), home to one of the world's largest collections of 'armoured cavalry' vehicles and tanks, and, soaring above the town's rooftops, the **Château de Saumur** (📞 02 41 40 24 40; www. chateau-saumur.fr; adult/child €7/5; ☺ 10am-1pm & 2-5.30pm Tue-Sun early Feb-Jun & Sep-Dec, 10am-1pm & 2-7pm daily Jul & Aug).

🍴 🛏 p156

The Drive ›› Southeast of Saumur on the south bank of the Loire, the D947 meanders for 10km through the villages of Souzay-Champigny and Parnay, home to several wineries offering tastings, including the Château Villeneuve, the Clos des Cordeliers, the Château de Parnay and the Château de Targé. Troglodyte dwellings burrow into the cliff face to your right as a hilltop windmill signals your arrival in Turquant.

°Gizeux

28 km to
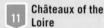

Parc
Naturel Régional Loire
Anjou Touraine

CENTRE

A85

Bourgueil

Île St-Martin

Rigny-Ussé

Indre

°Huismes

11

D751

D749 **6** **Chinon**   Forêt de Chinon

D751

7

°**Musée Rabelais**   La Roche-Clermault

euilly

Vienne

LINK YOUR TRIP

1

Essential France
Head east to Chambord to join this country-wide circuit of iconic French sights.

11

Châteaux of the Loire

In Chinon, connect to this classic tour of the Loire Valley's most famous châteaux.

❷ Turquant

Backed by chalk-coloured cliffs riddled with caves, picturesque Turquant is a showcase for the creative adaptation of historic troglodyte dwellings. The town's 'main street' runs parallel to the D947, past a handful of art galleries, restaurants and other enterprises featuring bespoke windows and colourful doors wedged into the cliff face. Turn right off the main road to **Les Pommes Tapées du Val de Loire** (📞02 41 51 48 30; https://pommes-tapees.fr; 11 rue des Ducs d'Anjou; adult/child €7.50/4; ⏰10am-5pm Tue-Sun Apr-Nov, plus Mon Jun-Sep, 10am-5pm Thu-Sun Feb & Mar), one of the last places in France producing the traditionally made dried apples known as *pommes tapées*. Tours begin at 10am, 11am, 2pm, 3pm and 4pm. Turquant's *tuffeau* cliffs have also been adapted for use as wine cellars by producers such as **La Grande Vignolle** (📞02 41 38 16 44; www.domaine-filliatreau.com; ⏰10am-6pm Apr-Oct & Dec, 2-6pm Thu & Fri, 10am-6pm Sat & Sun early Feb-Mar & Nov) and **Domaine des Amandiers** (www.domainedes-amandiers-viticulteur.fr).

🍴 🛏 p156

The Drive ≫ It's just a 3km hop, skip and jump southeast to Montsoreau along the D947 and D751. Alternatively, follow the narrow Route des Vins (parallel and slightly south of the D947) to the 16th-century windmill Moulin de la Herpinière, then continue northeast into Montsoreau via tiny Chemin de la Herpinière.

❸ Montsoreau

A surprising warning, written in huge letters in the gravel of the courtyard, greets you as you enter the Renaissance-style **Château de Montsoreau-Musée d'Art Contemporain** (📞02 41 67 12 60; www.chateau-montsoreau.com; passage du Marquis de Geoffre; adult/child €10.20/6.20; ⏰noon-6pm or 7pm Oct-Apr, 10am-7pm May-Sep, closed Jan), home to a museum of conceptual art specialising in the UK- and US-based Art & Language movement. Many works feature words, often in English, with intellectual and theoretical pretensions that range from profound to silly. For spectacular river views, climb to the roof of the tower.

Nearby, the **Regional Park Visitors Centre** (📞02 41 38 38 88; www.parc-loire-anjou-touraine.fr; 15 av de la Loire; ⏰9.30am-1pm & 2-6pm or 7pm daily Apr-Oct, Sat & Sun Mar, no midday closure Jul & Aug) provides information on activities throughout the 2708-sq-km **Parc Naturel Régional Loire-Anjou-Touraine**, established to protect the region's landscape, architecture and culture.

The Drive ≫ Follow the D751 1km southeast into Candes-St-Martin, enjoying pretty river views on your left.

❹ Candes-St-Martin

The picturesque village of Candes-St-Martin occupies an idyllic spot at the confluence of the Vienne and Loire Rivers. St Martin died here in 397, and the village's 12th- to 13th-century **church** is a major pilgrimage destination.

For great panoramas, climb the tiny streets above the church, past inhabited cave dwellings, or head down to the benches and path along the waterfront.

The Drive ≫ Snake 6km southwest along the D751, D7 and D947, following signs for Fontevraud-l'Abbaye.

❺ Abbaye Royale de Fontevraud

The highlight of this 12th-century **abbey complex** (📞02 41 51 45 11; www.fontevraud.fr; adult/child €11/7.50, audioguide €4.50; ⏰9.30am-6.30pm Apr-Oct, to 5.30pm Nov-Mar, closed mid-Jan) – turned into one of France's toughest prisons in the 19th century – is the vast but movingly simple **church**, notable for its soaring pillars, Romanesque domes and the polychrome stone tombs of four illustrious Plantagenets: Henry II, King of England (r 1154–89); his wife,

Turquant Troglodyte cave and house

Eleanor of Aquitaine (who retired to Fontevraud following Henry's death); their son Richard the Lionheart; and the wife of his brother King John, Isabelle of Angoulême. The **cloister** is surrounded by one-time dormitories, workrooms, prayer halls and a wonderful Gothic-vaulted refectory, while outside there are medieval-style gardens and a multi-chimneyed kitchen (restored in 2020). A major new **modern art museum** opened here in 2021 and features paintings and sculptures by Toulouse-Lautrec, Degas and many more.

🗶 🛏 p157

The Drive » Backtrack 5km to the D751 and follow it 13km southeast and then north towards Chinon. Immediately after crossing the Vienne River, take the D749 east 3km, paralleling the riverfront into town.

TRIP HIGHLIGHT

⑥ Chinon

Dominated by the vast **Forteresse Royale de Chinon** (☎02 47 93 13 45; www.forteressechinon. fr; adult/child €10.50/8.50; ⏰9.30am-7pm May-Aug, to 5pm or 6pm Sep-Apr), Chinon is etched into France's collective memory both as the favourite redoubt of Henry II (1133–89), king of England, and as the venue for Joan of Arc's first meeting with Charles VII, in 1429. Below the castle is an appealing medieval quarter, a warren of narrow lanes whose white tufa houses are topped with black slate roofs, giving the town its characteristic high-contrast aspect.

Surrounding the town is one of the Loire's main wine-producing areas; Chinon AOC (www.chi non.com) cabernet-franc vineyards stretch along the Vienne River. Chinon makes a good base for wine-cellar visits.

🗶 🛏 p147, p157

The Drive » Zigzag 8km southwest of Chinon through lovely rolling farmland along the D749A, D751E, D759, D24 and D117, following signs for La Devinière.

⑦ Musée Rabelais

La Devinière, the prosperous farm where François Rabelais (1483 or 1494–1553) – doctor, Franciscan friar, theoretician, author and all-around Renaissance man – lived for part of his childhood, inspired settings for some of his five satirical, erudite Gargantua and Pantagruel novels. Surrounded by vineyards and open farmland, the farmstead is now a **museum** (La

Devinière; 📞02 47 95 91 18;
www.musee-rabelais.fr; 4 rue
de la Devinière, Seuilly; adult/
child €6/5; ⏱10am-12.30pm
& 2-6pm or 7pm Wed-Mon
Apr-May & Sep, 10am-6pm or
7pm Jun-Aug, shorter hours
Oct-Mar), with exhibits on
Rabelais' life and genius
and an original 1951 Mat-
isse charcoal portrait.

The Drive » Follow the D117
west through the gorgeous
village of Seuilly, home to an
11th-century abbey. After 8km,
cross the D147 and continue
another 13km west-northwest
along the D48, D50, D310, D110
and D93 into Brézé.

---

⑧ Château de Brézé

The **Château de Brézé**
(📞02 41 51 60 15; www.
chateaudebreze.com; 2 rue
du Château, Brézé; adult/
child €11.80/6.20, incl tour
€17.90/10, audioguide €3;
⏱10am-6pm or 7pm Feb-
early Jan) sits on top of
a network of subterra-
nean rooms and passages
(1.5km of them open to
the public) that encom-
pass a bakery, wine cel-
lars, defensive bastions
and a troglodyte dwelling
dating from at least the
time of the Norman inva-
sions (early 10th century).
The dry moat is the
deepest (15m to 18m) in
Europe that completely
encircles a castle. Above
ground, much of the
U-shaped château dates
from the 19th century,
as do the many intri-
cately painted neogothic
and neo-Renaissance
interiors.

The Drive » Chart a meandering 22km course through
relatively flat farm country into
Doué-la-Fontaine via the D93,
D162, D163 and D960.

---

⑨ Doué-la-Fontaine

At the southeastern edge
of this small industrial
town, stop to visit the
fascinating **Troglodytes
et Sarcophages** (📞06
77 77 06 94; www.troglo-
sarcophages.fr; 1 rue de la Croix
Mordret, Doué-la-Fontaine;
adult/child €5.50/3.80;
⏱self-guided tours 10am-
12.30pm & 2.30-7pm early Jul-
late Aug, guided tours 2.30pm,
3.30pm & 4.30pm Thu-Mon
early Apr-early Jul, late Aug-Oct
& Christmas & Feb school
holidays), a Meroving-
ian quarry where stone
coffins were produced
from the 5th to the 9th
centuries and exported
all over western France.
Tours, in French with
printed information in
six languages, last one
hour.

Nearby at **Le Mystère
des Faluns** (Les Perrières;
📞02 41 59 71 29; https://le-
mystere-des-faluns.com; 7 rue
d'Anjou; adult/child €7/4.50;
⏱10am-noon or 12.30pm &
2-6pm Tue-Sun early Feb-1 Nov,
10am-7pm daily early Jul-mid-
Sep; ♿), creative light-
ing and sound effects
illustrating the origins
of *falun* stone and its
fossils turn the entire
600m walking route
here, though ancient
quarries (nicknamed
'cathedral caves' for their
lofty sloping walls), into

a glowing, ever-changing
work of art.

The Drive » Skirt the
southern edge of Doué-la-
Fontaine via the D960 for 4km,
then continue 5km north on
the D761 to the Rochemenier
exit. Follow signs the remaining
1.5km into Rochemenier.

TRIP HIGHLIGHT

⑩ Rochemenier

**Rochemenier Village
Troglodytique** (📞02 41
59 18 15; www.troglodyte.fr;
14 rue du Musée, Louresse-
Rochemenier; adult/child €7/5;
⏱9.30am-6pm May–mid-Sep,
10am-5pm Tue-Sun mid-Sep–
Nov & Feb-Apr, closed Dec &
Jan) is one of the Loire's
most evocative examples
of troglodyte culture.
You can explore the
remains of two adjacent
farmsteads, complete
with dwellings, stables
and a chapel, that were
originally excavated to
provide lime fertiliser.
Farm tools and photos
of former residents bring
alive the hard-working
spirit and simple pleas-
ures that defined life here
for many generations.

✖ p157

The Drive » Return to the
D761, then follow it 15km
northwest to Brissac-Quincé,
where signs direct you 1.5km
further to the château.

---

⑪ Château de Brissac

One of the Loire Valley's
most opulent castles, the
seven-storey **Château**

de Brissac ([☎]02 41 91 22 21; www.chateau-brissac. fr; Brissac-Quincé; adult/ child €12/4.50, gardens only €6/free; [⊙]10am-noon & 2-4.30pm or 5pm Wed-Mon Apr-Oct, 10am-4.30pm or 5pm daily Jul & Aug) – France's tallest – has been owned by the Brissac family for 18 generations (since 1502). Many of the 204 rooms are sumptuously furnished with antique furniture, Flemish tapestries and twinkling chandeliers. The serene 70-hectare grounds, whose vineyards boast four AOC vintages, can be visited on five themed paths.

The Drive ≫ Follow the D55 6km northeast, then wind 15km east-southeast on the D751 through forests and sunflower fields to rejoin the Loire at Gennes. From here, a particularly scenic stretch of the D751 follows the Loire's sandy banks 12km to St-Hilaire-St-Florent, passing by the villages of St-Georges-des-Sept-Voies and Chênehutte-Trèves-Cunault.

- - - - - - - - - - - - - - - - - -

⑫ St-Hilaire-St-Florent

This western suburb of Saumur is home to a number of wineries and cave-based attractions. Get acquainted with some fabulous fungi at the **Musée du Champignon** ([☎]02 41 50 31 55; www.musee-du-champignon. com; rte de Gennes, St-Hilaire-St-Florent; adult/child €9/7; [⊙]10am-6pm or 7pm

DETOUR: ANGERS

Start: ⑪ **Château de Brissac**

Angers' forbidding medieval **castle** ([☎]02 41 86 48 77; www.chateau-angers.fr; 2 promenade du Bout-du-Monde; adult/child €9.50/free, audioguide €3; [⊙]9.30am-6.30pm May-early Sep, 10am-5.30pm early Sep-Apr) – historic seat of the once-mighty counts and dukes of Anjou – is ringed by moats, 2.5m-thick walls made of dark schist, and 17 massive round towers. Inside is one of Europe's great medieval masterpieces, the stunning **Tenture de l'Apocalypse** (Apocalypse Tapestry), a 104m-long series of tapestries commissioned in 1375 to illustrate the story of the final bloody battle between good and evil, as prophesied in the New Testament's book of Revelation.

Just outside the château, learn about the region's 26 AOC wines – and taste them – at the **Maison des Vin de l'Anjou** ([☎]02 41 17 68 20; 5bis place Kennedy; [⊙]10.30am or 11.30am-1pm & 2.30pm or 3.30-6.30pm or 7.30pm Tue-Sat, open Mon & no midday closure Jul & Aug). Afterwards stroll through Angers' (pronounced ahn-ZHAY) pedestrianised centre, where you'll find cafes, restaurants, excellent museums and, behind the **cathedral**, the whimisical **Maison d'Adam** (place Ste-Croix), a medieval house decorated with bawdy carved figurines. Across the river, don't miss the stunning modern tapestries at the **Musée Jean Lurçat de la Tapisserie Contemporaine** ([☎]02 41 24 18 45; www.musees.angers.fr; 4 bd Arago; adult/child €6/free; [⊙]10am-6pm Tue-Sun).

To get here, head 28km northwest from Brissac on the D748, A87 and N260, following signs for Angers-Centre.

early Feb–mid-Nov), where a dozen varieties of mushroom grow in glowing shades of orange, yellow, tan, brown and white.

East towards Saumur, a short stretch of the D751 is home to a number of wineries offering cellar tours and *dégustation* (wine tasting), among them (from northwest

to southeast) **Acker-man** (www.ackerman. fr), **Langlois-Chateau** (www.langlois-chateau. fr), **Bouvet Ladubay** (www.bouvet-ladubay.fr) and **Veuve Amiot** (www. veuveamiot.fr). Look for Crémant de Loire and Saumur Brut, the region's very own bubblies.

Eating & Sleeping

Saumur ❶

✕ Le Boeuf Noisette — French €€

(☑09 81 73 73 10; www.leboeufnoisette.fr; 29 rue Molière; menus €25-30; ⊘ noon-2pm Tue, Thu, Fri & Sun, 7-10pm Tue-Sun; 🛜) Talented young chef Delphine Rémy has been earning enthusiastic reviews for cuisine she describes as *française, locale et fraîche* (French, local and fresh). Her flagship dish is tender, locally raised Rouge des Prés *boeuf* (beef) served with *beurre noisette* (hazelnut-coloured butter sauce made with drippings and spices) and out-of-this-world steamed veggies. For dessert, try the orange cake liberally doused with triple sec. Reserve ahead.

✕ Le Gambetta — Gastronomy €€€

(☑02 41 67 66 66; www.restaurantlegambetta. fr; 12 rue Gambetta; menus lunch from €32, dinner €39-115; ⊘ noon-1.30pm & 7.15-9pm Tue-Sat) Supreme elegance meets knock-your-socks-off creative French cuisine at Chef Mickaël Pihours' renowned establishment. Some *menus* include wine pairings perfectly chosen to complement the parade of gorgeously presented *gastronomique* dishes, punctuated by surprise treats from the kitchen. With the *carte blanche*, you choose the number of courses and the chef decides what each will be. Reserve ahead Friday night, Saturday and in summer.

🛏 Hôtel de Londres — Hotel €

(☑02 41 51 23 98; www.lelondres.com; 48 rue d'Orléans; d €80-110, q €120, apt €120-150; 🅿 ❄ @ 🛜) Built as an *hôtel de grand standing* (luxury hotel) and named in honour of the British capital in 1837, this family-run hotel has 29 spacious rooms decorated in jolly colours and two family-friendly apartments, all with big windows and gleaming bathrooms. Sunday brunch (adult/child €24/14) is served from 11.30am to 3pm. Excellent value.

🛏 Château de Beaulieu — B&B €€

(☑02 41 50 83 52; www.chateaudebeaulieu. fr; 98 rte de Montsoreau; d €120-160, q €190; ⊘ mid-Mar–mid-Nov; 🅿 🛜 ♨) Gregarious Dublin natives Mary and Conor welcome you with Irish warmth to their 1727 château. The five rooms are comfortably done up in classic style and the mood among guests is one of extended family. Sun yourself by the pool (next to the little vineyard) or play three-ball billiards in the grand salon. Situated 2.5km southeast of central Saumur.

🛏 Château de Verrières — Heritage Hotel €€€

(☑02 41 38 05 15; www.chateau-verrieres.com; 53 rue d'Alsace; d €189-349, ste €429; ⊘ closed Dec & Jan; 🅿 @ 🛜 ♨) Built by the widow of one of Napoleon III's generals, this splendid Belle Époque mansion (1896) is surrounded by a 2-hectare English-style park. It's sumptuous throughout, with carved-wood balustrades, marble fireplaces and, in the 10 spacious rooms, antique writing desks. The magnificent, wood-panelled Salle de Musique has a window directly over the fireplace (flues take the smoke around it).

Turquant ❷

✕ L'Hélianthe — French €

(☑02 41 51 22 28; www.restaurant-helianthe.fr; ruelle Antoine Cristal; mains €16.50; ⊘ noon-1.45pm Mon, Tue & Fri-Sun, 7-8.45pm Thu-Mon) Carved into the cliff behind Turquant's tiny *mairie* (town hall), this atmospheric troglodyte restaurant has a hearty menu firmly based on local products and classic French flavours. Specialities include Loire fish casserole and dishes made with *légumes oubliés* (heirloom vegetables) such as *panais* (parsnip), *topinambours* (Jerusalem artichoke) and *vitelottes* (purple potatoes).

🛏 Demeure de la Vignole — Design Hotel €€

(☑02 41 53 67 00; www.demeure-vignole. com; 3 impasse Marguerite d'Anjou; d €120-165, 4-person ste €220; ⊘ closed mid-Nov–mid-Feb; 🛜 ♨) This swish hotel has 11 richly decorated rooms, four of them inside caves. The 15m heated swimming pool is carved into the rock face, too. Very homey, and not just for hobbits. A refreshing change from the ordinary.

Fontevraud-l'Abbaye ⑤

✖ Chez Teresa   Cafe €

(📞02 41 51 21 24; www.lettersandlunchesfrom
theloire.com; 6 av Rochechouart; lunch menus
€12.50; 🕐noon-8pm; 📶) English expats
Teresa and Tony offer a cosy-warm welcome at
this frilly little tearoom, stuffed with bric-a-brac
from across the Channel. In the afternoon, pop
by for a cuppa, little triangular sandwiches,
scones with cream and jam, and cake, all for
€9.80. The double/triple room upstairs costs
€65/75, breakfast included. Just half-a-block
from the abbey.

🛏 Fontevraud L'Hôtel   Design Hotel €€

(📞02 46 46 10 10; www.hotel-fontevraud.com;
38 rue St Jean de l'Habit, Le Prieure St-Lazare;
d/q Fri & Sat €170/210, Sun-Thu €145/180;
🕐restaurant 7.30-9.30pm Thu & Fri, noon-2pm
& 7.30-9.30pm Sat, noon-2pm Sun, plus extra
days Apr-Oct; @📶) Ultramodern meets
medieval at this luxurious hotel, situated on
the abbey (p152) grounds in a one-time priory
(the vehicle entrance is around the side of the
complex). The 54 sleek rooms are decorated in
muted beiges and whites. The Michelin-starred
gastronomic restaurant (menus from €70)
serves seriously *haute* cuisine, conceived by
award-winning chef Thibaut Ruggeri.
Guests enjoy exclusive access to the abbey
grounds at night.

Chinon ⑥

✖ Les Années 30   French €€

(📞02 47 93 37 18; www.lesannees30.com;
78 rue Haute St-Maurice; weekday lunch menu
€19.50, dinner menus €28-46, veg menu €23;
🕐12.15-1.30pm & 7.30-8.45pm Thu-Mon;)

Expect the kind of meal you came to France
for, with exquisite attention to detail, served in
relaxed intimacy. The offerings range from *ris de
veau* (veal sweetbreads) to venison (during the
winter hunting season) to Guayaquil chocolate
mousse. There's a golden-lit downstairs
dining room and an elegantly grey-and-white
counterpart upstairs; in summer you can dine
outside.

🛏 Hôtel Diderot   Historic Hotel €

(📞02 47 93 18 87; www.hoteldiderot.com; 4
rue de Buffon; d €70-110, q €160; P📶) This
gorgeous town house is tucked amid luscious
rose-filled gardens and crammed with polished
antiques. The owners – Jean-Pierre, who's
French, and Jamie, who hails from Florida
– impart the sort of charm you'd expect for
twice the price. The 26 cheerful rooms are all
individually styled, some with 18th-century-
style *jouy* wallpaper. No lift. Situated 250m
north of place Jeanne d'Arc. Rates drop 30%
from November to April.

Rochemenier ⑩

✖ Les Délices de la Roche   French €€

(📞02 41 50 15 26; www.delicesdelaroche.
com; 16 rue du Musée, Louresse-Rochemenier;
weekday lunch menus €14.90-19.90, other
menus €29.90-43.90, child's menu €8.90;
🕐noon-2pm or 3pm Wed-Sun, 7-9pm or 10pm
Wed-Sat year-round, also open Tue Apr-Sep;
📶) Near Rochemenier's troglodyte village
(p154), friendly young hosts Henri and Sabrina
serve home-style French dishes, made with
quality local ingredients, in an airy dining room.
Favourites include fish, beef, mutton, burgers
and dishes made with Galet de Loire (a local
cheese made with raw cow's milk). They also
rent five simple, spacious rooms (doubles €67).

Volcanoes of the Auvergne

Mountains, meadows and ancient volcanoes form dramatic views on this tour of the Parc Naturel Régional des Volcans d'Auvergne. Get ready for invigorating hikes, acclaimed cheeses and family-friendly activities.

13

TRIP HIGHLIGHTS

START

12 km — ②

Puy de Dôme
The Auvergne's favourite lava dome

● Orcival

38 km — ⑤

Le Mont-Dore
A hiker's playground surrounded by stunning peaks

Puy de Sancy (1886m)

● St-Nectaire

200 km

Salers
Quaint cobbled streets and pastures producing superb beef and cheese

FINISH ⑨

Puy Mary (1787m)

4 DAYS
200KM / 125 MILES

GREAT FOR...

BEST TIME TO GO
May to September for warm weather and snow-free trails.

 ESSENTIAL PHOTO

The symmetrical crags of Roches Tuilière and Sanadoire framing the forests and farmland below Col de Guéry.

 BEST FOR FAMILIES

Geological site Volcan de Lemptégy and the Vulcania theme park.

13 Volcanoes of the Auvergne

Aeons ago, Europe's biggest volcanoes shaped the landscape of south-central France, blowing their tops with awe-inspiring force. On this trip you'll experience the wild beauty of the Auvergne's vestigial volcanoes – Puy de Dôme, Puy de Sancy and Puy Mary – but you'll also discover a tamer Auvergne whose picturesque patchwork of eroded cinder cones and verdant pastures is home to family-friendly walking trails, symphonies of cowbells and some of France's finest cheese.

① Volcan de Lemptégy

Fifteen kilometres west of Clermont-Ferrand, year-round guided walks lead visitors through the Auvergne's scorched-earth history. In summer, at weekends and during school holidays, a motorised 'train' chugs through the scarlet dust of **Volcan de Lemptégy** ([☎]04 73 62 23 25; www.auvergne-volcan.com; adult/child on foot €11.50/9.50, by train €15.70/12.70; [⊙]9.30am-6pm Apr-Sep, longer hours Jul & Aug, shorter hours Oct), weaving past boulders flung from the belly of this ancient volcano. Lemptégy's geological forces are fur-ther explained through a short **dynamic 3D film** (available in multiple languages) – expect bumps and jolts! If the kids are keen for more volcanic fun, rock on to **Vulcania** ([☎]04 73 19 70 00; www.vulcania.com; 2 rte de Mazayes, St-Ours-les Roches; adult/child €28.50/20.50; [⊙]10am-6pm Apr-Oct, closed Mon & Tue Apr, Sep & Oct; [♿]), 2km south. This educational theme park, the brainchild of two French geologists, includes the **Cité des Enfants** (Kids' City), with activities specially geared towards three- to seven-year-olds.

The Drive ›› Head southeast 7km along the D941 to the D942, where full-on views of Puy de Dôme beckon you 2km

southwest to the junction with
the D68 at the mountain's base.

TRIP HIGHLIGHT

② Puy de Dôme

Towering above the
surrounding landscape,
the distinctive volcanic
cone of **Puy de Dôme**
(1465m) was an icon long
before the Romans built
a temple to Mercury on
its summit in the 1st
century. Hop aboard
spiffy cog railway the
Panoramique des Dômes
(☏04 73 87 43 05; www.pano
ramiquedesdomes.fr; Orcines;
adult/child 1 way €12.10/7.30,
return €14.70/8.70; ☺9am-
7pm Apr-Jun & Sep, to 9pm Jul
& Aug, 10am-5pm Wed-Sun
Oct-Mar), inaugurated in
1907, to reach the sum-
mit. On clear days there
are sublime views of the
pouting cinder cones of
the 40km **Chaîne des
Puys**. If you're feeling

LINK YOUR TRIP

35 **Cave Art of the Vézère Valley**

Detour three hours west of
Le Mont-Dore to discover
France's oldest cave art.

36 **Dordogne's Fortified Villages**

Explore centuries-old
castles and fortified villages
along the Dordogne River,
three hours downstream
from Le Mont-Dore.

fit, there are bracing hikes to the top of Puy de Dôme. The steep, 6km **Chemin des Muletiers** takes roughly 1½ hours. A longer traverse with spectacular views is the north-facing **Chemin des Chèvres** (allow two to 2½ hours for the ascent). The summit is also prime hang-gliding territory; operators such as **Aero Parapente** ([☎]06 61 24 11 45; www.aeroparapente.fr; 1-/2-flight package €80/150; [☺]Feb-Oct) will take you soaring over the surrounding countryside.

The Drive » The 20km drive to Orcival weaves through the Chaîne des Puys on the D942, then continues southwest on the D216 and D27, passing through increasingly hilly and pastoral countryside dotted with lovely stone and slate barns.

❸ Orcival

Backed by a leafy green hillside and bisected by a rushing stream, photogenic Orcival clusters around a gorgeous Romanesque **basilica** (place de la Basilique; [☺]8.30am-6pm Oct-Mar, to 7.30pm Apr-Sep) that houses one of the Auvergne's most famous *Vierges noires* (black Madonnas, icons typical of the region). An object of veneration throughout the year, she's paraded through the streets with special fanfare on Assumption Day (15' August). The **tourist office** ([☎]04 73 65 89 77; www.auvergnevolcansancy.com;

place de la Basilique; [☺]9am-1pm & 2-6pm May-Sep, shorter hours rest of year; [☎]) just opposite loans tablets for lively self-guided tours of the basilica's hidden details (with a version suitable for kids). If you're sticking around, **Aluna Voyages** ([☎]06 78 40 36 79; www.aluna-voyages.com; [♿]) offers food-foraging tours into the meadows surrounding Orcival, along with donkey-accompanied walks geared towards young adventurers.

✕ p165

The Drive » The D27 climbs 8km through verdant hills and evergreen forest to a spectacular viewpoint just before Col de Guéry (1268m), where the dramatic volcanic crags Roche Tuilière (1288m) and Roche Sanadoire (1286m) rise in symmetry from the land below.

❹ Col de Guéry

This mountain pass, flanked by the Auvergne's highest lake, is enticing for walkers, fishers and winter sports fans; check in with the **Centre Montagnard Cap Guéry** ([☎]04 73 65 20 09; www.capguery. com; off D983, Col de Guéry; [☺]10am-6pm Jul & Aug, 10am-6pm Wed, Sat & Sun Jun & Sep, 9am-5pm daily Dec-Mar when snowy, weekends only Dec-Mar when not snowy) for maps of the wild hiking terrain. The countryside around picturesque **Lac de Guéry** (1268m) is laced with

walking trails, some of them suitable for snowshoeing in winter. Book a table at lakeside Auberge du Lac de Guéry (p165) for lunch with a view.

🛏 p165

The Drive » Spellbinding mountain views unfold as you approach the Massif du Sancy, soaring peaks that are often snowcapped late into the spring. A sinuous 9km drive along the D983 and D996 drops you straight into downtown Le Mont-Dore.

TRIP HIGHLIGHT

❺ Le Mont-Dore

Ringed by rugged peaks at the heart of the Parc Naturel Régional des Volcans d'Auvergne, this historic spa town makes a great base for exploring the surrounding high country. A **téléphérique** (Station du Mont-Dore; 1 way/return adult €7.70/10.20, child €5.70/7.60; [☺]9am-6pm Jul & Aug, 9am-noon & 1.30-5pm late Dec-Jun, Sep & Oct) whisks hikers through a landscape of precipitous crags to the foot of **Puy de Sancy** (1886m), the tallest peak in the Massif Central mountain range. Across town, a tortoise-slow but creakily atmospheric 1890s-vintage **funiculaire** ([☎]04 73 65 01 25; rue René Cassin, Le Mont-Dore; 1 way/return adult €6/7.50, child €5/6; [☺]10am-12.10pm & 2-5.40pm Wed-Sun May-Sep, to 6.40pm daily Jul & Aug) lumbers up to Les Capucins, an upland plateau (1245m)

Parc Naturel Régional des Volcans d'Auvergne Puy de Sancy

where well-marked trails fan out in all directions. Several fine hikes and mountain-biking routes also start in downtown Le Mont-Dore, including the **Chemin de la Grande Cascade**, which leads to a 32m-high waterfall. For trail info and high-resolution topo maps, visit Le Mont-Dore's **tourist office** (☏04 73 65 20 21; www.sancy.com; av de la Libération; ☺9am-noon & 2-6pm Mon-Sat, 10am-noon & 2-5pm Sun, longer hours Jul & Aug; ☏), in a riverside park downtown. Nearby streets are filled with outdoors-oriented shops and purveyors of local charcuterie and cheeses, such as dried sausage specialist **La Petite Boutique du Bougnat** (1 & 4 rue Montlosier, Le Mont-Dore; ☺9am-12.30pm & 2.30-7pm).

✗ ⊫ p165

The Drive ⟫ Begin with a spectacular traverse of 1451m Col de la Croix St-Robert, passing through 17km of wide-open high country along the D36. Next trundle along the D996 for 12km, enjoying pretty views of Lac Chambon, popular with boaters, hikers and campers, and Murol's hilltop castle, before reaching St-Nectaire.

----

⑥ St-Nectaire

Tiny St-Nectaire is famous for its 12th-century Romanesque church, stunningly set against a mountain backdrop, and its herds of happy bovines, who make this one of the Auvergne's dairy capitals. Buy a round of delectably creamy St-Nectaire cheese from **Maison du Fromage** (☏04 73 88 57 96; rte de Murol, St-Nectaire-le-Haut; tours adult/child €6.90/4.90; ☺10am-noon & 2-6pm), along with terrines, jams

and other picnic nibbles. To learn the secrets of how it's made, stay for a 35-minute guided tour of the cellars, complete with a swoony video presentation and cheese sampling.

The Drive ⟫ Follow the D996 7km downstream to tiny Rivallet, then head southwest 15km on the D978 into Besse. Overshoot the town centre by 4km to enjoy a scenic walk by Lac Pavin.

----

⑦ Besse-et-St-Anastaise

Basalt-brick cottages, cobbled lanes and a majestic old belfry are reason enough to visit this pretty mountain village. Hikers and bikers will also appreciate the fine network of trails uphill in **Super-Besse** and serene **Lac Pavin**, a crater lake 4km west of town. For a taste of mountain culture, visit during the

CHEESE COUNTRY

The Auvergne produces some of France's finest cheeses, including five Appellation d'Origine Protégée (AOP) varieties: the semihard, cheddar-like Cantal and nutty Salers, both made from the milk of high-pasture cows; St-Nectaire, creamy, tangy and semisoft; Fourme d'Ambert, a mild, smooth blue cheese; and Bleu d'Auvergne, a powerful, creamy blue cheese with a Roquefort-like flavour.

To taste them on their home turf, follow stretches of the signposted **Route des Fromages** (www. fromages-aop-auvergne.com), which links local farms and producers. A downloadable map is available on the website.

Local cheeses figure strongly in many traditional Auvergnat dishes. *Aligot* is a smooth blend of puréed potato with garlic and *tomme fraîche* or Cantal cheese. Heartier *truffade* mingles diced or crushed potatoes with melted Cantal cheese, usually accompanied by a generous helping of *jambon d'Auvergne* (local cured ham).

Transhumance de la Vierge Noire: on 2 July, a black Madonna icon is carried amid great fanfare from Besse-et-St-Anastaise up to the little village of Vassivière.

🛏 p165

The Drive ⟩⟩ Leave the Massif du Sancy behind and head south 75km towards the wilder, less populated Monts du Cantal. A curvy course through farmland and river valleys along the D978 and D678 leads to a supremely scenic, sustained climb along the D62 and D680, bringing you face to face with Puy Mary, the southernmost of the Auvergne's three classic peaks.

⑧ Puy Mary

Barely wide enough to accommodate parked cars, the vertiginous mountain pass of Pas de Peyrol (1589m) hugs the base of pyramid-shaped Puy Mary (1787m), the Cantal's most charismatic peak. A trail, complete with staircases for the steeper sections, leads to the summit (about one hour round-trip). Find walking routes for all abilities on www. puymary.fr.

The Drive ⟩⟩ The 20km descent along the D680 switchbacks steeply through a wonderland of high-country scenery before plunging into fragrant evergreen forest and following a long ridgeline into Salers.

TRIP HIGHLIGHT

⑨ Salers

Pretty Salers perches on a hilltop surrounded by fields full of long-horned brown cattle that produce the region's eponymous AOP cheese. With a compact core of 16th-century stone buildings and long views up towards Puy Mary, it's a relaxing place to linger. Central **place Tyssandier d'Escous** is lined with boutiques selling knives and handi-crafts and characterful restaurants that slosh Côtes d'Auvergne wine into glasses and sizzle up famously rich Salers beef. Learn more about the region's hallowed cattle, as well as its nutty local cheese, at **Maison de la Salers** (☎04 71 40 54 00; www.maisondelasalers. fr; Le Fau, St-Bonnet-de-Salers; adult/child €7/4.50; ⏱10am-noon & 2-6pm Feb-Oct & school holidays). Day hikes range from an easy 75-minute circuit of the stone-walled pastures surrounding town to high-mountain rambles through wide-open country around the base of 1592m-high **Puy Violent**.

🍴 🛏 p165

Eating & Sleeping

Orcival ③

✖ Auberge Le Cantou   French €

(☎04 73 65 82 07; www.aubergelecantou.com;
Le Bourg; menus from €16; ⏰noon-1.30pm &
7-9pm Tue-Sat) Dishing up cuisine as rustic as
its wood-and-stone dining room, Le Cantou is a
reliable spot to try classic Auvergnat dishes like
fondue of St-Nectaire cheese, pig's trotter in
mustard, and *pounti* (a savoury cake of potato
and prunes). Plain but nicely maintained double
rooms start at €67, with a decent breakfast
for €9.50.

Col de Guéry ④

🛏 Auberge du Lac de Guéry   Hotel €€

(☎04 73 65 02 76; www.auberge-lac-guery.
fr; d/f/ste from €98/155/185; ⏰Feb-mid-
Oct; 🅿🛜) In a scenic position on the lake's
southern edge, this cosy modern inn has chic
rooms with unbeatable access to hiking, fishing
and cross-country skiing. Staff are energetic
and brimming with tips, from snowshoeing
advice to sales of fishing permits. Say *oui, merci*
to breakfast (€14) or half board (around €47
per person extra) – naturally, lake fish are on
the menu.

Le Mont-Dore ⑤

✖ La Golmotte   French €€

(☎04 73 65 05 77; www.aubergelagolmotte.
com; rte D996, Le Barbier; menus €20-40;
⏰noon-1.30pm & 7-8.30pm Mon & Thu-Sat,
noon-1.30pm Sun; 👶) Reserve ahead for a
satisfying regional feast at this farm-style inn,
3km along the road to Lac de Guéry. Regional
classics like cheesy *truffade* and *pounti* are
offered beneath its wooden rafters, as are
refined recipes like scallops in orange butter
and seared steak with tangy blue-cheese sauce.
Rooms available, too (singles/doubles including
breakfast €52/65).

🛏 Grand Hôtel   Hotel €€

(☎04 73 65 02 64; www.hotel-mont-dore.com;
2 rue Meynadier; d/tr/q from €80/90/100;

⏰mid-Dec–mid-Nov; 🅿🛜) The romantic
ambience of this turreted 1850 hotel is amply
delivered within its rooms, which have a sharp
modern design and comfortable wrought-iron
beds. The best rooms have balconies looking
towards the mountains. Meanwhile, time
spent in the spa (€6) is the perfect balm for
calf muscles that ache from exertion up in the
mountains.

Besse-et-St-Anastaise ⑦

🛏 Auberge de la Petite Ferme   B&B €€

(☎04 73 79 51 39; www.auberge-petite-ferme.
com; Le Faux; d €55-125, f €105-175; 🅿🛜)
Fling open your shutters to reveal rolling
pastures from one of 32 snug rooms (most with
a balcony) at this converted farmhouse, 800m
from Besse's historic centre on the road to Lac
Pavin. The breakfast buffet (€11.50) is replete
with patisserie, yogurt and local honey, while
the snug on-site restaurant serves myriad melty
cheese dishes (from €14).

Salers ⑨

✖ La Diligence   French €€

(☎04 71 40 75 39; www.ladiligencesalers.com;
rue du Beffroi; menus €19-37; ⏰noon-2.30pm
& 7-9.30pm Apr-Oct) Loosen your belt for
generous servings of regional delicacies such as
pork with lentils and *coufidou* (beef marinated
in wine) at this restaurant in the historic centre.
Our pick: Salers beef served with cheesy
potato dish *truffade*. There's a children's
menu featuring crêpes and kid-sized regional
specialities.

🛏 La Maison
de Barrouze   Guesthouse €€

(☎04 71 40 78 08; av de Barrouze; d from €65;
🛜) With rough-hewn rooms stacked within a
grand old town house, La Maison de Barrouze
has charisma bouncing off every stone wall
and exposed timber beam. The hospitality is
beyond compare, as is the included breakfast of
homemade produce such as jams, yogurt and
fresh-baked cakes.

Medieval Burgundy

Fortified hill towns, medieval monasteries, exquisite Romanesque capitals and multicoloured tiled roofs share the stage with rolling vineyards and verdant hiking trails on this idyllic ramble.

14

TRIP HIGHLIGHTS

Noyers-sur-Serein

7

322 km

Abbaye de Fontenay
Tranquil end-of-the-road domain of 12th-century Cistercian monks

9 FINISH

Semur-en-Auxois

Dijon

4

178 km

Beaune
Burgundy's wine capital, crowned by kaleidoscopic roof tiles

Autun

Tournus

1 START

Vézelay
A hilltop treasury of Romanesque architecture

407 km

Cluny
Once Christendom's grandest abbey, reduced to peaceful ruins

0 km

6 DAYS
407KM / 252 MILES

GREAT FOR...

BEST TIME TO GO
From May wildflower season to the October wine harvest.

ESSENTIAL PHOTO

Vézelay's sinuous sweep of stone houses crowned by a hilltop basilica.

☑ BEST FOR OUTDOORS

The riverside walking trails around Noyers-sur-Serein.

14 Medieval Burgundy

Between the Middle Ages and the 15th century, Burgundy saw a tremendous flowering of ecclesiastical architecture, from Cistercian and Benedictine monasteries to Romanesque basilicas, accompanied by active patronage of the arts by the powerful Dukes of Burgundy. This medieval journey shows you the highlights while mixing in opportunities for wine tasting and walking in the gorgeous, rolling countryside that makes Burgundy one of France's most alluring regions.

① Cluny

The remains of Cluny's great **abbey** (Abbey Church; ☎03 85 59 15 93; www.cluny-abbaye.fr; place du 11 Août 1944; adult/child incl museum & Tour des Fromages €10.50/ free; ⊙9.30am-7pm Jul & Aug, to 6pm Apr-Jun & Sep, to 5pm Oct-Mar) – Christendom's largest church until the construction of St Peter's Basilica in the Vatican – are fragmentary and scattered, barely discernible among the houses and green spaces of the modern-day town. But with a bit of imagination, it's possible to picture how things looked in the 12th century, when

Cluny's Benedictine abbey, renowned for its wealth and power and answerable only to the pope, held sway over 1100 priories and monasteries stretching from Poland to Portugal.

Get oriented at the **Musée d'Art et d'Archéologie** (☎03 85 59 12 79; rue de l'Abbatiale; combined ticket with Église Abbatiale & Tour des Fromages adult/child €10.50/free; ⊙9.30am-6pm or 7pm Apr-Sep, to 5pm Oct-Mar), with its scale model of the Cluny complex and 3D 'virtual tour' of the abbey's original medieval layout, then climb the **Tour des Fromages** (rue Mercière; adult/child €2.80/1.50; ⊙9.30am-6.30pm May &

Jul-Sep, 9.30am-12.30pm & 2-6.30pm Apr & Jun, to 5pm Mon-Sat Oct-Mar) (access is through the tourist office) for a bird's-eye view of the abbey's remnants, including the striking octagonal **Clocher de l'Eau Bénite** (Tower of the Holy Water) and the **Farinier** (Granary), where eight splendid capitals from the original church are displayed.

 p173

The Drive » Head 13km north along the D981 to Cormatin, with its Renaissance-style château, then squiggle 25km east along the D14 past Chapaize's 11th-century Église St-Martin, Ozenay's château and the medieval hill village of Brancion before descending into Tournus.

---

2 **Tournus**

Tournus' superb 10th- to 12th-century Benedictine abbey, **Abbatiale St-Philibert** (www.tournus-

LINK YOUR TRIP

11 **Châteaux of the Loire**

Three hours west of Vézelay, explore the Loire Valley's classic châteaux.

15 **Route des Grands Crus**

Switch gears in Beaune to discover Burgundy's best wines.

tourisme.com; ☉8am-6pm or 7pm), makes a striking first impression, with its austere Romanesque façade peeking out through a medieval stone gate flanked by twin rounded towers. Its apse holds an extremely rare 12th-century **floor mosaic** of the calendar and the zodiac, discovered by chance in 2002. The medieval centre also boasts fine restaurants – good for a lunch stop.

The Drive >> From Tournus, zip 96km straight up the A6 and A31 to Dijon.

- - - - - - - - - - - - - - - -

❸ Dijon

Long-time capital of medieval Burgundy, Dijon was the seat of power for a series of enlightened dukes who presided over the region's 14th- and 15th-century golden age, filling the city with fine art and architecture and a wonderful medieval centre, best explored by foot.

Topping the list of must-see attractions are the early 13th-century **Église Notre Dame** (place Notre-Dame; ☉8am-7pm), with its remarkable façade of pencil-thin columns and leering gargoyles; the **Palais des Ducs et des États de Bourgogne** (Palace of the Dukes & States of Burgundy; place de la Libération), the Burgundy dukes' monumental palace,

which also houses Dijon's extraordinary fine arts museum, the **Musée des Beaux-Arts** (☎03 80 74 52 09; https://beaux-arts.dijon.fr; 1 rue Rameau; audioguide €4, guided tour €6; ☉10am-6.30pm Jun-Sep, 9.30am-6pm Oct-May, closed Tue year-round); and the **historic mansions** that line surrounding streets, especially rue des Forges, rue Verrerie, rue Vannerie and rue de la Chouette.

The Drive >> Zip 44km south on the A31 to Beaune, or take the slower but much more scenic Route des Grands Crus through the Côte de Nuits vineyards.

- - - - - - - - - - - - - - - -

TRIP HIGHLIGHT

❹ Beaune

Burgundy's supremely appealing viticultural capital, Beaune (pronounced 'bone'), is surrounded by vineyards producing some of the most renowned Côte d'Or appellations, grown on the slopes of the Côte de Nuits and Côte de Beaune (some AOC definitions were tweaked in 2020). Sipping local vintages at sunset on a cafe terrace here is one of France's great pleasures.

The architectural jewel of Beaune's historic centre is the **Hôtel-Dieu des Hospices de Beaune** (☎03 80 24 45 00; www.hospices-de-beaune.com; 2 rue de l'Hôtel-Dieu; adult/child €8.50/4; ☉9am-7.30pm late

Mar–mid-Nov, 9-11.30am & 2-6.30pm rest of year, last entry 1hr before closing), a 15th-century charity hospital topped by stunning turrets and pitched rooftops covered in multicoloured tiles. Interior highlights include the barrel-vaulted **Grande Salle**, with dragon-embellished beams; an 18th-century **pharmacy** lined with ancient flasks; and the mesmerising **Polyptych of the Last Judgement**, a 15th-century Flemish masterpiece that depicts the glory and utter terror of Judgement Day.

🍴 🛏 p173, p181

The Drive >> A super-scenic 49km drive along the D973 weaves southwest through gorgeous vineyard country, climbing past La Rochepot's striking 13th-century castle before turning west to Autun.

- - - - - - - - - - - - - - - -

❺ Autun

Two millennia ago, Autun (Augustodunum) was one of Roman Gaul's most important cities. Its next heyday came 1100 years later, when **Cathédrale St-Lazare** (place du Terreau; chapter room adult/child €2/free; ☉cathedral 8am-6pm year-round, chapter room 10am-noon Tue-Sat & 2-6pm Tue-Sun Apr-Oct) was built to house St Lazarus' sacred relics. Climb through the old city's narrow cobblestone streets to see the cathedral's fantastical

Beaune Hôtel-Dieu des Hospices de Beaune

Romanesque capitals and famous 12th-century **tympanum** depicting the Last Judgement, carved by Burgundy's master sculptor Gislebertus. Across the street, the **Musée Rolin** (☎03 85 54 21 60; www.museerolin.fr; 3 rue des Bancs; adult/child €6.50/free; ☺10am-1pm & 2-6pm Wed-Mon Apr-Sep, 10am-12.30pm & 2-5.30pm Wed-Mon Oct-Mar) houses Gislebertus' precociously sensual masterpiece, the *Temptation of Eve,* alongside Gallo-Roman artefacts and modern paintings.

Roman treasures around town include the town gates, **Porte d'Arroux** and **Porte St-André**; the 16,000-seat **Théâtre Romain**; the **Temple de Janus**; and the **Pierre de Couhard**, the 27m-high remnant of a Gallo-Roman pyramid.

Autun makes an excellent base for exploring the hills, forests, lakes and hamlets of the nearby **Parc Naturel Régional du Morvan** (www.parcdumorvan.org); there's a visitors centre in St-Brisson.

The Drive ≫ The D980 runs 70km north from Autun to Semur-en-Auxois; halfway along, there's a fine collection of Romanesque capitals at Saulieu's 12th-century Basilique de St-Andoche.

---

❻ Semur-en-Auxois

Perched on a granite spur, surrounded by a hairpin turn in the Armançon River and guarded by four massive pink-granite bastions, Semur was once an important religious centre boasting no fewer than six monasteries.

Pass through the two concentric medieval gates, **Porte Sauvigne** and **Porte Guillier**, onto pedestrianised **rue Buffon**; then meander west through the old town to **Promenade du Rempart** for panoramic views from atop Semur's medieval battlements. Semur is especially atmospheric at night, when the ramparts are illuminated.

Be sure to stop in at the historic **Pâtisserie Alexandre** (☎03 80 97 08 94; 1 rue de la Liberté; ☺7.30am-7pm Tue-Fri, 7am-1pm & 2-7pm Sat, 7am-1pm Sun) for some *granit rose de l'auxois* (a local pink confection laden with sugar, orange-infused chocolate, cherries, almonds and hazelnuts).

The Drive ≫ Follow the D980 20km north into Montbard, then hop 2km east on the D905 before joining the sleepy northbound D32 for the idyllic 3km home stretch into Fontenay.

TRIP HIGHLIGHT

7 Abbaye de Fontenay

Founded in 1118 and restored to its medieval glory a century ago, the Unesco-listed **Abbaye de Fontenay** (Fontenay Abbey; 📞03 80 92 15 00; www.abbayedefontenay.com; adult/child self-guided tour €10/7, guided tour €12.50/7.90; ⏰10am-6pm early Apr–mid-Nov, 10am-noon & 2-5pm mid-Nov–early Apr) offers a glimpse of the austere, serene surroundings in which Cistercian monks lived lives of contemplation, prayer and manual labour. Set in a bucolic wooded valley, the abbey includes an unadorned Romanesque church, a barrel-vaulted monks' dormitory, landscaped gardens and Europe's first metallurgical forge, with a reconstruction of a hydraulic hammer used by 13th-century monks.

From the parking lot, the **GR213 trail** forms part of two verdant walking circuits: one to Montbard (13km return), the other (11.5km) through Touillon and Le Petit Jailly. Maps and botanical field guides are available in the abbey shop.

The Drive » Backtrack to the D905, follow it 14km west-northwest to Rougemont, then take the westbound D956 21km into Noyers.

8 Noyers-sur-Serein

Tucked into a sharp bend in the Serein River, picturesque medieval Noyers is surrounded by pastureland and wooded hills. The town's cobbled streets, accessed via two imposing **stone gateways**, lead past 15th- and 16th-century gabled houses, wood and stone archways and several art galleries.

Noyers is a superb base for **walking**. Just outside the clock-topped southern gate, **Chemin des Fossés** threads its way between the Serein and the village's 13th-century fortifications, 19 of whose original 23 towers still remain. Continue along the Serein's right bank, joining the **Balade du Château** and climbing past Noyer's utterly ruined château to a series of belvederes with dreamy views over the town and the surrounding countryside.

The Drive » Snake 14km southward through the peaceful Serein valley via the D86, then head 11km west on the D11 from Dissangis to Joux-la-Ville before charting a southwest course down the D32, D9, D606 and D951 for the final 24km run into Vézelay.

TRIP HIGHLIGHT

9 Vézelay

Rising from lush rolling countryside and crowned by a fabulous medieval basilica, Vézelay is one of France's loveliest hilltop villages. Founded in the 9th century on a one-time Roman and then Carolingian site, **Basilique Ste-Madeleine** (www.basiliquedevezelay.org; ⏰7am-8pm) has served for almost a millennium as the starting point for one of the pilgrimage routes to Santiago de Compostela. Among its treasures are a 12th-century **tympanum**, with a carving of an enthroned Jesus radiating his holy spirit to the Apostles; several beautifully carved Romanesque **capitals**, including the Mystical Mill, which depicts Moses grinding grain into a flour sack held by St Paul; and a mid-12th-century **crypt** reputed to house one of Mary Magdalene's bones.

The **park** behind the basilica affords wonderful views of, and walking access to, the verdant Vallée de Cure. From **Porte Neuve**, Vézelay's old town gate, a footpath descends via the 12th-century chapel of **La Cordelle** to the village of **Asquins**. Another nice walk is the **Promenade des Fossés**, which circumnavigates Vézelay's medieval ramparts.

🍴 🛏 p173

Eating & Sleeping

Cluny ❶

✕ La Table d'Héloïse   Burgundian €€

(☎03 85 59 05 65; www.hostelleriedheloise.
com/restaurant-cluny; 7 rue de Mâcon; lunch
menu €21, dinner menus €35-52; ⊗12.15-
1.45pm Fri-Tue, 7.30-8.45pm Mon, Tue & Thu-Sat)
South of town, this family-run restaurant with
a charmingly cosy interior is a terrific place to
sample traditional Burgundian specialities, from
dexterously prepared *escargots de Bourgogne*
(Burgundy snails) to tender Charolais rib-eye
steak, and from ripe Époisses cheese to
the devastatingly delicious desserts. Book
ahead for a table on the light-filled verandah
overlooking the Grosne River.

✕ La Halte de l'Abbaye   Burgundian €€

(☎03 85 59 28 49; halte.cluny@gmail.com; 3 rue
Porte des Prés; menus from €20; ⊗noon-3pm
Wed-Sun & 7-9.15pm Tue-Sat, may close in
winter) Artisanal *andouillette* sausage, Charolais
steak tartare and even *tête de veau* (calf's head)
are among the classic Burgundian dishes on the
menu at this convivial, family-run spot a block
northeast of the abbey gates – look for the
green shutters. Hard-working owners Franck
and Séverine offer nonstop service throughout
the afternoon, making it a convenient break
between sightseeing stints.

Beaune ❹

✕ Caves Madeleine   French €€

(☎03 80 22 93 30; www.cavesmadeleine.com;
8 rue du Faubourg Madeleine; mains €23-25;
⊗noon-1.30pm & 7.15-9.45pm Mon, Tue &
Thu-Sat) Focusing on fresh-from-the-farm
vegetables and meat grown within a 100km
radius of Beaune, this cosy little restaurant
changes its menu daily. Reserve ahead for

a private table, or enjoy a more convivial
experience at the long shared table, backed by
well-stocked wine racks. Also rents out rooms.

🛏 Abbaye
de Maizières   Historic Hotel €€€

(☎03 80 24 74 64; www.hotelabbayede
maizieres.com; 19 rue Maizières; d €159-255, ste
€350-468; ✳ @ 🛜) Ensconced within a 14th-
century abbey, this atmospheric establishment
oozes history from every graceful Gothic arch.
Some of the 12 rooms and suites – luxuriously
modernised – boast Cistercian-style stained-
glass windows and exposed beams; those on
the top floor offer views over Beaune's famed
multicoloured tile roofs.

Vézelay ❽

✕ Restaurant SY La Terrasse   Bistro €

(☎03 86 33 25 50; www.vezelay-laterrasse.
com; place de la Basilique; mains €15-28, lunch
menus €19.50-24; ⊗noon-2pm & 7-8.30pm)
Stone walls, decorative tiled floors, smooth
jazz and a roaring fire on chilly nights make this
one of Vézelay's cosiest eateries. Menu options
include locally grown snails, bœuf bourguignon
and Charolais steak. The bar, well stocked with
whiskies, wines and rum, is a great spot for a
nightcap.

🛏 Cabalus   Guesthouse €

(☎03 86 33 20 66; www.cabalus.com; rue
St-Pierre; r €42-62) Cabalus offers four simple,
spacious rooms with sturdy beams, ancient
tiles and stone walls in a 12th-century building
half a block from the cathedral. Decoration is
sparse and cheaper rooms have shared toilets
(all rooms have private showers), but it's hard
to beat for location, price and quirky historic
charm.

Route des Grands Crus

15

The exquisite Route des Grands Crus brings together many of central Burgundy's most acclaimed vineyards, with plenty of opportunities to sample famous vintages in historic surrounds.

TRIP HIGHLIGHTS

START
● Gevrey-Chambertin

7 km

Château du Clos de Vougeot
A magnificent wine-growing estate

2

● Nuits-St-Georges

29 km

Beaune
The opulent capital of Burgundian wines

5

8

7

● Pommard

39 km

Château de La Rochepot ●

Puligny-Montrachet

FINISH

Château de Meursault
Wine tasting in a grandiose setting

St-Romain
Sensational views and a bucolic atmosphere

45 km

2 DAYS
62KM / 38 MILES

GREAT FOR...

BEST TIME TO GO

May, June, September and October for a symphony of colour and quiet roads.

ESSENTIAL PHOTO

Panoramic views of the countryside from the cliffs above St-Romain are exquisite.

BEST FOR FOODIES

Beaune is a great place to try Burgundian specialities such as snails.

15 Route des Grands Crus

Meandering through Burgundy's vine-carpeted countryside takes you to some of the most storied vineyards in the world and to ancient wine-growing villages whose names — engraved on labels or whispered during a romantic dinner — make oenophiles swoon. You'll visit legendary wine châteaux and wine cellars, redolent with the bouquet of fermenting grapes, that offer a golden opportunity to sample some of France's most prestigious reds and whites.

1 Gevrey-Chambertin

Kick off your epicurean adventure by visiting this picturesque village, which enjoys a world-class reputation among wine enthusiasts – it produces nine out of the 32 *grands crus* wines from Burgundy, all of them reds made from pinot noir.

The Drive >> From Gevrey-Chambertin it's a relaxed 7km drive south along the tertiary D122, via Morey-St-Denis and Chambolle-Musigny, to the Château du Clos de Vougeot.

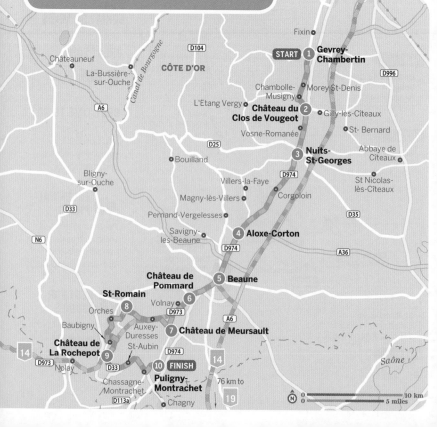

② Château du Clos de Vougeot

The magnificent wine-producing **Château du Clos de Vougeot** (03 80 62 86 09; www.closdevougeot. fr; rue de la Montagne, Vougeot; adult/child €7.50/2.50; ⊙10am-5pm Tue-Sun;), regarded by some as the birthplace of Burgundian wines, was originally the property of the Abbaye de Cîteaux, 12km southeast from here. Tours (€2.50; in French at 10.30am and 2.30pm) reveal the workings of enormous wine presses and casks.

The Drive » Pick up the D974 to Nuits-St-Georges, 4.5km south via Vosne-Romanée.

LINK YOUR TRIP

14 Medieval Burgundy

It's easy to combine this trip with our itinerary focusing on medieval Burgundy, either from Beaune or La Rochepot.

19 Beaujolais Villages

In the mood for more full-bodied wines? Motor 1¼ hours south to Villefranche-sur-Saône and make your way up to Roche de Solutré.

③ Nuits-St-Georges

It's worth spending a little time in attractive Nuits-St-Georges. Splashed around town are a dozen *domaines* selling superb reds and whites, but an informative port of call on any wine-tasting itinerary is **L'Imaginarium** (03 80 62 61 40; www.imaginarium-bourgogne.com; av du Jura; adult incl basic/grand cru tasting €10/21, child €7; ⊙2-7pm Tue, 10am-7pm Mon & Wed-Sun, last admission 5.15pm). This gleaming modern museum is a great place to learn about Burgundy wines and winemaking techniques. It's fun and entertaining, with movies, exhibits, interactive displays and tastings.

Architecture buffs might want to mosey over to the 17th-century **belfry** of the former town hall and the Romanesque **Église St-Symphorien**, slightly away from the town centre.

The Drive » Continue along the D974 southwestward towards Beaune. After passing through the village of Ladoix-Serrigny, look out for the sign to Château Corton-André on the right. The 11.5km drive takes about 10 minutes.

④ Aloxe-Corton

Surrounded by manicured vineyards, tiny Aloxe-Corton is a real charmer, especially for wine buffs – there are producers handily scat-

tered around the village. A good starting point is the **Caveau d'Aloxe Corton** (03 80 26 49 85; http://aloxe.corton.free.fr/ caveau-aloxe-corton.php; place du Chapitre; ⊙10am-1pm & 3-7pm Thu-Mon Easter–mid-Nov, no midday closure Sat & Sun), a wine shop representing eight producers of terrific local reds and whites.

The high-flying **Château Corton-André** (03 80 26 28 79; www. corton-andre.com; rue Cortons; ⊙10am-1pm & 2-6.30pm Apr-Oct, shorter hours & closed Sun afternoon Nov-Mar), aka Château Corton C, with its splendid cellars and multicoloured tile roof, is a wonderful place for a tasting session in atmospheric surrounds.

 p181

The Drive » Pick up the busy D974 to Beaune, 5.5km to the south.

⑤ Beaune

Beaune's *raison d'être* and the source of its unmistakable *joie de vivre* is wine: making it, ageing it, selling it, but most of all, drinking it. As a result, the attractive town is one of the best places in all of France for wine tasting.

The amoeba-shaped old city is enclosed by thick stone **ramparts**, which are lined with overgrown gardens and ringed by a pathway that makes for a lovely stroll. The most striking attraction of Beaune's old city is the magnificent **Hôtel-Dieu des Hospices de Beaune** (📞03 80 24 45 00; www.hospices-de-beaune.com; 2 rue de l'Hôtel-Dieu; adult/child €8.50/4; 🕐9am-7.30pm late Mar–mid-Nov, 9-11.30am & 2-6.30pm rest of year, last entry 1hr before closing).

Underneath Beaune's buildings, streets and ramparts, millions of dusty bottles of wine are being aged to perfection in cool, dark cellars. Stop in at **Patriarche Père et Fils** (📞03 80 24 53 78; www.patriarche.com; 7 rue du Collège; audioguide tour €17; 🕐tours begin 9.30-11.15am & 2-5.15pm), Burgundy's largest cellars, where 5km of corridors are lined with about three million bottles, the oldest a Beaune Villages AOC from 1904! Tour the premises in 60 to 90 minutes, sampling 10 wines along the way and taking the *tastevin* (tasting cup) home. Another excellent option for tours and *dégustation* is **Oenothèque Joseph Drouhin** (📞03 80 24 68 88; www.drouhin-oenotheque.com; place du Général Leclerc; tour & guided tasting from €38; 🕐tours 10am, 2pm & 4pm Mon-Sat).

🍴🛏 p173, p181

The Drive » Take the D974 (direction Autun), then the D973 to Pommard (5km).

⑥ Château de Pommard

For many red-wine lovers, a visit to the superb **Château de Pommard** (📞03 80 22 07 99; www.chateaudepommard.com; 15 rue Marey-Monge, Pommard; 1hr tour incl 5-wine tasting €26; 🕐10.30am-6.30pm or 7.30pm) – established in 1726 and American-owned since 2014 – is a true Burgundian pilgrimage.

The Drive » Take the D973 southwest, via Volnay, and follow the signs along the D23 to Meursault (5km). The Château de Meursault is signposted in the centre of the village.

`TRIP HIGHLIGHT`

⑦ Château de Meursault

One of the prettiest of the Côte de Beaune châteaux, the **Château de Meursault** (📞03 80 26 22 75; www.chateau-meursault.com; 5 rue du Moulin Foulot, Meursault; tour incl 6-/8-wine tasting €25/35; 🕐10am-noon & 2-6pm Oct-Apr, 10am-6.30pm May-Sep) has beautiful grounds and produces some of the most prestigious white wines in the world. Tours visit the estate's vast labyrinth of underground caves, the oldest dating to the 12th century.

The Drive » From the château, drive northwest on the D17E back to the D973. Turn left and head west on the D973 for 1.3km, through Auxey-Duresses, before turning right to rejoin the

LEONARD ZHUKOVSKY / SHUTTERSTOCK ©

D17E for 2.8km. Total distance: 6.5km.

`TRIP HIGHLIGHT`

⑧ St-Romain

Vineyards meet pastureland, forests and cliffs in the bucolic hamlet of St-Romain. For drop-dead views over the village and the valley, drive up to the panoramic viewpoint (it's signposted), perched

Château de Pommard The castle's ancient kitchen

atop a cliff near the ruins of a castle. Hiking trails from here include the spectacular **Sentier des Roches** circuit (13.9km).

The Drive » From the centre of St-Romain, head northeast on the D17E and turn left onto the D17, turning left again onto the D17l (direction Orches, Baubigny, Falaises). It's a lovely drive with scenic vistas until you reach Baubigny; then take the D111D to La Rochepot. Total distance: 8km drive.

- - - - - - - - - - - - - -

❾ Château de La Rochepot

With its spires and multi-coloured tile roofs rising dramatically from thick woods above the ancient village of La Roche-pot, the late medieval **Château de La Rochepot**

(📞07 60 50 25 62; www. chateau-de-la-rochepot.com; La Rochepot; adult/child self-guided €8.50/6.50; 🕙10am-5.30pm Wed-Mon Mar-Jun & Sep-Nov, 10am-6.30pm daily Jul & Aug) offers fab views of the surrounding coun-tryside. Inside you'll find Gothic and Renaissance furnishings, medieval weapons and even an old-time kitchen.

BURGUNDY WINE BASICS

Burgundy's epic vineyards extend approximately 250km from Chablis in the north to Beaujolais (almost!) in the south and comprise 84 Appellations d'Origine Contrôlée (AOC), some of which were changed a bit in 2020. Each micro-region has its own unique combination of characteristics – latitude, altitude, climate, sun exposure and, of course, soil – embodied in a concept called *terroir* (tair-WAHR) because it is the earth itself that imbues grapes with their unique, ethereal qualities.

Here's an ever-so-brief survey of some of Burgundy's major growing regions (from north to south):

Chablis & Grand Auxerrois Four renowned chardonnay white-wine appellations from 20 villages around Chablis. Part of the Auxerrois vineyards, Irancy produces excellent pinot noir reds.

Châtillonnais Approximately 20 villages around Châtillon-sur-Seine producing red and white wines.

Côte d'Or The northern section, the Côte de Nuits, stretches from Marsannay-la-Côte (near Dijon) south to Corgoloin and produces reds known for their robust, full-bodied character. The southern section, the Côte de Beaune, lies between Ladoix-Serrigny and Santenay and produces great reds and great whites. Appellations from the area's hilltops are the Hautes-Côtes de Nuits and Hautes-Côtes de Beaune.

Côte Chalonnaise The southernmost continuation of the Côte de Beaune's slopes is noted for its excellent reds and whites.

Mâconnais Known for rich or fruity white wines, like Pouilly-Fuissé chardonnay.

Want to Know More?

Sensation Vin (☎03 80 22 17 57; www.sensation-vin.com; 2A rue Paul Bouchard, Beaune; tasting sessions from €35, wine tour €275-495; ☺tasting classes 11am & 2.30pm Sun-Fri) Offers introductory tasting sessions (no appointment needed) as well as vineyard excursions and tailor-made courses.

École des Vins de Bourgogne (☎03 80 26 35 10; www.ecoledesvins-bourgogne.com; 6 rue du 16e Chasseurs, Beaune) Offers a variety of courses to refine your palate.

The Drive » Take the D973 direction Nolay; after 200m take a hard left onto the D33, which plunges down to St-Aubin. Turn left onto the D906 (direction Chagny) and left again onto the D113A to Puligny-Montrachet. Total distance: 10km.

- - - - - - - - - - - - - - - - - -

⑩ Puligny-Montrachet

Puligny-Montrachet makes a grand finale to your trip. Beloved of white-wine aficionados (no reds in sight), this bijou appellation is revered thanks to five extraordinary *grands crus*. At the relaxed **Caveau de Puligny-Montrachet** (☎03 80 21 96 78; www.caveau-puligny.com; 1 rue de Poiseul, Puligny-Montrachet; 6-wine tasting €20; ☺9.30am-noon & 2-7pm Mar-Oct, 10am-noon & 3-6pm Tue-Sun

Nov-Feb), a comfortable wine bar and cellar, you can sample the town's namesake vintages along with other fine local wines. Knowledgeable hosts Julien and Emilien provide excellent advice (in good English).

✕ 🛏 p181

Eating & Sleeping

Aloxe-Corton ④

🛏 Hôtel Villa Louise — Hotel €€

(☎03 80 26 46 70; www.hotel-villa-louise.fr;
9 rue Franche, Aloxe-Corton; d €109-205, ste
€235-275; Ⓟ @ 🛜 🏊) This tranquil mansion
– much of it from the 17th century – houses
elegant, modern rooms, each of them dreamily
different. The expansive garden stretches
straight to the edge of the vineyard, with a
sauna, *hammam* (Turkish steambath) and
indoor pool. Rents out bicycles for vineyard
rides.

Beaune ⑤

🍽 Food Market — Market €

(place de la Halle; ⊙7am-1pm Wed & Sat)
Beaune's Saturday food market is a sprawling
affair, with vendors displaying their wares both
indoors and on the cobblestones of place de la
Halle. There's a much smaller *marché gourmand*
(gourmet market) on Wednesday morning.

🍽 Loiseau des Vignes — Gastronomy €€€

(☎03 80 24 12 06; www.bernard-loiseau.com;
31 rue Maufoux; lunch menus €28-46, dinner
menus €59-119; ⊙noon-2pm & 7-10pm Tue-Sat)
Part of the family-run Bernard Loiseau group,
this *gastronomique* restaurant serves exquisite
concoctions ranging from *pigeonneau* (squab)
to *quenelles de sandre* (pike-fish dumplings).
Has reasonably priced midday *menus*. The
verdant garden is lovely in summer.

🛏 Hôtel des Remparts — Historic Hotel €€

(☎03 80 24 94 94; www.hotel-remparts-beaune.
com; 48 rue Thiers; d €70-150, ste €159-179;
Ⓟ ❋ 🛜) Set around two delightful courtyards,
rooms in this 17th-century townhouse have
red-tiled or parquet floors and simple antique
furniture, and some come with exposed beams
and a fireplace. Friendly staff can hire out bikes.

Puligny-Montrachet ⑩

🍽 Restaurant Olivier Leflaive — Bistro €€€

(☎03 80 21 37 65; www.olivier-leflaive.com; 10
place du Monumen; menus €33-49, wine pairings
€26-94; ⊙12.30-1.30pm & 7-8.30pm Wed-Sat)
Known for growing exceptional wines, Olivier
Leflaive also runs a bistro that marries seasonal
French classics with global flavourings, serving
exceptional pairings of delectable cuisine
and extraordinary wines from Burgundy and
beyond.

🛏 Hôtel Olivier Leflaive — Boutique Hotel €€€

(☎03 80 21 37 65; www.olivier-leflaive.com;
10 place du Monument; d €185-265; ⊙ closed
Christmas-early Feb; Ⓟ ❋ @ 🛜) Occupying
a 17th-century building in the heart of Puligny-
Montrachet, this boutique hostelry – renovated,
with art deco touches, in 2020 – delivers top
service and classy comfort. The 17 rooms and
suites are very spacious and come equipped
with charming furnishings, top-quality linens
and stylish bathrooms. The hotel offers
personalised wine tours and tastings, and
acclaimed dining right downstairs.

STRETCH YOUR LEGS
DIJON

Start/Finish Place de la Libération

Distance 1.5km

Duration Four hours

Discover the legacy of the Dukes of Burgundy on this easy stroll through Dijon's historic centre, taking in the city's grand old ducal palace, half-timbered houses and the bustling market, with an optional lunch break at one of Dijon's many fine restaurants.

Take this walk on Trip

Place de la Libération

Dijon's semicircular central square, dating from 1686, offers impressive views across the street to the **Palais des Ducs et des États de Bourgogne** (Palace of the Dukes & States of Burgundy), the monumental palace from which Burgundy's powerful dukes ruled the region during Dijon's 14th- and 15th-century heyday as a centre of art and culture.

The Walk » Cross rue de la Liberté, turn left and then right through the courtyard to reach Dijon's tourist office, starting point for climbing Tour Philippe Le Bon.

Tour Philippe Le Bon

For fantastic views over the old city's narrow streets and gracious squares, climb 316 winding steps to the top of this 46m-high, mid-15th-century **tower** (place de la Libération; adult/child €5/3; ☺ guided tours 11am & 2.30pm Mon, every 45min 10.30am-noon & 1.45-4.45pm Tue-Sun Apr–mid-Nov, 2 to 5 times a day mid-Nov–Mar). On clear days, views from the terrace up top extend all the way to Mont Blanc. Reserve guided tours at Dijon's **tourist office** (☎08 92 70 05 58 for €0.35 per minute; www.destinationdijon.com; 11 rue des Forges; ☺10am-6.30pm Mon-Sat, to 5.30pm Sun Apr-Sep, 10am-1pm & 2-6pm Mon-Sat, 10am-1pm & 2-4pm Sun Oct-Mar; ☜).

The Walk » Walk west along rue des Forges, admiring the attractive old *hôtels particuliers* (private mansions) at Nos 34, 38 and 40. Turn two blocks north on rue Odebert to place des Halles.

Les Halles Centrales

Dijon's **covered market** (rue Quentin; ☺8am-1pm Tue & Thu-Sat) buzzes with life four mornings a week, when vendors sell fruit, veggies, fish, meat, Dijon mustard and fine Burgundian cheeses such as Époisses and Chaource. Surrounding the square are restaurants, bars and cafes, perfect for a people-watching break.

The Walk » Opposite the market's southeastern corner, duck into impasse Quentin, a narrow alleyway, and follow its rightward bend towards rue Musette. A left turn here brings you face to face with the gargoyles of Église Notre Dame.

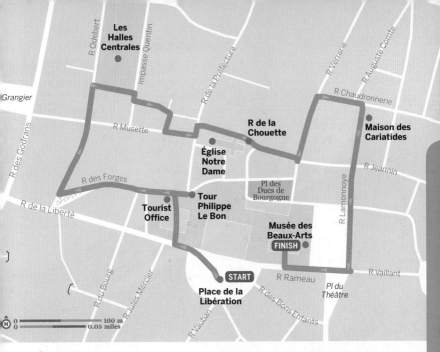

Église Notre Dame

Built between 1220 and 1240, this Gothic **masterpiece** (🕙8am-7pm) greets you with an extraordinary façade whose three tiers of gargoyles are separated by two rows of columns. High atop the façade, the 14th-century **Horloge à Jacquemart** – brought here from Belgium, as war booty, by Philip the Bold in 1383 – chimes every quarter-hour.

The Walk » Exiting the church, turn right and immediately right again onto rue de la Chouette.

Rue de la Chouette

This street is named after the small stone *chouette* (owl) carved into the exterior corner of the chapel diagonally across from No 24. Said to grant happiness and wisdom to those who stroke it, it has been worn smooth by generations of fortune-seekers. Try it for yourself!

The Walk » One block beyond (east of) the back of the church, turn left onto rue Verrerie, passing a picturesque series of half-timbered medieval houses before turning right on rue Chaudronnerie.

Maison des Cariatides

Its façade a riot of stone caryatids, soldiers and vines, this early-17th-century mansion is one of Dijon's most ornate and entrancing Renaissance buildings. Dating to the early 17th century, it was built by the Pouffiers, a wealthy family of local coppersmiths and merchants

The Walk » Walk south on rue Lamonnoye and then turn right (west) onto rue Rameau and enter the courtyard of Palais des Ducs, entry point to Dijon's art museum.

Musée des Beaux-Arts

This **fine arts museum** (📞03 80 74 52 09; https://beaux-arts.dijon.fr; 1 rue Rameau; audioguide €4, guided tour €6; 🕙10am-6.30pm Jun-Sep, 9.30am-6pm Oct-May, closed Tue year-round) is one of the most outstanding in France. Don't miss the wood-panelled **Salle des Gardes**, which houses the ornate, carved late-medieval sepulchres of dukes John the Fearless and Philip the Bold. Other sections focus on Egyptian art, the Middle Ages in Burgundy and six centuries of European painting.

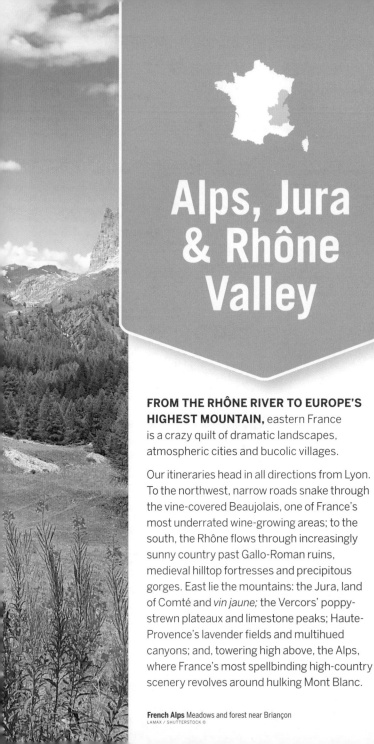

Alps, Jura & Rhône Valley

FROM THE RHÔNE RIVER TO EUROPE'S HIGHEST MOUNTAIN, eastern France is a crazy quilt of dramatic landscapes, atmospheric cities and bucolic villages.

Our itineraries head in all directions from Lyon. To the northwest, narrow roads snake through the vine-covered Beaujolais, one of France's most underrated wine-growing areas; to the south, the Rhône flows through increasingly sunny country past Gallo-Roman ruins, medieval hilltop fortresses and precipitous gorges. East lie the mountains: the Jura, land of Comté and *vin jaune;* the Vercors' poppy-strewn plateaux and limestone peaks; Haute-Provence's lavender fields and multihued canyons; and, towering high above, the Alps, where France's most spellbinding high-country scenery revolves around hulking Mont Blanc.

French Alps Meadows and forest near Briançon
LAMAX / SHUTTERSTOCK ©

The Jura 5 Days
Mellow out amid bucolic highlands and rolling vineyards in this off-the-beaten-track region. (p189)

 Alpine Adventure 6 Days
Revel in France's high-country grandeur, from lakeside Annecy to top-of-the-world Chamonix. (p197)

 Foothills of the Alps 6 Days
Hike verdant meadows and rugged canyons where the Alps and Provence meet. (p207)

Beaujolais Villages 2 Days
Explore the unhurried villages, gentle landscapes and renowned reds of the Beaujolais. (p215)

Rhône Valley 5 Days
Follow eastern France's great river from Lyon's bistros to Orange's Roman theatre. (p223)

 DON'T MISS

Château-Chalon

This is the perfect spot to sample the Jura's distinctive 'yellow' wine. Stay in a turreted B&B on Trip 16

Bonneval-sur-Arc

Hidden on Europe's highest mountain pass, this village in Parc National de la Vanoise is a nature-lover's hideaway. Escape here on Trip 17

Gîte d'Alpage de la Molière

Homemade raspberry pie and spectacular mountain views welcome hikers at this eatery. Rest your feet here on Trip 18

Domaine des Vignes du Paradis – Pascal Durand

This family-run domaine welcomes visitors. Stop in to sip award-winning St-Amour red on Trip 19

Sentier Aval des Gorges

Driving the Gorges de l'Ardèche scenic route is spectacular. Discover this easy-to-miss trail on Trip 20

The Jura

On this trip through the mountains of the Jura, you'll clamber over magnificent citadels, explore deep forests, taste the region's yellow wine and relax into its unhurried culture.

16

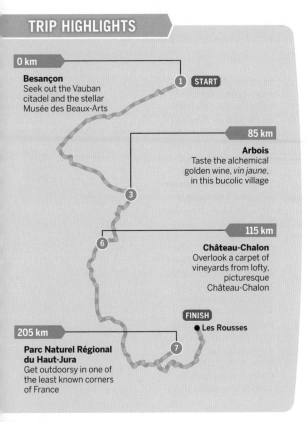

0 km

Besançon
Seek out the Vauban citadel and the stellar Musée des Beaux-Arts

① **START**

85 km

Arbois
Taste the alchemical golden wine, *vin jaune*, in this bucolic village

③

115 km

⑥

Château-Chalon
Overlook a carpet of vineyards from lofty, picturesque Château-Chalon

FINISH
● Les Rousses

205 km

Parc Naturel Régional du Haut-Jura
Get outdoorsy in one of the least known corners of France

⑦

5 DAYS
227KM / 141 MILES

GREAT FOR...

BEST TIME TO GO

Come between June and September, when the sun shines; winter is best left to cross-country skiers.

ESSENTIAL PHOTO

Snap the hawks' view from the Col de la Faucille.

BEST FOR FAMILIES

Camping and tramping in the Parc Naturel Régional du Haut-Jura.

16 The Jura

Subalpine, but still formidable, the high Jura mountains contrast starkly with the rolling, bucolic lowlands, famed for Comté cheese and golden wine. In fact, this trip is full of contrasts: one day you might check out Egyptian mummies, the next you'll be eating with vignerons at a cheery bistrot, and beyond that dangling above limestone escarpments in a chairlift. Despite such abundance, the Jura remains one of France's least visited territories.

50 km to 15

TRIP HIGHLIGHT

❶ Besançon

Home to a monumental Vauban citadel and France's first public museum, birthplace of Victor Hugo and the Lumière brothers, Besançon has an extraordinary background. Somehow, despite its graceful 18th-century old town and first-rate restaurants, it remains something of a secret.

The Unesco-listed **Citadelle de Besançon** (☎03 81 87 83 17; www.citadelle.com; 99 rue des Fusillés de la Résistance; adult/child €10.90/8.80; ☺9am-7pm Jul & Aug, shorter hours rest of year, closed Jan; Ⓟ)

is a formidable feat of engineering, designed by the prolific Marquis de Vauban for Louis XIV in the late 17th century. Inside (and included in the ticket price) are a number of **museums**.

The **Musée des Beaux-Arts et d'Archéologie** (☎03 81 87 80 67; www.mbaa.besancon.fr; 1 place de la Révolution; joint ticket with Musée du Temps adult/child €8/4; ☺10am-noon & 2-6pm Mon & Wed-Fri, 10am-6pm Sat & Sun) houses France's oldest public art collection, founded in 1694. The stellar displays include such archaeological exhibits as Egyptian mummies, neolithic tools and Gallo-Roman mosaics, as well as a wide range

of paintings and drawings, including works by Dürer, Delacroix, Rubens, Goya, Cranach and Bonnard.

✕ ⊨ p195

The Drive ›› From Besançon you can opt for the fast A36 (51km, 45 minutes) or the marginally slower but more enjoyable D673 (46km, 55 minutes) to Dole.

---

2 Dole

Almost every town in France has at least one street, square or garden named after Louis Pasteur, the great 19th-century chemist who invented pasteurisation and developed the first rabies vaccine. The Jura takes this veneration further: the illustrious

LINK YOUR TRIP

15 Route des Grands Crus

Need a drink before starting our Jura tour? Combine it with our Route des Grands Crus drive; its starting point of Gevrey-Chambertin is 62km from Dole along the A39.

17 Alpine Adventure

If the heights of the Jura appeal then you'll love our Alpine Adventure, which begins in Annecy, an 80km drive from Mijoux on the other side of Switzerland.

man was a local lad, born in 1822 in the well-preserved medieval town of Dole.

A scenic stroll along the Canal des Tanneurs in Dole's historic tanners' quarter brings you to Pasteur's childhood home, **La Maison Natale de Pasteur** (La Maison Natale de Pasteur; 📞03 84 72 20 61; www.amisdepasteur.fr; 43 rue Pasteur; adult/child €5.30/3.20; ⏰9.30am-12.30pm & 2-6pm May-Sep,

2-6pm Feb-Apr & Oct), now an atmospheric museum housing exhibits including his cot, first drawings and university cap and gown.

The Drive » It's a 45-minute, 36km doddle down the D905 and D469 to Arbois.

 TRIP HIGHLIGHT

❸ Arbois

The charming village of Arbois is well worth a visit. In 1827 the Pasteur

family settled here, and Louis' laboratory and workshops are on display at **La Maison de Louis Pasteur** (📞03 84 66 11 72; www.terredelouispasteur.fr; 83 rue de Courcelles; adult/child €6.80/4.20; ⏰9.30am-12.30pm & 2-6pm May-Sep, 2-6pm late Feb-Apr & Oct).

If science is a bit too dusty for you, then may we tempt you with a glass of wine? Arbois sits at the heart of the Jura wine region, renowned for its *vin jaune*. The history of this nutty 'yellow wine' is told in the **Musée de la Vigne et du Vin du Jura** (📞03 84 66 40 45; www.arbois.fr; rue des Fossés; adult/child €3.50/free; ⏰10am-noon & 2-6pm Jul & Aug, shorter hours Sep-Jun), housed in the whimsical, turreted Château Pécauld. Afterwards clear your head by walking the 2.5km-long **Chemin des Vignes** trail, which wends its way through the vines, starting from the steps next to the Château Pécauld.

🍴 🛏 p195

The Drive » Clamber steeply uphill for five minutes (3km) along the D246 to reach the spectacularly situated village of Pupillin.

❹ Pupillin

High above Arbois is tiny Pupillin, a cute yellow-brick village famous for its wine production. Some 10 *caves* (wine cellars) are open to visitors.

LIQUID GOLD

Legend has it that *vin jaune* (yellow wine) was invented when a winemaker found a forgotten barrel, six years and three months after he'd initially filled it, and discovered its contents miraculously transformed into a gold-coloured wine.

A long, undisrupted fermentation process gives Jura's signature wine its unique characteristics. Savagnin grapes are harvested late and their sugar-saturated juices left to ferment for a minimum of six years and three months in oak barrels. A thin layer of yeast forms over the wine, which prevents it from oxidising, and there are no top-ups to compensate for evaporation (called *la part des anges* – 'the angels' share'). In the end, 100L of grape juice ferments down to 62L of *vin jaune* (lucky angels), which is then bottled in special 0.62L bottles called *clavelin*. *Vin jaune* is renowned for its ageing qualities, with prime vintages easily keeping for more than a century. A 1774 vintage, a cool 220 years old at the time, was sipped by an awestruck committee of experts in 1994.

La Percée du Vin Jaune (www.percee-du-vin-jaune.com; entry & 10 tasting tickets €20; ⏰early Feb) festival takes place annually in early February to celebrate the first tasting of the vintage produced six years and three months earlier. Villages take it in turn to hold the two-day celebrations, at which the new vintage is blessed and rated, and street tastings, cooking competitions, cellar visits and auctions keep *vin jaune* aficionados fulfilled.

Château-Chalon Medieval village

The Drive » Head southwest out of Pupillin on the N83 and in 15 minutes (9km) you'll have dropped to the small town of Poligny.

- - - - - - - - - - - - - - - -

⑤ Poligny

Need a little cheese to accompany all that wine? Comté is the pre-eminent AOC cheese of the Jura, and the small town of Poligny is the 'capital' of an industry that produces 40 million tonnes of its sweet, nutty goodness a year. Learn how 450L of milk is transformed into a 40kg wheel, smell some of its 83 aromas, and have a nibble at the **Maison du Comté** (☎03 84 37 78 40; www.maison-du-comte.com; av de la Résistance; adult/child €5/3; ⏰2-5pm Tue-Sun Apr-Jun, Sep & Oct, 10am-5pm Jul & Aug). Dozens of *fruitières* (cheese cooperatives) are open to the public. Poligny's **tourist office** (☎03 84 37 24 21; www. poligny-tourisme.com; 20 place des Déportés; ⏰9.30am-1.30pm & 2.30-5.30pm Jul-Sep, shorter hours Oct-Jun) stocks an abundance of info on cheesemakers and wineries in the region.

🛏 p195

The Drive » Take the D68 out of town, and after about 4km veer right onto the D96. After a further 4km, make a sharp right onto the D5 and cruise through pretty countryside into Château-Chalon. It's 15km in total.

- - - - - - - - - - - - - - - -

TRIP HIGHLIGHT

⑥ Château-Chalon

Despite a name that conjures up images of grand castles, Château-Chalon is actually a pocket-sized medieval village of honey-coloured stone perched on a hilltop and surrounded by vineyards known for their legendary *vin jaune*.

🛏 p195

The Drive » Leave Château-Chalon in a northeasterly

193

SPECIALITY FOOD & DRINK

It's hot, it's soft and it's packed in a box. Vacherin Mont d'Or is the only French cheese to be eaten with a spoon – hot. Made between 15 August and 15 March with *lait cru* (unpasteurised milk), it derives its unique nutty taste from the spruce bark in which it's wrapped. Connoisseurs top the soft-crusted cheese with chopped onions, garlic and white wine, wrap it in aluminium foil and bake it for 45 minutes to create a *boîte chaude* (hot box). Only 11 factories in the Jura are licensed to produce Vacherin Mont d'Or.

Mouthe, 15km south of Métabief Mont d'Or, is the mother of *liqueur de sapin* (fir-tree liqueur). *Glace de sapin* (fir-tree ice cream) also comes from Mont d'Or, known as the North Pole of France due to its seasonal subzero temperatures (record low: -38°C). Sampling either is rather like ingesting a Christmas tree. Then there's *Jésus* – a small, fat version of *saucisse de Morteau* (Morteau sausage), easily identified by the wooden peg on its end, attached after the sausage is smoked with pinewood sawdust in a traditional *tuyé* (mountain hut).

direction on the D5 and then double back to the D70 and the town of Lons-le-Saunier. From here the D52, D470 and D436 will be your route into the high-mountain bliss of the Parc Naturel Régional du Haut-Jura and the village of Lajoux. In total it's 90km and 1½ hours.

TRIP HIGHLIGHT

7 Parc Naturel Régional du Haut-Jura

Experience the Jura at its rawest in the Haut-Jura Regional Park, an area of 757 sq km stretching from Chapelle-des-Bois in the north almost to the western tip of Lake Geneva.

A great place to learn more is the **Maison du Parc** (📞03 84 34 12 30; www.parc-haut-jura.fr; 29 Qua le Village, Lajoux; adult/child €5/3.50; ⊗9am-1pm & 2-6pm Tue-Fri & Sun, 9am-1pm Sat), a visitor centre that also has a kid-focused museum that explores the region and its history through sound, touch and smell. The Maison du Parc is in the village of Lajoux, 19km east of St-Claude and 5km west of Mijoux.

The Drive » From the Maison du Parc the D436 will have you switchbacking 5km down the valley into the village of Mijoux.

8 Mijoux

Close to the small ski resort of Mijoux there are some fabulous panoramas of Lake Geneva, framed by the French Alps and Mont Blanc. For the best views, drive to the **Col de la Faucille** (7km along the D936), high above the village. A 4km round-trip hike from the parking area up the Petit Montrond (1533m) makes the stop even better.

The Drive » It's a 20-minute, 20km drive along the D936 and D1005 to Les Rousses through forest and pastureland.

9 Les Rousses

The driving tour comes to a close in the resort of Les Rousses, on the north-eastern edge of the park and hard up against the Swiss border. This is the Haut-Jura's prime sports hub for winter (skiing) and summer (walking and mountain biking) alike. The resort comprises four small, predominantly cross-country ski areas: Prémanon, Lamoura, Bois d'Amont and the village Les Rousses. Find out more at the Maison du Tourisme, home to the **tourist office** (📞03 84 60 02 55; www.lesrousses.com; 495 rue Pasteur; ⊗9am-noon & 2-6pm mid-Jun–Aug, hours vary rest of year).

Eating & Sleeping

Besançon ❶

✕ Le Saint-Pierre   French €€€

(📞03 81 81 20 99; 104 rue Battant; menus
€45-82; 🕑noon-1.30pm Mon-Fri, 7.30-9pm
Mon-Sat) Crisp white tablecloths, exposed
stone and subtle lighting create an understated
backdrop for Le Saint-Pierre's intense flavours:
roast lamb in crushed tomato, sea bass with
forest mushrooms, and ornate dessert plates,
all expertly paired with regional wines.

🛏 Résidence
Charles Quint   Apartment, Guesthouse €

(📞03 81 82 00 21; www.residence-charlesquint.
com; 3 rue du Chapitre; d/apt €85/115; P 🛜)
Slumbering behind the cathedral, in the shade
of the citadel, this discreetly grand 18th-century
townhouse has double rooms with period
furniture and sumptuous fabrics, and self-
catering apartments with marbled bathrooms
and an antique feel. The highlight is the peaceful
private garden, erupting with flowers in summer
and shaded by huge trees. Minimum three-night
stay.

Arbois ❸

🛏 Closerie les Capucines   B&B €€

(📞07 70 09 07 37; www.closerielescapucines.
com; 7 rue de Bourgogne; d/f from €155/275;
🕑Feb-Dec; @ 🛜 🏊) A 17th-century stone
convent has been lovingly transformed into this
boutique B&B, with five rooms remarkable for

their pared-down elegance, tree-shaded garden
by the river, plunge pool and sauna.

Poligny ❺

🛏 Hôtel de la Vallée Heureuse   Hotel €€

(📞03 84 37 12 13; www.hotellavalleeheureuse.
com; rte de Genève; d €100-160, f €185;
P 🛜 🏊) Inside a converted 18th-century
mill, this eccentric country hotel overhangs
a babbling stream 1km south of Poligny. The
'Happy Valley' is a labyrinth of stairs and timber
beams, surrounded by gardens that brim with
flowers and fruit trees. The whitewashed rooms
are tasteful and trim, and the best have garden-
view balconies. The on-site **restaurant**
(evenings only, mains €17 to €22) doesn't
compete with Poligny's other dining options but
it's good value and the multilingual service is
friendly and efficient.

Château-Chalon ❻

🛏 Le Relais des Abbesses   B&B €

(📞03 84 44 98 56; www.relais-des-abbesses.fr;
36 rue de la Roche; s incl breakfast €75-100, d incl
breakfast €80-105; 🕑Mar-Nov; 🛜) Within this
elegantly restored farmhouse, five spacious,
en-suite rooms – all with either hardwood or
antique tile floors – are decorated with soothing
pastel colours and a candelabra, and equipped
with memory-foam mattresses. As well as
setting out an ample breakfast buffet spread,
kindly host Anne-Marie can prepare evening
meals of Jurassien produce by request.

Classic Trip

Alpine Adventure

17

Combining retina-burning splendour with the sturdy charms of time-worn mountain culture, France's Alps provide an incomparable setting for a summer road trip.

TRIP HIGHLIGHTS

START 1

95 km

Chamonix
Experience Mont Blanc's magnetic allure in Europe's mountaineering capital

Val d'Isère
Col de l'Iseran

6

0 km

Annecy
Wander flowery canal banks and swim a pure Alpine lake

215 km

Bonneval-sur-Arc
The quintessential Alpine village, tucked beyond Europe's highest paved pass

Col du Galibier

Briançon

St-Véran
FINISH

6 DAYS
363KM / 225 MILES

GREAT FOR...

BEST TIME TO GO

Mid-June to mid-September, when mountain passes are snow free.

ESSENTIAL PHOTO

Jagged peaks and glacial valleys from the top of the Aiguille du Midi.

BEST TWO DAYS

The section between Annecy and Chamonix, for classic French Alpine scenery.

Classic Trip

17 Alpine Adventure

A study in superlatives, this outdoorsy ramble through the heart of the French Alps runs from Annecy (perhaps France's prettiest lakeside city) to Mont Blanc (Western Europe's highest peak) to Col de l'Iseran (its highest mountain pass) to Bonneval-sur-Arc (an Alpine village of incomparable charm) to St-Véran (France's highest village). Along the way you'll have ample opportunity for adrenaline-laced mountain adventures: hiking, mountain biking, white-water rafting, riding knee-trembling cable cars and crossing the French Alps' most spectacular passes.

TRIP HIGHLIGHT

1 Annecy

There's no dreamier introduction to the French Alps than Annecy. The mountains rise steep, wooded and snow-capped above startlingly turquoise Lac d'Annecy, providing a sublime setting for the medieval town's photogenic jumble of geranium-strewn houses, romantic canals and turreted rooftops.

Summer is the prime time to visit, when everyone is outdoors, socialising at pavement cafes, swimming in the lake (among Europe's purest) and boating, walking or cycling around it. Evening street performers feature during July's **Les Noctibules** festival, and there are lakeside fireworks during August's **Fête du Lac**.

Wander through the narrow medieval streets of the **Vieille Ville** (Old Town) to find the whimsical 12th-century **Palais de l'Isle** (☎04 56 49 40 37; www.musees.annecy.fr; 3 passage de l'Île; adult/child €3.80/2; ☉10.30am-6pm

daily Jul-Sep, 10am-noon & 2-5pm Wed-Mon Oct-Jun) on a triangular islet in the Canal du Thiou. Next stroll the tree-fringed lakefront through the flowery **Jardins de l'Europe**, linked to the popular picnic spot **Champ de Mars** by the graceful **Pont des Amours** (Lovers' Bridge) and presided over by the dour, commanding **Château d'Annecy** (☏04 50 33 87 34; www.musees.annecy.fr; place du Château; adult/child €5.50/3; ⏱10.30am-6pm daily Jun-Sep, 10am-noon & 2-5pm Wed-Mon Oct-May).

Cycling paths encircle the lake, passing by several pretty **beaches** en route. **Boats** (per hour €15 to €50) can be hired along the canal-side quays, and several companies offer **adventure sports**. For details, visit Annecy's **tourist office** (☏04 50 45 00 33; www.lac-annecy.com; 1 rue Jean Jaurès,

LINK YOUR TRIP

16 The Jura

Discover the gentler pleasures of eastern France's 'other' mountains, 1½ hours north of Annecy.

18 Foothills of the Alps

Join this nature-lover's jaunt through high-country plateaux and dramatic canyons, two hours west of Briançon.

199

courtyard of Centre Bonlieu; ⏱9am-12.30pm & 1.45-6pm Mon-Sat year-round, plus Sun Apr-early Oct).

✕ 🛏 p205

The Drive ≫ This 70km drive starts with a pretty southeastwards run along Annecy's lakefront, passing through the wildlife-rich wetlands of Bout du Lac on the lake's southern tip before

continuing east on the D1508, then northeast on the D1212 and D909 into St-Gervais.

- - - - - - - - - - - - - - -

② St-Gervais-les-Bains

Basking in the shadow of Mont Blanc, St-Gervais-les-Bains is a peaceful Savoyard village, centred on a Baroque church and an old-fashioned carousel.

Panoramic **hiking trails** in the Bettex, Mont d'Arbois and Mont Joly areas head off from

HIKING CHAMONIX

Chamonix boasts 350km of spectacular high-altitude trails, many reached by cable car. In late June and July there's enough light to walk until at least 9pm. Here are a few recommended walks to get you started.

Lac Blanc From the top of **Télésiège de l'Index** (www.montblancnaturalresort.com; adult/child return from Les Praz €30/25.50; ⏱Dec-Apr & mid-Jun–Sep) or at **Télécabine de la Flégère** (35 rte des Tines; return adult/child from Les Praz €19/16.20; ⏱8.50am-4.30pm mid-Jun–mid-Sep, shorter hours rest of year), the line's midway point, gentle 1¼- to two-hour trails lead to 2352m Lac Blanc, a turquoise-coloured lake ensnared by mountains. Stargazers can overnight at the **Refuge du Lac Blanc** (📞06 02 05 08 82; www.refugedulacblanc.fr; dm incl half-board adult/child €56/50; ⏱mid-Jun–Sep), a wooden chalet favoured by photographers for its top-of-Europe Mont Blanc views.

Grand Balcon Sud This easygoing trail skirts the western side of the valley, stays at around 2000m and commands a terrific view of Mont Blanc. Reach it on foot from behind Le Brévent's *télécabine* station.

Grand Balcon Nord Routes starting from the Plan de l'Aiguille include the challenging Grand Balcon Nord, which takes you to the dazzling Mer de Glace, from where you can walk or take the **Montenvers train** (p201) down to Chamonix.

town. Some of the best mountain-biking terrain is marked between Val d'Arly, Mont Blanc and Beaufortain.

For spirit-soaring mountain views with zero effort, board the **Tramway du Mont Blanc** (📞04 50 53 22 75; www.montblancnaturalresort.com; av de la Gare, St-Gervais; return to Bellevue/Nid d'Aigle €33.50/38.50; ⏱4-6 departures daily mid-Dec–early Apr, 8 daily early Jun–mid-Sep), France's highest train. Since 1913 it has been labouring up to Bellevue (1800m) in winter and Mont Lachat (2113m) in summer.

Train buffs will also love the narrow-gauge **Mont Blanc Express** (www.mont-blanc-express.com), which trundles along a century-old rail line from St-Gervais to Martigny in Switzerland.

🛏 p205

The Drive ≫ The 24km route to Chamonix follows the D902, N205 and D243 into the heart of the Alps.

- - - - - - - - - - - - - - -

TRIP HIGHLIGHT

③ Chamonix

An outdoors playground of epic proportions, Chamonix sits directly at the foot of Western Europe's highest peak, the bone-white dome of Mont Blanc (4810m).

Climbers with the necessary skill and stamina flock here to tackle any number of iconic Alpine routes, including the incomparable **Mont Blanc ascent**. If you're not quite ready to scale the big one, consider circumnavigating it on the classic eight- to 11-day **Tour du Mont Blanc**, which takes in majestic glaciers and peaks in France, Italy and Switzerland; local outfitters organise excursions including half-board in *refuges* (mountain huts), lift tickets and luggage transport. Other peak experiences include Chamonix' dozens of **day hikes**, the unforgettable cable-car ascent to **Aiguille du Midi** and the **Montenvers train ride** (☎04 50 53 22 75; www.montblancnaturalresort.com; 35 place de la Mer de Glace; adult/child return €34/28.90; ☺10am-4pm late Dec–mid-Mar, to 5pm mid-Mar–Apr) to France's largest glacier, the 200m-deep **Mer de Glace** (Sea of Ice).

Chamonix has an unparalleled menu of adrenaline sports including **rafting**, **canyoning**, **mountain biking** and **paragliding** down from the heights of Planpraz (2000m) or Aiguille du Midi (3842m). For details, visit the **tourist office** (☎04 50 53 00 24; www.chamonix.com; 85 place du Triangle de l'Amitié; ☺9am-7pm mid-Jun–mid-Sep & mid-Dec–Apr, shorter hours rest of year; ☎).

✕ 🛏 p205

TOP TIP:
WINTER DRIVING

Parts of this route (notably the northern stretches around Annecy and Chamonix) are accessible to drivers in winter, but the high mountain passes further south are strictly off-limits outside summer.

The Drive ≫ From Chamonix, take the E25/N205 southeast 17km through the Mont Blanc Tunnel (€46.30) into Italy. From the Aosta/Courmayeur exit, continue 31km southwest back towards France along the SS26. Once across the border, follow the D1090 and D84 southwest, then the D902 southeast for a total of 40km into Val d'Isère.

- - - - - - - - - - - - - - - - - - -

④ Val d'Isère

This world-renowned, end-of-the-valley resort is home to the gargantuan **Espace Killy** (www.espacekilly.com; adult 1-/6-day pass €61/304, child €49/244) skiing area, named after French triple Olympic gold medallist Jean-Claude Killy. Even in July, you can ski the **Pisaillas Glacier** above town, though many summer visitors also come to hike, mountain bike and enjoy off-season hotel discounts.

The trails weaving into the nearby valleys of **Parc National de la Vanoise** are a hiker's dream. For more of a challenge, play among the peaks at neighbouring La Daille's two **via ferrata** (assisted climbing routes).

Mountain biking (VTT) is big in Val. Five lifts offer cyclists access to 16 downhill routes, seven endurance runs and two cross-country circuits. Bike rental is available at local sport shops. **Bureau des Guides** (☎03 77 08 09 76; www.guides-montagne-valdisere.com; Galerie des Cimes, 137 av Olympique, Val Village; ☺8.30am-12.30pm & 2.30-7.30pm Mon-Fri, 8.30am-7.30pm Sat & Sun) arranges guided hiking, mountain biking, canyoning and rock-climbing excursions.

Visit the **tourist office** (☎04 79 06 06 60; www.valdisere.com; place Jacques Mouflier, Val Village; ☺8.30am-7.30pm Sun-Fri, to 8pm Sat Dec-Apr & Jun-Aug; ☎) for details on family-friendly activities, from donkey trekking to farm visits.

The Drive ≫ Prepare for a dizzying climb as you leave Val d'Isère, steeply switchbacking 17km up the D902 to Col de l'Iseran.

- - - - - - - - - - - - - - - - - - -

⑤ Col de l'Iseran

No doubt about it, you've gained some serious altitude here! Indeed, the

Classic Trip

EVGENY SUBBOTSKY / SHUTTERSTOCK ©

La Ferme Angelina

MARISA ESTIVILL / SHUTTERSTOCK ©

WHY THIS IS A CLASSIC TRIP
CHRISTOPHER PITTS, WRITER

That a glacier's softly curving snowfields can hide fathomless crevasses and a sea of deep blue ice shards sums up all the drama contained in this magnificent mountain range. It's irresistibly beautiful, but with just enough danger lurking beneath the surface to send a frisson down your spine. Snowy pistes, jagged peaks, glittering Alpine lakes and pots of bubbling fondue – here, you truly do feel like you're on top of the world.

Above: Climbing Mont Blanc
Left: Bonneval-sur-Arc

D902 over Col de l'Iseran (2770m) is the highest paved through road in Europe. Meteorological conditions at the summit are notoriously fickle – witness the Tour de France stage that was supposed to pass through here on 8 July 1996 but had to be re-routed due to snow and -5°C temperatures!

The Drive » Spellbinding views unfold as you navigate the D902's hairpin turns 14km downhill into Bonneval-sur-Arc.

TRIP HIGHLIGHT

6 Bonneval-sur-Arc

Heralded as one of the *plus beaux villages de la France* (prettiest villages in France), this high mountain hamlet is filled with stone and slate cottages that wear their winter preparations proudly (notice all the woodpiles up on 2nd-floor porches).

Bonneval makes a tranquil base for exploring the 530-sq-km **Parc National de la Vanoise** (www.parcnational-vanoise.fr), whose rugged snowcapped peaks, mirror-like lakes and vast glaciers dominate the landscape between the Tarentaise and Maurienne Valleys. This incredible swath of wilderness was designated France's first national park in 1963, protecting habitat for marmots, chamois and France's

largest colony of ibexes, along with 20 pairs of golden eagles and the odd bearded vulture.

The park is a hiker's heaven between June and September. The **Grand Tour de Haute Maurienne** (www.hautemaurienne. com), a seven-day loop around the upper reaches of the valley, takes in national park highlights. For information on local day hikes, visit Bonneval-sur-Arc's **tourist office** (☏04 79 05 95 95; www.bonneval-sur-arc.com; Bonneval-sur-Arc; ☺9am-noon & 2-6.30pm late Dec-Mar, to 6pm Apr & late Jun-Aug).

🛏 p205

The Drive » Cruise 55km down the Arc River valley on the D902/D1006 through Lanslebourg and Modane to St-Michel de Maurienne, then climb 35km through the ski resort of Valloire to the ethereal heights of Col du Galibier.

7 Col du Galibier

The signposts say you're simply crossing the departmental border from Savoie into the Hautes Alpes. The landscape says that you've entered another universe. Col du Galibier (2642m) is a staggeringly beautiful Alpine pass, whose forbidding remoteness may make you feel like the last living person on earth. To the west lies the Parc National des Écrins, a 918-sq-km expanse of high-country wilder-

ness. Stop and savour the top-of-the-world feeling before returning to the squiggling ribbon of roadway below.

The Drive » Despite the distance on the signpost (35km), the incredibly twisty and scenic descent into Briançon on the D902 and D1091 feels longer; stupendous views will stop you in your tracks every couple of minutes. Enjoy every horn-tooting, head-spinning, glacier-gawping moment, with views of thundering falls, sheer cliffs and jagged peaks razoring above thick larch forests.

8 Briançon

Perched astride a high rocky outcrop, the fairy-tale walled city of Briançon affords views of the snowcapped Écrins peaks from almost every corner. The centre's Italian ambience is no coincidence; Italy is just 20km away.

Briançon's old town is a late-medieval time capsule, its winding cobbled lanes punctuated by shuttered, candy-coloured town houses and shops selling whistling marmots. The steep main street, **Grande Gargouille**, links two town gates, **Porte de Pignerol** and **Porte d'Embrun**. Crowning the old city is the massive **Fort du Château**. Daily **guided walks** (sometimes in English) are run by the **Service du Patrimoine** (☏04 92 20 29 49; www.ville-briancon.fr; Porte de Pignerol,

Classic Trip

Cité Vauban; tours adult/child €6.50/4.80; ⏰10am-noon & 2-5.30pm Mon-Fri Sep-Jun, Mon-Sat Jul & Aug).

Briançon's biggest drawcard is its ensem-ble of 17th- and early-18th-century structures designed by pioneering French military architect Vauban, including the old town's signature **star-shaped fortifications**, the coral-pink **Collégiale Notre Dame et St Nicolas**, several nearby **forts** and the **Pont d'Asfeld** bridge.

AIGUILLE DU MIDI

A great broken tooth of rock rearing above glaciers, snowfields and rocky crags, 8km from the hump of Mont Blanc, the Aiguille du Midi (3842m) is one of Chamonix' most distinctive landmarks. If you can handle the height, don't miss taking a trip up here; the 360-degree views of the French, Swiss and Italian Alps are breathtaking.

All year round the vertiginous **Téléphérique de l'Aiguille du Midi** (www.montblancnaturalresort.com; place de l'Aiguille du Midi; adult/child return to Aiguille du Midi €65/55.30, to Plan de l'Aiguille €33.50/28.50; ⏰6.30am-5pm Jul & Aug, shorter hours Sep-Jun), one of the world's highest cable cars, climbs to the summit. Halfway up, Plan de l'Aiguille (2317m) is a terrific place to start hikes or paraglide. In summer you'll need to obtain a boarding card (marked with the number of your departing *and* returning cable car) in addition to a ticket. Bring warm clothes; even in summer the temperature can drop below 0°C up top!

From the Aiguille du Midi, between late June and early September you can continue for a further 30 minutes of mind-blowing scenery – suspended glaciers, spurs, seracs and shimmering ice fields – in the smaller bubbles of the **Télécabine Panoramique Mont Blanc** (Aiguille du Midi; adult/child return from Chamonix €97/81; ⏰9am-4pm Jul & Aug, to 3pm late May, Jun & Sep) to Pointe Helbronner (3466m) on the France–Italy border. From there, the **SkyWay Monte Bianco** (www.montebianco.com; Pointe Helbronner; adult/child €52/36.40; ⏰Jun-Sep) can take you all the way to Courmayeur, in Italy's Val d'Aosta.

There are outstanding **hiking** opportunities in the mountains of nearby **Parc National des Écrins** (www.ecrins-parcnational.fr). Pick up maps and info at the **Maison du Parc** (☎04 92 21 42 15; www.ecrins-parcnational.fr; place du Médecin Général Blanchard; ⏰10.30am-6.30pm Jul & Aug, 2-6pm Mon-Fri Sep-Jun). For guided treks, glacier traverses, mountain biking, rafting, kayaking, canyoning and *via ferrate,* check with **Bureau des Guides et Accompagnateurs** (☎04 92 20 15 73; www.guides-briancon.com; 24 rue Centrale; ⏰10am-noon & 3-7pm Mon-Fri, 3-7pm Sat, 10am-1pm Sun summer, 5-7pm rest of year).

The Drive ›› From Briançon resume your way southeast along the D902, then via the D947 and D5 to your final stop, St-Véran. Only 28km as the crow flies, this last section of tightly folded mountain road works out to 55km, and around 1¾ hours behind the wheel.

⑨ St-Véran

What more fitting place to wind up a tour of the roof of Europe than France's highest village? Nestled a cool 2040m above sea level, in the midst of the Parc Naturel Régional du Queyras, St-Véran is listed as one of France's most beautiful villages and offers serene hiking in all directions.

Eating & Sleeping

Annecy ❶

✕ Kamouraska   French €€

(☎09 50 78 82 96; 6 passage de la Cathédrale; small plates €15-21; ⏱ noon-2pm & 6.30-10pm Thu-Sat, 6.30-10pm Wed) Named after a village in Québec, offbeat Kamouraska is a bit more fun-loving than the other gastronomic restaurants in town. Case in point: it's the only one with an organ and a single communal marble table (seating 13). Former painter Jérôme Bigot's creative small dishes are the order of the day: we recommend splitting all five, paired with a bottle of natural wine. Reserve.

🛏 Hôtel du Château   Hotel €€

(☎04 50 45 27 66; www.annecy-hotel.com; 16 rampe du Château; s/d/tr/q €69/99/119/129; P 🛜) Just across the square from the château's imposing gatehouse, this family-run hotel has a panoramic breakfast terrace and 16 neat rooms with rustic pine furniture and a sunny colour scheme. Four have lovely lake views.

St-Gervais-les-Bains ❷

🛏 Camping Les Dômes de Miage   Campground €

(Nature & Lodge Camping; ☎04 50 93 45 96; www.natureandlodge.fr; 197 rte des Contamines, St-Gervais; unpowered sites €22.20-27.60, powered sites €26.80-32.20; ⏱ mid-May–mid-Sep; 🛜) Mont Blanc is your wake-up call at this well-equipped campground, beautifully set in wooded hills, 900m above sea level. The first-rate facilities include 150 pitches, a restaurant, volleyball courts, table tennis and other diversions, as well as essentials like laundry and on-site ice-cream sales (we did say essentials).

Chamonix ❸

✕ Crèmerie du Glacier   French €

(☎04 50 54 07 52; www.lacremerieduglacier.fr; 766 chemin de la Glacière, Argentière; mains €7-15, fondues €15-20; ⏱ noon-2pm & 7-9pm mid-Dec–mid-May & late Jun–mid-Sep, closed Wed in winter) A wooden forest chalet is the setting for chef Claudy's *croûte aux fromages* (bread drenched in a secret white-wine sauce, topped with cheese and baked) and other cheesy Savoyard delights, including *gratin d'oeufs* (creamy baked eggs) and half a dozen kinds of fondue (the best with forest mushrooms). Reserve by phone and follow the signpost from the roundabout near the bridge at the southern entrance to Argentière.

🛏 Auberge du Manoir   Hotel €€€

(☎04 50 53 10 77; www.chalethotelchamonix. fr; 8 rte du Bouchet; d/f from €190/280; P 🛜) This beautifully converted farmhouse, ablaze with geraniums in summer, offers pristine mountain views, an outdoor hot tub, a sauna and a bar, whose open fire keeps things cosy. The 18 rooms at this family-owned hideaway vary greatly by size but all display the classic hallmarks of chalet chic: dainty patterns, flashes of crimson, and wood in every direction.

Bonneval-sur-Arc ❻

🛏 Auberge d'Oul   B&B €

(☎04 79 05 87 99; www.auberge-oul. com; Bonneval-sur-Arc; dm €27-29, d/tr/q €72/100/130; ⏱ mid-Jun–mid-Sep & mid-Dec–Apr) Smack on the village square, this flowery-balconied, slate-walled *gîte* (self-catering cottage) has a simple seven-person dorm and two plain but cosy *chambres d'hôte* (guest rooms) on the 2nd floor. The half-board option (per person €16) offers great-value mountain meals, from classic fondues to herbed lamb rack.

Foothills of the Alps

This exhilarating outdoor adventure links two gorgeous, wild landscapes: the high green meadows of the Vercors and the rugged canyon country of the Alpes de Haute-Provence.

18

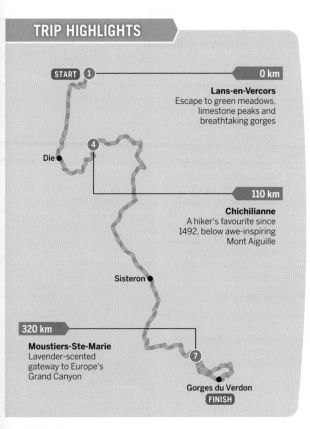

START ① ——————————— **0 km**

Lans-en-Vercors
Escape to green meadows, limestone peaks and breathtaking gorges

④

Die

110 km

Chichilianne
A hiker's favourite since 1492, below awe-inspiring Mont Aiguille

Sisteron

320 km

Moustiers-Ste-Marie
Lavender-scented gateway to Europe's Grand Canyon

⑦

Gorges du Verdon
FINISH

6 DAYS
475KM / 295 MILES

GREAT FOR...

BEST TIME TO GO
June and September, for good weather without peak summer crowds.

ESSENTIAL PHOTO
The dizzying view of the Gorges du Verdon from Belvédère de l'Escale.

BEST FAMILY HIKE
The high-country loop from La Molière, near Lans-en-Vercors.

18 Foothills of the Alps

In the transition zone between the Alps and Provence lie some of France's most magnificent and least explored landscapes. Extending from the Vercors plateau to the Verdon River, this trip starts in poppy-strewn pastures where cowbells jingle beneath limestone peaks and ends among the lavender fields and arid gorges of Haute-Provence. Along the way, there's plenty of outdoorsy excitement for the entire family.

TRIP HIGHLIGHT

❶ Lans-en-Vercors

Lans-en-Vercors (elevation 1020m) is idyllically set among the sloping pastures, plateaux and chiselled limestone formations of the 1750-sq-km **Parc Naturel Régional du Vercors**, 28km southwest of Grenoble. With stunning vistas and wildlife, including marmots, ibex and chamois, the park draws families seeking low-key outdoor adventure. Hikers of any age will enjoy the easy, supremely scenic 7km high-country loop from **La Molière** to **Pas de Bellecombe**, with

its built-in lunch stop at Gîte d'Alpage de la Molière (p213). To reach the trailhead, go 20km north of Lans-en-Vercors via Autrans, following the D106 and a partly unpaved forest road. Alternatively, **Les Accompagnateurs Nature et Patrimoine** (☎06 35 95 23 08; www.accompagnateur-vercors.com) offers **guided walks** (full day adult/child €28/21) throughout the Vercors.

✗ ⊨ p213

The Drive ›› Follow the D531 southwest from Lans-en-Vercors, descending to enter the magnificent Gorges de la Bourne after about 10km.

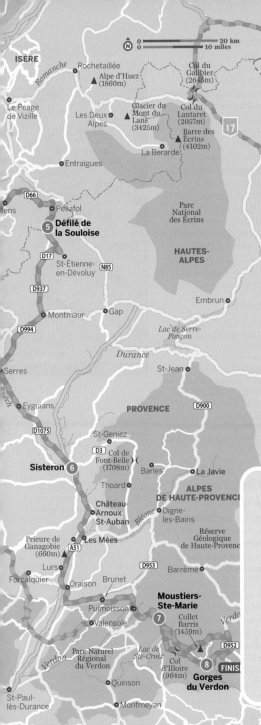

❷ Gorges de la Bourne

Cliff walls up to 600m high crowd around the road through these deep and dramatic gorges, cut by the eponymous Bourne as it rushes off the Vercors plateau. Watch for narrow turnouts alongside the roadway where you can pull off and admire the views.

The Drive » Near the end of the gorges, bear left on the D103 and proceed 20km south through the pretty mountain villages of St-Julien-en-Vercors and St-Martin-en-Vercors. At St-Agnan-en-Vercors continue 5km south on the D518 to the Grotte de la Luire.

❸ Grottes de la Luire

The Vercors was a hotbed of the French Resistance in WWII. This **cave** (📞04 75 48 25 83; www.grottedela luire.com; Le Passage, off D622,

LINK YOUR TRIP

17 **Alpine Adventure**
Head northeast from Lans-en-Vercors to explore France's most awe-inspiring peaks.

22 **Lavender Route**
Wander the purple-fringed back roads of Provence, west of Moustiers-Ste-Marie.

ROMRODPHOTO / SHUTTERSTOCK ©

St-Agnan-en-Vercors; adult/child €9/6.50; ☉ daily Jul & Aug, Wed-Sun Apr-Jun & Sep) outside the town of St-Agnan-en-Vercors served as a field hospital for Resistance fighters for five days in July 1944 before German troops raided it, killing many patients onsite and taking the rest to Grenoble to be shot or deported. Memorial plaques mark the site, and lantern-lit tours are offered in summer.

The Drive » The D518 travels 30km south to Die, culminating in a switchbacking descent from Col de Rousset. The D93 and D539 continue southeast 14km through sun-drenched farmland to Châtillon-en-Diois, a good lunch stop. The final 31km stretch along the D120 and D7 snakes over Col de Menée (1457m) to Chichilianne, affording spellbinding views of Mont Aiguille en route.

TRIP HIGHLIGHT

❹ Chichilianne

Its lovely hayfields strewn with red poppies in late spring, Chichilianne has deep roots in mountaineering history, dating back to 1492 when Antoine de Ville scaled massive cube-shaped Mont Aiguille by order of King Charles VIII (accompanied by stonemasons and master carpenters who helped build ladders and attach ropes!). Long nicknamed the 'inaccessible mountain', and celebrated by writers such as Rabelais, Mont Aiguille continues to capture the

imagination of all who venture near.

Superb high-country hikes around Chichilianne include the **Sentier des Charenches** up Mont Aiguille's southern flanks, and the six-hour loop to the Vercors plateau via **Pas de l'Essaure** and **Pas de l'Aiguille** (look for the monument to Resistance fighters who battled the Nazis at these high altitudes). Lower-elevation walks in surrounding valleys include the themed, family-oriented 5km walk, **Sentier des Artisans de la Terre**.

🛏 p213

The Drive » Follow the D7 and D526 east 17km to Mens, then cruise another 19km east on the D66 through hayfields backed by the Dévoluy massif's sawtooth ridgeline. Wind 8km south on the D66A and D537, descending to the Souloise River. Just before the bridge, turn left onto the D217, following signs for 'Sources des Gillardes' and parking at the trailhead.

---

❺ Défilé de la Souloise

Forming the border between the *départements* of Isère and Hautes-Alpes, the sheer-faced **Souloise Gorge** is an idyllic spot to get out and stretch your legs. From the parking area, an easy there-and-back hike (200m each way) leads to the **Sources des Gillardes**, France's second-largest natural spring. Alternatively,

continue downriver on the delightful **Canyon de l'Infernet** trail, through fragrant evergreen forest sandwiched between grey and orange rock walls. About 1km along, cross a bridge and loop back up the opposite bank to the parking area.

The Drive » Follow the D537 and D937 south through tiny St-Disdier, enjoying stunning views of the Massif de Dévoluy's austere rocky face, punctuated by the pencil-shaped spire of the 11th-century Mère Église. Zigzag south along the D117 (5km southeast), D17 (7km southwest) and D937 (16km south over Col de Festre). From here, follow the D994, D1075 and D4075 south 54km into Sisteron.

Gorges du Verdon The 'Grand Canyon of Europe'

---

6 Sisteron

Perched on a promontory high above the Durance River, Sisteron's stunner is its **citadel** (📞04 92 61 27 57; www.citadelledesisteron. fr; Montée de la Citadelle, Sisteron; adult/child €6.70/3; ⊙9am-6pm Apr, May & Oct, to 7pm Jun-Sep, 10am-5pm Nov). For centuries this imposing fortress guarded the strategic narrow passage between Dauphiné and Provence – though Napoléon did somehow sneak past here with 1200 soldiers after escaping Elba in 1815! Today it still commands bird's-eye perspectives of Sisteron's

medieval streets, the eye-catching stratified rock face **Rocher de Baume** and the Durance Valley beyond. Architectural highlights include a 13th-century *chemin de ronde* (parapet walk) and a powder magazine designed by French military architect Vauban. On summer evenings the hilltop comes alive with open-air dance and classical-music concerts performed during the **Festival des Nuits de la Citadelle** (www.nuitsdela citadelle.fr).

The Drive » Zip 39km down the A51 to Oraison. Take the D4 (5km), D907 (10km) and

D108 (4km) southeast, climbing through Brunet to the Valensole plateau. Cruise 7km east through lavender fields on the D8, take the D953 (4km) into Puimoisson (passing roadside lavender stand Maison du Lavandin), and wind 14km into Moustiers-Ste-Marie along the D56 and D952.

TRIP HIGHLIGHT

7 Moustiers-Ste-Marie

Nicknamed Étoile de Provence (Star of Provence), enchanting Moustiers-Ste-Marie straddles the base of towering limestone cliffs – the beginning of the Alps and the end of

211

DRIVING THE GORGES DU VERDON

This spine-tingling drive is one of France's classic road trips. A complete circuit of the Gorges from Moustiers-Ste-Marie involves 140km (about four hours without stops) of relentless hairpin turns on precarious rim-side roads, with spectacular scenery around every bend. The only village en route is La Palud-sur-Verdon (930m). Expect slow traffic and scant opportunities to overtake in summer.

From Moustiers, aim first for the **Route des Crêtes** (D952 & D23; ⊕mid-Mar–mid-Nov), a 23km-long loop with 14 lookouts along the northern rim – ensure you drive the loop clockwise: there's a one-way portion midway. En route, the most thrilling view is from **Belvédère de l'Escale**, an excellent place to spot vultures. After rejoining the D952, the road corkscrews eastward, past **Point Sublime**, which overlooks serrated rock formations dropping to the river.

Return towards Moustiers via the **Corniche Sublime** (D955 to D90, D71 and D19), a heart-palpitating route along the southern rim, passing landmarks including the **Balcons de la Mescla** (Mescla Terraces) and **Pont de l'Artuby**, Europe's highest bridge.

Haute-Provence's rolling prairies. Winding streets climb among tile-roofed houses, connected by arched stone bridges spanning the picturesque creek (Le Riou) that courses through the village centre.

A 227m-long chain bearing a shining gold star stretches high above the village, legendarily placed there by the Knight of Blacas upon his safe return from the Crusades. Below the star, the 14th-century **Chapelle Notre Dame de Beauvoir** clings to the cliff ledge like an eagle's nest. A steep trail climbs beside a waterfall to the chapel, passing 14 stations of the cross. On 8 September, a 5am Mass celebrates the Virgin Mary's nativity, followed by flutes, drums and breakfast on the square.

✖ ⊨ p213

The Drive » The trip to Gorges du Verdon is a classic. Follow the D952 19km southeast to La Palud-sur-Verdon, then the D23, winding from 9km above the western flank of the Verdon to your final destination.

- - - - - - - - - - - - - - - - - - - -

⑧ Gorges du Verdon

Dubbed the Grand Canyon of Europe, the breathtaking Gorges du Verdon slice 25km through Haute-Provence's limestone plateau. The narrow canyon bottom, carved by the Verdon's emerald-green waters, is only 8m to 90m wide; its steep, multihued walls, home to griffon vultures, rise as high as 700m – it's twice as tall as the Eiffel Tower! One of France's most scenic drives takes in staggering panoramas from the vertigo-inducing cliff-side roads on either side.

The canyon floors are accessible only by foot or raft. Dozens of blazed trails traverse untamed countryside between Castellane and Moustiers, including the classic **Sentier Martel**, which uses occasional ladders and tunnels to navigate 14km of riverbanks and ledges. For details on 28 walks, pick up the excellent English-language *Canyon du Verdon* (€4.70) at Moustiers' **tourist office** (☑04 92 74 67 84; www.moustiers.fr; passage du Cloître; ⊕10am-noon & 2-6pm Apr-Sep, closes around 5pm Oct-Mar; ☎). Rafting operators include **Guides pour l'Aventure** (www.guidesaventure.com) and **Aboard Rafting** (www.rafting-verdon.com).

Eating & Sleeping

Lans-en-Vercors ➊

🍴 Gîte d'Alpage
de la Molière   French €€

(📱06 09 38 42 42; http://gitedelamoliere.
aufilduvercors.org; 41 impasse des Frênes; plat
du jour €17; ⊗Jun-Oct & Dec-Mar) **High above**
Lans-en-Vercors, this welcoming trailside
refuge with incomparable views serves simple
mountain fare (savoury vegetable tarts, salad
with smoked trout, and raspberry, blueberry
and walnut pies) on umbrella-shaded picnic
tables astride an Alpine meadow. The picnic
hampers, only €13 per adult, are a great option
for ramblers.

🛏 À la Crécia   B&B €

(📱04 76 95 46 98; www.gite-en-vercors.
com; 436 chemin des Cléments, Les Cléments,
Lans-en-Vercors; s/d/tr/q €58/69/89/109)
Renovated by Véronique and Pascal, this
16th-century farm has been endowed with five
wood-panelled guest rooms and eco-conscious
additions like solar panels. Kids will adore
the on-site menagerie of sheep and pigs; and
optional dinners, served in a rustic dining room,
assemble farm-fresh produce like local cheeses
and homemade cakes (*menus* from €19). It's
2km south of Lans-en-Vercors' tourist office.

Chichilianne ➍

🛏 Au Gai Soleil
de Mont-Aiguille   Hotel €

(📱04 76 34 41 71; www.hotelgaisoleil.com; La
Richardière, Chichilianne; d €69-77; 🛜) At the
foot of striking Mont Aiguille, this simple inn has
fabulous views, superb access to local hiking
routes, a rustic country restaurant, a spa and

two massage rooms for treating weary muscles
at trail's end (spa access €15).

Moustiers-Ste-Marie ➐

🍴 La Grignotière   Provencal €

(📱04 92 74 69 12; rte de Ste-Anne; mains
€12-36; ⊗noon-2pm & 7-10pm Tue-Sun Apr-
Oct) Hidden behind the soft-pink façade of
Moustiers' Musée de la Faïence is this peaceful
garden restaurant. Tables sit between olive
trees and the colourful, eye-catching decor
– including the handmade glassware – is
the handiwork of talented, dynamic owner
Sandrine. Cuisine is 'picnic chic', meaning lots
of creative salads, tapenades, quiches, good
Corsican beer (Pietra) and so on.

🍴 La Ferme
Ste-Cécile   Gastronomy €€€

(📱04 92 74 64 18; www.ferme-ste-cecile.com;
D952; menu €40; ⊗noon-2pm & 7.30-10pm
Tue-Sat, noon-2pm Sun) Just outside Moustiers,
this wonderful *ferme auberge* (country inn)
immerses you in the full Provençal dining
experience, from the sun-splashed terrace and
locally picked wines right through to the chef's
meticulous Mediterranean cuisine. It's about
1.2km from Moustiers; look out for the signs as
you drive towards Castellane.

🛏 Ferme du Petit Ségriès   Farmstay €

(📱04 92 74 68 83; www.chambre-hote-verdon.
com; d €79-94; 🛜) This rural, vine-covered
farmhouse is a real bargain, with five pleasant
rooms and a lovely location deep in the
countryside, 5km west of Moustiers on the
D952 to Riez. It's not fancy, but it's extremely
good value considering that the rates include
breakfast.

Beaujolais Villages

With its lush green hills, cute villages and well-tended vineyards, Beaujolais is a landscape painting come to life. Explore its quaint localities, taste some excellent wines and enjoy the hush.

19

TRIP HIGHLIGHTS

95 km

Roche de Solutré
An exceptional panorama and a site rich in history

FINISH
12
11

90 km

Fuissé
A charming village with prestigious white wines

35 km

Mont Brouilly
Mesmerising views of the Beaujolais region

4

3

Vaux-en-Beaujolais
A super-scenic hilltop village

25 km

START
Villefranche-sur-Saône

2 DAYS
99KM / 61 MILES

GREAT FOR...

BEST TIME TO GO

April to June, September and October for a patchwork of colours.

 ESSENTIAL PHOTO

Enjoy a panorama over the entire region from Mont Brouilly.

 BEST FOR FOODIES

Vaux-en-Beaujolais prides itself on its Michelin-starred restaurant.

Beaujolais Church and vineyards

215

19 Beaujolais Villages

Ah, Beaujolais, where the unhurried life is complemented by rolling vineyards, beguiling villages, old churches, splendid estates and country roads that twist into the hills. Once you've left Villefranche-sur-Saône, a rural paradise awaits and a sense of escapism becomes tangible. Be sure to factor in plenty of time for wine tasting.

1 Villefranche-sur-Saône

Your trip begins with a stroll along lively rue Nationale, where you'll find most of the shops and the Gothic **Collégiale Notre-Dame des Marais**, which boasts an elegant façade and a soaring spire. An excellent starting point for oenophiles would be a visit to one of several wine bars and shops in town.

The Drive » At a roundabout about 800m south of the Collégiale, look out for the brown sign to 'Route des Vins du Beaujolais'. Pass through Gleizé, Lacenas, Denicé, St-Julien and Blacé before reaching Salles-Arbuissonas-en-Beaujolais.

Count on a good half hour to cover the 16km trip.

2 Salles-Arbuissonnas-en-Beaujolais

As you pass through Salles-Arbuissonnas, keep an eye out for the superb 10th-century **priory** (Musée le Prieuré; ☎04 74 07 31 94; www.salles-arbuissonnas.fr; 3 rue du Chapitre; museum adult/child €4.50/free; ⊙ museum 10am-12.30pm & 2-6pm Wed-Sun Mar-Dec) and the adjoining Roman **cloister**.

The Drive » Continue along the D35 to Vaux-en-Beaujolais (6.5km).

80 km to 15

Mâcon

FINISH

12 **Roche de Solutré**
D54

Fuissé
D31 11

D209

10
D17E

St-Amour Bellevue

Juliénas 9

D31

D68

La Chapelle-de-Guinchay

8 **Moulin à Vent**

Fleurie 7

Romanèche-Thorins

…les

D68

D86

6 **Villié-Morgon**

D9

A6

Saône

D337

Belleville-sur-Saône

…43

Odenas

D43

D76

D84

1 START

Villefranche-sur-Saône

30 km to 20

TRIP HIGHLIGHT

3 Vaux-en-Beaujolais

The village of Vaux-en-Beaujolais emerges like a hamlet in a fairy tale. You can't but be dazzled by the fabulous backdrop – it's perched on a rocky spur ensnared by a sea of vineyards. Don't leave Vaux without enjoying the fruity aroma of Beaujolais-Villages (the local appellation) at **La Cave de Clochemerle** (☎04 74 03 26 58; www.cavedecloch emerle.com; place de Petit Tertre; ⊗10.30am-12.30pm & 3-8pm Tue & Thu, to 9pm Fri, to 11pm Sat, from 10am Sun, from 3pm Mon & Wed), housed in atmospheric cellars.

🛏 p221

LINK YOUR TRIP

15 Route des Grands Crus

For more wine tasting and rolling vineyards, make a beeline for the Route des Grands Crus, which unfolds south of Dijon. Head to Mâcon and follow signs to Dijon.

20 Rhône Valley

For a change of scene, head to Lyon (via Mâcon) and discover the hidden gems of the Rhône Valley.

The Drive >> Take the D133 to Le Perréon, then follow signs to St-Étienne-des-Oullières and Odenas. In Odenas, follow signs to Mont Brouilly (13km from Vaux-en-Beaujolais).

RICHARD SEMIK / SHUTTERSTOCK ©

TRIP HIGHLIGHT

❹ Mont Brouilly

It would be a crime to explore the Beaujolais and not take the scenic road that leads to Mont Brouilly (485m), crowned with a small chapel. Hold on to your hat and lift your jaw off the floor as you approach the lookout at the summit – the view over the entire Beaujolais region and the Saône valley will be etched in your memory forever.

The Drive >> Drive down to St-Lager, then take the D68 to Cercié and continue along the D337 to Beaujeu (12km from Mont Brouilly).

❺ Beaujeu

The historic Beaujolais wine capital, Beaujeu is an enchanting spot to while away a few hours. **Le Comptoir Beaujolais** (☎04 74 04 81 18; www.face book.com/comptoirbeau jolais; place de L'Hôtel de Ville; tastings per person from €2; ⏰10.30am-1pm & 2.30-7pm, closed mid-Jan) **is a great place to sip some excellent Beaujolais-Villages and Brouilly. It's also worth popping your head into the rewarding La Maison du Terroir Beaujolais** (☎04 74 69 20 56; www.la

maisonduterroirbeaujolais.com; place de l'Hôtel de Ville, Beaujeu; ⏰10am-12.30pm & 2-7pm Jul & Aug, to 6pm Sep-Dec & Mar-Jun). Housed in a wonderful Renaissance building, this produce shop has a wide array of Beaujolais wines, cheeses, jams and charcuterie, among other items.

The Drive >> Head to Lantignié along the D78 and continue to Régnié-Durette, where you'll see signs to Villié-Morgon. The full drive covers just over 10km.

❻ Villié-Morgon

Morgon wine, anybody? Expand your knowledge

of the local appellation with a tasting session at the vaulted **Caveau de Morgon** (☎04 74 04 20 99; www.morgon-fr.cabanova. com; Château Fontcrenne, rue du Château de Fontcrenne; ⏰10am-noon & 2.30-7pm Feb-Oct, to 6pm Nov & Dec), which occupies a grandiose 18th-century château in the heart of town – it can't get more atmospheric than that.

🛏 p221

The Drive >> From Villié-Morgon, it's a relaxed 10km drive to Fleurie via Chiroubles. Follow the D18 and D86 to Chiroubles, then signs to Fleurie.

Moulin à Vent Windmill and vineyards

7 Fleurie

Beaujolais' rising star, Fleurie red wines are said to be sensuous, offering a combination of floral and fruity notes. A superb fine dining experience, Auberge du Cep (p221) features traditional Beaujolais cooking at its best with a range of regional specialities in a rustic dining room.

 p221

The Drive » Take the D68 towards Chénas; after about 3km turn right onto the D68e towards Romanèche-Thorins and you'll soon reach Moulin à Vent. It's a 4km drive from Fleurie.

8 Moulin à Vent

Reason itself to visit this drowsy hamlet is the heritage-listed **Moulin à Vent** (Windmill). Dubbed the 'King of Beaujolais', the Moulin à Vent appellation is a particularly charming wine to sample in situ: its **Caveau du Moulin à Vent** (☏03 85 35 58 09; www.moulin-a-vent.net; 1673 rte du Moulin à Vent, Moulin à Vent, Romanèche-Thorins; ⏱10am-12.30pm & 2.30-7pm Jul & Aug, 10am-12.30pm & 2.30-6pm Thu-Mon Sep–mid-Dec & Mar-Jun), across the road from the windmill, provides a prime wine-tasting opportunity.

The Drive » From Moulin à Vent retrace your route back towards Chénas and take the D68 to Juliénas. It's an easy 6.6km drive.

9 Juliénas

One of the best-kept secrets in Beaujolais is this delightful village famed for its eponymous vintage. A beauty of a castle, the 16th-century **Château de Juliénas** (☏06 85 76 95 41, 04 74 04 49 98; www.chateaudejulienas.com; rte de Vaux, Juliénas; free tour 4.30pm Tue-Fri mid-Jun–Oct, by reservation €8 Jan-Dec, aperi-vin €18, picnic €40; ⏱by reservation) occupies a delightful estate;

219

WHEN BEAUJEU GOES WILD

A colourful time to motor in Beaujeu (p218) is around the third week in November. At the stroke of midnight on the third Thursday (ie Wednesday night), the *libération* (release) or *mise en perce* (tapping; opening) of the first bottles of cherry-bright Beaujolais Nouveau is celebrated around France and the world. In Beaujeu there's free Beaujolais Nouveau for all as part of the Sarmentelles de Beaujeu – a giant street party that kicks off on the Wednesday leading up to the Beaujolais Nouveau's release for five days of wine tasting, live music and dancing.

tours can be arranged by phoning ahead. No doubt you'll be struck by the cellars, the longest in the region. Tours can be followed by an *aperi'vin* (tasting and snacks; €18) or a picnic among the grapes (€40). Another atmospheric venture set in a disused church, **Cellier de la Vieille Église** (☑04 74 04 42 98; Le Bourg, Juliénas; ⊙10am-12.30pm & 3-6pm, closed Tue Oct-Apr) is a great place to sip wines of the Juliénas appellation.

🛏 p221

The Drive » Follow the road to St-Amour Bellevue along the D17e and the D169 (3km from Juliénas).

- - - - - - - - - - - - - - - - - -

⑩ St-Amour Bellevue

Not to be missed in St-Amour: the **Domaine des Vignes du Paradis – Pascal Durand** (☑03 85 36 52 97; www.saint-amour-en-paradis.com; En Paradis, St-Amour Bellevue; ⊙10am-12pm & 2-6pm). This award-winning domaine run by the fifth generation of vintners welcomes visitors to its intimate cellars and sells St-Amour wines at unbeatable prices.

🛏 p221

The Drive » Follow the D186 towards Chânes. In Bourgneuf, take the D31 to St-Vérand. From St-Vérand, follow signs to Chaintré and continue to Fuissé. It's a 10km trip from St-Amour.

- - - - - - - - - - - - - - - - - -

TRIP HIGHLIGHT

⑪ Fuissé

If you like peace, quiet and sigh-inducing views, you'll love this absolutely picturesque stone town nestled in a small valley carpeted by manicured vineyards. You've now left Beaujolais – Fuissé is part of Burgundy. It's famous for its prestigious Chardonnay whites of the Pouilly-Fuissé appellation, parts of which were given Premier Cru status in 2020. You can attend tastings at various cellars around town or, for the ultimate experience, at the magnificent **Château de Fuissé** (☑03 85 35 61 44; www.chateau-fuisse.fr; Le Plan, Pouilly-Fuissé; ⊙9am-noon & 1.30-5.30pm Mon-Fri, by reservation Sat & Sun).

The Drive » From Fuissé follow signs to Chasselas along the D172. After about 3.5km, turn right onto the D31 (direction Tramayes). Drive another 2km to a right-hand turn onto the D54 (direction Solutré-Pouilly). Count on 15 minutes for the 7km trip.

- - - - - - - - - - - - - - - - - -

TRIP HIGHLIGHT

⑫ Roche de Solutré

A lovely 20-minute walk along the **Sentier des Roches** will get you to the top of the rocky outcrop known as the Roche de Solutré (493m), from where Mont Blanc can sometimes be seen, especially at sunset. For some cultural sustenance, make a beeline for the nearby **Musée Départemental de Préhistoire de Solutré** (☑03 85 35 82 81; http://rochedesolutre. com; chemin de la Roche, Solutré-Pouilly; adult/child incl audioguide €5/free; ⊙10am-6pm Apr-Oct, 1-5pm Nov-Mar), which displays finds from one of Europe's richest prehistoric sites.

🍴 p221

Eating & Sleeping

Vaux-en-Beaujolais ③

🛏 Auberge de Clochemerle   Hotel €€

(📞04 74 03 20 16; www.aubergedeclochemerle.
fr; 173 rue Gabriel Chevallier, Vaux-en-Beaujolais;
d €110-150, q €240, restaurant menus €48-84;
P 🛜) A pleasant combination of modern and
traditional, this atmospheric hotel smack dab
in the centre of Vaux-en-Beaujolais has 10
stylishly refitted rooms, some with vineyard
views. Dining at its decadent restaurant is a
treat. Chef Romain creates elaborate Beaujolais
meals using the best local ingredients, and
his wife Delphine is a renowned sommelier –
wine pairings are an adventure in themselves.
Brilliant value.

Villié-Morgon ⑥

🛏 Château de Bellevue   B&B €€

(📞04 74 66 98 88; www.chateau-bellevue.fr;
Bellevue, Villié-Morgon; d €100-160; P 🛜) For
the ultimate château experience, you can't
do better than this attractive venture nestled
amid seas of vineyards. The five rooms are
attractively set, with soft-toned fabrics and
sweeping vineyard views. Personalised tours of
the winery and the cellars are also on offer.

Fleurie ⑦

🍴 Auberge du Cep   French €€

(📞04 74 04 10 77; www.aubergeducep.com;
place de l'Église, Fleurie; mains €34-38, menus
lunch from €22, dinner €34-60; ⊙12.15-1.30pm
& 7.30-9pm Tue-Sat, 12.15-13.30pm Sun)
Traditional cooking at its best. Feast on regional
specialities such as pike-perch, snails, perfectly
fried frogs' legs and rosy tenderloin of Charolais
beef (France's best) in a rustic dining room.

Juliénas ⑨

🛏 Chez La Rose   Hotel €€

(📞04 74 04 41 20; www.chez-la-rose.fr; Le
Bourg, Juliénas; d €89-150, ste €220, menus €29

& €32; ⊙restaurant noon-2pm & 7-9pm, closed
Dec–mid-Mar; P ❄ 🛜 🍽) This charming inn
features 13 rooms in various buildings scattered
around the village. They're all equipped to the
highest standard, but the vast suites are the
ones to aim for. Dinner at the restaurant La
Table d'Alain Bleton is a gourmet affair, with
standouts like *coq au vin de Juliénas* (chicken
cooked in Juliénas wine) and *navarin de homard*
(lobster stew).

St-Amour Bellevue ⑩

🛏 Le Paradis de Marie   B&B €€

(📞03 85 36 51 90; www.leparadisdemarie.com;
Les Ravinets, St-Amour-Bellevue; d €100-120,
caravan €100; P 🛜 🍽) Have a decadently
bucolic rest at this relaxing place, a lovingly
restored stone mansion exquisitely situated
not far from the main street. The four rooms
open onto a courtyard, while the romantically
furnished gypsy caravan in the garden will
please those in search of an offbeat experience.

🛏 L'Auberge
du Paradis   Boutique Hotel €€

(📞03 85 37 10 26; www.aubergeduparadis.fr;
Le Plâtre Durand, Le Bourg, St-Amour-Bellevue; d
€150-260; ⊙restaurant noon-12pm & 7.30-9pm
Thu-Sat, 7.30-9pm Wed & Sun; P ❄ 🛜 🍽)
Beaujolais' iconic, much-beloved inn occupies
a village house restyled into an urban-chic,
design-led boutique hotel. Oh, and there's a
fantastic bistro and restaurant with creative,
inspired cooking (mains €11 to €18; expect top-
quality ingredients served with a symphony of
spices) drawing diners from afar.

Solutré ⑫

🍴 La Courtille de Solutré   French €€€

(📞03 85 35 80 73; www.lacourtilledesolutre.fr;
rte de la Roche, Solutré-Pouilly; menus lunch €24-
28, dinner €40-44; ⊙noon-2pm & 7-10pm Wed-
Sat, noon-2pm Sun) Chef Adrien Yparraguirre
does traditional dishes exceptionally well, with a
creative twist. Sit on the shady terrace or head
into the rustic-chic interior. The restaurant is
10km west of Mâcon via the D54.

Rhône Valley

20

The mighty Rhône flows from the Alps to the Mediterranean. Trace its course from Lyon to Provence, visiting gourmet restaurants, Gallo-Roman ruins and spectacular river gorges along the way.

TRIP HIGHLIGHTS

START

0 km — **1**

Lyon
Eat like a king and explore secret passageways of the silk weavers

2 — **35 km**

Vienne
A Gallo-Roman treasure trove by the Rhône's river banks

Valence

Mirmande

Montélimar

230 km — **6**

Gorges de l'Ardèche
Kayak down this dizzyingly beautiful river gorge

Mornas — **8**

FINISH

300 km

Orange
Gaze up at Caesar atop an ancient theatre wall

**5 DAYS
293KM / 182 MILES**

GREAT FOR...

BEST TIME TO GO

June and July for festivals in the Roman theatres of Lyon, Vienne and Orange.

 ESSENTIAL PHOTO

The Pont d'Arc, a stunning stone archway over the Ardèche River.

 BEST FOR FOODIES

Lyon's beloved *bouchons* (convivial neighbourhood bistros).

20 Rhône Valley

Food and history are recurring themes on this multifaceted meander down the Rhône, from the fabled eateries of Lyon to the Gallo-Roman museum at Vienne, the nougat factories of Montélimar and the ancient theatre at Orange. As you work your way downriver to Provence, you'll also encounter imposing hilltop fortresses, slow-paced southern villages and one of France's prettiest river gorges.

TRIP HIGHLIGHT

1 Lyon

This strategic spot at the confluence of the Rhône and Saône Rivers has been luring people ever since the Romans named it Lugudunum in 43 BCE. Climb Fourvière hill west of town to witness the successive waves of human settlement, spread out in chronological order at your feet: a pair of Gallo-Roman theatres in the foreground, Vieux Lyon's medieval cathedral on the Saône's nearby banks, the 17th-century *hôtel de ville* (town hall) on the peninsula between the rivers, and, beyond the Rhône, modern Lyon's skyscrapers backed by the distant Alps.

With its illustrious history and renowned gastronomy, France's third-largest city merits at least a two-day visit. Supplement a walking tour of Lyon's quintessential sights with a visit to Croix Rousse, the 19th-century silk-weavers' district where Jacquard looms still restore fabrics for France's historical monuments, and don't leave town without eating in at least one of the city's incomparable *bouchons*.

 p45, p229

The Drive » Shoot 33km down the A7 to Vienne, enjoying close-up views of the Rhône en route.

TRIP HIGHLIGHT

2 Vienne

France's Gallo-Roman heritage is alive and well in this laid-back riverfront city, whose back streets hide a trio of jaw-dropping ruins: the 1st-century-BCE **Temple d'Auguste et de Livie**, with its splendid Corinthian columns; the **Pyramide du Cirque**, a 15.5m-tall obelisk that once pierced the centre of a hippodrome; and the 1st-century-CE **Théâtre Romain** (04 74 78 71 17; www.theatreantiquevienne.com; rue du Cirque; adult/child €3/free; 9.30am-12.45pm & 1.30-6pm Tue-Sun Apr-Oct, 1-5.30pm Nov-Mar), which relives its glory days as a performance venue each summer during Vienne's two-week **jazz festival** (www.jazzavienne.com).

Across the river, a treasure trove of Gallo-Roman artefacts is displayed at the **Musée Gallo-Romain** (04 74 53 74 01; www.musees-gallo-romains.com; D502, St-Romain-en-Gal; adult/child €6/free; 10am-6pm Tue-Sun).

p229

The Drive » Follow the D386, D1086 and D86 for 48km south, threading the needle between the Rhône and the pretty mountains of the Parc Naturel Régional du Pilat. At Sarras cross the bridge to St-Vallier, then continue 32km south on the N7 through classic Côtes du

Rhône wine country around Tain l'Hermitage into Valence.

----

③ Valence

With its warm weather, honey-coloured light and relaxed cadence, it's easy to see why Valence advertises itself as the northern gateway to Provence. At lunchtime, make a beeline for André (p229), a stylish eatery with an excellent wine list that's part of the Pic family's award-winning, multigenerational restaurant empire, or pack yourself a picnic at the Pic-affiliated gourmet grocery, **L'Épicerie** (📞04 75 25 07 07; www.anne-sophie-pic.com/epicerie; 210 av Victor Hugo; ⏱10am-7pm Tue-Sat, 9am-noon Sun). Afterwards visit **Maison Nivon** (📞04 75 44 03 37; www.nivon.com; 17 av Pierre Semard; suisses from €12.50; ⏱6am-7pm Tue-Sun) for a *suisse*, Valence's classic orange-rind-flavoured pastry in the

⑧ LINK YOUR TRIP

13 Volcanoes of the Auvergne

Head west of Lyon for this pastoral meander among ancient green peaks.

21 Roman Provence

From Orange, head northeast and further south to delve deeper into Roman ruins.

shape of a Swiss Vatican guard. In the old town, gawk at the allegorical sculpted heads adorning the façade of the wonderful 16th-century **Maison des Têtes** (☎04 75 79 20 86; www.valenceromansagglo.fr; 57 Grande Rue; ☺8.30am-noon & 1.30-5.30pm Mon-Fri, 9.30am-12.30pm & 2-6pm Sat, 2-6pm Sun).

✖ 🛏 p229

The Drive ›› Cruise 28km south along the N7, then wind 4.5km through orchard-covered hills on the D57 into Mirmande.

---

④ Mirmande

Surrounded by pretty orchard country, this hilltop gem of stone houses and sleepy medieval streets was once a major centre of silkworm production. It then became an artists' colony in the 20th century, when cubist painter André Lhote made his home here. Volcanologist-cinematographer Haroun Tazieff later served as the town's mayor, adding to Mirmande's cultural cachet and earning it recognition as one of *les plus beaux villages de la France* (France's prettiest villages).

With a couple of charming hotels, Mirmande makes an inviting overnight stop. Wander up to the 12th-century Romanesque **Église de Ste-Foy**, where concerts and art exhibits are held in summertime and

beautiful Rhône Valley views unfold year-round.

The Drive ›› Snake 12km southeast on the D57 over Col de la Grande Limite (515m) into medieval Marsanne, then continue 15km southwest into Montélimar on the D105 and D6.

---

⑤ Montélimar

An obligatory stop for sweet tooths, Montélimar is famous for its delectable nougat made from almonds, lavender honey, pistachios, sugar, egg white and vanilla. To taste this sweet delight at the source, visit one of Montélimar's small producers, such as **L'Artisan Nougatier** (☎04 75 52 87 45; www.lartisannougatier.com; 35 bd Marre Desmarais; ☺9.30am-1pm & 2-7pm Mon-Sat, 9.30am-12.30pm & 2-6pm Sun). Afterwards burn off the calories with a climb to **Château des Adhémar** (☎04 75 91 83 50; www.chateaux.ladrome.fr; 24 rue du Château, Plateau du Narbonne; adult/child €6/free; ☺10am-12.30pm & 2-6pm Apr-Jul & Sep-Oct, 9.30am-6.30pm Jul & Aug, 1-5pm Tue-Sun Nov-Feb), whose 12th-century fortifications hold a Romanesque chapel and a rotating series of art exhibits.

The Drive ›› Follow the D73 southwest for 10km across the Rhône into Viviers, follow the river 15km south into Bourg-St-Andéol, then squiggle 30km along the D4 past St-Remèze's lavender museum to Vallon-Pont-d'Arc, western gateway to the Gorges de l'Ardèche.

SAMUEL BORGES PHOTOGRAPHY / SHUTTERSTOCK ©

TRIP HIGHLIGHT

⑥ Gorges de l'Ardèche

These steep and spectacular limestone gorges cut a curvaceous swath through the high scrubland along the Ardèche River, a tributary of the Rhône. The real showstopper, near the gorges'

Gorges de l'Ardèche Pont d'Arc

western entrance, is the **Pont d'Arc**, a sublimely beautiful natural stone arch. Stop here to camp, swim or join one of the many paddling tours down the river. Further east, the **Sentier Aval des Gorges** descends steeply for 2km to the heart of the gorges, granting hikers access to two primitive campgrounds at Bivouac de Gournier

and Bivouac de Gaud. Allow some time to visit the sensational **Grotte Chauvet 2** (☏04 75 94 39 40; www.grottechauvet2ardeche. com; Plateau du Razal; adult/child €17/8.50; ⊘10.30am-7pm mid-Jun–5 Jul, 9am-8pm 6 Jul-Aug, 9am-6.30pm Sep & Oct, 10.30am-5pm Nov & Dec) museum, which houses replicas of amazing prehistoric paintings.

🛏 p229

The Drive » From Vallon-Pont-d'Arc, the breathtaking D290 zigzags for 29km along the canyon's rim, with 11 viewpoints revealing dazzling vistas of horseshoe bends, and kayakers in formation far below. Exiting the gorges, take the D200 for 2km south through pretty medieval Aiguèze, then continue 22km southeast across the Rhône into Mornas via the D901, D6086, D994 and N7.

BOUCHONS

A *bouchon* might be a 'bottle stopper' or 'traffic jam' elsewhere in France, but in Lyon it's a cosy, traditional bistro specialising in regional cuisine. *Bouchons* originated in the first half of the 20th century when many bourgeois families had to let go their in-house cooks, who then set up their own restaurants.

Kick-start your meal with a *communard*, an aperitif of red Beaujolais wine and *crème de cassis* (blackcurrant liqueur), then move on to a *pot* – a 46cL glass bottle adorned with an elastic band to prevent wine drips – of local Brouilly, Beaujolais, Côtes du Rhône or Mâcon.

Next comes the entrée, perhaps *salade lyonnaise* (green salad with bacon, croutons and poached egg), or lentils in creamy sauce. Hearty main dishes include *boudin noir aux pommes* (blood sausage with apples), *quenelles de brochet* (pike dumplings served in a creamy crayfish sauce), *tablier de sapeur* (breaded, fried tripe) and *andouillette* (sausage made from pigs' intestines).

For the cheese course, choose between a bowl of *fromage blanc* (a cross between cream cheese and natural yoghurt); *cervelle de canut* ('brains of the silk weaver'; *fromage blanc* mixed with chives and garlic, a staple of Lyon's 19th-century weavers); or local St-Marcellin ripened to gooey perfection.

Desserts are grandma-style: think *tarte aux pommes* (apple tart), or the Lyonnais classic *tarte aux pralines*, a brilliant rose-coloured confection made with crème fraiche and crushed sugar-coated almonds.

Little etiquette is required in *bouchons*. Mopping your plate with a chunk of bread is fine, and you'll usually sit elbow-to-elbow with your fellow diners at tightly wedged tables (great for practising your French).

❼ Mornas

Perched on some precipitous cliffs, the 11th- to 14th-century **Forteresse de Mornas** (☎04 90 37 01 26; www.forteresse-de-mornas.com; 4 rue Thinel; tours adult/child €10/8; ⊙tours 10am, 11am, 2pm, 3pm, 4pm, 5pm daily Jul & Aug, Sat & Sun Apr-Jun & Sep) makes a dramatic backdrop for the pretty village below. Built by the medieval Counts of Toulouse, it commands outstanding views west to the Rhône and east to Mont Ventoux. A trail climbs 137 vertical metres from the village past the 12th-century Romanesque **Église Notre-Dame du Val-Romigier** to the fortress, where costumed guides offer historical re-enactments. Medieval fever also grips Mornas in July during **La Médiévale de Mornas**, a popular annual festival and crafts market.

The Drive ❯❯ Zip 12km southeast down the N7 into Orange, whose magnificent 2000-year-old Arc de Triomphe provides a fitting welcome.

TRIP HIGHLIGHT

❽ Orange

Sun-drenched Orange is a dream destination for fans of ancient ruins. The city's outstanding **Théâtre Antique** (Ancient Roman Theatre; ☎04 90 51 17 60; www.theatre-antique.com; rue Madeleine Roch; adult/child €9.50/7.50; ⊙9am-7pm Jun-Aug, to 6pm Apr, May & Sep, 9.30am-5.30pm Mar & Oct, 9.30am-4.30pm Nov-Feb), one of only three Roman theatres in the world with a perfectly preserved stage wall, shines brightest during summer performances such as the epic international opera festival **Chorégies d'Orange** (www.choregies.fr; ⊙Jul & Aug). North of town, Orange's second Roman treasure is the exquisitely carved 1st-century-CE **Arc de Triomphe**.

Eating & Sleeping

Lyon ❶

✕ Daniel et Denise · Bouchon €€

(📞04 78 42 24 62; www.danieletdenise.fr; 36 rue Tramassac, 5e; mains €17-29, 2-course lunch menu €21, dinner menus €37-60; 🕐noon-2pm & 7.30-9.30pm Tue-Sat; Ⓜ Vieux Lyon) One of Vieux Lyon's most dependable and traditional eateries, this classic spot is run by award-winning chef Joseph Viola. Come here for elaborate variations on traditional Lyonnais themes. You'll also find branches of Daniel et Denise in Croix Rousse and across the Rhône in the *troisieme*.

🛏 Cour des Loges · Hotel €€€

(📞04 72 77 44 44; www.courdesloges.com; 2-8 rue du Bœuf, 5e; d from €250, ste from €350; ❉ 🛜 🏊; Ⓜ Vieux Lyon) Four 14th- to 17th-century houses wrapped around a *traboule* (secret passage) with preserved features such as Italianate loggias make this an exquisite place to stay. Individually decorated rooms draw guests with designer bathroom fittings and bountiful antiques, while decadent facilities include a spa, a Michelin-starred restaurant (*menus* €105 to €145), a swish cafe and a cross-vaulted bar.

Vienne ❷

✕ L'Espace PH3 · French €€

(📞04 74 53 01 96; www.lapyramide.com; 14 bd Fernand Point; meat & fish €64-70, lunch menu €26, dinner menus €149-180; 🕐noon-1.30pm & 7.30-9.30pm) Overseen by two-Michelin-starred chef Patrick Henriroux, L'Espace PH3 offers a good-value gastronomic menu, serving a small selection of French classics with a creative twist. The lunch *menu* is an absolute steal. In summer, meals are served out on the superb garden terrace.

Valence ❸

✕ André · Bistro €€

(📞04 75 44 15 32; www.anne-sophie-pic.com/valence/#andre; 285 av Victor Hugo; mains €22-32, menus €39-72; 🕐noon-2pm & 7-10pm) André is the less formal but still stunning bistro side of Anne-Sophie Pic's gastronomic empire. The fabulous-value menu always involves seasonal, fresh ingredients, and dishes are imaginatively prepared and artfully presented. The Belle Époque–inspired decor, with wooden tables and old photos of the Pic family adorning the walls, is equally stunning.

🛏 La Maison de la Pra · B&B €€

(📞04 75 43 69 73; www.maisondelapra.com; 8 rue de l'Équerre; d €125-250; P ❉ 🛜) Such charm! If you've ever wanted to stay in a 16th-century *hôtel particulier* (private mansion), this bijou B&B enticingly positioned in a quiet alley near the town hall is the real deal. It offers five stadium-sized suites with beamed ceilings, period furniture and artworks. They're smack in the centre but still feel very quiet. Good English is spoken.

Gorges de l'Ardèche ❻

🛏 Le Belvédère · Hotel €

(📞04 75 88 00 02; www.hotel-ardeche-belvedere.com; D290, rte touristique des Gorges; d €65-135, q €140-190; 🕐Apr-5 Oct, restaurant Wed-Mon; P ❉ 🛜 🏊) Just 300m away from the Pont d'Arc, the aptly named Belvédère (Lookout) has 30 rooms that have been sleekly refitted. Half of the rooms have views of the gorges, and some come with a balcony. Facilities include a swimming pool, a canoe/kayak rental outlet and a well-regarded on-site restaurant (mains €17 to €22).

STRETCH YOUR LEGS
LYON

Start/Finish Opéra de Lyon

Distance 3km

Duration 2½ hours

Stroll through two millennia of Lyonnais history, from the Gallo-Roman settlement of Lugudunum to Lyon's avant-garde 20th-century opera house; along the way, three secret medieval passageways and a pedestrian bridge across the Saône River are thrown in just for fun.

Take this walk on Trip

20

Basilique Notre-Dame de Fourvière

Start at this massive hilltop **basilica** (☎04 78 25 13 01; www.fourviere.org; place de Fourvière, 5e; rooftop tour adult/child €12/5; ⏱basilica 7am-7pm, tours 2.30 & 4pm Wed, Sat & Sun Apr, May & Oct, 11am, 2.30pm & 4pm Mon-Sat, 2.30pm & 4pm Sun Jun-Sep, 2.30 & 3.30pm Wed, Sat & Sun Nov), whose terrace offers stunning panoramas of Lyon, the Rhône and Saône Rivers, and even distant Mont Blanc on clear days.

The Walk ≫ Head southwest along rue Roger Radisson for 250m to the Gallo-Roman Museum.

Musée Gallo-Romain de Fourvière

Gallo-Roman artefacts from the Rhône Valley are displayed at this **museum** (☎04 72 38 49 30; www.museegalloromain. grandlyon.com; 17 rue Cléberg, 5e; adult/child €4/free; ⏱11am-6pm Tue-Fri, 10am-6pm Sat & Sun). Next door are two ancient Roman theatres, the 10,000-seat **Théâtre Romain** and the smaller **odéon**.

The Walk ≫ Descend rue Cléberg 200m, turn left into Parc des Hauteurs, following the main path downhill 400m to Montée St-Barthélémy. Walk downhill about 50m on Montée St-Barthélémy and turn right into Montée des Chazeaux, down to rue du Bœuf. Turn right then immediately left into rue de la Bombarde. Take the first street to the right (rue des Antonins) to the cathedral.

Cathédrale St-Jean

This **cathedral** (www.cathedrale-lyon.fr; place St-Jean, 5e; ⏱cathedral 8.15am-7.45pm Mon-Fri, 8am-7pm Sat & Sun, treasury 9.30am-noon & 2-6pm Tue-Sat) was built between the 11th and 16th centuries. Don't miss the **astronomical clock** in the north transept, which chimes elaborately at noon, 2pm, 3pm and 4pm.

The Walk ≫ Go back to rue du Bœuf and stop at house number 27 (on your right).

Traboules

Throughout Vieux Lyon, secret passages known as *traboules* wind through apartment blocks and courtyards, up stairs and down corridors, connecting

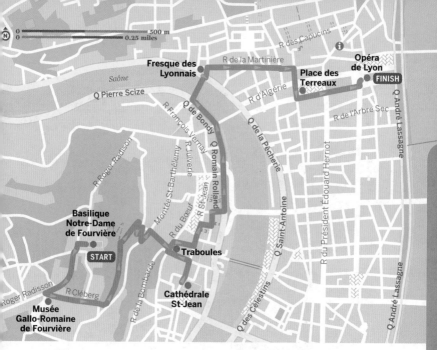

streets in unexpected ways. In all, 315 passages link 230 streets, with a combined length of 50km. Some date from Roman times, while others were constructed by *canuts* (silk weavers) in the 19th century to transport silk in inclement weather. Resistance fighters found them equally handy during WWII.

The Walk ❯❯ Enter the traboule at number 27 and navigate to its exit at 54 rue St-Jean; turn left into rue St-Jean until you reach number 27. Open the door and cross to 6 rue des Trois Maries. Turn left and walk until you reach place de la Baleine, which is lined with eateries and an iconic ice-cream parlour. Take the alley on your right to the main road along the Saône River. Now follow the river 600m north and cross the Passerelle St-Vincent bridge to Lyon's most famous mural.

Fresque des Lyonnais

Well-known Lyonnais peer out from this seven-storey **mural** (cnr rue de la Martinière & quai St-Vincent, 1er), including loom inventor Joseph-Marie Jacquard, superchef Paul Bocuse and the Little Prince, created by author-aviator Antoine de Saint-Exupéry.

The Walk ❯❯ Head 400m east on rue de la Martinière, then go south one block on rue Paul Chenavard into place des Terreaux.

Place des Terreaux

The centrepiece of Lyon's beautiful **central square** is a 19th-century **fountain** sculpted by Frédéric-Auguste Bartholdi (of Statue of Liberty fame). Fronting the square's eastern edge is the ornate **hôtel de ville** (town hall).

The Walk ❯❯ From the south side of the square head 250m east on rue Joseph Serlin to the Opéra.

Opéra de Lyon

Lyon's neoclassical 1831-built **opera house** (www.opera-lyon.com; 1 place de la Comédie, 1er) sports a semi-cylindrical glass-domed roof, added in 1993 by renowned architect Jean Nouvel. On summer evenings, free jazz concerts are performed under the arches up front.

The Walk ❯❯ From Hôtel de Ville station, where you're now standing, ride the metro three stops back to Vieux Lyon station, then return to Fourvière via funicular.

Provence & Southeast France

WITH ITS SHIMMERING COAST AND RUSTIC PROVENÇAL HEART, the Mediterranean south has a timeless allure. Driving here you'll travel through wildly divergent landscapes: cinematic coastline, rugged hinterland and bucolic valleys. And there are loads of charming villages that beg to be explored.

The Cote d'Azur's glamorous cities, deep-blue Med and chic hilltop villages never fail to delight. Inland, you'll weave between fragrant fields, forested gorges and Roman ruins. Skip over the sea to the unspoilt island delights of Corsica or be engulfed in the lush green wetlands of the Camargue.

Along the way you'll connect with the poets, painters and writers who flocked here during the 20th century, chasing sun and inspiration.

The Var Calanque de Port-Miou
PAVEL SZABO / SHUTTERSTOCK ©

Provence & Southeast France

Roman Provence 7 Days
21 Provence's impressive Roman treasures line up along this leisurely drive. (p237)

Lavender Route 4–5 Days
22 The region at its prettiest, with flowery fields and rustic villages. (p247)

Riviera Crossing 4 Days
Classic Trip **23** The best beaches, cities, villages and nature along the Med coast. (p255)

Var Delights 5 Days
24 Expect an incredible array of viewpoints and spectacular landscapes. (p267)

Southern Seduction en Corse 10 Days
25 This jaunt along Corsica's southern coast takes in plenty of history. (p277)

Corsican Coast Cruiser 5 Days
26 Discover western Corsica's majestic mountain peaks and covetable sandy coves. (p287)

The Camargue 4 Days
27 Loop through the wild, lush wetlands where bulls and white horses roam. (p297)

DON'T MISS

The Road up Mt Ventoux

Relive gruelling Tour de France ascents from behind the wheel. Feel the cycling love on Trip **22**

Fenocchio

Enjoy some original flavours at this iconic ice-cream parlour on Trip **23**

Grand Hôtel Nord Pinus, Arles

What other hotel (or city) boasts embedded Roman columns and bullfighters' trophies? Visit on Trip **27**

Orange's Roman Arc de Triomphe

This monument's detailed carvings are a fascinating peek into what got your average Roman foot soldier excited. Get close on Trip **21**

Pastis

Always ask for this aniseed-flavoured liqueur by brand. We like the herbal Henri Bardouin or the spicy Janot. Sip on Trips **21**
22 **23** **24** **25** **26** **27**

Roman Provence

Survey Provence's incredible Roman legacy as you follow ancient routes through the region's river gorges and vineyards, gathering provisions as you go.

21

TRIP HIGHLIGHTS

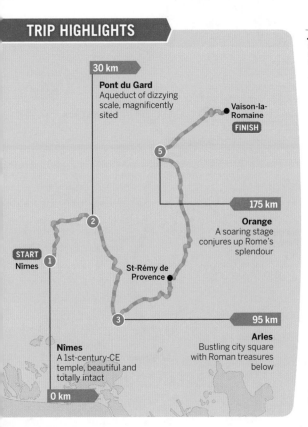

30 km

Pont du Gard
Aqueduct of dizzying scale, magnificently sited

Vaison-la-Romaine

FINISH

⑤

175 km

Orange
A soaring stage conjures up Rome's splendour

②

START
Nîmes
①

St-Rémy de Provence ●

③ **95 km**

Arles
Bustling city square with Roman treasures below

Nîmes
A 1st-century-CE temple, beautiful and totally intact

0 km

**7 DAYS
205KM / 127 MILES**

GREAT FOR...

BEST TIME TO GO
Ruins open year-round, but avoid August's heat and crush.

ESSENTIAL PHOTO
The Pont du Gard, illuminated every night in summer.

BEST FOR CULTURE
Balmy nights at Orange's Théâtre Antique are magical; July includes the Chorégies d'Orange.

21 Roman Provence

Provence was where Rome first truly flexed its imperial muscles. Follow Roman roads, cross Roman bridges and grab a seat in the bleachers at Roman theatres and arenas. Thrillingly, you'll discover that most of Provence's ancient ruins aren't ruins at all. Many are exceptionally well preserved, and some are also evocatively integrated into the region's modern cities. With Provence's knockout landscape as a backdrop, history never looked so good!

TRIP HIGHLIGHT

1 Nîmes

Although Nîmes isn't strictly speaking in modern Provence, a long, shared regional history means it has to feature in this Roman tour. The city's bizarre coat of arms – a crocodile chained to a palm tree! – recalls the region's first, but definitely not last, horde of sun-worshipping retirees. Julius Caesar's loyal legionnaires were granted land here to settle after

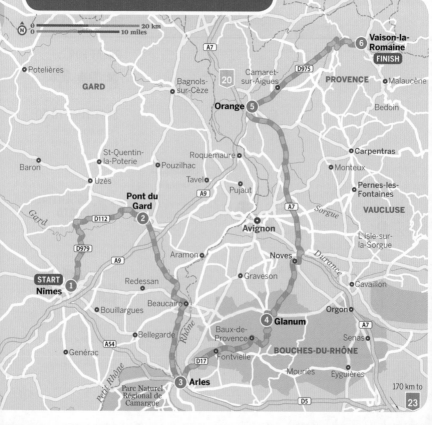

hard years on the Nile campaigns. Two millennia later, their ambitious town blends seamlessly with the bustling, workaday French streetscapes of the modern city. **Les Arènes** (📞04 66 21 82 56; www.arenes-nimes.com; place des Arènes; adult/child incl audio guide €10/8; ⏰9am-8pm Jul & Aug, to 7pm Jun, to 6.30pm Apr-Jun & Sep, to 6pm Mar & Oct, 9.30am-5pm Nov-Feb), an impressively intact 1st-century-CE amphitheatre, lies across the road from the outstanding **Musée de la Romanité** (📞04 48 21 02 10; 16 bd des Arènes; adult/child €8/3; ⏰10am-8pm Jul & Aug, to 7pm Sep-Nov & Apr-Jun, to 6pm Wed-Mon Dec-

LINK YOUR TRIP

20 **Rhône Valley**
Join up with this trip in Orange for several great Roman sites in Vienne and Lyon's Roman theatres and great Gallo-Roman museum.

23 **Riviera Crossing**
The Cote d'Azur shares the Roman treasures, and many of them are in superb locations; head east from Arles to Aix, then take the E80 to Cannes to join this trip.

Mar), which houses more than 5000 archaeological exhibits uncovered around Nîmes. North of there, locals nonchalantly skateboard or window-shop on the elegant plaza that's home to a beautiful and preciously intact 1st-century-CE temple, the **Maison Carrée** (📞04 66 21 82 56; www.maisoncarree. eu; place de la Maison Carrée; adult/child €6/5; ⏰9.30am-8pm Jul & Aug, 10am-6.30pm Apr-Jun & Sep, 10am-6pm Mar & Oct, 10am-1pm & 2-4.30pm Jan, Feb, Nov & Dec). Afterwards, stroll over to the pleasant **Jardins de la Fontaine** (quai de la Fontaine; entry to Tour Magne adult/child €3.50/3, garden free; ⏰9am-8pm Jul & Aug, to 5pm Sep-Jun). The remains of the **Temple de Diane** are in its lower northwest corner and a 10-minute uphill walk brings you to the crumbling, 30m-high **Tour Magne** overlooking the gardens. Built in 15 BCE as a watchtower and display of imperial might, it is the only one that remains of several that once spanned the 7km-long ramparts.

✗ 🏠 p244

The Drive » The D6086 is direct, but sacrifice 15 minutes and take route d'Uzès (D979). This way, leave Nîmes' snarly traffic behind and suddenly find yourself on a quiet stretch of winding road skirting grey rocky gorges and honey-stone villages. Cut east via Sanilhac-Sagriès on the D112, then turn off at Begude's roundabout.

TRIP HIGHLIGHT

② Pont du Gard

You'll get a glimpse of the **Pont du Gard** (📞04 66 37 50 99; www.pontdugard. fr; adult/child €9.50/free, guided tour to top tier €6/free; ⏰9am-11pm Jul & Aug, to 10pm Jun & Sep, to 9pm May, to 8pm Apr & Oct, to 6pm Nov-Mar; ♿) as you approach. Nature (and clever placement of car parks and visitor centres) has created one bravura reveal. Spanning the gorge is a magnificent three-tiered aqueduct, a marvel of 1st-century engineering. During the Roman period, the Pont du Gard was (like Nîmes) part of the Roman province of Gallia Narbonensis. It was built around 19 BCE by Agrippa, Augustus' deputy, and it's huge: the 275m-long upper tier, 49m above the Gard, has over 50 arches. Each block (the largest weighs over 5 tonnes) was hauled in by cart or raft. It was once part of a 50km-long system that carried water from nearby Uzès down to thirsty Nîmes. It's a 400m wheelchair-accessible walk from car parks on both banks of the river to the bridge itself, with a shady cafe en route on the right. Swim upstream for unencumbered views, though downstream is also good for summer dips, with shaded wooden platforms set in the flatter banks.

Want to make a day of it? There's an interactive, high-tech museum, a hands-on discovery space for kids, and a peaceful 1.4km botanical walk, **Mémoires de Garrigue**.

📑 p244

The Drive » Kayaking to the next stop would be more fun, and more direct, but you'll need to return south via the D986L to Beaucaire, then the D90 and D15 to Arles.

TRIP HIGHLIGHT

③ Arles

Arles, formerly known as Arelate, was part of the Roman Empire from as early as the 2nd century BCE. It wasn't until the 49–45 BCE civil war, however, when nearby Massalia (Marseille) supported Pompey (ie backed the wrong side), that it became a booming regional capital.

The town today is delightful, Roman cache or no, but what a living legacy it is. Its **Les**

Arènes (Amphithéâtre; ☎08 91 70 03 70; www.arenes-arles. com; Rond-Point des Arènes; adult/child incl Théâtre Antique €9/free; ☉9am-8pm Jul & Aug, to 7pm May, Jun & Sep, shorter hours Oct-Apr) is not as large as Nîmes', but it is spectacularly sited and occasionally still sees blood spilled, just like in the old gladiatorial days (it hosts gory bullfights and *courses Camarguaises,* which is the local variation). Likewise, the 1st-century **Théâtre Antique** (☎04 90 49 59 05; rue de la Calade; adult/child, incl entry to Les Arènes, €9/ free; ☉9am-7pm May-Sep, to 6pm Mar, Apr & Oct, 10am-5pm Nov-Feb) is still regularly used for open-air performances.

Just as social, political and religious life revolved around the forum in Arelate, the busy plane-tree-shaded **Place du Forum** buzzes with cafe life today. Sip a pastis here and spot the remains of a 2nd-century

temple embedded in the façade of the **Hôtel Nord-Pinus**. Under your feet are **Cryptoportiques** (place de la République, Hôtel de Ville; adult/child €4.50/ free; ☉9am-7pm May-Sep, to 6pm Mar, Apr & Oct, 10am-5pm Nov-Feb) – subterranean foundations and buried arcades. Access the underground galleries, 89m long and 59m wide, at the **Hôtel de Ville** (Town Hall; place de la République).

Emperor Constantin's partly preserved 4th-century private baths, the **Thermes de Constantin** (☎04 90 49 59 05; rue du Grand Prieuré; adult/child €4/ free; ☉9am-7pm May-Sep, to 6pm Mar, Apr & Oct, 10am-5pm Nov-Feb), are a few minutes' stroll away, next to the *quai.* Southwest of the centre is **Les Alyscamps** (av des Alyscamps; adult/child €4.50/free; ☉9am-7pm May-Sep, shorter hours rest of year), a necropolis founded by the Romans and adopted by Christians in the 4th century. It contains the tombs of martyr St Genest and Arles' first bishops. You may recognise it: Van Gogh and Gauguin both captured the avenues of cypresses on canvas (though only melancholy old Van Gogh painted the empty sarcophagi).

✕ 📑 p244, p303, p409

The Drive » Take the D17 to Fontvieille, follow the D78F/D27A to Baux-de-Provence, then the D5. This detour takes you past beautiful dry white rocky hills

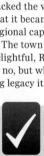
**TOP TIP:
PADDLING THE GARD RIVER**

Get your first glimpse of the Pont du Gard from the river by paddling 8km downstream from Collias, 4km west of the D981. **Kayak Vert** (☎04 66 22 80 76; www. kayakvert.com; 8 chemin de St-Vincent, Collias; adult/child from €24/20; ☉9am-6pm mid-May–Oct) and **Canoë Le Tourbillon** (☎04 66 22 85 54; www.canoeletourbillon.com; 3 chemin du Gardon, Collias; adult/child from €24/18; ☉9am-7pm Apr-Sep), both based near the village bridge, run guided river trips by canoe or kayak from March/April to October.

ALEXANDRE ROTENBERG / SHUTTERSTOCK ©

Arles Théâtre Antique

dotted with scrubby pine; the trip will still only take around 45 minutes. There's on-site parking at Glanum. If heading into St-Rémy, there's parking by the tourist office (place Jean-Jaurès) and north of the periphery (place Général-de-Gaulle).

- - - - - - - - - - - - - - - -

❹ Glanum

Such is the glittering allure of the gourmet delis, interiors boutiques and smart restaurants

that line St-Rémy-de-Provence's circling boulevards and place de la République that a visit to the **Site Archéologique de Glanum** (☎04 90 92 23 79; www.site-glanum.fr; rte des Baux-de-Provence; adult/child €7.50/free, parking €4; ⏰9.30am-6pm Apr-Sep, 10am-5pm Oct-Mar, closed Mon Oct-Mar) is often an afterthought. But the **triumphal arch** (20 CE) that

marks Glanum's entrance, 2km south of St-Rémy, is far from insignificant. It's pegged as one of France's oldest and is joined by a towering **mausoleum** (30–20 BCE). Walk down the main street and you'll pass the mainstays of Roman life: baths, a forum and marketplace, temples and town villas. And beneath all this Roman handiwork lies the remnants of an older Celtic and Hellenic settlement, built to take advantage of a sacred spring. Van Gogh, as a patient of the neighbouring asylum, painted the olive orchard that covered the site until its excavation in the 1920s.

 p245

The Drive » It's the A7 all the way up to Orange, 50km of nondescript driving if you're not tempted by a detour to Avignon on the way.

TRIP HIGHLIGHT

⑤ Orange

It's often said if you can only see one Roman site in France, make it Orange. And yes, the town's Roman treasures are gobsmacking and unusually old; both are believed to have been built during Augustus Caesar's rule (27 BCE–14 CE). Plus, while Orange may not be the Provençal village of popular fantasy, it's a cruisy, decidedly untouristy town, making for good-value accommodation and hassle-free sightseeing (such as plentiful street parking one block back from the theatre).

At a massive 103m wide and 37m high, the stage wall of the **Théâtre Antique** (Ancient Roman Theatre; ☏04 90 51 17 60; www.theatre-antique.com; rue Madeleine Roch; adult/child €9.50/7.50; ☺9am-7pm Jun-Aug, to 6pm Apr, May & Sep, 9.30am-5.30pm Mar & Oct, 9.30am-4.30pm Nov-Feb) dominates the surrounding streetscape. Minus a few mosaics, plus a new roof, it's one of three in the world still standing in their entirety, and originally seated 10,000 spectators. Admission includes an informative audioguide and access to the **Musée d'Art et d'Histoire** (www.theatre-antique.com; rue Madeleine Roch; entry incl with Théâtre Antique; ☺9.15am-7pm Jun-Aug, to 6pm Apr, May & Sep, shorter hours Oct-Mar) across the road. Its collection includes friezes from the theatre with the Roman motifs we love: eagles holding garlands of bay leaves, and a cracking battle between cavalrymen and foot soldiers.

For bird's-eye views of the theatre – and phenomenal vistas of rocky Mont Ventoux and the Dentelles – follow montée Philbert de Chalons, or montée Lambert, up **Colline St-Eutrope**, once the ever-vigilant Romans' lookout point.

To the town's north, the **Arc de Triomphe** stands on the ancient Via Agrippa (now the busy N7), 19m high and wide, and a solid 8m thick. Restored in 2009, its richly animated reliefs commemorate 49 BCE Roman victories with images of battles, ships, trophies, and chained, naked and utterly subdued Gauls.

 p245

The Drive » Northeast, the D975 passes through gentle vineyard-lined valleys for 40 minutes, with views of the Dentelles de Montmirail's limestone ridges along the way (the D977 and D23 can be equally lovely). Parking in Vaison can be a trial; park by the tourist office (place du Chanoine Sautel), or west of the Cité Médiévale (along Chemin de la Haute-Ville), if you don't mind walking.

⑥ Vaison-la-Romaine

Is there anything more telling of Rome's smarts than a sturdy, still-used Roman bridge? Vaison-la-Romaine's pretty little

---

ROMAN PROVENCE READING LIST

» *The Roman Provence Guide* (Edwin Mullins; 2012)

» *The Roman Remains of Southern France* (James Bromwich; 1993)

» *Southern France: An Oxford Archaeological Guide* (Henry Cleere; 2001)

» *Ancient Provence: Layers of History in Southern France* (Jeffrey Wolin; 2003)

SALVE, PROVINCIA GALLIA TRANSALPINA

It all starts with the Greeks. After founding the city of Massalia, now Marseille, around 600 BCE, they spent the next few centuries establishing a long string of ports along the coast, planting olives and grapes as they went. When migrating Celts from the north joined forces with the local Ligurians, resistance to these booming colonies grew. The Celto-Ligurians were a force to be reckoned with; unfortunately, they were about to meet ancient history's biggest bullies. In 125 BCE the Romans helped the Greeks defend Massalia, and swiftly took control.

Thus begins the Gallo-Roman era and the region of Provincia Gallia Transalpina, the first Roman *provincia* (province), from which Provence takes its name. Later Provincia Narbonensis, it embraced all of southern France from the Alps to the Mediterranean and the Pyrenees.

Roads made the work of empire possible, and the Romans quickly set about securing a route that joined Italy and Spain. Via Aurelia linked Rome to Fréjus, Aix-en-Provence, Arles and Nîmes; the northbound Via Agrippa followed the Rhône from Arles to Avignon, Orange and onwards to Lyon. The Via Domitia linked the Alps with the Pyrenees by way of the Luberon and Nîmes.

With Julius Caesar's conquest of Gaul (58–51 BCE), the region truly flourished. Under the emperor Augustus, vast amphitheatres, triumphal arches and ingenious aqueducts – the ones that propel this trip – were constructed. Augustus celebrated his final defeat of the ever-rebellious Ligurians in 14 BCE, with the construction of the monument at La Turbie on the Côte d'Azur.

The Gallo-Roman legacy may be writ large and loud in Provence, but it also persists in the everyday. Look for it in unusual places: recycled into cathedral floors or hotel facades, in dusty cellars or simply buried beneath your feet.

Pont Romain has stood the test of time and severe floods. Stand at its centre and gaze up at the walled, cobbled-street hilltop **Cité Médiévale**, or down at the fast-flowing Ouvèze River.

Vaison-la-Romaine is tucked between seven valleys and has long been a place of trade. The ruined remains of **Vasio Vocontiorum**, the Roman city that flourished here between around 100 BCE and 450 CE, fill two central **Gallo-Roman sites** (☏04 90 36 50 48; www.provenceromaine.com; adult/child incl all ancient sites, museum & cathedral €9/4;

🕑9.30am-noon & 2-6pm). Two ancient neighbourhoods lie on either side of the tourist office and av du Général-de-Gaulle. The Romans shopped at the colonnaded boutiques and bathed at **La Villasse**, where you'll find **Maison au Dauphin**, which has splendid marble-lined fish ponds.

In **Puymin**, see noblemen's houses, mosaics, a workmen's quarter, a temple, and the still-functioning 6000-seat **Théâtre Antique** (c 20 CE). To make sense of the remains (and gather your audioguide), head for the **archaeological museum**,

which revives Vaison's Roman past with an incredible swag: superb mosaics, carved masks, and statues that include a 3rd-century silver bust and marble renderings of Hadrian and his wife, Sabina. Admission includes entry to the soothing 12th-century Romanesque cloister at **Cathédrale Notre-Dame de Nazareth** (🕑9.30am-noon & 2-6pm Mar-Dec), a five-minute walk west of La Villasse and, like much of Provence, built on Roman foundations.

🍴 🛏 p245

Eating & Sleeping

Nîmes ❶

✕ Les Halles   Market €

(www.leshallesdenimes.com; rues Guizot, Général Perrier & des Halles; ⏱7am-1pm Mon-Sat, to 1.30pm Sun) With over 100 stalls in 3500 sq metres, Nîmes' covered market is a wonder: local specialities include *picholine* (a local green olive) and *brandade* (salt cod). One of the best lunch spots is **La Pie qui Couette** (📞04 66 23 59 04; www.facebook.com/la.pie.qui. couette; 1 rue Guizot; mains €12-18; ⏱noon-2pm Tue-Sat) – 'The Snoozing Magpie' – a no-frills, no-reservations spot for super tapas, salt cod and grilled meats.

✕ Bird   Bistro €€

(📞04 11 83 45 80; www.facebook.com/ thebirdnimes; 2 rue Tedenat; mains €15-19; ⏱7-10pm) If it's just good, honest French bistro food you're craving, The Bird is a beaut. With walls lined with wine bottles, plants dangling from the ceiling and an open kitchen hatch emblazoned above with the words 'Home Made Cuisine', this is a fine Nîmes diner. Reserve.

🛏 Appart' City
Nîmes Arènes   Historic Hotel €€

(📞04 56 60 26 70; www.appartcity.com; 1 bd de Bruxelles; d €98-185; 🌐🛜) A stroll away from the Arènes, this grand 19th-century Hausmann-style building has been converted into a modern aparthotel, with smart, parquet-floored rooms complete with kitchenettes and city views. There's also a sauna, laundry and gym, and a glorious double-flight staircase from the lobby. Public parking available nearby.

🛏 Hôtel des Tuileries   Hotel €

(📞04 66 21 31 15; www.hoteldestuileries.com; 22 rue Roussy; d €65-110, tr €74-140, ste €112-160; 🅿🌐🛜) This well-priced 11-room hotel within strolling distance from Les Arènes (p239) features simple but attractively furnished rooms, some with covered balconies. Splashes of art liven up the decor. Breakfast costs €9, and there's a garage (€10-15), but you need to reserve spaces.

Pont du Gard ❷

🛏 Hôtel Le Colombier   Hotel €

(📞04 66 37 05 28; www.hotelrestaurant-pontdugard.fr; 24 av du Pont du Gard, Remoulins; s/d/tr/q €75/89/122/139; 🅿🌐🛜�) Le Colombier's location just 200m from the Pont du Gard (p239) car park means you save on bridge parking costs – the hotel has its own free car park and a bike garage. Rooms are simple but comfortable, there's a decent on-site restaurant (*menus* – fixed-price meals – €15 to €35), and it's very family-friendly, with a fenced swimming pool and a large garden.

Arles ❸

✕ Le Gibolin   Bistro €€

(📞04 88 65 43 14; 13 rue des Porcelets; 2-/3-course menus €29/36; ⏱12.30-2pm & 8-10.30pm Tue-Sat Apr-Jul & Oct, shorter hours rest of year) After spending three decades plying Paris with their passion for organic wines, owners Brigitte and Luc decided to head south and do the same for Arles. Unsurprisingly, it's become a much-loved local fixture, known for its hearty home cooking and peerless wine list (racked up temptingly behind the bar and mostly available by the glass).

✕ L'Atelier
Jean-Luc Rabanel   Gastronomy €€€

(📞04 90 91 07 69; www.rabanel.com; 7 rue des Carmes; menus €95-165; ⏱seatings 12.15-1pm & 7.30-8.15pm Wed-Sun) As much an artistic experience as a double-Michelin-starred adventure, this is the gastronomic flagship of charismatic chef Jean-Luc Rabanel. Many products are sourced from the chef's veggie patch, and wine pairings are an experience in themselves. Saturday-morning cooking classes are also available, working with the kitchen brigade (€200). Next door, Rabanel's **À Côté** (📞04 90 47 61 13; www.bistro-acote.com; 21 rue des Carmes; mains €28-32, menu €49; ⏱seatings 12.15-1pm & 7.30-8.15pm Wed-Sun) offers bistro fare.

Beautiful rooms and apartments are available (from €150 per night), and can be combined with dining packages.

🛏 Hôtel de l'Amphithéâtre   Historic Hotel €€

(☎04 90 96 10 30; www.hotelamphitheatre. fr; 5-7 rue Diderot; s from €80, d €95-175; ❄ @ 🛜) This elegant address across from the amphitheatre is quite a bargain: the standard of design here far outreaches the reasonable price tag. Antiques, rugs, fireplaces and staircases speak of the building's history, while minimal rooms nod to modern trends, and several have super views over Les Arènes and Arles' rooftops (although you'll pay for the privilege).

🛏 Le Cloître   Design Hotel €€

(☎04 88 09 10 00; www.hotelducloitre.com; 18 rue du Cloître; r €185; ❄ @ 🛜) The traditional Mediterranean courtyard that greets you on arrival at 'The Cloister' is charming enough, but doesn't betray the inventiveness of the warm, colourful design within. Its 19 rooms are all distinct, with Italian showers and unusual furniture that sacrifices no comfort. There's a panoramic rooftop terrace and excellent meals are available from the neighbouring Épicerie du Cloître.

Glanum ④

✗ La Cuisine des Anges   Bistro €€

(☎04 90 92 17 66; www.angesetfees-stremy. com; 4 rue du 8 Mai 1945; 2-course menu €28-30, 3-course menu €34; ⊙ noon-2.30pm & 7.30-11pm Mon, Wed, Sat & Sun, 7.30-11pm Thu & Fri; ❄ 🛜) You can't really go wrong at the Angels' Kitchen – at least if you're looking for solid, Provençal cooking with a hearty dash of creativity. Tuck into dishes like poached sea bream with saffron, ravioli with ricotta and white truffle, or baked St-Marcellin cheese with thyme, and dine either in the courtyard or the stone-walled dining room. Upstairs is a cute B&B, **Le Sommeil des Fées** (☎04 90 92 17 66; www. angesetfees-stremy.com; 4 rue du 8 Mai 1945; incl breakfast s €55-70, d €70-90; 🛜).

Orange ⑤

🛏 Hôtel l'Herbier d'Orange   Hotel €

(☎04 90 34 09 23; www.lherbierdorange.com; 8 place aux Herbes; s/d/tr/q €56/68/85/98; P ❄ @ 🛜) On a quiet, tree-shaded square, this simple hotel makes a pleasant enough base in Orange, with 20 bright, colourful rooms, livened up with jolly fabrics and tiled floors. The stone-walled breakfast room is attractive too.

Vaison-la-Romaine ⑥

✗ Bistro du'O   Bistro €€

(☎04 90 41 72 90; www.bistroduo.fr; rue Gaston Gévaudan; lunch/dinner menus from €28/39; ⊙ noon-2pm Tue, noon-2pm & 7.30-10pm Wed-Sat; 🛜) For fine dining in Vaison, this is everyone's tip. The setting is full of atmosphere, in a vaulted cellar in the medieval city (once the château stables), and chef Philippe Zemour takes his cue from Provençal flavours and daily market ingredients. Top-class food, top setting, tops all round. Owners Philippe and Gaëlle Zemour also offer lodging in three handsomely furnished guestrooms, which includes an excellent breakfast served on the panoramic terrace (double €120 to €140).

✗ La Lyriste   French €€

(☎04 90 36 04 67; 45 cours Taulignan; mains €15-24, menu €15-28; ⊙ noon-1.30pm Wed, noon-1.30pm & 7.15-9pm Tue, Thu & Fri, 7.15-9.30pm Sat; ✈) Nothing world-changing here, but tasty regional food from *bourride* (fish stew) to *brandade de cabillaud* (cod kebabs), laced with lashings of olive oil, tomatoes and Provençal herbs. The plane-tree-shaded terrace tables are the ones to ask for.

🛏 Hôtel Burrhus   Hotel €

(☎04 90 36 00 11; www.burrhus.com; 1 place de Montfort; d €69-98, apt €140; P ❄ 🛜) From the outside, this looks like a classic town hotel: shutters, stonework and a prime spot on the town square. But inside, surprises await: the arty owners have littered it with modern art, sculptures, funky furniture and colourful decorative details, although the white-walled rooms themselves sometimes feel stark. On sunny days, take breakfast on the plane-tree-shaded balcony overlooking the square.

Lavender Route

Banish thoughts of grandma's closet. Get out among the purple haze, sniff the heady summer breezes and navigate picturesque hilltop towns, ancient churches and pretty valleys.

22

TRIP HIGHLIGHTS

4 km

Abbaye Notre-Dame de Sénanque
Dreamy 12th-century abbey framed by rows of lavender

50 km

Sault
Stop off for wonderful sweets and nougat

Banon

Forcalquier

Plateau de Valensole

Gordes

START

FINISH

Coustellet
Rolling lavender fields and a lavender-themed museum

0 km

Prieuré de Salagon
Wander round a medieval herb garden

135 km

4–5 DAYS
217KM / 135 MILES

GREAT FOR...

BEST TIME TO GO

July is purple prime time, but June's blooms still impress.

 ESSENTIAL PHOTO

The road just north of Sault is a particularly stunning spot.

 BEST FOR OUTDOORS

Mont Ventoux has brilliant hiking trails and is hallowed ground for cycling fans.

22 Lavender Route

The Luberon and Vaucluse may be well-trodden (and driven) destinations, but you'll be surprised at how rustic they remain. This trip takes you to the undoubtedly big-ticket (and exquisitely beautiful) sights but also gets you exploring back roads, sleepy villages, big skies and one stunner of a mountain. And yes, past fields and fields of glorious purple blooms.

TRIP HIGHLIGHT

① Coustellet

Our lavender trail begins just outside the village of Coustellet at the **Musée de la Lavande** (📞04 90 76 91 23; www.museedelalavande. com; 376 rte de Gordes, D2; adult/child €8/free; ⏰9am-7pm Jun-Aug, to 1pm & 2-6pm Apr, May, Sep & Oct, 10am-1pm & 2-5.30pm Nov-Mar, closed Jan), an excellent eco-museum and working lavender farm, where you can immerse yourself in the traditions and history of the Provençal

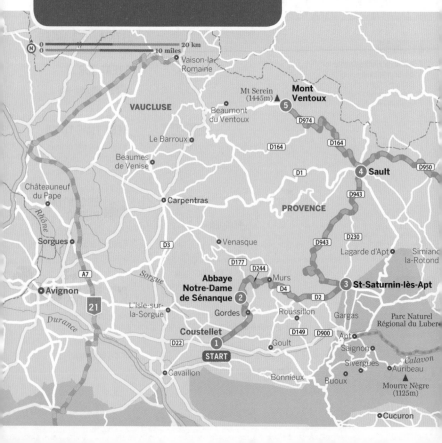

icon and buy lavender goodies in the on-site boutique. Afterwards the hilltop village of Gordes is worth a detour, especially at sunset, followed perhaps by a drink on the panoramic terrace at the lavish **Bastide de Gordes** (☎04 90 72 12 12; www.aire lles.com; 61 rue de la Combe; r from €310; ❄☎☎) hotel.

The Drive » The museum is just off the D2. From here, it's another 7km to Gordes along the D2, then a turn-off onto the D177 for 4km till you reach the abbey. You'll pass plenty of lavender photo ops en route, so feel free to stop if you can find an appropriate spot.

TRIP HIGHLIGHT

② Abbaye Notre-Dame de Sénanque

Isolated and ridiculously photogenic, this 12th-century Cistercian **abbey** (☎04 90 72 18 24; www.senanque.fr; off D177; guided/unguided tour €8/9.50; ❂10-11.30am & 1-5.30pm Mon-Sat, 1.30-5.30pm Sun) is famously framed by lavender from mid-June through July. The abbey was founded in 1148 and is still home to a small number of monks. The cloisters have a haunt-

ing, severe beauty; reservations are essential whether on a guided tour or independently (in the latter, visitors borrow an info-packed tablet that shows what abbey life was like in the 13th century). Conservative dress and silence are required. Be sure to build in some extra time to enjoy the meditative beauty of the lavender fields (most striking from mid-June to mid-July).

The Drive » The more scenic route from the abbey heads north. Continue up the D177 then turn right onto the D244 and follow the signs to Murs, a very winding 9.5km drive accompanied by wheat fields and vineyards. From here it's about 25 minutes to the next stop.

LINK YOUR TRIP

18 Foothills of the Alps

Swap rolling hills for spectacular gorges and then alpine air: take the D6 and D852 to Moustiers-Ste-Marie, or drop in at Sisteron from Forcalquier.

21 Roman Provence

From Roman Provence's last stop in Vaison-la-Romaine, it's a gorgeous drive to Gordes via Carpentras and Venasque.

③ St-Saturnin-lès-Apt

St-Saturnin-lès-Apt is a refreshingly ungentrified village, with marvellous views of the surrounding Vaucluse plateau punctuated by purple fields – climb to the **ruins** atop the village for a knockout vista. At **Moulin à Huile Jullien** (📞04 90 75 56 24; www.moulin-huile-jullien.com; rte d'Apt; ⏰10am-noon & 2-6pm Tue-Fri Mar-Sep, to 5pm Oct-Feb) see how olives are milled into oil (with honey and oil tastings thrown in).

✕ 🛏 p253

The Drive » Take the scenic, narrow D943 west and north towards Sault. Along the way, look out for the magnificent views of the red-tinged escarpment and the rust-coloured village of Roussillon. The views of Mont Ventoux only get more spectacular as you approach Sault, a 35-minute drive away.

④ Sault

This drowsily charming, isolated hilltop town mixes its lavender views with plum orchards and scattered forest. The town hot spot is **André Boyer** (📞04 90 64 00 23; www.nougat-boyer.fr; place de l'Europe), which has kept farmers, cyclists and mountaineers in honey and almond nougat since 1887; its lavender marshmallows and the

local speciality *pognes* (an orange-scented brioche) are also must-tries. Head to **Les Lavandes de Champelle** (📞06 82 53 95 34; www.lavandes-champelle. fr; rte de Ventoux; ⏰9am-7pm Mon-Fri, from 10am Sat & Sun), a roadside farm stand northwest of town, whose products include great buys for cooks. The lavender up here is known for its dark, OK... deep purple, hue.

The Drive » Exit town on the D164; when you hit the D974, fields give way to dense, fragrant forest. Above the treeline, strange spots of alpine scrub are gradually replaced by pale bald slopes. These steep gradients have often formed a hair-raising stage of the Tour de France – the road is daubed with Tour graffiti and many fans make a brave two-wheeled homage.

⑤ Mont Ventoux

If fields of flowers are intoxicating, Mont Ventoux (1910m) is awe-inspiring. Nicknamed *le géant de Provence* – Provence's giant – its great white hulk is visible from much of the region. *Le géant* sparkles all year round – once the snow melts, its lunarstyle limestone slopes glimmer in the sun. From its peak, clear-day vistas extend to the Alps and the Camargue.

Even summer temperatures can plummet by 20°C at the top; it's also twice as likely to rain, and the relentless mistrals blow 130 days

a year, sometimes exceeding 250km/h. Bring a cardigan and scarf!

🛏 p253

The Drive » Go back the way you came to Sault, then head east to Banon on the D950 for another 40 minutes.

⑥ Banon

A tasty, nonfloral diversion: little village, big cheese. Bustling Banon is famous for its chèvre de Banon, a goat's-milk cheese wrapped in a chestnut leaf. Fromagerie de Banon sells its cheese at the Tuesday morning market and in wonderful cheese-and-sausage shop **Brindille Melchio** (📞04 92 73 23 05; place de la République; ⏰9am-12.30pm & 2.30-6pm Fri-Tue Sep-Jun, daily Jul & Aug), which is unbeatable for picnic supplies. Tuck into cheese-and-charcuterie plates at **Les Vins au Vert** (📞04 92 75 23 84; www.restaurant-caviste-banon-04.fr; rue Pasteur; menus €14.50-16; ⏰10am-3pm & 5.30-10pm Thu-Sat, 10am-3pm Wed & Sun); make reservations for Thursday to Saturday nights.

The Drive » Follow the D950 southeast for 25km to Forcalquier, as the scenery alternates between gentle forested slopes and fields.

⑦ Forcalquier

Forcalquier has an upbeat, slightly bohemian vibe, a holdover from

TRIP HIGHLIGHT

Coustellet Musée de la Lavande

the 1960s and '70s, when artists and back-to-the-landers arrived, fostering a now-booming organics ('*biologiques*' or bio) movement. Saffron is grown here, absinthe is distilled, and the town is also home to L'Université Européenne des Senteurs & Saveurs (UESS; European University of Scents and Flavours). To see it all in action, time your visit for the Monday morning market.

Climb the steep steps to Forcalquier's gold-topped **citadel** and octagonal **chapel** for more sensational views; on the way down note the once-wealthy seat's ornately carved wooden doorways and grand bourgeois town houses. Pop in for a drink, a Michelin-starred meal and (if budget allows) an overnight stay at the luxurious Couvent des Minimes (p253), owned by fragrance house L'Occitane.

✕ ⊨ p253

The Drive ≫ Find yourself in a gentle world, all plane-tree arcades, wildflowers and, yes, lavender. Around 4km south on the D4100 you'll come to our next stop, just before the pretty town of Mane.

TRIP HIGHLIGHT

⑧ Prieuré de Salagon

This beautiful 13th-century priory, located on the outskirts of Mane, is today home to lovely gardens and a **museum** (☎04 92 75 70 50; www. musee-de-salagon.com; adult/child €8/6; ⊙10am-7pm May-Sep, to 6pm Oct–mid-Dec & Feb-Apr; ♿). This is ethno-botany at its most poetic and sensual: wander through recreated medieval herb gardens, fragrant with native lavender, mints and mugworts. Inside

251

DETOUR:
THE LUBERON

Start: ⑧ Prieuré de Salagon

The Luberon's other, southern, half is equally florally blessed. Lavender carpets the **Plateau de Claparèdes** between **Buoux** (west), **Sivergues** (south), **Auribeau** (east) and **Saignon** (north). Cycle, walk or motor through the lavender fields and along the northern slopes of **Mourre Nègre** (1125m) – the Luberon's highest point, accessible from Auribeau. The D113 climbs to idyllic lavender distillery **Les Agnels** (📱04 90 04 77 00; www.lesagnels.com; rte de Buoux, btwn Buoux & Apt; adult/child €6/free; ⊘10am-1pm & 3-6pm Tue, Wed, Fri & Sat Jun, 10am-1pm & 2-7pm Jul & Aug, 10am-1pm & 3-6pm Sep & Oct), which distils lavender, cypress and rosemary. The small on-site spa has a lavender-scented swimming pool. Stay at **L'Auberge du Presbytère** (📱04 32 52 15 28; www. laubergedupresbytere.com/en; place de la Fontaine; d €95-140, q €165-200; 🅿@🛜🏊) in tiny Saignon, which perches on high rocky flanks, its narrow streets crowning a hill ringed with craggy scrub and petite lavender plots, with incredible vistas across the Luberon to Mont Ventoux.

the medieval walls, the museum's permanent and temporary exhibitions provide a fascinating insight into rural life in Haute-Provence.

The walled town of **Mane** is lovely for strolling. The **Pont Roman de Mane** is also worth a look. This triple-arched stone bridge over the trickling Laye dates from the 12th or 13th century and makes a fine spot for a picnic. Head 800m south of Mane to the Hôtel Mas du Pont Roman, then turn right and look for the tiny lane just after passing the hotel.

The Drive » Get on the D13, then follow the signs to the D5 for the forest-lined drive to Manosque (roughly 30 minutes in total).

---

⑨ Manosque

Manosque has two lovely fountains and a historic cobblestoned core, but the traffic and suburban nothingness make visiting a nuisance. Why swing by? Just southeast is the home of **L'Occitane** (📱04 92 70 32 08; http:// fr.loccitane.com; chemin St-Maurice; ⊘10am-7pm Mon-Sat year-round, 10am-6pm Sun Apr-Oct), the company

that turned traditional lavender-, almond- and olive oil–based Provençal skincare into a global phenomenon. Factory tours can be booked online; the shop offers a flat 10% discount and there's also a small Mediterranean garden to peruse.

The Drive » Leave the freeways and ring roads behind and cross the Durance River towards the quieter D6. You'll pass farmland and lavender fields on the 20-minute drive to the town of Valensole.

---

⑩ Plateau de Valensole

Things get very relaxed once you hit the D6, and the road begins a gentle climb. Picnic provisions packed, wind down your windows. This dreamily quiet plateau has Provence's greatest concentration of lavender farms. Once you reach Valensole village make your way to **MEA Provence** (📱07 82 67 92 73; http://lavande-valensole. com; rte de Gréoux). Here you'll find lavender fields, an aromatic garden and a few exhibition panels about the history of lavender growing on the Valensole plateau. At the shop, you can browse essential oils, soaps, skincare products, dried bouquets, honey, candy, ice cream and other lavender-tinged products.

Eating & Sleeping

St-Saturnin-lès-Apt ❸

✗ La Coquillade   French €€€

(📞04 90 74 71 71; www.coquillade.fr; Le
Perrotet; meals €25-95; ⊗ noon-3pm & 7.30-
10pm mid-Apr–mid-Oct) Overnighting at this
luxurious hilltop estate won't suit everyone's
budget, but three excellent restaurants make a
fine destination for culinary-minded travellers.
It offers fine dining on innovative small plates at
La Coquillade, a more casual Italian-style bistro
(with a wood-burning oven) called Il Ristorante,
and a lovely outdoor terrace restaurant
featuring garden-to-table Provençal cuisine at
Les Vignes et Son Jardin.

🛏 Le Mas Perréal   B&B €€

(📞04 90 75 46 31; www.masperreal.com;
Quartier la Fortune; d €140, studios €150;
🛜🌊) Surrounded by vineyards, lavender
fields and cherry orchards, on a vast 7-hectare
property outside St-Saturnin-lès-Apt, this
farmhouse B&B offers a choice of cosy rooms
or self-catering studios, both filled with country
antiques and Provençal fabrics. There's a
heavenly pool and big garden with mountain
views. It's 2km southwest of town along the D2.

Mont Ventoux ❺

🛏 Le Domaine des Tilleuls   Hotel €€

(📞04 90 65 22 31; www.hotel-
domainedestilleuls.com; rte de Mont Ventoux; s
or d €90-114, tr €116-130, q €136; 🅿❄🛜🌊) A
favourite stop-off for cyclists and hikers heading
for Mont Ventoux' summit, this fine country
hotel makes a perfect base in Malaucène. Once
a silk farm, it's been totally overhauled into a
spacious, friendly hotel, with beamed rooms in
the main building, and pastel-tinted ones in an
annexe. Outside there are pretty grounds and a
pool shaded by lime trees.

Forcalquier ❼

✗ Aux Deux Anges   Bistro €€

(📞04 92 75 04 36; 3 place St-Michel; menus
from €20; ⊗ noon-1.30pm Wed-Sun, 7-10.30pm
Wed-Mon) Beside a fountain in Forcalquier's
old town, this homespun place is as traditional
as it gets. All the dishes are made to timeworn
recipes *comme à la maison* (like you'd have
at home) – hearty stews, slow-cooked lamb,
roast chicken and the like, simply served with
vegetables. Far from fancy, but flavoursome –
and the junk shop interior is fun.

🛏 Relais d'Elle   B&B €

(📞06 75 42 33 72; www.relaisdelle.com;
rte de la Brillane, Niozelles; s/d/q/apt from
€70/80/100/135; 🅿🛜🌊) For peace and
tranquillity, you can't really quibble with this
cosy, ivy-covered farmhouse, surrounded by
lovely gardens and a cracking pool. The rooms
err towards the traditional rather than the
fashionable, with old furniture and rather dated
decor – but the gorgeous grounds and friendly
owners make up for what the house lacks in
luxury. *Table d'hôte* dinners are available by
reservation, and are served in the garden in
summer.

🛏 Couvent des Minimes   Hotel €€€

(📞04 92 74 77 77; www.couventdesminimes-
hotelspa.com; chemin des Jeux de Maï, Mane;
r from €315; ❄🛜🌊) This medieval convent
has been turned into one of Provence's most
indulgent country retreats courtesy of the
luxury Occitane brand. It's a no-expense-
spared affair: luminous rooms incorporating
the building's ecclesiastical architecture, a
wonderful spa and pool, a belt-buster Michelin-
starred restaurant, **Le Cloître** (menus
from €95) and a more affordable bistro, **Le
Pesquier** (menus €38 to €48). It's in Mane,
3.5km south of Forcalquier on the D4100.
Off-season deals sometimes reduce the hefty
price-tag.

Classic Trip

Riviera Crossing

23

French road trips just don't get more glamorous than this: cinematic views, searing sunshine, art history aplenty and the Med around every turn.

TRIP HIGHLIGHTS

4 DAYS
110KM / 68 MILES

GREAT FOR...

110 km
Èze
End with a sundowner in a dreamy hilltop village

62 km
La Grande Corniche
Cruise the Côte d'Azur's most famous road

FINISH
Menton

Roquebrune-Cap-Martin
Monaco

Nice
Delve into busy markets and an atmospheric old town
48 km

St-Paul de Vence
Paint your own pictures in this hilltop artists' hideaway
28 km

Antibes
Juan-les-Pins

START

Cannes
Cinematic heritage and cinematic views to match
0 km

BEST TIME TO GO

Anytime, but avoid July and August's crowds.

 ESSENTIAL PHOTO

Standing by Augustus' monumental Trophée des Alpes, with Monaco and the Mediterranean far below.

BEST FOR GLAMOUR

Strolling La Croisette in Cannes and fulfilling your film-star fantasies.

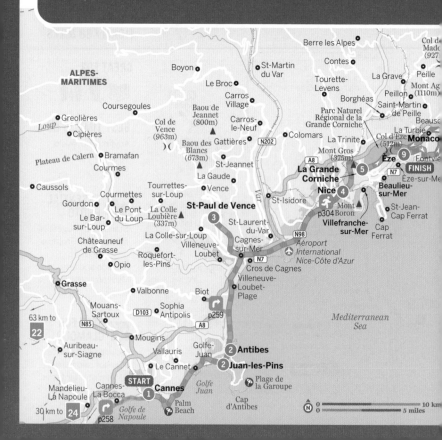

Classic Trip

23 Riviera Crossing

Cruising the Côte d'Azur is as dazzling and chic as road trips get. From film town Cannes to sassy Nice via the corkscrew turns of the Corniches and into millionaire's Monaco, it's a drive you'll remember forever. Filmmakers, writers, celebs and artists have all had their hearts stolen by this glittering stretch of coastline: by the end of this trip, you'll understand why.

Berre les Alpes

ALPES-
MARITIMES

Boyon

St-Martin
du Var

Contes

Col de
Mado
(927

La Grave

Peille

Le Broc

Carros
Village

Tourette-
Levens

Mont Ag
(1110m)

Peillon

Courseg oules

Baou de
Jeannet
(800m)

Carros-
le-Neuf

Borghéas

Saint-Martin-
de Peille

Beausc

Greolières

Col de
Vence
(963m)

Gattières

N202

Colomars

Parc Naturel
Régional de la
Grande Corniche

La Turbie
Col d'Èze
(512m)

Monaco

Cipières

Loup

Plateau de Calern

Bramafan

Baou des
Blancs
(673m)

St-Jeannet

La Trinite

Mont Gros
(375m)

Èze

Fontvie

FINISH

Èze-sur-Me

Courmes

Tourrettes-
sur-Loup

La Gaude

A8

La Grande
Corniche

N7

Caussols

Courmettes

Vence

Beaulieu-
sur-Mer

Gourdon

Le Pont
du Loup

La Colle
Loubière
(337m)

St-Paul de Vence

St-Isidore

Nice

Var

Mont
Boron

St-Jean-
Cap Ferrat

Le Bar-
sur-Loup

p304

Villefranche-
sur-Mer

Châteauneuf
de Grasse

La Colle-sur-Loup

St-Laurent-
du-Var

Cap
Ferrat

Opio

Roquefort-
les-Pins

Villeneuve-
Loubet

Cagnes-
sur-Mer

N98

Grasse

Valbonne

Biot

Cros de Cagnes

Aéroport
International
Nice-Côte d'Azur

N7

Mouans-
Sartoux

D103

Sophia
Antipolis

Villeneuve-
Loubet-
Plage

Mediterranean
Sea

63 km to
22

N85

A8

p259

Auribeau-
sur-Siagne

Mougins

Vallauris

Golfe-
Juan

Antibes

Le Cannet

Juan-les-Pins

Plage de
la Garoupe

Mandelieu-
La Napoule

Cannes-
La Bocca

START

Cannes

Golfe
Juan

30 km to
24

p258

Golfe de
Napoule

Palm
Beach

Cap
d'Antibes

N 0
0

10 km

5 miles

TRIP HIGHLIGHT

❶ Cannes

What glitzier opening could there be to this Côte d'Azur cruise than Cannes, as cinematic as its reputation suggests. Come July during the film festival, the world's stars descend on **boulevard de la Croisette** (aka La Croisette) to stroll beneath the palms, plug their latest opus and hobnob with the media and movie moguls. Getting your picture snapped outside the

Palais des Festivals (Festival & Congress Palace; www.palaisdesfestivals.com; 1 bd de la Croisette; guided tour adult/child €6/free) is a must-do, as is a night-time stroll along the boulevard, illuminated by coloured lights.

Outside festival time, Cannes still feels irresistibly ritzy. Private beaches and grand hotels line the seafront; further west lies old Cannes. Follow rue St-Antoine and snake your way up **Le Suquet**, Cannes' atmospheric original village. Pick up the region's best produce at **Marché Forville** (www.marcheforville.com; 11 rue du Marché Forville; ⏲7.30am-1pm Tue-Fri, to 2pm Sat & Sun), a couple of blocks back from the port.

Need nature? Then head to the **Îles de Lérins**, two islands located a 20-minute boat ride away. Tiny and traffic-free, they're perfect for walks or a picnic. Boats for the islands leave from quai des Îles, on the western side of the harbour.

 p264

The Drive » The most scenic route to Antibes is via the coastal D6007. Bear right onto av Frères Roustan before Golfe Juan. With luck and no traffic jams, you should hit Juan-les-Pins in 30 minutes or so.

---

❷ Antibes & Juan-les-Pins

A century or so ago, Antibes and Juan-les-Pins were a refuge for artists, writers, aristocrats and hedonistic expats looking to escape the horrors of post-WWI Europe. They came in their droves – F Scott Fitzgerald wrote several books here, and Picasso rented a miniature castle (it's now a museum dedicated to him).

First stop is the beach resort of **Juan-les-Pins**. It's a long way from the fashionable resort of Fitzgerald's day, but the beaches are still good for sun-lounging (even if you do have to pay).

Then it's on around the peninsula of **Cap d'Antibes**, where many

Castellar
-Agnès
Roverino
LIGURIA
Ventimiglia
bio Garavan   Mortola
uebrune ❼ **Menton**
Carnolès
❻ **Roquebrune-**
Cap **Cap-Martin**
Martin
e d'Azur

LINK YOUR TRIP

22 **Lavender Route**
After the coast, head into the lavender-filled hills of Haute-Provence.

24 **Vars Delights**
Mediterranean coast and Provençal countryside: a natural extension west.

DETOUR:
CORNICHE DE L'ESTEREL

Start: ❶ Cannes

West of Cannes, the winding coast road known as the **Corniche de l'Estérel** (sometimes known as the Corniche d'Or, the Golden Road) is well worth a side trip if you can spare the time. Opened in 1903 by the Touring Club de France, this twisting coast road is as much about driving pleasure as getting from A to B; it runs for 30 unforgettable coastal kilometres all the way to St-Raphael. En route you'll pass seaside villages, secluded coves (sandy, pebbled, nudist, you name it) and the rocky red hills of the Massif de l'Estérel, dotted with gnarly oaks, juniper and wild thyme. Wherever you go, the blue Mediterranean shimmers alongside, tempting you to stop for just one more swim. It's too much to resist.

of the greats had their holiday villas: the Hotel Cap du Eden Roc was one of their favourite fashionable haunts. Round the peninsula is pretty **Antibes**, with a harbour full of pleasure boats and an old town ringed by medieval ramparts. Aim to arrive before lunchtime, when the atmospheric **Marché Provençal** (cours Masséna; ⏰7.30am-1pm Tue-Sun Sep-Jun, daily Jul & Aug) will still be in full swing, and then browse the nearby **Musée Picasso** (☎04 92 90 54 26; www.antibes-juanlespins.com/culture/musee-picasso; Château Grimaldi, 4 rue des Cordiers; adult/concession €8/6; ⏰10am-6pm Tue-Sun mid-Jun–mid-Sep, 10am-1pm & 2-6pm Tue-Sun rest of year) to see a few of the artist's Antibes-themed works.

🛏 p264

**The Drive ›› ** Brave the traffic on the D6007 and avoid signs to turn onto the A8 motorway: it's the D2 you want, so follow signs for Villeneuve-Loubet. When you reach the town, cross the river. You'll pass through a tunnel into the outskirts of Cagnes-sur-Mer; now start following signs to St-Paul de Vence.

TRIP HIGHLIGHT

❸ St-Paul de Vence

Once upon a time, hilltop St-Paul de Vence was just another village like countless others in Provence. But then the artists moved in: painters such as Marc Chagall and Pablo Picasso sought solitude here, painted the local scenery and traded canvases for room and board. This is how the hotel **La Colombe d'Or** (☎04 93 32 80 02; www.

la-colombe-dor.com; place de Gaulle; d €225-480; ❋ 🛜 🅿) came by its stellar art collection.

It's now one of the Riviera's most exclusive locations, a haven for artists, film stars and celebrities, not to mention hordes of sightseers, many of whom are here to marvel at the incredible art collection at the **Fondation Maeght** (☎04 93 32 81 63; www.fondation-maeght.com; 623 chemin des Gardettes; adult/child €16/11; ⏰10am-7pm Jul-Sep, to 6pm Oct-Jun). Created in 1964 by collectors Aimé and Merguerite Maeght, it boasts works by all the big 20th-century names – including Miró sculptures, Chagall mosaics, Braque windows and canvases by Picasso, Matisse and others.

While you're here, it's worth taking a detour northwards to Vence, where the marvellous **Chapelle du Rosaire** (Rosary Chapel; ☎04 93 58 03 26; http://chapellematisse.fr; 466 av Henri Matisse; adult/child €7/4; ⏰10am-noon & 2-6pm Tue, Thu & Fri, 2-6pm Wed & Sat Apr-Oct, to 5pm Nov-Mar) was designed by an ailing Henri Matisse. He had a hand in everything here, from the stained-glass windows to the altar and candlesticks.

**The Drive ›› ** Return the way you came, only this time follow the blue signs onto the A8 motorway to Nice. Take exit 50 for Promenade des Anglais, which will take you all 18km along the Baie des Anges. The views are great, but you'll hit nightmare traffic at rush hour.

TRIP HIGHLIGHT

④ Nice

With its mix of real-city grit, old-world opulence and year-round sunshine, Nice is the undisputed capital of the Côte d'Azur. Sure, the traffic is horrendous and the beach is made entirely of pebbles (not a patch of sand in sight!), but that doesn't detract from its charms. It's a great base, with loads of hotels and restaurants, and character in every nook and cranny.

Start with a morning stroll through the huge food and flower markets on **cours Saleya** (cours Saleya; ☉6am-5.30pm Tue-Sat, 6.30am-1.30pm Sun), then delve into the winding alleyways of the old town, **Vieux Nice**, where there are many backstreet restaurants at which you can try local specialities such as *pissaladière* (onion tart topped with olives and anchovies) and *socca* (chickpea-flour pancake). Stop for an ice cream at famous Fenocchio (p264) – flavours include tomato, lavender, olive and fig – then spend the afternoon sunbathing on the beaches along the seafront **Promenade des Anglais** (🚌8, 52, 62) before catching an epic sunset.

If you have the time, the city has some great museums too – you'll need at least an afternoon to explore all of the modern masterpieces at the **Musée d'Art Moderne et d'Art Contemporain** (MAMAC; ☎04 97 13 42 01; www.mamac-nice.org; place Yves Klein; museum pass 24hr/7 days €10/20; ☉10am-6pm Tue-Sun late Jun–mid-Oct, from 11am rest of year; 🚊1 to Garibaldi).

🍴 🛏 p264, p409

The Drive » Exit the city through Riquier on the D2564. You don't want the motorway – you want bd Bischoffsheim, which becomes bd de l'Observatoire as it climbs to the summit of Mont Gros. The next 12km are thrilling, twisting past the Parc Naturel Régional de la Grande Corniche. Stop for a picnic or a hilly hike, then continue towards La Turbie.

TRIP HIGHLIGHT

⑤ La Grande Corniche

Remember that sexy scene from Hitchcock's *To Catch a Thief,* when Grace Kelly and Cary Grant cruised the hills in a convertible, enjoying sparkling banter and searing blue Mediterranean views? Well you're about to tackle the very same drive – so don your shades, roll down the windows and hit the asphalt.

It's a roller coaster of a road, veering through hairpins and switchbacks

DETOUR: BIOT

Start: ② Antibes & Juan-les-Pins

About an 8km drive from Antibes along the coast road and the D4, this 15th-century hilltop village was once an important pottery-manufacturing centre. The advent of metal containers brought an end to this, but Biot is still active in handicraft production, especially glassmaking. At the foot of the village, the **Verrerie de Biot** (☎04 93 65 03 00; www.verreriebiot. com; chemin des Combes; guided tour adult/child €6/3, museum adult/child €3/1.50; ☉10am-8pm Mon-Sat, 10.30am-1.30pm & 2.30-7.30pm Sun May-Sep, to 6pm Oct-Apr) produces bubbled glass by rolling molten glass into baking soda; bubbles from the chemical reaction are then trapped by a second layer of glass. You can watch skilled glass-blowers at work and browse the adjacent art galleries and shop. There are also guided tours (€6), during which you get the chance to try your hand at a spot of glass-blowing – and learn why it's probably best left to the professionals.

Classic Trip

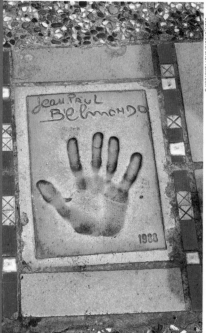

WHY THIS IS A CLASSIC TRIP
CELESTE BRASH, WRITER

With light that inspired Picasso and Matisse, history you can feel in your soul and a view over the Mediterranean at every hairpin turn, this drive takes in every dreamy hue of the Côte d'Azur. Each kilometre is special, from the glamour of Cannes and perfumeries of Grasse to the brassiness of Nice, audaciousness of Monaco and all the hilltop villages between.

Above: Menton
Left: Boulevard de la Croisette, Cannes
Right: Èze

OLENA Z/SHUTTERSTOCK ©

as it heads into the hills above Nice. There are countless picnic spots and photo opportunities along the way, including the **Col d'Èze**, the road's highest point at 512m. Further on you'll pass the monumental Roman landmark known as the **Trophée des Alpes** (☎04 93 41 20 84; www.trophee-auguste.fr; 18 av Albert 1er; adult/child €6/free; ☉9.30am-1pm & 2.30-6.30pm Tue-Sun mid-May–mid-Sep, 10am-1.30pm & 2.30-5pm rest of year), a magnificent triumphal arch built to commemorate Augustus' victory over the last remaining Celtic-Ligurian tribes who had resisted conquest. The views from here are jaw-dropping, stretching all the way to Monaco and Italy beyond.

The Drive » Monte Carlo may sparkle and beckon below, but keep your eyes on the road; the principality will keep for another day. Stay on the D2564 to skirt Monaco for another amazing 10km, then turn right into the D52 to Roquebrune.

- - - - - - - - - - - - - - - - - -

⑥ Roquebrune-Cap-Martin

This village of two halves feels a world away from the glitz of nearby Monaco: the coastline around **Cap Martin** remains relatively unspoilt, as if Roquebrune had left its clock on medieval time. The historic half of the town, Roquebrune itself, sits 300m high on

PERFUME IN GRASSE

Up in the hills to the north of Cannes, the town of Grasse has been synonymous with perfumery since the 16th century, and the town is still home to around 30 makers – several of whom offer guided tours of their factories, and the chance to hone your olfactory skills.

It can take up to 10 years to train a *perfumier*, but since you probably don't have that much time to spare, you'll have to make do with a crash course. Renowned maker **Molinard** (MIP; 🖉 04 92 42 33 21; www.molinard.com; 60 bd Victor Hugo; 20min/1hr/2hr workshops €30/69/199; ⏱9.30am-6.30pm) runs workshops where sessions range from 30 minutes to two hours, during which you get to create your own custom perfume (sandalwood, vanilla, hyacinth, lily of the valley, civet, hare and rose petals are just a few of the potential notes you could include). At the end of the workshop, you'll receive a bottle of *eau de parfum* to take home. **Galimard** (🖉 04 93 09 20 00; www.galimard.com; 73 rte de Cannes; workshops from €55; ⏱9am-12.30pm & 2-6pm) and **Fragonard's Usine Historique** (🖉 04 93 36 44 65; www.fragonard.com/fr/usines/musee-du-parfum; 20 bd Fragonard; ⏱9am-6pm) offer similar workshops.

For background, make time to visit the excellent **Musée International de la Parfumerie** (MIP; 🖉 04 97 05 58 11; www.museesdegrasse.com; 2 bd du Jeu de Ballon; adult/child €4/free, combo ticket incl Les Jardins du MIP €6/free; ⏱10am-7pm May-Sep, to 5.30pm Oct-Apr; 🚻) and its nearby **gardens** (🖉 04 92 98 62 69; www.museesdegrasse.com; 979 chemin des Gourettes, Mouans-Sartoux; adult/child €4/free, combo ticket incl MIP €6/free; ⏱10am-7pm May-Aug, to 5.30pm Apr & Sep-Nov, closed Dec-Mar), where you can see some of the many plants and flowers used in scent-making. Needless to say, the bouquet is overpowering.

a pudding-shaped lump. It towers over the Cap, but they are, in fact, linked by innumerable, very steep steps.

The village is delightful and free of tack, and there are sensational views of the coast from the main village square, **place des Deux Frères**. Of all Roquebrune's steep streets, **rue Moncollet** – with its arcaded passages and stairways carved out of rock – is the most impressive. Scurry upwards to find architect Le Corbusier's grave at the cemetery at the top of the village (in section J, and yes, he did design his own tombstone).

The Drive » Continue along the D52 towards the coast, following promenade du Cap-Martin all the way along the seafront to Menton. You'll be there in 10 minutes, traffic permitting.

- - - - - - - - - - - - - - - - - - - -

7 Menton

Last stop on the coast before Italy, the beautiful seaside town of Menton offers a glimpse of what the Riviera once looked like, before the high-rises, casinos and property developers moved in. It's ripe for wandering, with peaceful gardens and Belle Époque mansions galore, as well as an attractive yacht-filled

harbour. Meander the historic quarter all the way to the **Cimetière du Vieux Château** (montée du Souvenir; ⏱7am-8pm Apr-Oct, 8am-5pm Nov-Mar) for the best views in town.

Menton's miniature microclimate enables exotic plants to flourish here, many of which you can see at the **Jardin Botanique Exotique du Val Rahmeh** (🖉 04 93 35 86 72; www.mnhn.fr/fr/visitez/lieux/jardin-botanique-exotique-menton; av St-Jacques; adult/child €7/5; ⏱9.30am-12.30pm & 2-6pm Wed-Mon Apr-Sep, 10am-12.30pm & 2-5pm Wed-Mon Oct-Mar), where terraces overflow with fruit trees, and the beautiful, once-abandoned **Jardin de la Serre de la Madone** (☏04 93 57 73 90; www.serredelamadone.com; 74 rte de Gorbio; adult/child €8/4; ⌚10am-6pm Tue-Sun Apr-Oct, to 5pm Jan-Mar, closed Nov & Dec), overgrown with rare plants. Spend your second night in town.

 p265

The Drive » Leave Menton on the D6007, the Moyenne Corniche, skirting the upper perimeter of Monaco. When you're ready, turn off into Monaco. All the car parks charge the same rate. Good options include the Chemin des Pêcheurs and Stade Louis II for old Monaco, or the huge underground Casino car park by allées des Boulingrins for central Monte Carlo.

---

⑧ Monaco

This pint-sized principality (covering barely 200 hectares) is ridiculous, absurd, ostentatious and fabulous all at once. A playground of the super-rich, with super-egos to match, it's the epitome of Riviera excess – especially at the famous **Casino de Monte Carlo** (☏98 06 21 21; www.casinomontecarlo.com; place du Casino; morning visit incl audio guide adult/child Oct-Apr €17/8, May-Sep €17/12, salons ordinaires gaming €17; ⌚visits 9am-1pm, gaming 2pm-late), where cards turn, roulette wheels spin and eye-watering sums are won and lost.

For all its glam, Monaco is not all show. Up in the hilltop quarter of **Le Rocher**, shady streets surround the **Palais Princier de Monaco** (☏93 25 18 31; www.palais.mc; place du Palais; adult/child €10/5, incl Collection de Voitures Anciennes car museum €8/4, incl Musée Océanographique €16/10; ⌚10am-6pm Apr-Jun & Sep–mid-Oct, to 7pm Jul & Aug), the wedding-cake castle of Monaco's royal family (time your visit for the pomptastic changing of the guard at 11.55am).

Nearby is the impressive **Musée Océanographique de Monaco** (☏93 15 36 00; www.oceano.mc; av St-Martin; adult/child high season €16/10; ⌚9.30am-8pm Jul & Aug, 10am-7pm Apr-Jun & Sep, to 6pm Oct-Mar), stocked with all kinds of deep-sea denizens. It even has a 6m-deep lagoon complete with circling sharks.

Round things off with a stroll around the cliffside **Jardin Exotique** (☏93 15 29 80; www.jardin-exotique.mc; 62 bd du Jardin Exotique; adult/child €8/4; ⌚9am-7pm mid-May–mid-Sep, to 6pm rest of year) and the obligatory photo of Monaco's harbour, bristling with over-the-top yachts.

The Drive » Pick up where you left off on the Moyenne Corniche (D6007), and follow its circuitous route back up into the hills all the way to Èze.

TRIP HIGHLIGHT

⑨ Èze

This rocky little village perched on an impossible peak is outrageously romantic. The main attraction is technically the medieval village, with small higgledy-piggledy stone houses and winding lanes (and, yes, galleries and shops). It's undoubtedly delightful, but it's the ever-present views of the coast that are truly mesmerising. They just get more spectacular from the **Jardin Exotique d'Èze** (☏04 93 41 10 30; www.jardinexotique-eze.fr; rue du Château; adult/child €6/3.50; ⌚9am-7.30pm Jul-Sep, to 6.30pm Apr-Jun & Oct, to 4.30pm Nov-Mar), a surreal cactus garden at the top of the village, so steep and rocky it may have been purpose-built for mountain goats. It's also where you'll find the old castle ruins; take time to sit, draw a deep breath and gaze, as few places on earth offer such a panorama.

Èze gets very crowded between 10am and 5pm; if you prefer a quiet wander, plan to be here early in the morning or before dinner. Or even better, treat yourself to a night and supper at the swish Château Eza (p265), a fitting finish to this most memorable of road trips.

 p265

263

Eating & Sleeping

Cannes ❶

✕ Bobo Bistro   Mediterranean €€€

(☏04 93 99 97 33; www.facebook.com/
BoboBistroCannes; 21 rue du Commandant
André; pizzas €15-18, mains €18-32; ☺noon-
3pm & 7-11pm Mon-Sat) Predictably, it's a
'bobo' (bourgeois bohemian) crowd that
gathers at this achingly cool bistro in Cannes'
fashionable Carré d'Or. Decor is stylishly retro,
with attention-grabbing objets d'art including a
tableau of dozens of spindles of coloured yarn.
Cuisine is local, seasonal and invariably organic:
including artichoke salad, dorado ceviche with
avocado, or rotisserie chicken with mash *fait
masion* (homemade).

⊨ Hôtel Le Mistral   Boutique Hotel €€

(☏04 93 39 91 46; www.mistral-hotel.com; 13 rue
des Belges; d €118-168; ❋ 🛜) For super-pricey
Cannes, this little three-star offers amazing
value. The 10 rooms are small but decked out in
flattering red and plum tones – Privilege rooms
have quite a bit more space, plus a fold-out sofa
bed. There are sea views from two rooms on
the 4th floor, and the hotel is just 50m from La
Croisette. There's no lift, though.

⊨ Villa Garbo   Boutique Hotel €€€

(☏04 93 46 66 00; www.villagarbo-cannes.
com; 62 bd d'Alsace; d €220-800; ❋ @ 🛜) For
a taste of Cannes' celeb lifestyle, this indulgent
stunner is hard to beat. Rooms are more like
apartments, offering copious space, plus
kitchenettes, king-size beds, sofas and more.
The style is designer chic – acid tones of puce,
orange and lime contrasted with blacks and
greys, supplemented by quirky sculptures and
objets d'art. Unusually, rates include breakfast.

Antibes ❷

⊨ Hôtel La Jabotte   B&B €€

(☏04 93 61 45 89; www.jabotte.com; 13 av Max
Maurey; d €87-130, ste €254; ❋ @ 🛜) Just
150m inland from Plage de la Salis and 2km
south of the old town towards Cap d'Antibes,
this pretty little hideaway makes a cosy base.
Hot pinks, sunny yellows and soothing mauves

dominate the homey, feminine decor, and
there's a sweet patio where breakfast is served
on sunny days. There's a minimum stay of three
nights in summer.

Nice ❹

✕ Fenocchio   Ice Cream €

(☏04 93 80 72 52; www.fenocchio.fr; 2 place
Rossetti; 1/2 scoops €3/5; ☺9am-midnight
Mar-Nov) There's no shortage of ice-cream
sellers in the old town, but this *maître glacier*
(master ice-cream maker) has been king of
the scoops since 1966. The array of flavours is
mind-boggling – cactus, cinnamon, fig, lavender
and rosé to name a few. Dither too long over the
98-plus flavours and you'll never make it to the
front of the queue.

✕ Le Bistrot d'Antoine   French €€

(☏04 93 85 29 57; 27 rue de la Préfecture; mains
€17-32; ☺9am-1.45pm & 7-10pm Tue-Sat) A
quintessential French bistro, right down to
the checked tablecloths, streetside tables
and impeccable service – not to mention the
handwritten blackboard, loaded with classic
dishes such as rabbit pâté, pot-cooked pork,
blood sausage and duck breast. If you've never
eaten classic French food, this is definitely the
place to start; no matter what, you're in for a
treat.

⊨ Hôtel Le G   Hotel €€

(☏04 93 56 84 79; www.le-g-chineurs.
com; 1 rue Cassini; r €121-297; ❋ 🛜; 🚇1 to
Garibaldi) Location, location, location! Nice's
best nightlife is right outside your door at this
renovated corner hotel off place Garibaldi, bang
in the heart of the lively Petit Marais district.
Bedrooms look sleek in cool greys, crimsons
and charcoals; bathrooms are modern and
well-appointed. Breakfast is served in the
ground-floor cafe, brimful of vintage bric-a-brac
and mismatched furniture.

⊨ Hôtel Windsor   Boutique Hotel €€

(☏04 93 88 59 35; www.hotelwindsornice.
com; 11 rue Dalpozzo; d €137-225; ❋ @ 🛜 🏊;
🚌7, 9, 22, 27, 59, 70 to Grimaldi or Rivoli) Don't
be fooled by the staid stone exterior: inside,

owner Odile Redolfi has enlisted the collective creativity of several well-known artists to make each of the 57 rooms uniquely appealing. Some are frescoed and others are adorned with experimental chandeliers or photographic murals. The garden and pool out the back are delightful, as are the small bar and attached restaurant.

Menton ❼

✘ Au Baiser du Mitron   Bakery €

(The Baker's Kiss; ☎04 93 57 67 82; www.aubaiserdumitron.com; 8 rue Piéta; items from €1; ⏱7.30am-1pm Wed-Sun) This one-of-a-kind *boulangerie* showcases breads from the Côte d'Azur, inland Provence and other favourite spots from baker-owner Kevin Le Meur's world travels. Everything is baked in a traditional *four à bois* (wood bread oven) from 1906, using 100% natural ingredients and no preservatives. The *tarte au citron de Menton* (Menton lemon tart) is the best there is.

🛏 Hôtel Napoléon   Boutique Hotel €€

(☎04 93 35 89 50; www.napoleon-menton.com; 29 porte de France; d €170-340, junior ste €298-462; ❄ @ 🛜 ☒) Standing tall on the seafront, the Napoléon is Menton's most stylish sleeping option. Everything from the pool to the restaurant-bar and the back garden (a haven of freshness in summer) has been beautifully designed. Rooms are decked out in white and blue, with Cocteau drawings on headboards. Sea-facing rooms have balconies but are a little noisier because of the traffic.

Èze ❾

🛏 Château Eza   Luxury Hotel €€€

(☎04 93 41 12 24; www.chateaueza.com; rue de la Pise; d €215-580; ❄ 🛜) If you're looking for a place to propose, well, there can be few more memorable settings than this wonderful clifftop hotel, perched dramatically above the glittering blue Mediterranean. There are only 14 rooms, so it feels intimate, but the service is impeccable, and the regal decor (gilded mirrors, sumptuous fabrics, antiques) explains the sky-high price tag.

Var Delights

Varied is the Var: on this drive you'll encounter bleached cliffs, tropical gardens, idyllic islands, pristine forests, secret beaches and a few gorges for good measure.

24

TRIP HIGHLIGHTS

128 km

St-Tropez
Watch old men play *pétanque* near place des Lices

FINISH

Moustiers-Ste-Marie

95 km

Bormes-les-Mimosas
Wander the streets of this atmospheric village

St-Raphaël

START
● Marseille

② ⑦

Bandol

⑤

Sanary-sur-Mer

Domaine du Rayol

The Calanques
Explore this wild and spectacular protected area near Marseille

9 km

5 DAYS
310KM / 192 MILES

GREAT FOR...

BEST TIME TO GO
Early spring and late autumn to dodge summer traffic.

📷 ESSENTIAL PHOTO
Standing on the dazzling white cliffs above the Calanque d'En Vau.

✅ BEST FOR FAMILIES
Snorkelling in sapphire waters at the Domaine du Rayol.

The Calanques Calanque d'En Vau

24 Var Delights

This is the other side of the Côte d'Azur: snazzy in spots, stark and wild in others, taking in everything from seaside towns to hilltop villages and big, busy cities. While parts of the coast have been heavily developed, finding solitude is still possible – you can hike to deserted coves in the Calanques, explore the forested trails of the Massif des Maures or get lost in the wild hills of the Var.

1 Marseille

Long dismissed as the Riviera's troublesome cousin – crime-ridden, industrial, downright dirty – Marseille has enjoyed a long-overdue renaissance since its stint as European Capital of Culture in 2013. Though it retains its grittier, rough-and-ready feel compared to the coast's more genteel towns, it also has character in abundance.

Take a stroll around the **Vieux Port**, then swing by the city's

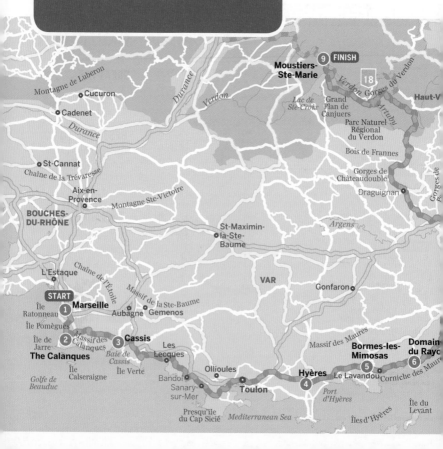

spangly Mediterranean-themed museum, **Musée des Civilisations de l'Europe et de la Méditerranée** (MuCEM, Museum of European & Mediterranean Civilisations; ☎04 84 35 13 13; www.mucem.org; 7 promenade Robert Laffont; adult/child incl exhibitions €11/free; ◷11am-6pm Nov-Apr, to 7pm May, Jun & Oct, 10am-8pm Jul-Sep, closed Tue year-round; ♿), which helped kick-start the city's revival in 2013. It's attached to the formidable **Fort St-Jean**, which once protected the city's harbour from attack. Afterwards, head

uphill to the city's oldest quarter, **Le Panier** (from the French for basket), which is criss-crossed by graffiti-clad alleyways and full of quirky shops and neighbourhood cafes. Reward yourself with a black vanilla ice cream from **Vanille Noire** (☎07 77 33 68 19; www.vanillenoire.com; 13 rue Caisserie; ice cream €3-6; ◷12.30-7pm Apr-Oct, to 10.30pm Fri & Sat Jun–mid-Jul & Sep, to 10.30pm daily mid-Jul–Aug), then head off for dinner at one of the city's excellent bistros around rue Sainte.

 ⊨ p274

The Drive » To get to the Calanques, follow av du Prado south from the Vieux Port; it winds up into the hills and becomes the D559, the main road through the national park. There are loads of places to stop, but you'll have to do some walking to see any coves. It gets hot in summer, so set out early.

- - - - - - - - - - - - - - - - - -

TRIP HIGHLIGHT

❷ The Calanques

East of Marseille, a range of bone-white, parched cliffs towers above glittering turquoise coves. Known as the **Calanques**

(☎04 20 10 50 00; www.calanques-parcnational.fr; 141 av du Prado, Bâtiment A, Marseille), these craggy inlets run for around 20km all the way to the seaside village of Cassis. They've been protected since 1975 and were designated as a national park in 2014. They're a favourite place for Marseillais to hike and picnic; Marseille's tourist office runs regular guided hikes, although trails are closed in July and August due to fire risk.

Of the many *calanques* along the coastline, the most accessible are **Calanque de Sormiou** and **Calanque de Morgiou**, while remote inlets such **Calanque d'En Vau** and **Calanque de Port-Miou** take dedication and time to reach – either on foot or by kayak. The roads into each *calanque* are usually closed to drivers, but a sneaky workaround is to make a booking at one of the cove restaurants: good options are **Le Château** (☎04 91 25 08 69; www.lechateausormiou.fr; 226 chemin de Sormiou; menu €28-50; ◷noon-2.30pm

ALPES-MARITIMES

○Grasse

Lac de St-Cassien

23 Cannes○

Golfe de Napoule

Massif de l'Estérel

Fréjus ○

St-Raphaël

Corniche de l'Estérel

○Les Issambres

-Maxime

Golfe de St-Tropez

Côte d'Azur

7

t-Tropez

Mediterranean Sea

▲ 0 ⎯⎯⎯⎯⎯⎯ 20 km
➲ 0 ⎯⎯⎯⎯ 10 miles

§ LINK YOUR TRIP

18 Foothills of the Alps
From Haute-Provence on into the wilds of the Vercors.

23 Riviera Crossing
Cut out the gorges and stick to the coast for Cannes.

& 7.30-9.30pm Apr-Sep) in Sormiou and **Nautic Bar** (📞04 91 40 06 37; Calanque de Morgiou; mains €20-32; 🕙noon-2.30pm & 7.30-9.30pm Tue-Sun Apr-Oct) in Morgiou.

The Drive » You'll see signs for Cassis not long after you drive out of the national park. Bandol is another 25km along the D559, and Sanary-sur-Mer is 8km further on.

---

③ Cassis, Bandol & Sanary-sur-Mer

East of Marseille, the coast road passes a handful of lovely seaside villages, all with their own reason for a stop, not least the area's excellent wines. First comes **Cassis**, nestled at the foot of a dramatic rocky outcrop crowned by a 14th-century château (now a pricey hotel). Still a working fishing port, its harbourside is crammed with seafood restaurants, perfect for a plate of grilled sardines or a copious shellfish platter. Neighbouring **Bandol** is well-known for its wines, too: stop in at the **Maison des Vins de Bandol** (📞04 94 90 29 59; www.vinsde bandol.com; 238 chemin de la Ferrage, Le Castellet; 🕙10am-1pm & 3-7pm Tue-Sat), where knowledgeable staff will happily give you a crash course on recommended wines, vineyards and vintages. Last comes seaside **Sanary-sur-Mer**, perhaps the prettiest and most

authentic of all: here you can still watch the fishermen unload their catch on the quayside, and pick up local produce at the lively **Wednesday market** (held 8am to 1pm).

🍴 🛏 p274

The Drive » There's no compelling reason to stop in Toulon, so skip it and zoom past on the motorway (A50, A57 and A570).

---

④ Hyères

The coastal town of Hyères is split in two: there's the attractive **old town**, centring on a medieval castle, and the T-shaped **peninsula**, home to a busy pleasure port and some fine sandy beaches (perfect for a day's leisurely swimming and sunbathing). In between are several lagoons that are great for birdwatchers. But the main reason to visit Hyères is (rather ironically) to leave: it's the main harbour for trips over to the idyllic **Îles d'Hyères**, a tiny archipelago of islands fringed by white sand and criss-crossed by nature trails. **Transport Littoral Varois** (📞04 94 58 21 81; www.tlv-tvm.com) runs ferries, including a two-island day trip (return €32) to Île de Port-Cros and Le Levant.

🍴 🛏 p274

The Drive » It's an easy 22km along the D98 to Bormes-les-Mimosas, although the climb up

MARINA VN / SHUTTERSTOCK ©

to the village can be trafficky in summer. There's a large free car park on place St-François off rte de Baguier, a short walk from the village centre.

TRIP HIGHLIGHT

⑤ Bormes-les-Mimosas

This 12th-century hilltop village is heralded for its horticultural splendour: dazzling yellow mimosas in winter, deep-fuchsia bougainvilleas in summer. Generally, though, it's just a lovely place to stop for a wander: a browse around the many art galleries, a spot of souvenir shopping in the

Bormes-les-Mimosas Hilltop village

smart boutiques, or a leisurely lunch at a village bistro. On the peninsula, there's also an 11th-century fortress to visit, the **Fort de Brégançon** (📞04 94 01 38 38; www.bormeslesmimosas.com; av Guy Tezenas, Cap de Brégançon; adult/child €10/free, parking €7-10; 🕙9am-5.45pm late Jun–mid-Oct, shorter hours rest of year), used as a private state residence for the French president since 1968 and opened to the public in 2014. Book a ticket at Bormes' tourist office, which also arranges guided nature walks in the nearby forests.

The Drive » Pick up the coast road again (D559) and follow its curves as it becomes the Corniche des Maures. There are numerous swimming spots along here, so keep your eyes peeled and your bathing suit handy. The Domaine du Rayol is clearly signed when you hit Le Rayol-Canadel.

- - - - - - - - - - - - - - - - - -

6 Domaine du Rayol

East of Bormes, the coastal Corniche des Maures twists past sandy beaches and seaside settlements like Le Lavandou and Rayol-Canadel-sur-Mer, where you'll find one of the gems of this stretch of the coastline: the dazzling gardens of the **Domaine du Rayol** (Le Jardin des Méditerranées; 📞04 98 04 44 00; www.domainedurayol.org; av des Belges, La Rayol-Canadel; adult/child €12/9; 🕙9.30am-7.30pm Jul & Aug, to 6.30pm Apr-Jun, Sep & Oct, to 5.30pm Nov-Mar; 🅿️ ♿), filled with plants from Mediterranean climates from across the globe. It's a riot of fragrance and colour, most impressive in April and May when the flowers are in full bloom. In summer, the estate's lovely beach also runs guided snorkelling sessions, during which you get to spot some of the colourful flora and

THE VILLAGE OF TORTOISES

About 20km north of Collobrières, the **Village des Tortues** (☎04 89 29 14 10; www.villagedestortues.fr; 1065 rte du Luc/D97, Carnoules; adult/child €15/10; ☻10am-7pm Apr-Aug, to 6pm Sep & Oct, to 5pm Wed, Sat & Sun Nov-Mar; ⓟ✚) protects one of France's most endangered species, the Hermann tortoise (*Testudo hermanni*). Once common along the Mediterranean coast, it is today found only in the Massif des Maures and Corsica. A viewing trail travels through the reserve (look out for vicious-looking models of the tortoise's ancestors lurking among the bushes). Along the way, you'll also visit the tortoise clinic, where wounded tortoises are treated before being released back into the wild, and the nurseries, where precious eggs are hatched and young tortoises spend the first three of their 60 to 100 years.

In summer, the best time to see the tortoises is in the morning and late afternoon. Hatching season is from mid-May to the end of June; from November to early March, they're all tucked up during hibernation.

sea life that lie beneath the Mediterranean waves; reserve ahead for snorkelling, which costs €30 per person (€22 for children).

The Drive » The D559 meanders nearly all the way to swish St-Tropez, although, unfortunately, if you're here in summer, you're pretty much guaranteed to hit jams the nearer you get to town. There's a big car park by the port (av du Gaulle).

TRIP HIGHLIGHT

❼ St-Tropez

Sizzling actress Brigitte Bardot came to St-Tropez in the '50s and transformed the peaceful fishing village into a jet-set favourite. Tropeziens have thrived on their sexy image ever since. At

the **Vieux Port**, yachts like spaceships jostle for millionaire moorings, while out on the beaches, cashed-up kids dance until dawn and the restaurants are really fabulous, as long as you aren't picking up the tab.

Swamped by more than 100,000 visitors a day in summer, outside the peak season St-Tropez rediscovers its soul. Now's the time to wander the cobbled lanes in the old fishing quarter of **La Ponche**, or sip a pastis and watch a game of *pétanque* on lovely **place des Lices** – preferably with a generous slice of *tarte tropézinenne,* the town's famous orange-perfumed cake. Whenever you come, don't miss the

Citadelle de St-Tropez

(☎04 94 97 59 43; www.saint-tropez.fr/culture/citadelle; 1 montée de la Citadelle; adult/child €3/free; ☻10am-12.30pm & 1.30-5.30pm; ✚), a 17th-century fortress that offers dazzling views from its hillside perch just east of the centre. Its dungeons are home to the excellent Musée de l'Histoire Maritime, an interactive museum with a focus on Provence's seafaring history.

✗ 🛏 p275

The Drive » Back onto our old friend again, the D559, through Port-Grimaud and Ste-Maxime, along the coast, and into Fréjus after 38km. Allow more time than you think you'll need; traffic is inevitable. St-Raphaël is just round the bay.

❽ Fréjus & St-Raphaël

They might not be quite on a par with many of Provence's Roman ruins, but the little town of **Fréjus** is still worth a detour if you're an archaeology enthusiast, as it includes the remains of an amphitheatre, Roman theatre and various arches and portals. Even if you're not, the old town is lovely: make sure you stop in at heavenly Le Palais du Fromager (p275) for a gourmet tour of local cheeses. Just along the coast is Fréjus' sister town, **St-Raphaël**, a beachy, boaty kind of place and a good overnight base.

 p275

The Drive » Zip along the A8 before exiting onto the D1555 and heading northwards towards Draguignan. Turn off onto the D955 before you reach town, which will take you via the Gorges de Châteaudouble, and stay on the road all the way to Comps-sur-Artuby. Here you turn left onto the D71 and enter the wild, sky-high world of the Gorges du Verdon.

- - - - - - - - - - - - - - - - - -

 Haut-Var

From the coast, it's time to head inland into the hills of the Haut-Var, a rocky, wild landscape that feels a world away from the chichi towns of the coast. Dry and sparsely populated, studded with hill villages and riven by gorges, it makes for spectacular driving. Your ultimate destination is the majestic **Gorges du Verdon**, sometimes called Europe's Grand Canyon – but it's worth making a detour via one of the lesser-known valleys, like the **Gorges de Châteaudouble**, 12km north of the military town of Draguignan.

From the coast, it's about a 90-minute drive before you enter the gorges near Comps-sur-Artuby, then climb past the impressive **Pont d'Artuby**, Europe's highest bridge, and track the southern side of the gorges along a route that's sometimes known (appropriately enough) as **La Corniche Sublime** (D955 to D90, D71 and D19). The drops are dizzying and it's single-file most of the way, but there aren't many more memorable drives. Eventually, you'll pass the emerald-green waters of the Lac de Ste-Croix before reaching the journey's end in **Moustiers Ste-Marie**.

 p275

DETOUR:
MASSIF DES MAURES

Start: Rayol-Canadel-sur-Mer

A wild range of wooded hills rumpling the landscape inland between Hyères and Fréjus, the **Massif des Maures** is a pocket of surprising wilderness just a few kilometres from the summer hustle of the Côte d'Azur. Shrouded by pine, chestnut and cork oak trees, its near-black vegetation gives rise to its name, derived from the Provençal word *mauro* (dark pine wood). Traditional industries (chestnut harvests, cork, pipe-making) are still practised here, and the area is criss-crossed by hiking trails that offer wraparound views of the coastline. From June to September, access to many areas is limited due to the risk of forest fire, but at other times of year, it's a haven of peace and nature.

It can be approached from the east from St-Tropez along the D14, but a more entertaining route is to head inland from Rayol-Canadel-sur-Mer along the switchbacking D27, over the Col du Canadel and along the tortuous rte des Crêtes onto the D98.

If you want to extend the drive, you can follow the D41 north up to the leafy village of **Collobrières** (population 1910); it's renowned for its chestnuts and hosts its own chestnut festival in October. The tourist office offers guided forest walks and can point you in the direction of the Châtaignier de Madame, the biggest chestnut tree in Provence, measuring a mighty 10.4m round.

Alternatively, you can head south down the D41 and rejoin the coast road at Le Lavandou.

Eating & Sleeping

Marseille ❶

✕ L'Arôme   French €€

(📞04 91 42 88 80; 9 rue de Trois Rois; menus €23-30; ⏱7.45-11.30pm Mon-Sat; Ⓜ Notre Dame du Mont) **Reserve ahead to snag a table** at this fabulous little restaurant just off cours Julien. From the service – relaxed, competent and friendly without over familiarity – to the street art on the walls and the memorable food, it's a complete winner. Well-credentialled chef-owner Romain achieves sophisticated simplicity in dishes such as roast duckling served with polenta and a pecorino *beignet* (doughnut).

✕ L'Epuisette   Provençal €€€

(📞04 91 52 17 82; www.l-epuisette.com; 158 rue du Vallon des Auffes; lunch/bouillabaisse menu €75/105; ⏱noon-1.30pm & 7.30-9.30pm Tue-Sat; 🚌83) This swanky restaurant has a Michelin star and knockout water-level views from an elegantly austere dining room. Many splurge on what may be Marseille's top bouillabaisse – which comes as part of a decadent multi-course *menu* – and on the superb cellar, which leans heavily towards French whites.

🛏 Hôtel Edmond Rostand   Design Hotel €€

(📞04 91 37 74 95; www.hoteledmondrostand. com; 31 rue Dragon; s/d/tr €100/120/140; ❉ @ 🛜; Ⓜ Estrangin-Préfecture) Push past the unassuming facade of this great-value hotel in the Quartier des Antiquaires to find a stylish interior in olive-grey and citrus, with a communal lounge area, a cafe and 15 rooms dressed in crisp white and soothing natural hues. Some rooms overlook a tiny private garden and others the Basilique Notre Dame de la Garde.

🛏 Mama Shelter   Design Hotel €€

(📞04 84 35 20 00; www.mamashelter.com; 64 rue de la Loubière; d €122-195; P ❉ 🛜; Ⓜ Notre Dame du Mont-Cours Julien) Part of a funky mini-chain of design-forward hotels, Marseille's Mama Shelter offers 125 Philippe Starck–imagined rooms over five floors. It's all about keeping the cool kids happy here – with

sleek white-and-chrome colour schemes, a live stage and bar, and a giant *babi foot* (fussball) table. Smaller rooms are oddly shaped, however, and it's a walk from the Vieux Port.

Cassis ❸

✕ La Villa Madie   Gastronomy €€€

(📞04 96 18 00 00; av de Revestel-anse de Corton; mains €78-98, menus €115-220; ⏱noon-1.15pm Thu-Mon & 7-9.15pm Thu-Sat & Mon) This double Michelin-starred restaurant with fantastic coastal views has become one of the destination addresses on the Riviera, renowned for its creative seafood and refined setting. Top-drawer ingredients like Aubrac beef and locally caught sea urchins, turbot and blue lobster form the core of the menu, with more exotic ingredients such as kaffir lime making judicious appearances. Dress nicely.

🛏 Le Clos des Arômes   Hotel €

(📞04 42 01 71 84; www.leclosdesaromes.fr; 10 rue Abbé Paul Mouton; s/d from €60/85; ❉ 🛜) If you're keen to save some centimes, this old-fashioned hotel just five minutes' stroll from the waterfront is a decent bet. It's set around a lovely little garden, where breakfast is served in summer, and the rooms, though simple, have big windows and a cheery colour scheme. The on-site restaurant provides more-than-serviceable Provençal food.

Hyères ❹

✕ Le Béal   Provençal €€

(📞04 94 20 84 98; www.lebeal.com; 24 rue de Limans; mains €17-27, menus €32-45; ⏱noon-1.15pm & 7-9.30pm Fri-Mon, 7-9.30pm Thu) The Béal is the name of the 15th- to 16th-century canal that brought water 10km to Hyères, which still functions and can be seen at points around the old town. Its namesake restaurant also nourishes the citizens of Hyères, with delightful modern French food such as octopus salad, and chorizo-crusted cod on creamy risotto. It's friendly, tastefully designed, and generally joyful.

🛏 Hôtel Bor
Boutique Hotel €€

(📞04 94 58 02 73; www.hotel-bor.com; 3 allée Émile Gérard, Hyères Beach; d from €170; ⊙Mar-Oct; ❄@🛜🌊) Right beside Plage Bona, this Scandi-tinged, palm-fringed hotel is a stylish place to stay, with its cedar-clad exterior, sun-loungers, potted plants and seafront deck. Rooms are modern and minimal, with gloss-wood floors, monochrome photos and steel-grey walls. The on-site bar and restaurant (mains €26 to €32) is good for beef tenderloin or grilled seafood.

St-Tropez ❼

🍴 La Tarte Tropézienne
Cafe €

(📞04 94 97 94 25; www.latartetropezienne.fr; place des Lices; tarts/snacks from €5.50/3; ⊙6.30am-10pm; 🛜) This smart, bustling cafe-bakery is the creator of St Tropez' eponymous sugar-crusted, orange-perfumed cake, but also does decent breads and light meals. There are smaller branches on **rue Clémenceau** (📞04 94 97 71 42; 36 rue Clémenceau; tarts/snacks €5.50/3; ⊙7am-9.30pm) and near the **new port** (📞04 94 97 19 77; 9 bd Louis Blanc; tarts/snacks €5.50/3; ⊙7am-7pm), plus various other towns around Provence and the Île de France.

🛏 Hôtel Lou Cagnard
Hotel €€

(📞04 94 97 04 24; www.hotel-lou-cagnard.com; 30 av Paul Roussel; d €86-188; ⊙Apr-late Oct; 🅿❄🛜) This old-school hotel stands in stark contrast to most of the swanky hotels around St-Tropez. Located in an old house shaded by lemon and fig trees, its 18 rooms are unashamedly frilly and floral, but some have garden patios, and the lovely jasmine-scented garden and welcoming family feel make it a home away from home. The cheapest rooms share toilets.

🛏 Hôtel Ermitage
Boutique Hotel €€€

(📞04 94 81 08 10; www.ermitagehotel.fr; 14 av Paul Signac; r from €320; ❄🛜) Well, if you really want to hang with the jet set, the hip Hermitage is your kind of place. Self-consciously retro, the decor draws inspiration from St-Tropez' midcentury heyday: bold primary colours, vintage design pieces and big prints of '60s icons on the walls. The bar's as cool as they come, with sweeping views over St-Trop.

Fréjus ❽

🍴 Le Palais du Fromager
Deli €

(📞04 94 40 67 99; www.mon-fromager.fr; 38 rue Siéyès; plat du jour €16, 5-cheese platter €13; ⊙shop 9am-9pm Tue-Fri, to 7pm Sat, lunch noon-2pm Tue-Sat; 🍴) Enterprising cheesemonger Philippe Daujam not only sells cheese – he also cooks it into tasty lunches in his deli-style restaurant by the cheese counter and on the street outside. Locals flock for the excellent-value *plat du jour* and can't-go-wrong cheese platters with salad.

🛏 Hôtel Les Calanques
Hotel €€

(📞04 98 11 36 36; www.hotel-les-calanques.com; rue du Nid au Soleil, Les Issambres; d €93-149, f €149-169) Thirteen kilometres south of Fréjus towards St-Tropez along the winding coast road, this family-run three-star sits on the rocks above its own quiet cove, accessed via the hotel's palm-filled garden. Many of the 12 simple rooms sport brand-new bathrooms and other upgrades from a recent makeover, and 10 boast stunning sea views – don't even consider the two facing the busy road.

Moustiers-Ste-Marie ❾

🍴 La Ferme Ste-Cécile
Gastronomy €€€

(📞04 92 74 64 18; www.ferme-ste-cecile.com; D952; menu €40; ⊙noon-2pm & 7.30-10pm Tue-Sat, noon-2pm Sun) Just outside Moustiers, this wonderful *ferme auberge* (country inn) immerses you in the full Provençal dining experience, from the sun-splashed terrace and locally picked wines right through to the chef's meticulous Mediterranean cuisine. It's about 1.2km from Moustiers; look out for the signs as you drive towards Castellane.

🛏 La Fabrique
B&B €€

(📞06 95 36 08 31; www.lafabrique04360.com; La Maladrerie, rte de Riez; d €98-135, f €135-150; 🅿🛜) Inside the handsome brick shell (a former factory) are gorgeous, clean-lined, screamingly elegant rooms, with industrial touches like exposed brick and sliding doors. Downstairs is the former factory floor, now a design-mag dream. There's a vast refectory table where a hearty dinner is available (€25 including drinks) and breakfast is served.

Southern Seduction en Corse

From edgy urban vibe to tranquil green lanes and cliff-carved coastline, this trip takes history fiends and culture vultures on a dramatic spin around the best of southern Corsica.

25

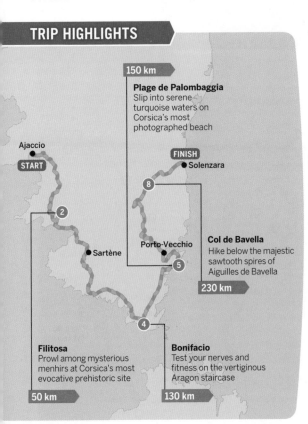
10 DAYS
260KM / 160 MILES

GREAT FOR...

BEST TIME TO GO
Spring or late summer to beat the crowds and the heat.

ESSENTIAL PHOTO
The cliffs of Bonifacio from a boat.

BEST FOR HEART-POUNDING HIKES
Nothing beats the hike down the 'king's staircase' in Bonifacio.

25 Southern Seduction en Corse

Starting with your foot on the pedal in the Corsican capital, this 10-day journey ducks and dives along the island's most dramatic coastal roads and mountain passes in southern Corse (Corsica). Mellow green hikes, gold-sand beaches and crisp turquoise waters to break the drive and stretch your legs are never far away, and for archaeology buffs there's the added bonus of some of France's most extraordinary prehistoric sites.

1 Ajaccio

Napoléon Bonaparte's hometown and the capital of France's ravishing Île de Beauté (aka Corsica), this charismatic city on the sea thoroughly spoils with fine art in **Palais Fesch – Musée des Beaux-Arts** (☎04 95 26 26 26; www.musee-fesch.com; 50-52 rue du Cardinal Fesch; adult/child €8/5; ☺9.15am-6pm May-Oct, 9am-5pm Nov-Apr) and a beautiful bay fringed with palm trees. After sampling these delights, hike 12km west to **Pointe**

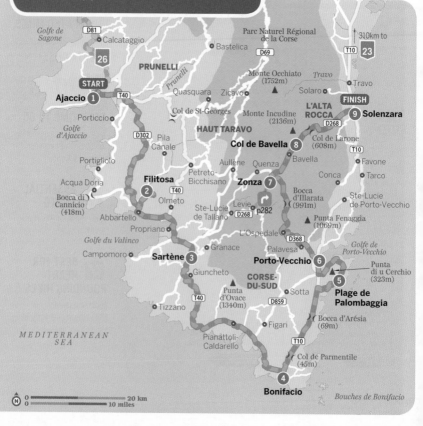

de la Parata to watch the sunset turn the **Îles Sanguinaires** (Bloody Islands) vivid crimson. Later, savour drinks beneath the stars on a trendy waterfront terrace at Port Tino Rossi.

 p284, p295

The Drive » From Ajaccio port, pick up the N193 and subsequent T40 to Bonifacio. After 12km turn right onto the D302, direction Pila Canale (a brown sign reads 'Filitosa'), and prepare for the sudden grand view of Ajaccio city below as the road climbs. Bear right onto the D255 and wind along peaceful green lanes via the D55, D355, D757 and D57 to Filitosa.

- - - - - - - - - - - - - - - - - -

TRIP HIGHLIGHT

❷ Filitosa

Nowhere is more evocative of ancient Corsican civilisation than this

 LINK YOUR TRIP

 23 Riviera Crossing
Pop your car on the ferry in Bastia and sail to Nice for more mountainous, hairpin-laced corniches (coastal roads) with giant blue views.

26 Corsican Coast Cruiser
Completely smitten? Motor north from Ajaccio and up to Île Rousse to cruise the island's west coast.

archaeological site (📞04 95 74 00 91; www.filitosa.fr; D57, Sollacaro; adult/child €9/7; ⏰9am-1hr before sunset Apr-Oct) ripe with olive trees, pines and the intoxicating scent of maquis (herbal scrub). Visit around noon when the sun casts dramatic shadows on the carved statues and menhirs woven around trees and circling sheep pastures.

Corsica developed its own megalithic faith around 4000 to 3000 BCE, and many of the stones at Filitosa date from this period. The menhirs are particularly unusual, including some with detailed faces, anatomical features like rib cages, even swords and armour.

The Drive » Wind your way back to the D57 and meander south to the sea along the D157 to join the southbound T40 just north of Propriano. Count on about 40 minutes to cover the 30km trip to Sartène.

- - - - - - - - - - - - - - - - - -

❸ Sartène

With its ramshackle granite houses, shaded shabby streets and secretive alleys, this sombre town evokes the rugged spirit of rural Corsica, notorious for banditry and bloody vendettas in the 19th century.

A colourful time to motor in is on Good Friday during the **Procession du Catenacciu**, celebrated since the

Middle Ages. Barefoot, red-robed and cowled, the Catenacciu (literally 'chained one'; penitent) lugs a massive 35kg wooden cross through town in a re-enactment of Christ's journey to Calvary. The rest of the year, cross and 17kg penitent chain hang inside **Église Ste-Marie** (place Porta).

Don't leave town without filling your picnic hamper with cheese, sausage, honey and wine from **La Cave Sartenaise** (📞06 88 65 50 49; www.lacavesartenaise.com; place Porta; ⏰10am-9.30pm Mon-Sat, to 8.30pm Sun May-Oct, shorter hours and closed Sun rest of year).

 p284

The Drive » From Sartène it is an easy one-hour drive along the southbound T40 to Bonifacio. Slow down along the final leg – coastal views are glittering and you might well want to jump out for a dip.

- - - - - - - - - - - - - - - - - -

TRIP HIGHLIGHT

❹ Bonifacio

With its glittering harbour, incredible clifftop perch and stout citadel teetering above the cornflower-blue waters of the **Bouches de Bonifacio**, this Italianate port is an essential stop. Sun-bleached town houses, dangling washing lines and murky chapels secreted in a postcard-worthy web of alleyways hide within the old citadel, while down at the harbour, kiosks tout must-do boat trips through gin-clear waters to **Îles Lavezzi**.

Park at the harbour and walk up **montée du Rastello** and **montée St-Roch** to the citadel gateway with its 16th-century drawbridge. Inside is the 13th-century **Bastion de l'Étendard** (www.bonifacio.fr/visite-decouverte/bastion-de-letendard; adult/child €3.50/1, incl Escalier du Roi d'Aragon €4.50/1.50; ⏲10am-4.30pm Apr-Dec) with a history museum. Stroll the ramparts to **place du Marché** and **place de la Manichella** for jaw-dropping views of the legendary cliffs. Then hike down the **Escalier du Roi d'Aragon** (www.bonifacio.fr/visite-decouverte/escalier-roy-daragon; adult/child €3.50/1, incl Bastion de l'Étendard €4.50/1.50; ⏲9am-sunset Apr-Dec), a steep staircase cut into the southern cliff-face to the water. Legend says its 187 steep steps were carved in a single night by Aragonese troops during the siege of 1420. In truth, the steps led to an underground freshwater well, in a cave on the seashore.

✗ ⌂ p284

The Drive ≫ From the harbour, head north along the T10 towards Porto-Vecchio. Count on about 45 minutes to cover the 35km from Bonifacio to the Plage de Palombaggia turn-off, signposted on the large roundabout south of Porto-Vecchio town proper.

PAWEL KAZMIERCZAK / SHUTTERSTOCK ©

Corsica Cliffs of Bonifacio

⑤ Plage de Palombaggia

When it comes to archetypal 'idyllic beach', immense Plage de Palombaggia is near impossible to top. This pine-fringed beach stars on most Corsica postcards, with sparkling turquoise water, long stretches of sand and splendiferous views

over the **Îles Cerbicale**. Melting into its southern fringe are the equally picture-perfect expanses of sand and lapping shallow waters of **Plage de la Folacca**. This irresistible duo is sure to set your heart aflutter.

✕ 🖺 p284

The Drive » Follow rte de Palombaggia on its anticlockwise loop around the peninsula, afterwards joining the busy T10 briefly for its final

sprint into Porto-Vecchio. Spend a pleasant hour mooching along at a relaxed, view-savouring pace.

⑥ Porto-Vecchio

Shamelessly seductive and fashionable, Porto-Vecchio is the Corsican St-Tropez, the kind of place that lures French A-listers and wealthy tourists. Its picturesque backstreets, lined with restaurant terraces and

DETOUR: PREHISTORIC CORSICA

Start: ⑦ Zonza

This short but startling detour dives into the heart of ancient Corsica. To create a perfect weekend, combine it with an overnight stay at the island's best boutique-farm spa.

From Zonza drive 9km south along the D268 to **Levie**, unexpected host to the **Musée de l'Alta Rocca** (📞04 95 78 00 78; www.corsedusud.fr/nos-competences/patrimoine-et-culture; quartier Prato; adult/child €4/2.50; ☺10am-6pm Jun-Sep, to 5pm Tue-Sat Oct-May), a local history and ethnographical museum.

Continue south along the D268 and after 3km turn right onto rte du Pianu (D20), a narrow lane signposted 'Cucuruzzu Capula Site Archéologique'. Soon after, you arrive at **A Pignata** (📞04 95 78 41 90; www.apignata.com; rte de Cucuruzzu; incl half-board d €260-420, cabin €480-680; ☺Apr-Dec; 🅿🛜🏊), a chic mountain retreat where you can gorge on Alta Rocca mountain views crossed by swirling clouds from a poolside chaise longue. Fronted by brothers Antoine and Jean-Baptiste, the farmhouse spa with vegetable garden and pigs (and the most mouth-melting charcuterie) is first-class. Its 18 rooms are contemporary and its restaurant (*menu* €53) is the best in southern Corsica. For heaven on earth, go for the impossibly romantic treehouse for two.

Next morning, continue along the same D20 road for five minutes to the **Site Archéologique Cucuruzzu Capula** (📞04 95 51 64 29; www.isula.corsica/musees; Levie; adult/child €4/free; ☺9.30am-7pm Jun-Sep, to 6pm Apr, May & Oct), 3.7km in all from the D268. Allow two hours to explore the archaeological site. Enthralling for kids and adults alike, an evocative 3km interpretive trail takes you on foot between giant boulders coloured bright green with moss to the Bronze Age *castelli* (castles) of Cucuruzzu and Capula. Along the way, kids can duck into the earliest natural-rock shelters used by prehistoric humans (who were small in stature) and poke around the remaining rooms of a stronghold where, a few centuries later, they butchered wild boar, cooked broth, spun wool and fashioned thongs from stretched animal skins.

Backtrack to the D268 and turn left (north) back to Levie and beyond to Zonza.

designer shops, have charm in spades – presided over with grace by the photogenic ruins of an old Genoese **citadel**.

Small and sleepy by day, Porto-Vecchio sizzles in season when it dons its dancing shoes and lets rip for hot nights of partying. Cafes and bars cluster place de la République and along the seafront.

 p285

The Drive » Leave Porto-Vecchio by the winding D368 and follow it through the heavily wooded Forêt de l'Ospédale – excellent walks and picnic spots – to the rural hamlet of L'Ospédale (1000m), 18km northeast. Continue on the same road through more forest and loads more exhausting wiggles to Zonza, 20km north again. It'll take a good hour for the entire journey.

- - - - - - - - - - - - - - - -

❼ Zonza

The chances are you've had a temporary surfeit of superb seascapes, so take a couple of days out to explore the **Alta Rocca** wilderness, a world away from the bling and glitz of the coast. At the south of the long spine that traverses Corsica, the area is an exhilarating combination of dense, mixed evergreen–deciduous forests and granite villages strung over rocky ledges.

No mountain village plunges you more dramatically into its heart than Zonza, a

hamlet overshadowed by the iconic **Aiguilles de Bavella** (Bavella Needles), granite pinnacles like shark's teeth that jab the skyline at an altitude of more than 1600m. Hiking is the thing to do in this wild neck of the woods.

🛏 p285

The Drive » Allow up to 20 minutes for the go-slow, bend-laced D268 that climbs slowly and scenically up from Zonza to the mountain pass at 1218m, 9km north.

- - - - - - - - - - - - - - - -

TRIP HIGHLIGHT

❽ Col de Bavella

No number of hairpins or sheer drops can prepare you for the spectacular drama that awaits you atop the Bavella Pass (1218m), the perfect perch for marvelling close-up at the Aiguilles de Bavella. Depending on the time of day and weather, these gargantuan granite spikes glimmer red, gold, crimson, ginger or dark broody burgundy.

Short and long hikes are a dime a dozen, and when you've finished savouring the outdoor action and intoxicating alpine views, there is unforgettable feasting on roasted baby goat and wild pig stew at the **Auberge du Col de Bavella** (📞04 95 72 09 87; www.auberge-bavella.com, D268; menu €26; ⏱noon-3pm & 7-9.30pm Apr-Oct) on the pass. If you want to stay

overnight, this Corsican inn has dorm beds (per person including half-board €47).

The Drive » Steady your motoring nerves for relentless hairpins on the perilously steep descent along the D268 from the Col de Bavella to the Col de Larone, 13km northeast, and onwards north through the hills to Solenzara on the coast. Allow at least an hour for the entire 30km trip.

- - - - - - - - - - - - - - - -

❾ Solenzara

The town itself is not particularly postcard-worthy. What gives this seaside resort on Corsica's eastern coast natural appeal is its handsome spread of sandy beaches and the journey to the resort – one of the most stunning (and nail-biting) drives on Corsica. So steep and narrow is the road in places that it's not even single lane, while hazy views of the tantalising Mediterranean far below pose an unnerving distraction. Once through the thick pine forest of the **Forêt de Bavella**, the road drops across the **Col de Larone** (608m) to eventually meet the banks of the **River Solenzara**. When the extreme driving gets too much, pull over and dip your toes in the crystal-clear river water – there are swimming and picnic spots aplenty.

Eating & Sleeping

Ajaccio ❶

✖ Le 20123 — Corsican €€

(☑️04 95 21 50 05; www.20123.fr; 2 rue du Roi de Rome; menu €38.50; ☺ noon-2.30pm Mon-Sat, 7-11pm daily Apr-Oct, closed Mon Nov-Mar) This fabulous, one-of-a-kind restaurant originated in the village of Pila Canale (postcode 20123). When the owner moved to Ajaccio, the village came too – water fountain, life-sized dolls, central square and all. That might sound tacky, but it works; lively year-round, it's a charming, characterful night out, where everyone feasts on a seasonal four-course menu that's rich in meaty traditional cuisine. The price might seem a little steep, but given the sheer quantity of food that's served, you won't feel short-changed.

🛏 Hôtel Napoléon — Hotel €€

(☑️04 95 51 54 00; www.hotel-napoleon-ajaccio. fr; 4 rue Lorenzo Vero; d €115-149; 🌑🛜) The warmth of a family-run hotel, coupled with a prime location on a side street in the heart of town, make the Napoléon an excellent midrange choice. Rooms are clean, bright and comfortable, despite their rather uninspiring decor; some of the nicest are on the 7th floor, with high ceilings and tall shuttered windows looking out on a leafy backyard.

🛏 Hôtel San Carlu Citadelle — Hotel €€

(☑️04 95 21 13 84; www.hotel-sancarlu.com; 8 bd Danièle Casanova; d/q from €109/159; 🌑🛜) This cream-coloured townhouse, smack opposite the citadel and featuring matching oyster-grey shutters, is a solid bet. Rooms are clean and modern, while the views over citadel and sea get better with every floor. The family room sleeps up to five comfortably. Traffic noise could be an issue for light sleepers.

Sartène ❸

🛏 Domaine de Croccano — B&B €€

(☑️04 95 77 11 37; www.corsenature.com; rte de Granace/D148, km 3; d €100-120, cottage per week €420-630; ☺ Feb-Nov; 🌑🛜)

Set amid rolling maquis 5km northeast of town, this charming stone farmhouse offers end-of-the-road tranquillity. The rooms are very old-fashioned but the pastoral views are stunning, and picnic facilities and horse-riding are available. Rates drop for multi-night stays. A self-catering cottage is also available for weekly rentals.

Bonifacio ❹

✖ Kissing Pigs — Corsican €€

(☑️04 95 73 56 09; www.facebook.com/ kissingpigs; 15 quai Banda del Ferro; mains €11-23.50, menus €21-23; ☺11.30am-3pm Thu-Tue, 6.30-11pm Thu-Sat, Mon & Tue) At the water's edge beneath the citadel, and festooned with swinging sausages, this seductively cosy and friendly restaurant-cum–wine-bar serves wonderfully rich and predominantly meaty Corsican dishes. Hearty casseroles include pork stewed with muscat and chestnuts, while the cheese and charcuterie platters are great for sharing. The Corsican wine list is another hit.

🛏 Hôtel Colomba — Hotel €€

(☑️04 95 73 73 44; www.hotel-bonifacio-corse. fr; 4-6 rue Simon Varsi; d €132-167; ☺Apr-Oct; 🅿🌑🛜) Occupying a tastefully renovated 14th-century building, this hotel enjoys a prime location on a picturesque (steep) street, bang in the heart of the old town. Rooms are simple and smallish, but fresh and decorated with amenities including wrought-iron bedsteads, country fabrics, carved bedheads and/or chequerboard tiles. Other pluses include friendly staff and breakfast served in a medieval vaulted cellar.

Plage de Palombaggia ❺

✖ Tamaricciu — Mediterranean €€

(☑️04 95 70 49 89; www.tamaricciu.com; mains €19-32; ☺9am-7pm mid-Apr–mid-Jun & Sep–mid-Oct, to 10.30pm mid-Jun–Aug) Chic beach restaurant, on the Palombaggia sands 10km southeast of Porto-Vecchio. The setting is unsurpassable, with first-class views of the turquoise surf from the wood-decked terrace, while the Mediterranean cuisine, with salads, pasta, and lots of grilled fish and meat in the evening especially, is well prepared and beautifully presented.

🛏 A Littariccia   B&B €€

(📞04 95 70 41 33; www.littariccia.com; rte de Palombaggia; d €115-225; 🅿🛜🏊) The twin trump cards here are the fabulous hillside location, overlooking Plage de Palombaggia 9km southeast of Porto-Vecchio, and the dreamy pool. Spread through adjacent villas, which can also be rented in their entirety, the rooms are pretty and bright, but not all come with a sea view. Wi-fi is available in the pool area only.

🛏 Le Belvédère   Hotel €€€

(📞04 95 70 54 13; www.hbcorsica.com; rte de Palombaggia; d €250-350, ste €375-700; 🕐late Apr-late Nov; 🅿🛜🏊) This divine 15-room hotel, 5km east around the bay from Porto-Vecchio, occupies a former family estate amid the seafront eucalyptus, palm and pine. Its modern decor mixes traditional stone with wood, marble and wrought iron, and the public areas spill across natural rock and sand, with a wonderful sea-facing pool. Rates tumble in low season.

Porto-Vecchio

🍴 A Cantina di l'Orriu   Corsican €€

(📞04 95 70 26 21; www.lorriu.fr; 5 cours Napoléon; mains €20-35; 🕐6-10pm Mon, noon-2pm & 6-10pm Tue-Fri, noon-11pm Sat mid-Mar–Oct) The atmospheric old-stone interior of this wine-bar-turned-restaurant is packed to the rafters with sausages and cold meats hung up to dry, cheeses, jars of jam and honey, and other tasty Corsican produce, and there's a spacious outdoor terrace too. Lunch platters range from light to feisty – ravioli is a speciality – and desserts are sumptuous.

Zonza ⑦

🛏 Les Hauts de Cavanello   B&B €€

(📞06 09 50 05 01; www.locationzonza.com; Hameau de Cavanello; s/d €88/98; 🕐May–late Oct; 🅿🛜🏊) Also let under the name 'Hameau de Cavanello', this rural B&B 2km northeast of Zonza offers five cosy, well-equipped modern rooms plus a pool and stone terrace, all nestling in hectares of green meadows and forests with magical views of the Aiguilles de Bavella.

🛏 Chez Pierrot   B&B €

(📞04 95 78 63 21; http://gitechezpierrot.free.fr; Hameau de Jallicu, Quenza; dm/d €47/124, both incl half-board) For a quintessential Corsican experience in an utterly tranquil setting, on the Mare a Mare trail at 1200m altitude, bookmark Chez Pierrot, 5km uphill from Quenza. Three-dorm *gîte*, four-room B&B, restaurant and equestrian centre, all rolled into one, it's run by the idiosyncratic, charismatic Pierrot, who's lived here since early childhood. Horse riding is available April to October (€47, one hour).

Corsican Coast Cruiser

26

Few coastlines are as ravishing or varied as the seashore ribbon that unfurls on this five-day trip around western Corsica. For some daredevil action, detour inland to the island's deepest canyon.

TRIP HIGHLIGHTS

10 km	

Algajola
Discover dreamy secret coves aboard the rickety 'trembler' train

Île Rousse
START

Calvi

20 km

Plage de l'Arinella
Lunch on the sand at one of Corsica's most coveted beach dining spots

90 km

Porto
Cruise from Porto to the dazzling Réserve Naturelle de Scandola

100 km

Les Calanques de Piana
Weave through fantastic red rock formations above the deep blue Mediterranean

185 km

Ajaccio
Enjoy sweeping bay views and explore the sights of Napoléon Bonaparte's hometown

FINISH

**5 DAYS
185KM / 115 MILES**

GREAT FOR...

BEST TIME TO GO

April to July and September for quiet roads and blue-sky views.

 ESSENTIAL PHOTO

Snap blazing-red rock formations at Les Calanques de Piana.

 BEST FOR BOAT TRIPS

Set sail from Porto for some of Corsica's most breathtaking coastal scenery.

Corsican Coast Cruiser

Keep both hands firmly on the wheel during this high-drama ride along Corsica's hairpin-laced west coast. Dangerously distracting views out the window flit from glittering bay and bijou beach to sawtooth peak, blazing-red rock and maquis-cloaked mountain. Meanwhile, the road — never far from the dazzling big blue — gives a whole new spin to the concept 'go slow': you won't average much more than 35km/h for the duration of the trip.

---

1 Île Rousse

Sun-worshippers, celebrities and holidaying yachties create buzz in this busy beach town straddling a long, sandy curve of land backed by mountains and herb-scented maquis (herbal scrubland).

Begin the day on Île Rousse's central tree-shaded square, **place Paoli**, overlooked by the 21 classical columns of the Greek temple–styled **food market**, built around 1850. Get lost in the rabbit warren of old-town alleys around the square, and at noon sip a pre-lunch aperitif on the terrace of venerable **Café des Platanes**

(www.balagne-corsica.com/cafe-des-platanes; place Paoli; ⊙6am-2am Jun-Sep, 7am-8.30pm Oct-May) and watch old men play boules.

Later, take a sunset stroll past a Genoese watchtower and lighthouse to the russet-coloured rock of **Île de la Pietra**, from which the town, founded by Pascal Paoli in 1758, gets its colourful name. **Sea kayaking** (☎04 95 60 22 55; www.cnir.org; rte du Port; per hr kayak/SUP/sailboard/catamaran €14/15/20/40; ⊙9am-7pm daily Jul & Aug, 2-5pm Wed & Sat & by arrangement Sep-Jun) around the promontory and its islets is an outdoor delight.

✗ ⊨ p294

The Drive » From the roundabout at the western end of town, pick up the T30 towards Calvi; buy fresh fruit for the journey from the open-air stall signposted 'Marché Plein Air' on the roundabout.

TRIP HIGHLIGHT

2 Algajola

This gloriously old-fashioned, bucket-and-spade address makes a great base. Its golden-sand beach is one of Corsica's longest and loveliest, and budget accommodation options are superb. If your idea of luxury is drifting off to the orchestra of crashing waves and frolicking on the sand in pyjamas fresh out of bed at dawn, there is no finer place to stay.

Next morning, jump aboard the *trinighellu* (trembler), aka the **Tramway de la Balagne**, a dinky little seaside train that trundles along sand-covered tracks between Île Rousse and Calvi, stopping on request only at hidden coves and bijou beaches en route.

✗ ⊨ p294

The Drive » Continue towards Calvi on the coastal T30 and in the centre of Lumio, 6km south of Algajola, turn right following signs for 'Plage de l'Arinella'. Twist 2.6km downhill past leafy walled-garden *residences secondaires* (holiday homes) to where the turquoise water laps Plage de l'Arinella.

MEDITERRANEAN
SEA

START

Île Rousse ①

T30

Algajola ②

○ Pigna

Plage de l'Arinella

○ Lumio

③

Calvi ④

○ Cateri

T30

Pointe de la
Ravelleta ⑤

Feliceto ○

LA BALAGNE

Figarella

○ Calenzana

D81B

Suare ○

Baie de
Crovani

Argentella ○

Ferayola ○

FILOSORMA

Galeria ○   ○ Le Fango

D81

Haut
Asco ○

Girolata ○

Parc Naturel
Régional
de la Corse

○ Curzu

⑥

○ Portinellu

Vergio ○

**Col de
la Croix**

Gorges de Spelunca

Golfe de Porto

Porto

⑦

○ Ota   ○ Évisa

**Les Calanques
de Piana ⑧**

○ Cristinacce

p293

○ Piana

○ Marignana

Soccia ○

D81

Vico ○   ○ Murzo

○ Muna

Cargèse ○

D81

Salice ○

○ Sagone

Golfe de
Sagone

Tiuccia ○

Sant' Andrea-
d'Orcino ○

○ Calcataggio

D81

Afa ○

Castagnola ○

PRUNELLI

Prunelli

Ajaccio ⑨

FINISH

Porticcio ○

24

Golfe
d'Ajaccio

25

300 km to

N ⊿
0 ――――――― 10 km
0 ――――――― 5 miles

TRIP HIGHLIGHT

③ Plage de l'Arinella

If there is one crescent of sand in Corsica you must not miss, it's this serene, rock-clad cove with one of the island's finest beach restaurants and dramatic views of the citadel of Calvi. Lunch here is a trip highlight.

From the stylish, shabby-chic interior of **Le Matahari** (☏04 95 60 78 47; mains €18-37, dinner menu €45; ☻11am-3pm Apr-Sep, 6-10pm Tue-Sun Jun-Sep) to the big windows looking out to Calvi beyond the waves, this hip beach spot is one very special hideaway. Wooden tables, strung on the sand and topped with straw parasols, immediately evoke a tropical paradise, while

**LINK
YOUR
TRIP**

24 **Var Delights**
Sail by car ferry to Marseille and enjoy the coastal treasures of the Var.

25 **Southern
Seduction en Corse**
Corsica is so seductive you might well find yourself extending your trip with this 10-day motor from Ajaccio around the island's southern tip to Porto-Vecchio on the east coast and beyond.

cuisine is creative – think penne *à la langouste* (lobster), squid, fresh *morue* (codfish) or a simple tuna steak pan-fried to pink perfection.

The Drive ≫ Motor back up the hill to join the coastal T30 and continue south for another 15 minutes, around the Golfe de Calvi, to Calvi. The best spot to park is at the top of town, across from the entrance to the citadel.

----

④ Calvi

Basking between the fiery orange bastions of its 15th-century citadel and the glittering waters of a moon-shaped bay, Calvi feels closer to the chichi sophistication of a French Riviera resort than a historic Corsican port. Palatial yachts and private cruisers jostle for space along its harbourside, while high above the quay the watchtowers and battlements of the town's Genoese stronghold stand guard, proffering sweeping views inland to Monte Cinto (2706m).

Set atop a lofty promontory, Calvi's massive fortified **citadel** has fended off everyone down the centuries, from Franco-Turkish raiders to Anglo-Corsican armies. Wraparound views from its five feisty bastions certainly have the wow-factor, and **Chez Tao** (☎04 95 65 00 73; www.cheztao.com; rue St-Antoine; ◷10.30pm–6am Jun–Sep), a wildly hip and lavish music bar around since 1935,

is the spot to lap them up, cocktail in hand.

✗ ⊨ p294

The Drive ≫ Across from the citadel, pick up the coastal road D81B signposted 'Rte de Porto – Bord de Mer'. Before driving off, don't miss the old shabby square shaded by rare ombu trees with gnarled and knotted trunks, and sweet honey-producing flowers.

----

⑤ Pointe de la Revellata

Within seconds of leaving town, you're deep in the hot sun-baked maquis, with a low stone wall being the only separator between white-knuckled passenger and green drop down to emerald water below. After 4km the magnificent cape of Pointe de la Revellata – the nearest Corsican point to the French mainland – pops into view, with a toy-like white lighthouse at its tip and dusty walking trails zigzagging between the scrub and the ocean. Park and indulge in a signposted 1.5km hike to **Chapelle Notre Dame de la Serra**, where drop-dead views of the peninsula, its beaches and the mountains of Corsica's interior unfold.

The Drive ≫ Continue south on the D81B. After the *champ de tir* (military shooting range), savour a brief reprieve from the big coastal views as the road ducks inland between the mountainous 703m hulk of Capu di a Veta and fields of

Calvi Citadel and harbour

grazing sheep. At the first road fork, 35km south of Calvi, bear right along the D81 signposted 'Galeria 5km, Porto 49km', and at the second fork, bear left.

- - - - - - - - - - - - - - - - - -

❻ Col de la Croix

Having driven for a good hour around relentless hairpins, you might be tempted to stop on **Col de Palmarella** (405m), a mountain pass with fine views of the W-shaped bay of the Golfe de Girolata far below. Pull over to photograph the blazing blue Mediterranean ensnared by the flaming-red rock of **Punta Rossa**, the dollhouse-sized hamlet of Girolata tucked in the crook of the bay, and the menacing dark green of forested **Capo d'Osani**. But save the picnic lunch and sun-fuelled siesta for **Col de la Croix** (260m), about 10km further south.

Park in the car park and pick up the dusty footpath behind the snack bar signposted 'Panorama – Table d'Orientation'. Climbing gently uphill for 20 minutes through typical Corsican maquis, the path suddenly staggers out of the Mediterranean bush into a mind-blowing panorama of fiery red and smouldering black-green capes, blue bay and the spaghetti road you've successfully navigated to get here. An orientation table tells you what's what.

Back at the roadside *buvette* (snack bar), longer walking trails lead downhill to the seaside hamlet of **Girolata** (1¾ hours, 7km) and **Plage de Tuara** (45 minutes, 3km).

The Drive ❱❱ Count on a good half-hour of relentlessly bend-laced motoring to cover the 25km from Col de la Croix south to Porto. The final five minutes reward you with a sudden narrowing of the road and dramatic roadside rock formations that flame a brilliant red. Go even slower than slow.

- - - - - - - - - - - - - - - - - -

 TRIP HIGHLIGHT

❼ Porto

The crowning glory of the west coast, Porto sits sweet at the foot of a thickly forested valley trammelled on either side by crimson peaks. Split by a promontory, the village itself is topped by a restored **Genoese tower** (€2.50; ☺9am-7pm Apr-Oct, to 8pm Jul & Aug) built in the 16th century to protect the gulf from Barbary incursions. Scale the russet-coloured rocks up to the square tower, take in the tiny local-history exhibition inside, then stroll to the bustling marina, where a footbridge crosses the estuary to a eucalyptus grove and pebble beach. April to October, boats sail from the marina to the shimmering seas around the magnificent, Unesco-protected marine reservation of **Réserve Naturelle de Scandola**.

✕ ⊨ p295

The Drive ❱❱ Cruise 12km south along the same coastal D81 towards the village of Piana. When you see red, you'll know you've hit the next stop.

- - - - - - - - - - - - - - - - - -

TRIP HIGHLIGHT

❽ Les Calanques de Piana

No amount of hyperbole can capture the astonishing beauty of these sculpted cliffs teetering above the Golfe de Porto. Rearing up from the sea in staggering scarlet pillars, teetering columns, towers and irregularly shaped boulders of pink, ochre and ginger, Les Calanques flame red in the sunlight and are among Corsica's most iconic, awe-inspiring sights. And as you sway around switchback after switchback along the rock-riddled 12km stretch of the D81 south of Porto towards the village of **Piana**, one mesmerising vista piggybacks another.

For the full Technicolor experience of this natural ensemble of gargantuan proportion, park up and savour Les Calanques on foot. Several trails wind their way around these dramatic rock formations, which are uncannily shaped like dogs' heads, dinosaurs and all sorts; trails start near **Pont de Mezzanu**, a road bridge on the D81 about 3km north of Piana. Afterwards, splurge

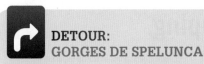

DETOUR:
GORGES DE SPELUNCA

Start: ⑦ Porto

If you crave a break from the blue, head inland into the hills to reach **Ota** and **Évisa**, a twin set of enigmatic mountain villages that dangle defiantly above a plunging canyon blanketed with thick woods of pine, oak and chestnut. Quintessentially Corsican, these magical mountain hideaways are a haven for hikers, positioned halfway along the **Mare e Monti hiking trail** and within striking distance of Corsica's answer to the Grand Canyon, the unforgettable **Gorges de Spelunca**. Until the D84 was carved into the mountainside, the only link between the two villages was a tiny mule track via two Genoese bridges, the **Ponte Pianella** (also called **Ponte Vecchju**) and **Ponte Zaglia**. The trail between the villages is a fantastic day hike (five hours return), winding along the valley floor past the rushing River Porto and soaring orange cliffs, some more than 1km high. Or follow the shorter two-hour section between the bridges; pick up the trail at the arched road-bridge 2km east of Ota.

Carpeting the slopes east of Évisa is **Forêt d'Aïtone**, home of Corsica's most impressive stands of *laricio* pines. These arrow-straight, 60m-high trees once provided beams and masts for Genoese ships.

South of Porto, the D84 wiggles direct to Évisa, 22km east and a good 30 minutes of go-slow, blind-bend driving. Or opt for the narrower, slower D124 to the north that detours to the village of Ota before hooking up with the same D84.

on lunch at Corsica's most mythical hotel, **Les Roches Rouges** (☎04 95 27 81 81; www.lesrochesrouges. com; D81; ☺Apr-Oct; ❄🐾).

The Drive » The driving drama is done with: it's a relatively easy 70km drive south along the D81 to the Corsican capital of Ajaccio.

- - - - - - - - - - - - - - - - - -

TRIP HIGHLIGHT

⑨ Ajaccio

Corsica's capital is all class – and seduction. Commanding a lovely sweep of the bay, the city breathes confidence and has a real whiff of the Côte d'Azur. Mosey around the centre with its mellow-toned build-

ings and vibrant cafe culture, stroll the marina and trendy beach-clad rte des Sanguinaires area, and congratulate yourself on arriving in the city – several hundred hairpin bends later – in one piece!

Napoléon Bonaparte was born here in 1769, and the city is dotted with sites relating to the diminutive dictator. You can visit his childhood home, which is now a museum, the **Maison Bonaparte** (☎04 95 21 43 89; www.musees-nationaux-malmaison.fr; rue St-Charles; adult/child €7/free; ☺10am-12.30pm & 1.15-5.30pm Tue-Sun Apr-Sep, 10.30am-12.30pm &

1.15-4.30pm Tue-Sun Oct-Mar). Though little of the original decor remains, it has interesting memorabilia – including a glass medallion containing a lock of the general's own hair.

The Oscar for most fascinating museum goes to Ajaccio's fine-arts museum, established by Napoléon's uncle, inside **Palais Fesch** (☎04 95 26 26 26; www.musee-fesch.com; 50-52 rue du Cardinal Fesch; adult/child €8/5; ☺9.15am-6pm May-Oct, 9am-5pm Nov-Apr). France's largest collection of Italian paintings outside the Louvre hangs here.

🍴 🛏 p284, p295

Eating & Sleeping

Île Rousse ❶

✖ A Casa Corsa   Corsican €

(☎04 95 60 23 63; 6 place Paoli; sandwiches & salads €5-10; ☺9am-midnight mid-Mar–mid-Nov; ✎) With a prime location – and outdoor tables – on gorgeous place Paoli, this wine bar does a brisk trade in salads, cheese and charcuterie platters and other stalwart Corsican dishes. All the excellent, all-Corsican wines are available by the glass.

⌂ L'Escale Côté Sud   Hotel €€

(☎04 95 63 01 70; www.hotel-ilerousse.com/escale-cote-sud; 22 rue Notre-Dame; d €85-210) Open year-round and right in the heart of town, this well-equipped modern hotel is an excellent midrange option. Four of its rooms enjoy dreamy views of limpid turquoise waters lapping the beach, just across the promenade. Besides the large lounge bar downstairs, the place also has a good **restaurant** (☎04 95 60 10 53; www.hotel-ilerousse.com; 28 rue Notre-Dame; mains €25-30, menu €29; ☺noon-3pm & 6-10pm) just down the street.

Algajola ❷

✖ Le Padula   Seafood, Pizza €

(☎04 95 60 75 22; www.facebook.com/lepadula.algajola; Plage d'Aregno; pizza from €12, mains €16-25; ☺8am-11pm Easter-Oct) Spectacular views and tasty, unpretentious food bring the crowds flocking to this informal beach terrace restaurant, 1km east of the centre. The menu ranges from pizza – served day and night – and the daily *plat du jour* (€16) to classic seafood snacks like fried squid or mussels cooked in wine.

⌂ U Castellu   B&B €€

(☎04 95 36 26 13; www.ucastelluchambres dhotes.com; 8 place du Château; d incl breakfast €90-173; ☺late Mar–early Nov; ❄🤖) The five light-filled rooms in this lovely B&B, set in an old village home on the main square and right beside the ancient castle, are a wonderful blend of old and new. Maud's welcome is another drawcard, as is the panoramic rooftop terrace where they lay out the copious buffet breakfast.

Calvi ❹

✖ A Candella   Corsican €€

(☎04 95 65 42 13; 9 rue St-Antoine; mains €18-30; ☺noon-2.30pm & 7-10.30pm mid-May–Sep) Of the few eating options within the citadel, A Candella stands out for the stupendous views from its romantic, golden-hued stone terrace, strewn with pretty flowers in pots and olive trees. The food tends to be Corsican hearty, with rich sauces on chunks of meat and fish, but they do decent salads if you fancy lingering over a light lunch.

✖ U Casanu   Corsican €€

(☎04 95 65 00 10; 18 bd Wilson; mains €16-25; ☺noon-1.30pm & 8-10pm Mon-Sat Jan-Oct) For an unforgettable lunch, grab a booth at this cosy hole-in-the-wall, cheerily decorated in yellow and green, and hung with watercolours by septuagenarian artist-owner Monique Luciani. Tuck into home-cooked fish couscous, roast lamb, codfish aioli or octopus salad, and don't miss the exquisite *fiadone*, a classic Corsican cheesecake made with lemon-scented Brocciu cheese soaked in *eau de vie* (brandy).

⌂ Hôtel Le Magnolia   Hotel €€

(☎04 95 65 19 16; www.hotel-le-magnolia.com; rue Alsace Lorraine; d €107-220; ☺late Mar-Oct; ❄🤖) Right by the church in the heart of town, this attractive mansion sits in a beautiful high-walled courtyard garden adorned by a handsome magnolia tree. Pretty much every room has a lovely outlook – rooftops, garden or sea – while connecting doubles make it a hit with families.

Porto ⑦

✖ Le Maquis
Corsican €€

(☏04 95 26 12 19; rte de Calvi; mains €25-30; ☺noon-2pm & 7-10pm, closed Mon Oct-Apr) Propped on the hillside beside the main road, this welcoming restaurant is much loved by locals and tourists alike. The food is a delight, with a changing daily menu that's rooted in traditional Corsican recipes but extends to Mediterranean classics like seafood risotto. Sit in the cosy interior or, for brilliant views, reserve a table on the balcony.

🛏 Hôtel-Restaurant Le Belvédère
Hotel €€

(☏04 95 26 12 01; www.hotelrestaurant-lebelvedere-porto.com; rte de la Marine; d/q €100/165; 🛜) In a great location beside the harbour, near the steps up to the little watchtower, this small hotel holds bright, clean, tiled-floor rooms; several have full-on sea views, some have private terraces. Family rooms sleep up to five, with a double bed, two bunks and a trundle bed.

Ajaccio ⑨

✖ L'Altru Versu
Bistro €€

(☏04 95 50 05 22; www.facebook.com/mezzacquiresto; rte des Sanguinaires; mains €20-40, menus from €29; ☺noon-2pm & 8-10pm, closed Jan & Feb) At this perennial favourite on Ajaccio's waterfront, 2.5km west of the old town, magnificent sea views complement the exquisite gastronomic creations of the Mezzacqui brothers (Jean-Pierre front of house, David powering the kitchen), from crispy minted prawns with pistachio cream to pork with honey and clementine zest.

🛏 Hôtel Demeure Les Mouettes
Boutique Hotel €€€

(☏04 95 50 40 40; www.hotellesmouettes.fr; 9 cours Lucien Bonaparte; d €185-595; ☺Apr-Oct; ❄🛜🏊) Nestled right at the water's edge, 1.5km west of the old town, this colonnaded, peach-coloured 19th-century mansion is a dream. Views of the bay from its terraces – some rooms have their own private ones – and (heated) pool are exquisite; you may spot dolphins at dawn or dusk. Inside, the decor is elegantly understated and the service superb.

🛏 Hôtel Marengo
Hotel €€

(☏04 95 21 43 66; www.hotel-marengo.com; 2 rue Marengo; d €87-119; ☺Apr-Oct; ❄🛜) Hôtel Marengo is a charmingly eccentric little hotel, a block up from Trottel beach 1km west of the old town. Its plain but comfortable rooms lack sea views but have balconies overlooking a quiet flower-filled courtyard, while reception is an agreeable clutter of tasteful prints and personal objects. Find it down a cul-de-sac off bd Madame Mère.

The Camargue

27

Take this semicircular tour from Arles to the coast and loop back to experience Provence at its most wild, lush and lovely. Welcome to a watery, dreamlike landscape like no other.

TRIP HIGHLIGHTS

35 km

Stes-Maries-de-la-Mer
A 12th-century church houses the town's namesakes

START/FINISH
1

0 km

Arles
Home to Provence's hippest square

Étang de Vaccarès ●

● Le Sambuc

5

3

105 km

Salin de Badon
Flamingos swoop over wetlands as you walk

Saltworks Observation Point

7

125 km

Plage de Piémanson
End-of-the-earth feel with miles of windswept beach

4 DAYS
190KM / 118 MILES

GREAT FOR...

BEST TIME TO GO

Spring and early autumn are ideal for viewing huge flocks of migratory birds.

 ESSENTIAL PHOTO

Saltworks Observation Point for its pink-tinged backdrop and flocks of flamingos taking flight.

✓ **BEST FOR ROMANTICS**

Dinner by the hearth in the timber-beamed 17th-century kitchen of Le Mas de Peint.

Réserve Nationale de Camargue Camargue horses

27 | The Camargue

Leave Arles and the highway behind and suddenly you're surrounded by the Camargue's great yawning green and an equally expansive sky. It won't be long until you spot your first field of cantering white horses or face off with a black bull. This is not a long trip, but one that will plunge you into an utterly unique world of cowboys, fishers, beachcombers, the Roma, and all their enduring traditions.

TRIP HIGHLIGHT

❶ Arles

Befitting its role as gateway to the Camargue, Arles has a delightfully insouciant side. Long home to bohemians of all stripes, it's a great place to hang up your sightseeing hat for a few languorous hours (or days). Soak it in from the legendary bar at the Hôtel Nord-Pinus (p303), with its bullfighting trophies and enthralling photography collection, or pull up a table on lively **place Paul**

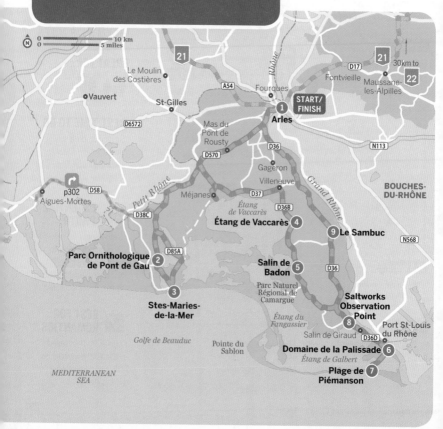

Doumer, where Arles' new generation makes its mark. Make a beeline for the Saturday-morning **market** (bd des Lices) and pack a Camargue-worthy picnic basket with local goat's cheese, olives and *saucisson d'Arles* (bull-meat sausage), or do likewise on Wednesday mornings on bd Émile Combes.

There's precious little parking within the old town, though you will find ample free parking near the train station off rue Pierre-Louis Rouillard.

 p244, p303, 409

The Drive » Take the D35A across the Grand Rhône at the Pont de Trinquetaille, then follow signs to the D570 – you'll soon be in no doubt you've entered the Camargue. Continue south on the D570 until Pont de Gau, 4km before you hit the coast, around 30 minutes all up.

 LINK YOUR TRIP

21 **Roman Provence**
Slot in the Camargue trip's loop south from either Nîmes or Arles.

22 **Lavender Route**
From Arles, take the 570N and the D28 (direction Châteaurenard), then the D900 to Coustellet.

② Parc Ornithologique du Pont de Gau

Itching to get in among all that green? **Parc Ornithologique de Pont de Gau** (🖉 04 90 97 82 62; www.parcornithologique.com; D570, Pont du Gau; adult/child €7.50/5; ⊙9am-7pm Apr-Sep, 10am-6pm Oct-Mar; P 🖐), a 60-hectare bird park, makes for a perfect pit stop. As you meander along 7km of trails, flamingos pirouette overhead; the pink birds can't help play diva. Secreted away in the marshes, though, is every bird species that calls the Camargue wetlands home, including herons, storks, egrets, teals and raptors.

The Drive » Continue south on the D570. The last stretch of road into Stes-Maries-de-la-Mer is dotted with stables – little-white-horse heaven, so get out your camera.

TRIP HIGHLIGHT

③ Stes-Maries-de-la-Mer

Apart from a stretch of fine-sand beaches – some 30km – the main attraction at this rough-and-tumble beach resort is the hauntingly beautiful **Église des Stes-Maries** (🖉04 90 97 80 25; www.sanctuaire-des-saintesmaries.fr; 19 place Jean XXIII; rooftop €3; ⊙8am-7pm), a 12th-century church that's home to a statue of Sara-la-Kali,

or black Sara. The crypt houses her alleged remains, along with those of Marie-Salomé and Marie-Jacobé, the Maries of the town's name. Shunned by the Vatican, this paleo-Christian trio has a powerful hold on the Provençal psyche, with a captivating backstory involving a boat journey from Palestine and a cameo from Mary Magdalene. Sara is the patron saint of the *gitans* (Roma people), and on 24 and 25 May each year, thousands come to town to pay their respects and party hard. Don't miss the ex-voto paintings that line the smoke-stained walls, personal petitions to Sara that are touching and startlingly strange in turns.

This town is the easiest spot to organise *promenades à cheval* (horseback riding); look for Fédération Française d'Equitation (FFE) accredited places, such as the friendly **Cabanes de Cacharel** (🖉04 90 97 84 10, 06 11 57 74 75; www.cabanesdecacharel.com; rte de Cacharel, D85A; horse trek per hour/day €22/70) on the easterly D85A.

 p303

The Drive » The scenic D85A rejoins the D570. After 10 minutes or so, turn right onto the D37. Stop at Méjanes for supplies or to visit the legendary fish restaurant Le Mazet du Vaccarès. The D36B dramatically skims the eastern lakeshore; it's a 20-minute journey but is worth taking your time over.

④ Étang de Vaccarès

This 600-sq-km lagoon, with its watery labyrinth of peninsulas and islands, is where the wetlands are at their most dense, almost primordial. Much of its tenuous shore forms the **Réserve Nationale de Camargue** and is off-limits, making the wonderful nature trails and wildlife observatories at **La Capelière** (📞04 90 97 00 97; www.snpn.com/reservedecamargue; C134,

rte de Fiélouse, La Capelière; permits adult/child €4/2; ⊗9am-1pm & 2-6pm Apr-Sep, to 4.30pm Wed-Mon Oct-Mar) particularly precious. The 1.5km-long **Sentier des Rainettes** (Tree-Frog Trail) takes you through tamarisk woodlands and the grasses of brackish open meadows.

The Drive » Continue on the D36B past Fiélouse for around 10 minutes.

TRIP HIGHLIGHT

⑤ Salin de Badon

Before you leave La Capelière, grab your permits for another outstanding

reserve site, once the **royal salt works** (adult/child €4/2). Around the picturesque ruins are a number of observatories and 4.5km of wild trails – spy on flamingos wading through springtime iris. Avid birdwatchers mustn't miss a night in the **gîte** (www.snpn.com/reservedecamargue; off the D36B; dm €16) here, a bare-bones cottage in a priceless location.

The Drive » Continue south until you meet the D36, turning right. Stop in Salin de Giraud for bike hire and fuel (there's a 24/7 petrol station on ave Joseph Imbert) or visit the salt works. The D36 splits off to cross the Rhône via punt, but you continue south on the D36D, where it gets exciting: spectacular salt pans appear on your right, the river on your left.

DETOUR: AIGUES-MORTES

Start: ③ Stes-Maries-de-la-Mer

Located over the border from Provence in the Gard, Aigues-Mortes sits a winding 28km northwest of Stes-Maries-de-la-Mer at the Camargue's far western extremity. Its central axis of streets often throngs with tourists, and shops spill out Camargue-themed tack, but the town is nonetheless magnificent, set in flat marshland and completely enclosed by rectangular ramparts and a series of towers. Come sundown, things change pace, and its squares are a lovely place to join locals for a relaxed *apéro* (pre-dinner drink). It was established by Louis IX in the mid-13th century to give the French crown a Mediterranean port, and it was from here that the king launched the seventh Crusade (and persecuted Cathars). The **Tour de Constance** (www.aigues-mortes-monument.fr; adult/child €8/free; ⊗10am-7pm May-Aug, to 5.30pm Sep-Apr; 🚻) once held Huguenot prisoners; today it's the start of the 1.6km wall-top circuit, a must-do for heady views of salt mountains and viridian plains. Park on bd Diderot, on the outside of the northeastern wall.

⑥ Domaine de la Palissade

Along the D36D, **Domaine de la Palissade** (📞horse riding 06 27 13 63 41, info 04 42 86 81 28, kayak tour 06 73 11 28 99; www.palissade.fr; 36 chemin Départemental; adult/child €3/free, horse trekking 1hr/2hr €30/55, kayak tour 90min €24; ⊗9am-6pm Jul-Sep, to 5pm Mar-Jun & Oct, to 5pm Wed-Sun Feb & Nov; 🅿) organises horse treks and kayaking excursions where you'll find yourself gliding across brackish lakes and through a purple haze of sea lavender. You can also explore the lagoons and scrubby glasswort on foot; pick

Salin de Badon Nature trail

up a free map of the estate's marked walking trails, which range from 1.5km to 8km. Book horse riding or kayaking excursions at least one day ahead.

The Drive » The next 3.7km along the rte de la Mer is equally enchanting, with flocks of birds circling and salt crystals flashing in the sun. Stop when you hit the sea.

TRIP HIGHLIGHT

7 Plage de Piémanson

Just try to resist the urge to greet the Med with a wild dash into the waves at this lovely, windswept beach anchoring the southern end of rte de la Mer. Located just west of the mouth of the Rhône, the sands stretch for 6km, which means it's not hard to find your own private space. Head 1km east for the popular nudist beach. There's ample free parking and lifeguards in July and August, but no facilities of any kind, so bring food and drinks (the nearby village of Salin de Giraud has all the essentials).

The Drive » Backtrack north along the D36D. Just before Salin de Giraud, look for a signed turnoff off to your left, which leads to a small car park and viewing spot.

8 Saltworks Observation Point

This lookout provides a rare vantage point to take in the stunning scene of pink-stained *salins* (salt pans) and soaring crystalline mountains. As fruitful as it is beguiling, this is Europe's largest salt works, producing over 340,000 tonnes per year. A microalgae gives the water its pinkish hue and also provides nourishment for the shrimp. This also gives the pinkish colour to the flamingos which feed upon the shrimp.

The Drive » Heading north on D36 for 20 minutes, Le Mas de Peint is on your right before Le Sambuc, while the fork-and-trowel shingle of La Chassagnette is on the left to its north.

9 Le Sambuc

This sleepy town's outskirts hide away one of the region's most luxurious places to stay and one of its best restaurants. **Le Mas de Peint** (📞04 90 97 20 62; www.masdepeint.com; rte de Salin de Giraud, Le Sambuc, Manade Jacques Bon; d from €275; ☾mid-Mar–mid-Nov; ❋ 🤶 ☀) is owned by the Bon family, who have been in the *gardian* (cowboy) business for decades. Along with superb Provençal food and lovely rooms, the 500-hectare estate also offers flamenco, bull-herding and birdwatching weekends.

✗ p303

The Drive » Continue north on the D36, where you'll re-meet the D570 heading to Arles, a 25km stretch in all.

10 Arles

Back in Arles, last stop is **Les Arènes** (Amphithéâtre; 📞08 91 70 03 70; www.arenes-arles.com; Rond-Point des Arènes; adult/child incl Théâtre Antique €9/free; ☾9am-8pm Jul & Aug, to 7pm May, Jun & Sep, shorter hours Oct-Apr), the town's incredibly well-preserved Roman amphitheatre. Dating from around 90 CE, this great arena would once have held more than 21,000 baying spectators, and it's still used for many events. The structure itself hasn't survived the centuries entirely intact, but it's still an evocative insight into the Roman psyche. Entry is on the northern side.

✗ 🛏 p244, p303, p409

Eating & Sleeping

Arles ❶

✕ Le Comptoir du Calendal Cafe €

(☎04 90 96 11 89; www.lecalendal.com; 5 rue Porte de Laure; mains €12-20; ⊙8am-8.30pm; 🛜) Based on the ground floor of **Le Calendal** (☎04 90 96 11 89; www.lecalendal.com; 5 rue Porte de Laure; s/d/tr/q €109/149/159/209; ❄🛜🏊), this bright and breezy cafe does a nice line in lunchtime sandwiches and salads, plus offers a tempting choice of cakes and teas post-sightseeing. Takeaway is available and the ice cream is pretty good too.

🛏 Hôtel de l'Amphithéâtre Historic Hotel €€

(☎04 90 96 10 30; www.hotelamphitheatre. fr; 5-7 rue Diderot; s from €80, d €95-175; ❄@🛜) This elegant address across from the amphitheatre is quite a bargain: the standard of design here far outreaches the reasonable price tag. Antiques, rugs, fireplaces and staircases speak of the building's history, while minimal rooms nod to modern trends, and several have super views over Les Arènes and Arles' rooftops (although you'll pay for the privilege).

🛏 Grand Hôtel Nord Pinus Heritage Hotel €€€

(☎04 90 93 44 44; www.nord-pinus.com; place du Forum; s/d €240/395; ❄🛜) This Arlésian landmark has housed everyone from Picasso and Hemingway to Cocteau and Fritz Lang. Its style is 1930s opulence: wrought-iron beds, art deco sinks, designer furniture, vintage *féria* posters, black-and-white Peter Beard photographs and a chichi bar and restaurant. This is not the place to stay if you baulk at paying €25 for parking and €24 per person for breakfast.

Stes-Maries-de-la-Mer ❸

✕ La Cabane aux Coquillages Seafood €

(☎06 10 30 33 49; 16 av Van Gogh; seafood €10-22; ⊙noon-3pm & 5-11pm Apr-Nov) Attached to the excellent Ô Pica Pica restaurant, this informal little *cabane* (hut) specialises, unsurprisingly, in *coquillages* (shellfish): oysters, *palourdes* (clams), *coques* (cockles), and *tellines* (a type of local shellfish known elsewhere in France as *pignons*). Or, you could opt for perfectly cooked *fritures* (battered baby prawns, baby squid or anchovies) and a very cooperative glass of wine.

🛏 Lodge Sainte Hélène Boutique Hotel €€€

(☎04 90 97 83 29; www.lodge-saintehelene. com; chemin Bas des Launes; d for 2 nights from €510; ⊙Jan–mid-Nov; ❄@🛜🏊) These pearly-white terraced cottages on a peninsula on the Étang des Launes are prime real estate for birdwatchers and romance seekers. It's so quiet you can hear flamingos flapping past. The charming rooms have terraces overlooking the water (perfect spot for a sundowner, with tapas and drinks available). Staff can arrange horse riding and mountain biking, and there's also a heated pool. Prices drop outside high season, when single-night stays are also possible.

Le Sambuc ❾

✕ La Chassagnette Gastronomy €€€

(☎04 90 97 26 96; www.chassagnette.fr; rte du Sambuc, Domaine de L'Armellière; menu lunch/dinner €67/105; ⊙noon-1.30pm & 7-9.30pm Jun-Sep, noon-1.30pm Thu-Mon & 7-9.30pm Sat Oct-May; 🍴) Surrounded by a vast *potager* (kitchen garden), which supplies practically all the restaurant's produce, this renowned gourmet table is run by Armand Amal, a former pupil of Alain Ducasse. The multicourse *menus* are full of surprises, and the bucolic setting is among the loveliest anywhere in the Camargue. There's a vegetarian *menu* (unfortunately available only at lunch).

STRETCH YOUR LEGS
NICE

Start Hotel Negresco, Promenade des Anglais

Finish Promenade des Anglais

Distance 5.8km

Duration 2 hours

Get to know Nice's bustling heart with this walk that begins with a seaside stroll, then takes you into the tangled alleys of the old town, and finally up and over the city's soaring headland to the port. Along the way shop, eat and drink in Niçois style.

Take this walk on Trips

Promenade des Anglais

Nice personified, the Prom seductively blends hedonism with history, pumping beach clubs with quiet seaside gazing. Why 'Anglais'? English expats paid out-of-work citrus farmers to build the Prom in 1822. Don't miss the palatial façades of Belle Époque **Hôtel Negresco** and art deco **Palais de la Méditerranée**.

The Walk » Turn up av de Verdun to place Masséna. Take in the elegant architecture, then head down the steps. Take rue de l'Opéra to our next stop.

Rue St-François de Paule

Window-shop or gift shop on this elegant street just back from the seaside. First stop: **Moulin à Huile d'Olive Alziari** (☎04 93 62 94 03; www.alziari.com.fr; 14 rue St-François de Paule; ⊙9am-7pm Mon-Sat, from 10am Sun) for superb local olive oil. Head west to the florid **Opera House**; then shop for soap and sweets along the charming pedestrianised street.

The Walk » Continue on past soap sellers into the open square. This eventually becomes cours Saleya.

Cours Saleya

A top tourist destination that remains Niçois to the core, this bustling market square is the place to greet the day with espresso and banter with flower sellers, lunch with locals or getting rowdy after dark with the town's cool kids.

The Walk » Any of the streets running away from the beach take you to rue de la Préfecture.

Vieux Nice

Soak in the labyrinthine streets of Nice's old town, stumbling upon Baroque gems like **Cathédrale Ste-Réparate** (☎04 93 92 01 35; https://cathedrale-nice.fr; place Rossetti; ⊙2-6pm Mon, 9am-noon & 2-6pm Tue-Sun). Stop to eat – book **Le Bistrot d'Antoine** (☎04 93 85 29 57; 27 rue de la Préfecture; mains €17-32; ⊙9am-1.45pm & 7-10pm Tue-Sat), or grab an aperitif at **Les Distilleries Idéales**

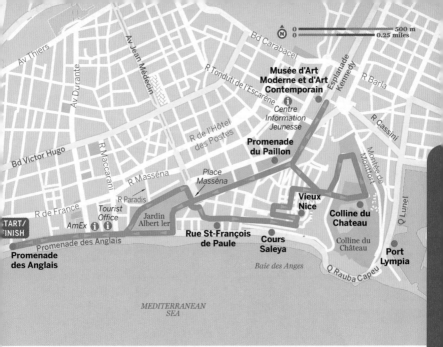

(📞04 93 62 10 66; www.facebook.com/ldinice;
24 rue de la Préfecture; 🕙9am-12.30am).
Snacks, ice cream, gift shopping and
more are ubiquitous.

The Walk » Take the stairs at rue Rossetti
(or if you can't face the climb, the lift at rue des
Ponchettes).

Colline du Château

On a rocky outcrop towering over Vieux
Nice, the **Parc de la Colline du Château**
(Castle Hill; 🕙8.30am-8pm Apr-Sep, to 6pm
Oct-Mar; 🚌1 to Garibaldi/Le Château) offers
a panorama of the whole city – Baie
des Anges on one side, the port on the
other. Fabulous for picnics (there's a
waterfall) or to let kids loose in the
playground.

The Walk » Head towards the cemetery, then
follow Allée Font aux Oiseaux and the Montée du
Château back into the old town. Take backstreets to
bd Jean Jaurès and cross to Promenade du Paillon.

Promenade du Paillon

The grounds of this lovely park unfold
from the Théâtre National to place

Masséna with a succession of green
spaces, play areas and water features.
It's a favourite among Niçois for evening strolls.

The Walk » Follow the park as it heads
northeast and exit onto av St-Sébastien.

Musée d'Art Moderne et d'Art Contemporain

Nice's modern art **museum** (MAMAC;
📞04 97 13 42 01; www.mamac-nice.org;
place Yves Klein; museum pass 24hr/7 days
€10/20; 🕙10am-6pm Tue-Sun late Jun–mid-
Oct, from 11am rest of year; 🚌1 to Garibaldi)
focuses on the European and American
avant-garde from the 1950s to the
present, with works by artists such as
Yves Klein and César. The building's
rooftop works as an exhibition space
(with knockout panoramas of the city).
Then it's back to the Promenade des
Anglais for a post-walk *pastis* (aniseed-
flavoured aperitif).

Pyrenees & Southwest France

PEAKS TO PLAINS, VALLEYS TO VILLAGES, MOUNTAINS TO MED: the southwest encompasses the French landscape in all its drama and diversity. Stretching from the lion's-tooth peaks of the Pyrenees all the way to the scrubby, sun-baked plains of the Languedoc, it's a region that's made for driving, with lots of scenic roads punctuated by fabulous viewpoints.

In the west, you'll meander across mountain passes and delve into remote valleys where life still feels timeless and traditional. As you move east, you'll discover the two sides of the Languedoc: Bas-Languedoc, with its flat plains, sprawling vineyards and laid-back coastal cities, and Haut-Languedoc, home to the wild hills and rocky gorges of the Parc National des Cévennes.

Le Puy-en-Velay Chapelle St-Michel d'Aiguilhe
MIHAI-BOGDAN LAZAR / SHUTTERSTOCK ©

Pyrenees & Southwest France

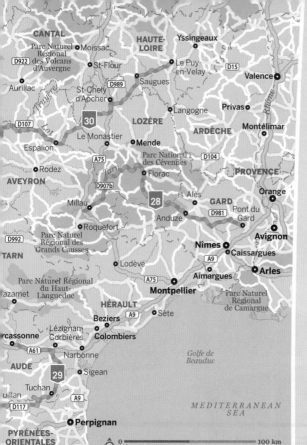

 DON'T
MISS

Le Puy-en-Velay

Climb inside a giant statue of the Virgin Mary for views across this Auvergnat town. Take them in on Trip **30**

Lac de Gaube

One of the Pyrenees' most beautiful valleys centres on the glittering Lac de Gaube. Catch the cable car to the lake on Trip **31**

La Cité des Pierres

An otherworldly landscape of limestone pillars has been created here by centuries of natural erosion. Walk it on Trip **28**

Col d'Aubisque

The col is one of the Pyrenees' highest road passes. Competitors in the Tour de France have to pedal it, so count yourself lucky to just drive it on Trip **31**

Roquefort

Descend into murky, mould-covered cellars to find out how this pungent fromage is made. Sample a piece on Trip **28**

Pont du Gard to Viaduc de Millau

28

This trip begins and ends with a river, traversing hills and gorges in between. Start at the Pont du Gard, France's greatest Roman aqueduct, and finish by crossing the space-age Viaduc de Millau.

TRIP HIGHLIGHTS

142 km

Gorges du Tarn
Canoes are great for exploring the gorges at your own pace

100km

Florac
Hike the wild hills of the Cévennes

5 **4**

FINISH
7

Anduze

1
START

Viaduc de Millau
Enjoy the unforgettable drive across France's futuristic road-bridge

223 km

Pont du Gard
Marvel at a mighty Roman aqueduct

0 km

5 DAYS
223KM / 139 MILES

GREAT FOR...

BEST TIME TO GO
April to July.

 ESSENTIAL PHOTO

The Pont du Gard Roman aqueduct from the water below.

 BEST FOR FAMILIES

Canoeing beneath the towering cliffs of the Gorges du Tarn.

28 Pont du Gard to Viaduc de Millau

Languedoc's known for its fine coastline and even finer wines, but on this trip you'll explore a different side to this peaceful corner of France. Inland, the landscape climbs into the high hills and river ravines of the Parc National des Cévennes, beloved by walkers, kayakers and nature-lovers alike. The scenery is truly grand, but keep your eyes on the tarmac, as some of the roads are hairy.

TRIP HIGHLIGHT

❶ Pont du Gard

The trip begins 21km northeast of Nîmes at the **Pont du Gard** (☎04 66 37 50 99; www.pontdugard. fr; adult/child €9.50/free, guided tour to top tier €6/free; ☺9am-11pm Jul & Aug, to 10pm Jun & Sep, to 9pm May, to 8pm Apr & Oct, to 6pm Nov-Mar; ♿), France's finest Roman aqueduct. At 50m high and 275m long, and graced with 35 arches, it was built around 19 BCE to transport water from Uzès to Nîmes. A

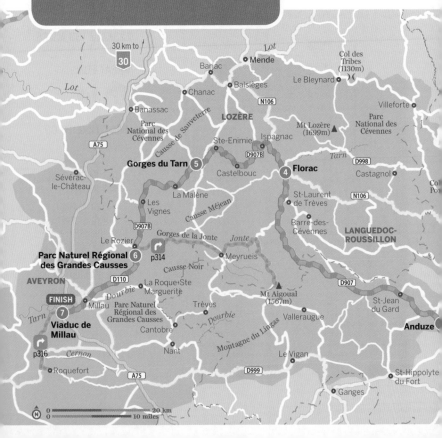

museum explores the bridge's history. You can walk across the tiers for panoramic views over the Gard River, but the best perspective on the bridge is from downstream, along the 1.4km **Mémoires de Garrigue** walking trail.

For a unique perspective on the Pont du Gard, you need to see it from the water. Canoe and/or kayak rental companies are plentiful.

There are large car parks on both banks of the river, a 400m level walk from the Pont du Gard. Early evening is a good time to visit, as admission is cheaper and the bridge is stunningly illuminated after dark.

The Drive » Drive northwest from the Pont du Gard along the D981 for 15km to Uzès.

----

② Uzès

Northwest of the Pont du Gard is Uzès, a once-wealthy medieval town that grew rich on the proceeds of silk, linen and liquorice. It's also home to the **Duché Château** (📞04 66 22 18 96; www.uzes.com; place du Duché; €13, incl tour €20; ⌚10am-12.30pm & 2-6.30pm Jul & Aug, 10am-noon & 2-6pm Sep-Jun), a castle that belonged to the powerful Dukes of Uzès for more than 1000 years. You can climb 135 steps to the top of the Tour Bermonde for a magnificent view across the town's rooftops.

Built in 1090 on the site of a Roman temple, Uzès' **Cathédrale St-Théodont** (place de l'Évêché; ⌚9am-6pm May-Sep, to 5pm Oct-Apr) was partially destroyed in both the 13th and 16th centuries and stripped during the French Revolution. All that remains of the 11th-century church is its 42m-high round tower, Tour Fenestrelle, the only round bell tower in France, which resembles an upright Leaning Tower of Pisa.

LINK YOUR TRIP

21 Roman Provence
Our tour through southern France's Gallo-Roman legacy also passes through Pont du Gard, so it's a perfect add-on.

30 Cheat's Compostela
Our Chemin de Compostela drive is an ideal route to the Atlantic Coast. It starts 180km northeast of Millau in Le Puy-en-Velay.

If you've got a sweet tooth, don't miss the nearby **Musée du Bonbon Haribo** (Sweets Museum; 04 66 22 20 25; www.museeharibo.fr; Pont des Charrettes; adult/child €8/6; ⏰10am-7pm Jul, to 8pm Aug, to 7pm Tue-Sun Sep-Jun), a candy museum belonging to the Haribo brand. Join in with a tasting session, or just pick up some treats for the road.

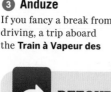 p317

The Drive » From Uzès, travel 44km west on the D982 and D907 to Anduze; the Train à Vapeur des Cévennes is well signposted.

- - - - - - - - - - - - - - - - - - -

❸ Anduze

If you fancy a break from driving, a trip aboard the **Train à Vapeur des Cévennes** (04 66 60 59 00; www.trainavapeur.com; Anduze; adult/child/bike return €16.50/11.50/3; ⏰Apr-Oct) is just the ticket. This vintage steam train chugs 13km between Anduze and St-Jean du Gard, a journey of 40 minutes each way. En route, you'll stop at a 150-year-old bamboo garden, the **Bambouseraie de Prafrance** (04 66 61 70 47; www.bambouseraie. com; 552 rue de Montsauve, Générargues; adult/child €12.50/8.90; ⏰9.30am-7pm mid-Mar–Sep, to 6pm early-mid-Mar & Oct, to 5pm early Nov, closed mid-Nov–Feb).

The Drive » The 74km stretch between Anduze and Florac along the D907 follows the river and slowly loops up through the forested hillsides into the high Cévennes. Petrol stations are few and far between, so remember to fill your tank.

- - - - - - - - - - - - - - - - - - -

❹ Florac

It's a long, winding drive up into the **Parc National des Cévennes** (www. causses-et-cevennes. fr). Created in 1970, it's a wild range of rumpled hills, forested ravines and quiet hamlets. Famously featured in Robert Louis Stevenson's classic 1878 travelogue, *Travels with a Donkey in the Cévennes*, it's still a remote and sparsely populated landscape, home to rare species including vultures, beavers, otters, roe deer and golden eagles. Since 2011, it has formed part of one of France's largest Unesco World Heritage Sites, the Causses and Cévennes.

The riverside town of Florac makes an ideal base, draped along the west bank of the Tarnon River, a tributary of the Tarn. There's not much to see in town, but it's a good place to stretch your legs: Florac's **Maison du Parc National des Cévennes** has comprehensive information on hiking and other activities.

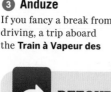 p317

The Drive » Head on from Florac along the N106, and keep your eyes open for the sharp left turn onto the D907B towards Ispagnac. The road teeters

---

DETOUR:
GORGES DE LA JONTE

Start: ❻ Parc Naturel Régional des Grandes Causses

The 20km-long Gorges de la Jonte cleave east–west from Meyrueis to Le Rozier, dividing Causse Noir from Causse Méjean. They're much more lightly trafficked – though busy enough in summer – than the more famous Gorges du Tarn, and make for a spectacular loop drive in combination with their better-known neighbour. Just west of Le Truel on the D996, more than 200 reintroduced vultures have taken up residence on the limestone cliffs. You can watch them gliding above the Gorges de la Jonte from the viewing point at the **Maison des Vautours** (05 65 62 69 69; www.lozere-tourisme.com/maison-des-vautours/meyrueis/loiloz048fs0005a; adult/child €6.20/2.70; ⏰9.30am-7.30pm Jul & Aug, to 6pm Tue-Sun Apr-Jun, Sep & Oct), which also has a live video feed from the nesting sites.

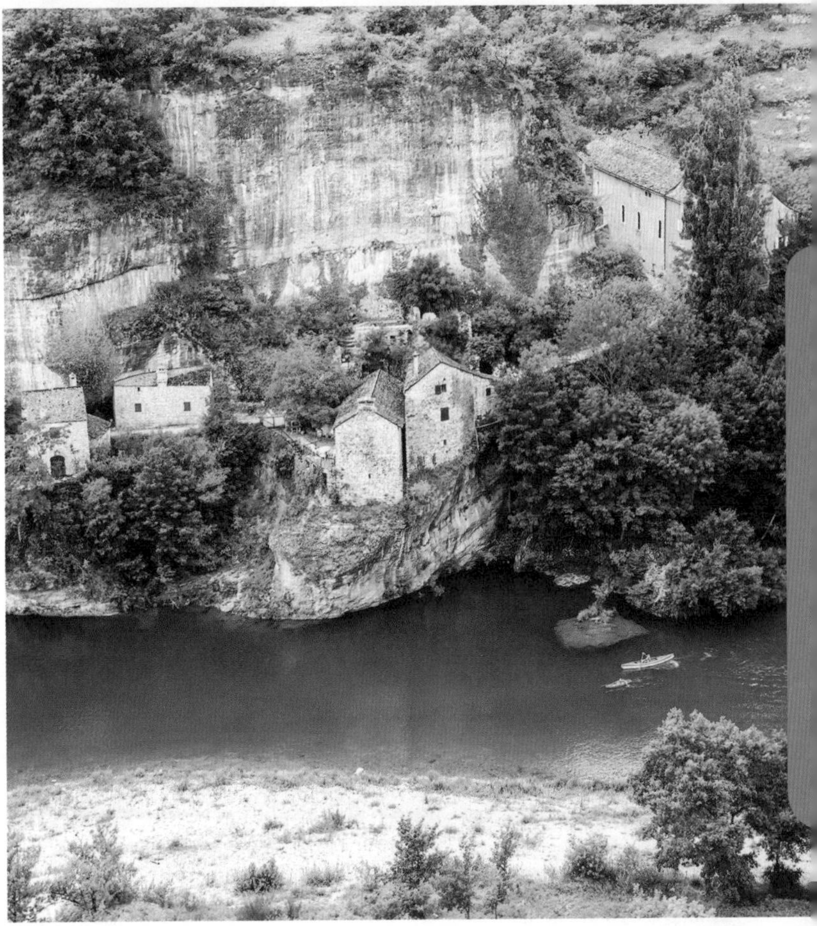

Gorges du Tarn

along the edge of the gorge as it passes through Ispagnac and tracks the river to Ste-Énimie, 28km northwest of Florac.

TRIP HIGHLIGHT

5 Gorges du Tarn

West of Florac, the rushing Tarn River has carved out a series of sheer slashes into the limestone known as the Gorges du Tarn. Running southwest for 50km from Ispagnac, this spectacular ravine provides one of Languedoc's most scenic drives. In summer the cliffside road becomes one long traffic jam, though – you'll find spring or autumn are more relaxing times to travel.

Until the road was constructed in 1905, the only way through the gorges was by boat. Piloting your own kayak is still the best way to experience the scenery; the villages of **Ste-Énimie** and **La Malène** both have lots of companies offering river trips.

The Drive » The cliff-side D907B runs all the way to Le Rozier, 36km to the southwest of Ste-Énimie. It's a superbly scenic drive, so don't rush, and leave ample time for photo ops.

DETOUR: ROQUEFORT

Start: ⑦ Millau

The village of Roquefort, 25km southwest of Millau via the D992 and the D999, is synonymous with its famous blue cheese, produced from the milk of local ewes who live in natural caves around the village. Marbled with distinctive blue-green veins caused by microscopic mushrooms known as *Penicillium roquefort*, this powerfully pungent cheese has been protected by royal charter since 1407, and was the first cheese in France to be granted AOC (Appéllations d'Origines Contrôlées) status in 1925. There are seven AOC-approved producers in the village, three of which (La Société, Gabriel Coulet and Papillon) offer cellar visits and tasting sessions. The cellars of four other producers aren't open to the public, but they all have shops where you can sample the village's illustrious cheese.

When you get to Le Rozier, crawl your way up the hairpin bends of the D29 and turn left onto the D110 to La Cité des Pierres, another 9km.

⑥ Parc Naturel Régional des Grandes Causses

Around the gorges of the western Cévennes, the Tarn, Jonte and Dourbie Rivers have created four high *causses* ('plateaux') in the local lingo): Sauveterre, Méjean, Noir and Larzac, each slightly different in geological character. You could spend several days touring along the tangled roads that cut between them, but the D996 along the **Gorges de la Jonte** (p314) is particularly detour-worthy.

South of Le Rozier is the **Cité des Pierres** (Montpellier-le-Vieux; ☎05 65 60 66 30; www.lacitedepierres. com; Le Maubert; adult/child €7.90/4.90, combination ticket with Aven Armand €17/10.70; ☺9.30am-6.30pm mid-Jul–Aug, to 5pm or 5.30pm May–mid-Jul & Sep-Oct), where centuries of erosion have carved out a landscape of amazing limestone formations, often given fanciful names, such as the Sphinx and the Elephant. Several walking trails cover the site, or you can cheat and catch a tourist train instead.

The Drive » Continue along the narrow D110 towards Millau, 18km to the southwest. There are a couple of great roadside lookouts on the way, as well as a trail to the top of the local peak known as Puncho d'Agast.

TRIP HIGHLIGHT

⑦ Viaduc de Millau

Finish your road trip with a spin over the gravity-defying Viaduc de Millau, the famous road bridge that hovers 343m above the Tarn River. Designed by the British architect Norman Foster, the bridge contains over 127,000 cu metres of concrete and 19,000 tonnes of steel, but somehow still manages to look like a gossamer thread, seemingly supported by nothing more than seven needle-thin pylons.

It's such a wonderful structure, it's worth seeing twice. Begin with the drive across: head north of Millau on the D911, and then turn south onto the A75 motorway.

Once you've crossed the bridge, turn off at exit 46 and loop back to Millau along the D999 and D992, which passes directly underneath the bridge and gives you an unforgettable ant's-eye view. En route, you'll pass the bridge's visitor centre, **Viaduc Expo** (☎05 65 61 61 54; www. leviaducdemillau.com; Aire du Viaduc de Millau, A75; guided tour adult/child €4.50/2.50; ☺visitors centre 9am-7pm Jul & Aug, 9am-6pm Apr-Jun, Sep & Oct, 9am-5pm Nov-Mar).

✕ ☞ p317

Eating & Sleeping

Uzès ❷

🍴 Le Tracteur
Bistro €€

(📞04 66 62 17 33; Off D3B, Bord Nègre; mains €17-25; 🕑noon-2pm Mon-Thu, noon-2pm & 7.30-9.30pm Fri & Sat) A cracking lunch stop just off the D981 from Uzès, this recommended restaurant in the village of Argilliers is well worth a detour for its first-rate Mediterranean food. Sit out in the sandy courtyard garden under a majestic tree, or head inside to the art-filled warehouse space, full of quirky artworks and upcycled furniture. The namesake Massey-Ferguson tractor is outside.

🛏 La Maison d'Uzès
Boutique Hotel €€€

(📞04 66 20 07 00; www.lamaisonduzes.fr; 18 rue du Dr Blanchard; d from €240; 🅿❄🛜🏊) In a 17th-century *hôtel particulier* (private mansion) in Uzès' historical centre, this jewel has beautiful rooms filled with light-toned vintage and contemporary furnishings, and a Michelin-starred **restaurant** (menus €34-86; 🕑12.15-1.30pm & 7.30-8.30pm Wed-Sun), opening to a gorgeous linden-tree-shaded courtyard with a fountain at its centre. The pièce de résistance is the in-house spa with swimming pool set in an old Roman cellar.

Florac ❹

🍴 Les Tables de la Fontaine
French €€

(📞04 66 65 21 73; www.tables-de-la-fontaine. com; 31 rue du Therond; 2-/3-course menu €20/23; 🕑noon-1.30pm & 7-8.30pm Mon, Tue & Thu-Sat, noon-1.30pm Sun) Red-umbrella-shaded tables are scattered around a natural spring in the courtyard adjoining this homely regional restaurant, which serves delicacies

such as locally caught trout and Aubrac beef. Upstairs are four simple guest rooms (doubles half-board €120).

🛏 Hôtel Les Gorges du Tarn
Hotel €

(📞04 66 45 00 63; www.hotel-gorgesdutarn. com; 48 rue du Pêcher; d €70-95; 🕑Easter-Oct; 🅿❄🛜) This modern Logis de France hotel in Florac is a reliable choice, with three room categories – the nicest are the Florales, which are smart, functional and colourful. Its restaurant is among the best in town.

Millau ❼

🍴 La Mangeoire
French €€

(📞05 65 60 13 16; www.restaurantmillau.com; 10 bd de la Capelle; 2-/3-course menu €17/25, mains from €16; 🕑noon-1.30pm & 7-9.30pm Tue-Sun; 🍷) Fronted by a shady pavement terrace strung with fairy lights and opening to a romantic vaulted-stone dining room, Millau's best restaurant refines the rich flavours of the region: wood-fire-grilled Trénels tripe sausage with *aligot* (mashed potato and melted sheep's cheese); lamb with honey-mustard sauce; and spicy spit-roasted local hare (in winter).

🛏 Château de Creissels
Hotel €€

(📞05 65 60 16 59; www.chateau-de-creissels. com; place du Prieur, Creissels; d €88-148, ste €144-188; 🕑early Mar-late Dec; 🅿❄🛜🏊) In Creissels, 2km southwest of Millau on the D992, this castle's rooms are split between the 12th-century tower (parquet floors, fireplaces, oil paintings) and modern wings (sleek showers, stripped-wood floors, designer lamps; some with garden-view balconies). Excellent regional cuisine (*menus* from €28) is served in the restaurant's brick-vaulted cellar, and there's a swimming pool with knockout views of the bridge.

The Cathar Trail

29

From the fairy-tale towers of Carcassonne to the tumbledown walls of Montségur, this cross-country trip explores the main Cathar strongholds of sun-baked southwest France.

TRIP HIGHLIGHTS

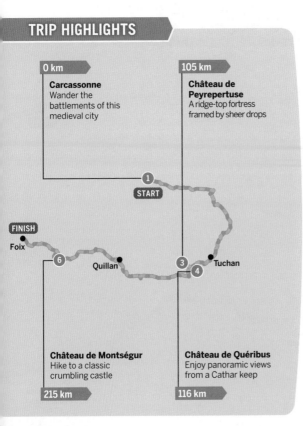

0 km

Carcassonne
Wander the battlements of this medieval city

START ①

FINISH
Foix

⑥

Quillan ③ ④ Tuchan

105 km

Château de Peyrepertuse
A ridge-top fortress framed by sheer drops

Château de Montségur
Hike to a classic crumbling castle

215 km

Château de Quéribus
Enjoy panoramic views from a Cathar keep

116 km

**3 DAYS
247KM / 153 MILES**

GREAT FOR...

BEST TIME TO GO
September and October when the summer heat has passed.

 ESSENTIAL PHOTO
The view from the ramparts of Carcassonne.

BEST FOR HISTORY
Go in search of the Holy Grail in Montségur.

29 The Cathar Trail

The parched land between Perpignan and the Pyrenees is known as Le Pays Cathare (Cathar Land), a reference to the Christian order that escaped persecution here during the 12th century. Its legacy remains in a string of hilltop castles, flanked by sheer cliffs and dusty scrubland. Most can be reached after a short, stiff climb, but this is wild country and fiercely hot in summer, so be sure to pack a hat.

TRIP HIGHLIGHT

❶ Carcassonne

Jutting from a rocky spur of land and ringed by battlements and turrets, the fortress of Carcassonne was one of the Cathars' most important strongholds. After a notorious siege in August 1209, the castle crumbled into disrepair, but was saved from destruction in the 19th century by Viollet-le-Duc, who rebuilt the ramparts and added the turrets' distinctive pointy roofs.

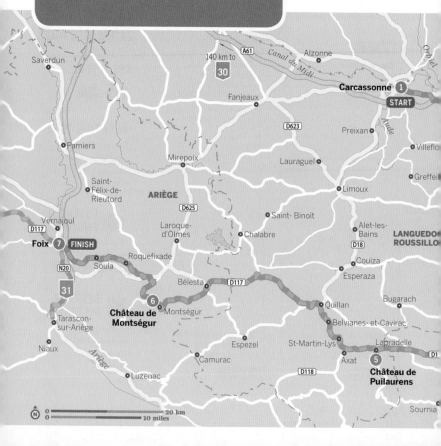

These days Carcassonne is one of the Languedoc's biggest tourist draws, and its cobbled streets can feel uncomfortably crowded in summer. Try to time your visit for early or late in the day when it's at its most peaceful.

✖️ 🛏️ p325

The Drive » From Carcassonne, take the A61 east for 36km towards Narbonne. Turn off at exit 25, signed to Lezignan-Corbières, and follow the D611 across the sun-baked countryside for 46km. Just before you reach Tuchan, look out for a white sign with a blue castle pointing to 'Aguilar'. Drive up this minor track to the car park.

----

② Château d'Aguilar

When the Albigensian Crusade forced the Cathars into the mountains between France and the province of Aragon, they sought refuge in a line of frontier strongholds. The first of these is the **Château d'Aguilar** (📞04 68 45 51 00; www.tuchan. fr; Tuchan; adult/child €4/2; 🕙10am-7pm Jul & Aug, 10.30am-5.30pm May, Jun & Sep, 11am-5pm Apr & Oct,

11am-4pm Feb & Mar), which squats on a low hill near the village of Tuchan. It's the smallest of the castles and is crumbling fast – but you can still make out the corner turrets along with the hexagonal outer wall.

The Drive » Take the D611 through Tuchan, emerging from the narrow streets onto dry, vine-covered slopes. You'll reach a roundabout; turn left onto the D14, signed to Padern and Cucugnan. (After 15km, note the turn-off to the Château de Quéribus on the D123 as you bypass Cucugnan; you'll be returning here following your next stop.) Continue 9km northwest towards Duilhac-sous-Peyrepertuse.

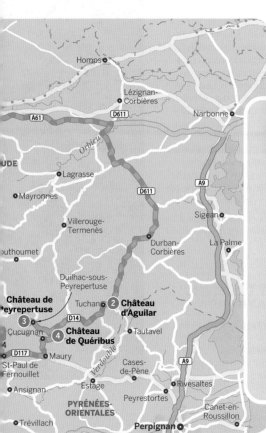

🔗 **LINK YOUR TRIP**

30 Cheat's Compostela

Make a longish detour off our version of the Chemin de St-Jacques by driving northwest of Carcassonne for 165km to Moissac, with an optional stop in Toulouse en route.

31 The Pyrenees

Foix sits on the eastern edge of the Pyrenees, so our Pyrenean tour makes a natural next stage – although you'll have to do it in reverse.

❸ Château de Peyrepertuse

The largest and perhaps most dramatic of the Cathar castles is **Peyrepertuse** (📞04 30 37 00 77; www.chateau-peyrepertuse. com; Duilhac-sous-Peyrepertuse; adult/child €7/4; ⏰9am-8pm Jul & Aug, 9am-7pm Apr-Jun & Sep, 10am-6pm Mar & Oct, 10am-4.30pm or 5pm rest of year), spanning a narrow ridge with a dizzying drop of 800m on either side. Several of the original towers and many sections of ramparts are still standing. In mid-August, the castle holds falconry displays and a two-day medieval festival, complete with knights in armour.

The Drive » Backtrack along the D14 for 9km to the turn-off onto the D123 near Cucugnan. The road twists and turns steeply into the dusty hills. Keep your eyes peeled for the Quéribus turn-off as you drive another 3km uphill.

❹ Château de Quéribus

Perilously perched 728m up on a rocky hill, **Quéribus** (📞04 68 45 03 69; www. cucugnan.fr; Cucugnan; adult/child €7.50/4.50; ⏰9am-8pm Jul & Aug, 9.30am-7pm May, Jun & Sep, 10am-6pm or 6.30pm Apr & Oct, 10am-5pm Nov-Mar) was the site of the Cathars' last stand in 1255. Its interior structure is fairly well preserved: the **Salle du Pilier** inside the central keep still features its original Gothic pillars, vaulting and archways. There's also a small house that has been converted into a theatre which shows a film documenting the story of the castle through the eyes of one of the castle's curates.

The top of the keep is reached via a narrow staircase and offers a truly mind-blowing view stretching to the Mediterranean and the Pyrenees on a clear day.

The Drive » Drive back down to the turn-off, and turn

TOP TIP: PASSEPORT DES SITES DU PAYS CATHARE

The **Passeport des Sites du Pays Cathare** (www. payscathare.org; €4) gives a €1 reduction off 21 local sites, including medieval abbeys at St-Hilaire, Lagrasse and Villelongue. Pick it up at tourist offices throughout the region.

Cathar Land Château de Peyrepertuse

DETOUR:
GORGES DE GALAMUS

Start: ④ Château de Quéribus

Languedoc's soft limestone has created plenty of eye-popping gorges, but for heart-in-the-mouth views, the Gorges de Galamus near the village of Saint-Paul-de-Fenouillet are hard to beat. Gouged out by the River Agly, the gorge is spanned by a terrifyingly narrow road, cut by hand into the cliff-face at the end of the 19th century. There are car parks at either end, from where you can hike up to the photogenic Ermitage St-Antoine de Galamus, clinging halfway up the cliff-face. If you don't feel like walking, in summer, electric shuttles called *diablines* can be hired for €1 per person each way.

Look out for the turn-off to the right near St-Paul de Fenouillet as you drive along the D117 from Quéribus towards Puilaurens.

left. Continue along this road (the D19) for 8km to the small town of Maury. Take the D117 for 25km to Puilaurens. The next castle is signed from here, another 3km south.

---

❺ Château de Puilaurens

If it's the classic hilltop castle you're after, **Puilaurens** (☎04 68 20 65 26; www.chateau-puilaurens. com; Lapradelle; adult/child €7/4; ◷9am-6pm Jul & Aug, 10am-6pm May, Jun & Sep, 10am-5pm Apr & Oct–mid-Nov) is it. With its turrets and lofty location, it's one of the most visually striking of the Cathar fortresses, with all the classic medieval defences: double defensive walls, four corner towers and crenellated battlements. It's also said to be haunted by the

White Lady, a niece of Philippe le Bel.

The Drive » Backtrack to the D117 and follow it west for 49km to Bélesta, skirting through hills, fields and forests. As you drive through town, spot signs onto the D9 to 'Fougax et B/Querigut/Château de Montségur'. The village is another 14km further along this road; follow it through the village to the castle's roadside car park.

TRIP HIGHLIGHT

❻ Château de Montségur

For the full Monty Python medieval vibe – not to mention a good workout (bring your own water!) – tackle the steep 1207m climb to the ruins of the **Château de Montségur** (www.montsegur.fr; Montségur; adult/child Jul & Aug €6.50/3.50, other times

€5.50/3; ◷9am-6pm Jul & Aug, 10am-6pm Apr-Jun & Sep, 10am-5pm Mar & Oct, 11am-4pm Nov-Dec & Feb). It was here, in 1242, that the Cathar movement suffered its heaviest defeat; attacked by a force of 10,000 royal troops, the castle fell after a gruelling nine-month siege, and 220 of the defenders were burnt alive when they refused to renounce their faith.

Montségur has also been cited as a possible location for the Holy Grail, which was supposedly smuggled out of the castle in the days before the final battle.

The original castle was razed to rubble after the siege, and the present-day ruins largely date from the 17th century.

The Drive » Continue on the D117, turning onto the busy N20 to Foix, 32km northwest.

---

❼ Foix

Complete your trip through Cathar country with a visit to the **Château de Foix** (☎05 61 05 10 10; rue du Rocher; adult/child €11.50/8; ◷9am-6pm summer, shorter hours rest of year), nestled among the foothills of the Pyrenees. It's in a more complete state of repair than many of the Cathar fortresses you've seen, and gives you some idea of how they may have looked in their medieval heyday.

 p325, 343

Eating & Sleeping

Carcassonne ①

✖ Brasserie à Quatre Temps
Brasserie €€

(📞04 68 11 44 44; www.brasseriea4temps.com; 2 blvd Barbès; 3-course lunch/dinner menu €19/32, mains €21-30; ⏱7am-10pm) The prices at Franck Putelat's double Michelin-starred Le Parc may be out of reach, but a smidgen of the chef's magic dust is sprinkled over his brasserie in the Ville Basse. Tuck into dishes like lamb cutlets, beef fillet, cassoulet, pan-fried scallops and poached sea bass, with a view over place du Géneral de Gaulle. It's popular: bookings advised.

✖ La Barbacane
Gastronomy €€€

(📞04 68 71 98 71; www.cite-hotels.com/en/etablissements/restaurant-la-barbacane.html; place Auguste-Pierre-Pont, Cité Médiévale; lunch menu €41, dinner mains €50-68; ⏱12.30-2pm & 7.30-9.30pm) Jérôme Ryon's Michelin-starred premises at the grand Hôtel de la Cité is the town's most regal place to dine, with an antique-filled dining room gleaming with carved wood and stained glass. Rich, indulgent, classical French cookery is the MO – dinner is eye-wateringly expensive, but the lunch menu (including two glasses of wine) offers real value.

🛏 Carcassonne Townhouse
B&B €€

(📞06 88 48 59 39; www.carcassonnetownhouse.com; 4 rue Bellevue; d €99-135; 🛜) Without doubt the most beautifully presented B&B in Carcassonne, run by English couple Rachael and Mark. The 1850 townhouse has been renovated with painstaking attention to period detail – old-school radiators, decorative floor tiles, retro armchairs, heritage bedsteads and all. The two Cité-view suites are the pick, but all rooms are lovely, and breakfast is a spoil. Free parking is available on nearby Quai Bellevue.

🛏 Hotel Le Pont-Levis
Boutique Hotel €€€

(📞04 68 72 08 08; www.pontlevishotel.com; 40 chemin des Anglais; d €160-280, ste €220-335; 🅿❄🛜🏊) Carcassonne has plenty of upscale hotels, but this stylish place (co-owned by super-chef Franck Putelat) offers the best price-to-pamper ratio, especially out of season. The 12 rooms are spacious, private and colour-splashed; all have sleek bathrooms and Nespresso machines, some in-room bathtubs. The terraced garden is a joy (complete with outdoor pool) and there are dreamy Cité views. A spoil.

Foix ⑦

🛏 Château de Beauregard
Hotel €€

(📞05 61 66 66 64; www.chateaubeauregard.net; av de la Résistance, St-Girons; d €100-1200, ste €200-220, d incl half-board €184-300; 🅿🛜🏊) In St-Girons, halfway between St-Gaudens and Foix along the D117, this grand château with pointy roof turrets is surrounded by 2.5 hectares of beautiful gardens and has grand rooms named after writers (some have their bathrooms hidden in the castle's corner towers). There's also a pool, spa and a restaurant (menus €30 to €54) serving traditional Gascon meals.

Cheat's Compostela

Follow in the age-old footsteps of pilgrims on this holiest of road trips, where the scallop-shell symbol of St James traces a classic route right across southwestern France.

30

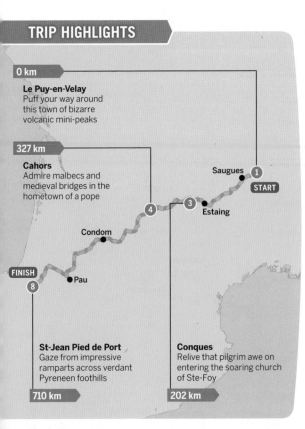

0 km

Le Puy-en-Velay
Puff your way around this town of bizarre volcanic mini-peaks

327 km

Cahors
Admire malbecs and medieval bridges in the hometown of a pope

Saugues **1**

START

Condom

4 **3** **Estaing**

FINISH

8 **●Pau**

St-Jean Pied de Port
Gaze from impressive ramparts across verdant Pyreneen foothills

710 km

Conques
Relive that pilgrim awe on entering the soaring church of Ste-Foy

202 km

7 DAYS
710KM / 440 MILES

GREAT FOR...

BEST TIME TO GO

May to September, to make the most of the summer sunshine.

📷 **ESSENTIAL PHOTO**

Being dwarfed beside Le Puy's huge statue of the Virgin Mary.

☑ **BEST FOR CULTURE**

Comparing churches in Condom, Cahors and Moissac, each with a grand carved tympanum (decorative arch).

30 Cheat's Compostela

Known in French as the Chemin de St-Jacques, the 'Camino' or 'Way of St-James' is one of Europe's greatest pilgrimages. It was originally undertaken on foot by those seeking credit in the afterlife. We can't promise equal spiritual merit if you're driving, but this classic French branch-route does present many lovely villages, iconic churches and historic cities, plus a giant iron statue of the Virgin Mary on a tower of volcanic rock.

TRIP HIGHLIGHT

❶ Le Puy-en-Velay

Your journey begins at the striking town of Le Puy-en-Velay, where pilgrims would traditionally have earned a blessing at the **Cathédrale Notre-Dame** (☎04 71 09 79 77; www.cathedraledupuy.org; rue de la Manécanterie; ⏱6.30am-7pm) with its Romanesque archways and Byzantine domes. Older and much more distinctive is the 10th-century **Chapelle St-Michel d'Aiguilhe** (☎04 71 09 50 03; www.

rochersaintmichel.fr; adult/child €5/3.50; ⊘9am-6.30pm May–Sep, shorter hours Oct–mid-Nov, early–mid-Apr & school holidays), perched on top of a remarkable 85m-high needle of volcanic rock. Its cave-like interior and 12th-century frescoes create an otherworldly atmosphere. On another rocky crag is an enormous cast-iron statue of the Virgin Mary, aka **Notre Dame de France** (adult/child €4/2; ⊘9am-7pm May–Sep, to 6pm mid-Mar–Apr, 10am-5pm Feb–mid-Mar & Oct–mid-Nov, 2-5pm Sun late Nov–Jan). A creaky spiral staircase

winds its way to the top of the 835-tonne structure, which is 22.7m-tall if you include the pedestal. Peep through portholes for dizzying vistas over the town.

🛏 p333

The Drive ⟫ From Le Puy, it's a memorable day's drive of around 160km to Estaing with plenty of village stops en route. The D589 winds down across the Allier Valley just bypassing Monistrol-d'Allier, where a pilgrims' chapel is set into a cliffside. The D589 continues west to Saugues, famed for its sheep market and the tall if stunted Tour Anglais fortress tower. From there head south on the D585

to castle-hamlet Esplantas, then southwest on the D587. On the A75 motorway, zip one exit south to Aumont Aubrac, from which the D987 closely follows the Camino via charming pilgrim villages Nasbinals, Aubrac and (with a small detour) St-Chely d'Aubrac. At lovely St-Côme-d'Olt, you finally reach the River Lot, which you follow downstream through Espalion with its 14th-century bridge.

---

② Estaing

Especially memorable when seen reflected across the river, Estaing is a pyramidal cluster of old stone buildings enfolding a Tolkeinesque 15th-century church. Inside are the relics of St Fleuret, a 5th-century miracle-working bishop.

🛏 p333

LINK YOUR TRIP

31 **The Pyrenees**
For fantastic mountain scenery, join our Pyrenees trip at Pau, just 12km off the A65/64 junction that you'll pass between Condom and St-Jean Pied de Port.

37 **The Lot Valley**
Between Figeac and Cahors you can combine this itinerary with the most beautiful section of our Lot Valley trip.

The Drive » For the 42km route to Conques, follow the Lot downstream. Turn left across the river at the second dam, zigzagging up the narrow D135 to hilltop Golinhac with its panoramic viewpoint. Go 1.5km west on the D519, dogleg 150m south on the D904, then continue west to Conques (24km) on the similarly narrow, winding D42 via Espeyrac and Senergues.

TRIP HIGHLIGHT

❸ Conques

The next major stop for medieval pilgrims would have been the magical hillside-village of Conques – or more specifically, the **Abbey Church of Ste-Foy**, built to house the holy relics of its namesake saint. It's a classic example of a pilgrimage church: simple and serene, with few architectural flourishes except for the carved **tympanum** (decorative arch) above the main doorway depicting the Day of Last Judgment.

🛏 p333

The Drive » Head northwest on the D901, recrossing the Lot River in a beautiful wide valley. Follow signs to Decazeville (21km), where you turn west onto the D840. Around 50km from Conques you reach Figeac, whose medieval heart is a fine place to spend at least half a day. From there, it's a slow but delightful 75km drive to Cahors along the Lot Valley. A faster alternative is via the D13 and D653, which takes about an hour from Figeac.

TRIP HIGHLIGHT

❹ Cahors

Now best known for its rich red Malbec wines, the city of Cahors sits on an excentric loop of the Lot River. In the Middle Ages it was a rare crossing point on the wide river and its fortified 14th-century bridge, the **Pont Valentré**, formed part of its defences with three soaring towers that give the Unesco-listed structure an unmistakable grandeur.

Cahors also retains an impressive Romanesque cathedral, the **Cathédrale St-Étienne**. Consecrated in 1119, the cathedral's airy nave is topped by two huge cupolas which, at 18m wide, are the largest in France. The tympanum of the cathedral's north portal sees an ascending Christ surrounded by fluttering angels and swooning saints.

🛏 p333

The Drive » The lovely 61km route to Moissac crosses a sparsely populated area of gently rolling fields and woodlands. Leave central Cahors on the southbound D620, turning right onto the D653 after 4km at a poorly signed suburban roundabout. After 39km, consider detouring up into the pretty little hill town of Lauzerte for a coffee on the arcaded central square. Then head south on the D2, forking right on the D16 and entering Moissac on the D957.

WESRERBE / SHUTTERSTOCK ©

❺ Moissac

Moissac is a large riverside town, partly on an 'island' formed between the Tarn and the Garonne Canal. Its one crowning glory is the Unesco-listed **Abbaye St-Pierre** (☎05 63 04 01 85; www.tourisme.moissac. fr; 6 place Durand de Bredon; ⏱8am-7pm), a monumental abbey church built from a curious mixture of brick, stone and wood cladding. Its Gothic interior was repainted in the 1960s to recreate the original wallpaper-like effect and contains the superb 15th *Mise*

Conques Abbey Church of Ste-Foy

au Tombeau, a large polychrome wooden sculpture of Jesus' body being placed in the tomb. Above the south portal, the 1130 **tympanum** depicts St John's vision of the Apocalypse. Behind the abbey's main entrance you can access the 'world's oldest' **cloister** (adult/child €6.50/4.50; ⊙10am-noon & 2-5pm Apr-Jun & Oct, 10am-7pm Jul-Sep, 1.30-5pm Nov-Mar), which was completed in 1100. Its slender stone columns are topped with carved capitals, many of them depicting animals, plants and biblical scenes, such as Samuel

pouring holy oil over a kneeling David.

The Drive » Head westbound on the D813 through flat, agricultural lands following the canal to forgettable Valence. Cross the canal on the D116 then the Garonne on the D953, which becomes the D88 south of the motorway. Turn right at Masonville onto the D40, then head west on the D7 to reach the arty citadel-village of Lectoure, in total 57km from Moissac.

- - - - - - - - - - - - - - - - - -

⑥ Lectoure

This fortified hilltop town retains an almost complete set of medieval lower ramparts and quite a few stone mansions dating back to the 13th-

century era of English rule. The colonades and painted chapel of the former lords' palace are now filled with bric-a-brac stalls, with artists' workshops in the cellars below. There's also a scattering of other craft, antique and decor shops dotted around town. The giant cathedral-church of St-Gervais, built on the site of an ancient pagan temple, holds the relics of St-Clair of Aquitaine, the first bishop of Albi.

🛏 p333

The Drive » By the D7, Condom is a straight 24km drive from Lectoure. However,

CHEMIN ST-JACQUES

In 9th century Spain, a hermit named Pelayo stumbled across what he believed to be the tomb of the Apostle James, brother of John the Evangelist. Ever since, the Galician town of Santiago de Compostela has been one of Christendom's holiest sites. In the Middle Ages, millions of pilgrims were inspired to walk there from the far corners of Europe. Their arduous journey, known as the 'Camino' (*Chemin St-Jacques* in French), was an act of piety and penance that might earn a reduced spell in purgatory after death. As the centuries proceeded, plague, wars and changing religious ideas meant that numbers waned significantly. Barely 3000 souls undertook the journey in 1987, the year that Paolo Coelho wrote about the experience in his reflective classic *The Pilgrimage*, but since then its popularity has ballooned again to over 300,000 annually.

Today, walkers or horse riders who complete the final 100km to Santiago aren't promised merit in heaven but do qualify for a Compostela Certificate, issued on arrival at the cathedral. Cyclists need to do 200km. Within France, there are four main routes starting at Paris, Vezelay, Arles and notably Le Puy-en-Velay, a route known as the Via Podensis and marked as the GR65 hiking route. Find out more at www.webcompostella.com and www.csj.org.uk/voie-du-puy.

pilgrims follow a prettier 34km route via tiny Marsolan, with its glorious panorama point, and La Romieu, with a superb former abbey church and charming gardens.

---

❼ Condom

Despite its snigger-inducing name, Condom actually has nothing to do with contraceptives – its name dates from Gallo-Roman times, when it was known as Condatomagus. The town's Flamboyant Gothic **Cathédrale St-Pierre** was the main point of interest for pilgrims who could take wet-weather protection in the covered cloisters. Condom's other claim to fame is as the home of Armagnac, a potent brandy brewed since medieval times, originally as a medicinal

tonic. The tourist office has a list of local producers in the surrounding area that offer tastings.

 p333

The Drive » The last day's drive is 230km, 100km of that on motorway as for part of the way roads don't really parallel the footpaths of the true Camino. Leave Condom via the citadel-hamlet of Larressingle (9km) and the beautifully preserved bastide town of Montreal-du-Gers. The D29 then leads southwest to cathedral-town Éauze, from which the N524 and D931 take you to Air sur-l'Adour. Air's distinctive, Unesco-listed Church of Ste-Quitterie honours a 4th-century Visigoth princess who was decapitated for refusing to give up Christianity. From here take the A65 and A64 toll highways to junction 7, then head south on the D933, which rejoins the original pilgrim route at Ostobat. The final 22km to St-Jean Pied de Port passes through the

attractive Basque town of St-Jean-le-Vieux.

TRIP HIGHLIGHT

❽ St-Jean Pied de Port

St-Jean Pied de Port wows with cobbled lanes, impressive ramparts, stone-and-whitewash houses and a Vauban citadel all set amid pretty green foothills. Here, three important branches of the Camino converge before crossing into Spain via the Roncevalles Pass, 8km away. While you might be ending your drive here, spare a thought for the real pilgrims who still have another 800km to walk before journey's end at Santiago de Compostela's famous cathedral.

🍴🛏 p333, p357

Eating & Sleeping

Le Puy-en-Velay ①

🏠 L'Epicurium   B&B €

(📞 04 43 07 27 11; www.l-epicurium.com; 5 rue
du Bessat; d €64-69, ste €72-99; 🕒 reception
5.30-7pm; 🛜) This gastronomy-obsessed
guesthouse has six spacious lodgings renovated
with minimalist flair: ceilings are high, tones are
neutral, and period features include wooden
beams and chimney places. Creaky floors are
part of the old-world charm. Breakfast involves
a toothsome range of homemade jams, and you
can reserve a three-course meal (€18) or a picnic
box (€10). Call ahead with your arrival time.

Estaing ②

🏠 Auberge St-Fleuret   Hotel €

(📞 05 65 44 01 44; https://auberge-st-fleuret.
com; 19 rue François d'Estaing; d €48-58; 🛜🏊)
Unpretentious but managed with love, this is
an ideal freshen-up stop for pilgrims, complete
with an outdoor pool, right in the heart of super-
quaint Estaing.

Conques ③

🏠 Auberge St Jaques   Hotel €

(📞 05 65 72 86 36; www.aubergestjacques.fr;
rue Gonzagues Florent; d €60-74) Right in the
heart of medieval Conques, this traditional 13-
room pilgrims' lodge has simple, en-suite rooms
at excellent prices, so long as you can manage
several flights of stairs. Dine at the 1st-floor
restaurant, whose €21 pilgrim menu has an
unexpectedly gourmet edge.

Cahors ④

🏠 Grand Hôtel Terminus   Hotel €€

(📞 05 65 53 32 00; www.balandre.com; 5 av
Charles de Freycinet; d €75-115; ❄🛜) Built in
1911, Cahors' original train-station hotel has
retained much of the original atmosphere,
including Tiffany glasswork and creaking oak
stairs (though there's a lift, too). Room styles
vary considerably between slightly faded floral

and very pleasantly updated shades of grey.
With chandeliers and stained glass, the deeply
traditional family-run restaurant, Balandre, is
a gastronomic treat (two-/three-/six-course
menus €36/50/69), but it only opens on Friday
night and Saturday.

Lectoure ⑥

🏠 L'Hôtel
Particulier Guilhon   B&B €€

(📞 06 27 17 81 65; www.hotel-particulier-guilhon.
com; 95 rue Nationale; ste incl breakfast €160-
270; 🅿 ❄ 🛜 🏊) Stunning! Discreetly hidden
behind a large grey door, this stylishly restored
17th-century mansion feels like a luxurious
private club with its splendid lounge, honesty
bar and veritable gallery of 20th-century art. The
five gigantic suites are all individually designed
around musical themes, there's a small pool in
the yard, and another, with a Jacuzzi, lies indoors
within a former medieval kitchen.

Condom ⑦

🍴 Le Balcon   International €

(📞 05 62 28 44 06; 1 place St-Pierre; mains
€13.50-21, menu €26; 🕒 noon-2pm Tue-Sun
& 7-9.30pm Tue-Sat; ❄ 🛜) Upstairs, facing
the cathedral, this buzzing, unfussy bistro
creates delicious meals that combine locally
sourced meats with wok-fried vegetable
accompaniments and delectable desserts like
caramel-vanilla cream with Armagnac.

St-Jean Pied de Port ⑧

🏠 Hôtel Ramuntcho   Hotel €€

(📞 05 59 37 03 91; www.hotel-ramuntcho.
com; 1 rue de France; d €72-96; 🕒 closed Dec;
🛜) In the same hands for generations – and
with a suitably old-fashioned feel – this is the
only hotel proper inside the walled town. It's
in a typical Béarn half-timbered house, with
16 peach-coloured rooms; some overlook the
street, others the Pyrenean foothills. From
May to September there's also a ground-floor
restaurant serving local dishes.

Classic Trip

The Pyrenees

31

Traversing hair-raising roads, sky-top passes and snow-dusted peaks, this roller coaster of a trip ventures deep into the sublime beauty of the Pyrenees mountains.

TRIP HIGHLIGHTS

277 km

Cauterets
Hit the trails at this chic and historic ski resort

522 km

Tarascon-sur-Ariège
See prehistoric art in a Pyrenean cavern

START
Oloron Ste-Marie ● Pau

St-Girons ● Foix

FINISH

Vallée d'Aspe
Escape the outside world in this wonderfully rural valley

80 km

Col du Tourmalet
Marvel at the mountain panorama from the Pic du Midi

322 km

7 DAYS
522KM / 324 MILES

GREAT FOR...

BEST TIME TO GO
June to September, when roads are snow-free. October for fiery autumn colours.

ESSENTIAL PHOTO
Posing in the imposing Cirque de Gavarnie.

BEST FOR OUTDOORS
Hiking to the Lac de Gaube or Refuge Wallon near Cauterets.

31 The Pyrenees

They might not have the altitude of the Alps, but what the Pyrenees do have is an unsurpassed beauty. The mountains are laced through with deep, green valleys punctuated by pretty stone villages. The lower slopes glow red and orange in autumn, thanks to vast beech forests, and higher up lies a wilderness of snow-dusted peaks and glittering lakes. With every valley and massif offering something new it's a thrilling region to travel through and even the most hardened driver will feel the urge to get out of the car and take to a hiking trail.

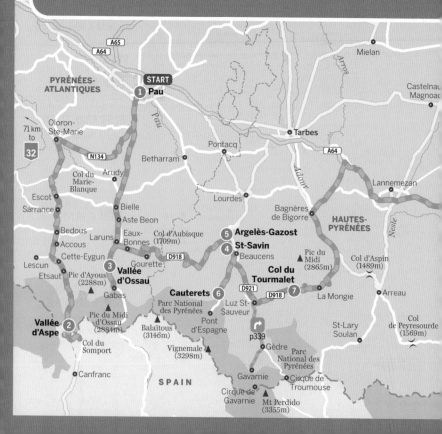

❶ Pau

Palm trees might seem out of place in this mountainous region, but Pau (rhymes with 'so') has long been famed for its mild climate. In the 19th century this elegant town was a favourite wintering spot for the wealthy, and their legacy is visible in the town's grand villas and smart promenades.

Its main sight is the **Château de Pau** (☎ 05 59 82 38 00; www.chateau-pau.fr; 2 rue du Château; adult/child €7/free; ⏰ 9.30am-12.15pm & 1.30-5.45pm, gardens open longer hours), built by the monarchs of Navarre and transformed into a Renaissance château in the 16th century. It's home to a fine collection of Gobelins tapestries and Sèvres porcelain.

Pau's tiny old centre extends for around 500m around the château, and boasts many attractive

LINK YOUR TRIP

29 The Cathar Trail
From Foix, it's only a short drive from the mountains before you reach the heart of the Cathar lands and their amazing châteaux.

32 Basque Country
This Pyrenean trip makes a natural extension of our themed trip through the French Basque country. From St-Jean Pied de Port, it's 71km to Oloron-Ste-Marie, or 103km to Pau.

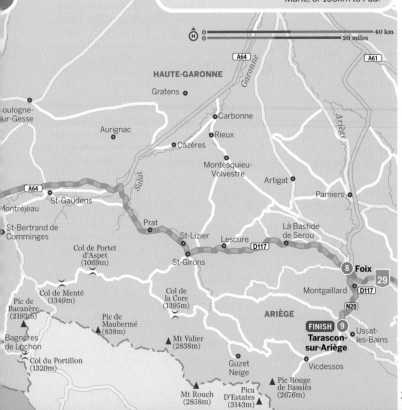

medieval and Renaissance buildings.

Central street parking in Pau is mostly *payant* (chargeable), though there's limited free parking at the central Stadium de la Gare.

 p343

The Drive >> To reach the Vallée d'Aspe from Pau, take the N193 to Oloron-Ste-Marie. The first 30km are uneventful, but over the next 40km south of Oloron the mountain scenery unfolds in dramatic fashion, with towering peaks stacking up on either side of the road.

TRIP HIGHLIGHT

❷ Vallée d'Aspe

The westernmost of the Pyrenean valleys makes a great day trip from Pau. Framed by mountains and bisected by the Aspe River, it's awash with classic Pyrenean scenery. Allow yourself plenty of time for photo stops, especially around pretty villages such as **Sarrance**, **Borce** and **Etsaut**.

Near the quiet village of **Bedous**, it's worth detouring up the narrow road to **Lescun**, a tiny hamlet perched 5.5km above the valley, overlooking the peak of **Pic d'Anie** (2504m) and the **Cirque de Lescun**, a jagged ridge of mountain peaks that close out the head of the valley.

The return drive to Pau is just over 80km.

The Drive >> To reach the Vallée d'Ossau from Pau, take the N134 south of town, veering south onto the D934 towards Arudy/Laruns. From Pau to Laruns, it's about 42km.

❸ Vallée d'Ossau

More scenic splendour awaits in the Vallée d'Ossau, which tracks the course of its namesake river for a spectacular 60km. The first part of the valley as far as Laruns is broad, green and pastoral, but as you travel south the mountains really start to pile up, before broadening out again near Gabas.

Halfway between Arudy and Laruns, you can spy on some of the mightiest birds of the western Pyrenees, griffon vultures, at the **Falaise aux Vautours** (Cliff of the Vultures; ☎05 59 82 65 49; www.falaise-aux-vautours. com; Aste-Béon; adult/child €6/4; ⏲10.30am-12.30pm & 2-6.30pm daily Jul & Aug, 1.30-5.30pm Mon-Fri Apr-Jun & Sep). Live CCTV images are beamed from their nests to the visitors centre in Aste-Béon. Griffon vultures are common throughout the western part of the Pyrenees. Much rarer cousins include the Egyptian vulture and the massive lammergeier.

The ski resort of **Artouste-Fabrèges**, 6km east of Gabas, is linked by cable car to the **Petit Train d'Artouste** (☎05 59 05 36 99; https://artouste.fr; adult/child/family €25/18/80; ⏲mid-May–mid-Oct), a miniature mountain railway built for dam workers in the 1920s. The train is only open between June and September; reserve ahead and allow four hours for a visit.

The Drive >> The D918 between Laruns and Argelès-Gazost is one of the Pyrenees' most breathtaking roads, switchbacking over the lofty Col d'Aubisque. The road feels exposed, but it's a wonderfully

---

THE TRANSHUMANCE

If you're travelling through the Pyrenees between late May and early June and find yourself stuck behind a cattle-shaped traffic jam, there's a good chance you may have just got caught up in the Transhumance, in which shepherds move their flocks from their winter pastures up to the high, grassy uplands.

This ancient custom has been a fixture on the Pyrenean calendar for centuries, and several valleys host festivals to mark the occasion. The spectacle is repeated in October, when the flocks are brought back down before the winter snows set in.

scenic drive. You'll cover about 52km, but allow yourself at least 1½ hours. Once you reach Argelès-Gazost, head further south for 4km along the D101 to St-Savin.

----

④ St-Savin

After the hair-raising drive over the Col d'Aubisque, St-Savin makes a welcome refuge. It's a classic Pyrenean village, with cobbled lanes, cafes and timbered houses set around a fountain-filled main square.

It's also home to one of the Pyrenees' most respected hotel-restaurants, **Le Viscos** (☎05 62 97 02 28; www.hotel-leviscos.com; 1 rue Lamarque, St-Savin; menus €32-75; ⏰12.30-1.30pm Tue-Sun, 7.30-8.30pm Tue-Sat; **P ❋ 🛜**), run by celeb chef Jean-Pierre St-Martin, known for his blend of Basque, Breton and Pyrenean flavours (as well as his passion for foie gras). After dinner, retire to a cosy country-style room and watch the sun set over the snowy mountains.

🛏 p343

The Drive » From St-Savin, travel back along the D101 to Argelès-Gazost. You'll see signs to the Parc Animalier des Pyrénées as you approach town.

----

⑤ Argelès-Gazost

The Pyrenees has a diverse collection of wildlife, but spotting it in the wild isn't always simple. Thankfully, **Parc**

Animalier des Pyrénées (☎05 62 97 91 07; www.parc-animalier-pyrenees.com; 60bis av des Pyrénées, Argelès-Gazost; adult/child €20/14.50; ⏰9.30am-6pm or 7pm Apr-Oct) does all the hard work for you. It's home to endangered Pyrenean animals including wolves, marmots, lynxes, ravens, vultures, beavers and a few brown bears (whose limited presence in the Pyrenees is highly controversial).

The Drive » Take the D921 south of Argelès-Gazost for 6km to Pierrefitte-Nestalas. Here, the road forks; the southwest branch (the D920) climbs up a lush, forested valley for another 11km to Cauterets.

TRIP HIGHLIGHT

⑥ Cauterets

For alpine scenery, the century-old ski and spa resort of Cauterets is perhaps the signature spot in the Pyrenees. Hemmed in by mountains and forests, it has clung on to much of its fin de siècle character, with a stately spa and grand 19th-century residences.

To see the scenery at its best, drive through town along the D920 (signed to the 'Pont d'Espagne'). The road is known locally as the **Chemins des Cascades** after the waterfalls that crash down the mountainside; it's 6.5km of nonstop hairpins, so take it steady.

At the top, you'll reach the giant car park at **Pont d'Espagne** (cable cars adult/child €15/12). From here, a combination *télécabine* and *télésiege* ratchets up the mountainside allowing access to the area's trails, including the popular hike to sapphire-tinted **Lac de Gaube** and the even more beautiful, but longer walks to the **Refuge Wallon** (4 hours return) and **Refuge**

DETOUR: CIRQUE DE GAVARNIE

Start: ⑥ Cauterets

For truly mind-blowing mountain scenery, it's well worth taking a side trip to see the Cirque de Gavarnie, a dramatic glacially formed amphitheatre of mountains 20km south of Luz-St-Sauveur. It's a return walk of about two hours from the village, and you'll need to bring sturdy footwear. There's another spectacular – and quieter – circle of mountains 6.5km to the east, the **Cirque de Troumouse**. It's reached via a hair-raising 8km toll road (€5 per vehicle; open April to October). There are no barriers and the drops are really dizzying, so drive carefully.

Classic Trip

OKS.MIT/GETTY IMAGES ©

RAPHAEL GAILLARDE/GAMMA-RAPHO VIA GETTY IMAGES ©

WHY THIS IS A CLASSIC TRIP
STUART BUTLER,
WRITER

The craggy peaks of the Pyrenees are home to some of France's rarest wildlife and most unspoilt landscapes, and every twist and turn in the road seems to reveal another knockout view. I've spent the past two decades living at the western foot of these mountains and still never tire of exploring them. For me, there is simply no more beautiful mountain range on earth. This west-to-east drive through the mountains showcases some of its finest, and most easily accessible, sights, views and experiences.

Above: Cauterets
Left: Grotte de Niaux, Tarascon-sur-Ariège
Right: Griffon vulture, Pyrenees

Oulette de Gaube (5 to 6 hours return).

✕ ⇐ p343

The Drive » After staying overnight in Cauterets, backtrack to Pierrefitte-Nestalas and turn southeast onto the D921 for 12km to Luz-St-Sauveur. The next stretch on the D918 is another mountain stunner, climbing up through Barèges to the breathtaking Col du Tourmalet.

TRIP HIGHLIGHT

⑦ Col du Tourmalet

At 2115m, Col du Tourmalet is the highest road pass in the Pyrenees, and it usually only opens between June and October. It's often used as a punishing mountain stage in the Tour de France, and you'll feel uncomfortably akin to a motorised ant as you crawl up towards the pass.

From the ski resort of La Mongie (1800m), a cable car climbs to the top of **Pic du Midi** (www.picdu midi.com; rue Pierre Lamy de la Chapelle; adult/child €45/27; ⊙9.30am-7pm Jun-Sep, 10am-5.30pm Oct-Apr). This high-altitude observatory commands otherworldly views – but it's often blanketed in cloud, so make sure you check the forecast before you go.

The Drive » The next stage to Foix is a long one. Follow the D918 and D935 to Bagnères de Bigorre, then the D938 and D20 to Tournay, a drive of 40km. Just before Tournay, head west onto the A64 for 82km. Exit onto the D117, signed to St-Girons. It's another 72km to Foix, but with twisting roads all the way and

ROAD PASSES IN THE PYRENEES

The high passes between the Vallée d'Ossau, the Vallée d'Aspe and the Vallée de Gaves are often closed during winter. Signs are posted along the approach roads indicating whether they're *ouvert* (open) or *fermé* (closed). The dates given below are approximate and depend on seasonal snowfall.

Col d'Aubisque (1709m, open May-Oct) The D918 links Laruns in the Vallée d'Ossau with Argelès-Gazost in the Vallée de Gaves. An alternative that's open year-round is the D35 between Louvie-Juzon and Nay.

Col de Marie-Blanque (1035m, open most of year) The shortest link between the Aspe and Ossau valleys is the D294, which corkscrews for 21km between Escot and Bielle.

Col du Pourtalet (1795m, open most of year) The main crossing into Spain generally stays open year-round except during exceptional snowfall.

Col du Tourmalet (2115m, open Jun-Oct) Between Barèges and La Mongie, this is the highest road pass in the Pyrenees. If you're travelling east to the Pic du Midi (for example from Cauterets), the only alternative is a long detour north via Lourdes and Bagnères de Bigorre.

---

lots of 30km/h zones this last part takes at least 1½ hours.

- - - - - - - - - - - - - - -

8 Foix

Looming above Foix is the triple-towered **Château de Foix** (📞05 61 05 10 10; rue du Rocher; adult/child €11.50/8; ⊙9am-6pm summer, shorter hours rest of year), constructed in the 10th century as a stronghold for the counts of the town. The view from the battlements is wonderful and a refurbishment has spruced up the displays on medieval life. There's usually at least one daily tour in English in summer.

Afterwards, head 4.5km south to **Les Forges de Pyrène** (📞05 34 09 30 60; www.forges-de-pyrene. com; rte de Paris, Montgailhard; adult/child €10.20/6.80; ⊙10am-6pm Tue-Sat Jul-Oct; 👪), a fascinating 'living museum' that explores Ariège folk traditions.

Spread over 5 hectares, it illustrates traditional trades such as glass blowing, tanning, thatching and nail making, and even has its own blacksmith, baker and cobbler.

🛏 p325, 343

The Drive » Spend the night in Foix, then head for Tarascon-sur-Ariège, 17km south of Foix on the N20. Look out for brown signs to the Parc de la Préhistoire.

- - - - - - - - - - - - - - -

TRIP HIGHLIGHT

9 Tarascon-sur-Ariège

Thousands of years ago, the Pyrenees were home to thriving communities of hunter-gatherers, who used the area's caves as shelters and left behind many stunning examples of prehistoric art.

Near Tarascon-sur-Ariège, the **Parc de la Préhistoire** (📞05 61 05 10 10; Tarascon-sur-Ariège; adult/child €11.50/8; ⊙10am-7pm Jul & Aug, to 6pm Sep, Oct & Apr-Jun) provides a handy primer on the area's ancient past. It explores everything from prehistoric carving to the arts of animal-skin tent making and ancient spear-throwing.

About 6.5km further south, the **Grotte de Niaux** (📞05 61 05 10 10; www.sites-touristiques-ariege. fr; adult/child €14/10; ⊙tours hourly 10.15am-4.15pm, extra tours in summer) is home to the Pyrenees' most precious cave paintings. The centrepiece is the **Salon Noir**, reached after an 800m walk through the darkness and decorated with bison, horses and ibex. The cave can only be visited with a guide. From April to September there's usually one daily tour in English at 1.30pm. Bookings are advisable.

Eating & Sleeping

Pau ①

✕ Les Papilles Insolites French €€

(📞05 59 71 43 79; www.lespapillesinsolites.
blogspot.co.uk; 5 rue Alexander Taylor; tapas
€8-12; ⊘3-10pm Wed, 11am-1.30pm & 7-10pm
Thu-Sat) Run by a former Parisian sommelier,
this cosy wine bar serves beautifully prepared
small plates like Galician-style octopus, scallops
with leeks or lamb with cumin. Complete the
experience with the owner's choice of one of
the 350-odd wines stacked around the shop.
Gorgeously Gallic.

🛏 Hôtel Bristol Hotel €€

(📞05 59 27 72 98; www.hotelbristol-pau.
com; 3 rue Gambetta; s €80-100, d €90-110, f
€120-130; 🅿🛜) A classic old French hotel but
with up-to-date rooms, all wrapped in a grand
19th-century building. Each room is uniquely
designed, with stylish decor, bold artwork and
elegant furniture, while big windows fill the
rooms with light. Ask for a mountain-view room
with balcony. Breakfast is pricey at €12.

St-Savin ④

🛏 Hôtel des Rochers Hotel €

(📞05 62 97 09 52; www.lesrochershotel.com;
1 place du Castillou, St-Savin; d €68-76, f €110;
🅿🛜) In the idyllic village of St-Savin, 16km
south of Lourdes, this handsomely landscaped
hotel makes a perfect mountain retreat. It's
run by an expat English couple, John and
Jane, who have renovated the rooms in clean,
contemporary fashion – try for one with a
mountain view. Half-board is available and the
hotel can provide picnic lunches that will satisfy
the hungriest hiker.

Cauterets ⑥

✕ La Grande Fache French €€

(📞06 06 44 99 55; 5 rue Richelieu; fondue per
person €19-24; ⊘noon-2.30pm & 7-10pm)
You're in the mountains, so really you should be
eating artery-clogging, cheese-heavy dishes
such as *tartiflette* (potatoes, cheese and bacon
baked in a casserole), *raclette* and fondue.
This family-run restaurant will oblige, served
in a dining-room crammed with mountain
memorabilia.

🛏 Hôtel du Lion d'Or Hotel €€

(📞05 62 92 52 87; www.liondor.eu; 12 rue
Richelieu; d €84-168; 🛜) This country-cottage-
style hotel oozes mountain character from
every nook and cranny. In business since 1913,
it is deliciously eccentric, with charming old
rooms in polka-dot pinks, sunny yellows and
duck-egg blues, and mountain-themed knick-
knacks dotted throughout, from antique sleds
to snowshoes. Breakfast includes homemade
honey and jams, and the restaurant serves
hearty Pyrenean cuisine.

Foix ⑧

🛏 La Ciboulette B&B €

(📞05 61 01 10 88; www.laciboulette.net; rte
St Pierre-de-Rivière, Lieu-Dit La Rochelle; s
€49-69, d €64-89, f €109) In a peaceful setting
some 3km west of Foix, this small family-run
guesthouse has several attractive rooms
decorated with artwork and elegant furnishings.
Views over the mountains add to the charm.
Don't miss a meal of creatively prepared local
dishes in the excellent restaurant on-site (open
Thursdays to Mondays, mains €14.50-18.50).

STRETCH YOUR LEGS
TOULOUSE

Start Place de la Capitole

Finish Place de la Capitole

Distance 5km

Duration 3 hours

Toulouse is France's fourth-largest city, a vibrant modern metropolis now famed for its space and aeronautical industries (such as the Airbus). However, the old core is contrastingly historic and well worth strolling amid the brick and red-stone architecture that gives Toulouse its nickname 'La Ville Rose' (The Pink City).

Take this walk on Trips

38

Place du Capitole

Park beneath place du Capitole, Toulouse's grand main square. Order a coffee or an early aperitif at one of the Belle Èpoque brasserie-cafes that face the 128m-long façade of the **Capitole**. That neoclassical masterpiece contains what's essentially a free art gallery, its walls and ceilings lavished with work by excellent local artists of the late 19th and early 20th centuries, notably post-impressionist Henri Martin.

The Walk » In gardens directly east of the Capitole, ask the tourist office for a free map then head north up the grand, Parisian-style shopping street rue d'Alsace-Lorraine. Wiggle west onto rue du Perigord and dog-leg past the 1935 art deco city library to rue Bellegarde.

Basilique St-Sernin

As you turn the corner, you get a great view of the **basilica** (www.basilique-saint-sernin.fr; place St-Sernin; ☺ cathedral 8.30am-7pm Jun-Sep, to 6pm Oct-May, ambulatory 10am-noon & 2-5.30pm or 6pm mid-summer), one of France's finest Romanesque structures, topped by a spired octagonal tower in five stages. Inside, St Sernin's tomb is sheltered beneath a sumptuous canopy. Across the square, the **Musée St-Raymond** holds a remarkable collection of Roman statuary.

The Walk » Return to place du Capitole via rue du Taur, continue southeast on rue de la Pomme, with a minor detour via the pretty triangular fountain-square of place Salengro to cafe-ringed place St-Georges. Rue d'Astog leads on to the cathedral.

Cathédrale de St-Étienne

Toulouse's cathedral has a wide, vaulted choir in classic Gothic style thrust incongruously together with a heavy nave barely half the width and considerably older. The result is a compulsively fascinating sense of architectural schizophrenia.

The Walk » Head west on rue Croix Baragnon, turn right on rue des Arts and find the entrance to the imposing museum on rue de Metz.

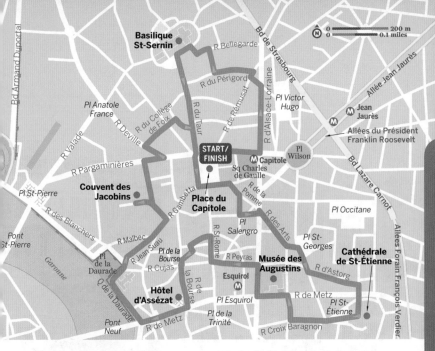

Musée des Augustins

Within a former Augustinian monastery, this fabulous **gallery** (www.augustins. org; 21 rue de Metz; adult/child €5/free; ⏰10am-6pm Thu-Mon, to 9pm Wed) has art spanning two millennia, from Roman to modern. Don't miss 18th-to-20th-century masterpieces by Delacroix, Ingres, Toulouse-Lautrec and Monet, nor the statuary housed in 14th-century cloister gardens.

The Walk » Stroll west wandering randomly through the smaller laneways that contain some of Toulouse's most elegant 16th- and 17th-century mansions, as well as tempting bars around place de la Bourse.

Hôtel d'Assézat

The 1555 **Hôtel d'Assézat**, built as a home for a wealthy wood merchant, now houses the **Fondation Bemberg** (☎05 61 12 06 89; www.fondation-bemberg. fr; place d'Assézat; adult/under 26yr €8/5; ⏰10am-12.30pm & 1.30-6pm Tue-Sun, to 8.30pm Thu) with a superb collection of impressionist and expressionist art.

The 1st floor's velvet-walled rooms are packed with period furniture.

The Walk » Continue to the elegant Pont Neuf. Despite its name (neuf = new), it's the city's oldest surviving bridge. Swing north, enjoy views across the Garonne from the plane-tree shaded quai de la Daurade, pass the statue-fronted Ecole des Beaux-Arts and the Doric columns of the Église Daurade. At place de la Daurade, descend to river level if you fancy a boat ride on the River Garonne (March to October). Otherwise head northeast via rue Jean Suau.

Couvent des Jacobins

Though it looks austere and forbidding from outside, the soaring church of this former **convent** (☎05 61 22 23 82; www.jacobins.toulouse.fr; rue Lakanal; church/cloister free/€5; ⏰10am-6pm Tue-Sun) has a light-filled interior housing a simple altar beneath which lie the relics of St Thomas Aquinas. For a small fee you can enter the beautiful cloister.

The Walk » Rue Gambetta leads back to place de la Capitole but the indirect route via rue du Collège de Foix is more interesting.

Atlantic Coast

THE ATLANTIC COAST IS WHERE FRANCE GETS BACK TO NATURE. Much more laid-back than the Med, this is the place to slow the pace right down.

Driving through this region is all about quiet country roads winding through vine-striped hills, glimpsed views of dead-at-noon villages and the occasional foray into dynamic, inventive cities such as Bordeaux.

The region's wine is famous worldwide, and to wash it down you'll find fresh-from-the-ocean seafood wherever you go, plus plenty of regional delicacies, including snails in the north, foie gras further south and, in the unique Basque regions, chilli-tinted dishes filled with hints of Spain.

St-Jean de Luz Waterfront houses
VOUVRAYSAN / SHUTTERSTOCK ©

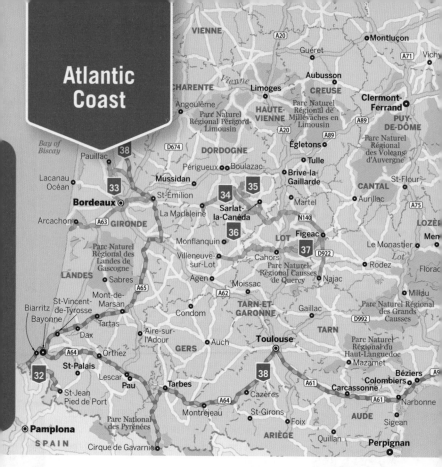

Atlantic Coast

 DON'T
MISS

Musée National de Préhistoire

A brilliant place to do your homework on the Vézère Valley's cave art. Bone up on Trip 35

Domme

Explore this spectacular hilltop village, with its views over the Dordogne valley. Take it all in on Trip 36

Najac

This fairy-tale castle offers some of the most breathtaking views in southwest France. Explore it on Trip 36

Tapas

Tuck into these tasty bites and wonder whether you're in France, Spain or somewhere else altogether. Indulge yourself on Trip 32

Basque Country

Feisty and independent, France's Basque Country is famous for glitzy Biarritz. But on this tour you'll also uncover fishing ports, chocolate-box villages and rolling hills.

32

TRIP HIGHLIGHTS

30 km

St-Jean de Luz
Taste traditional Basque seafood dishes

2

START
Bayonne

13 km

Biarritz
Treat yourself to tapas and watch surfers tackle the waves

5

8

Sare

Ainhoa

72 km

Espelette
Potter about a picturesque Basque village

St-Étienne de Baïgorry

11

FINISH

St-Jean Pied de Port
Walk in the footsteps of millions of pilgrims

117 km

7 DAYS
117KM / 73 MILES

GREAT FOR...

BEST TIME TO GO

September and October offer the best combination of weather and low crowds.

 ESSENTIAL PHOTO

Looking across Grande Plage in Biarritz from the southern headland.

 BEST FOR CULTURE

Absorbing the Basque spirit of old Bayonne.

32 Basque Country

Driving into the village of Espelette you'll be struck by how different everything is from other parts of the country. The houses are all tarted up in the red and white of Basque buildings, streamers of chilli peppers hang from roof beams, and from open windows comes a language you don't recognise. As you'll discover on this tour, being different from the rest of France is exactly how the proud Basques like it.

❶ Bayonne

Surrounded by sturdy fortifications and splashed in red and white paint, Bayonne is one of the most attractive towns in southwest France. Its perfectly preserved old town and riverside restaurants are an absolute delight to explore, but the town is best known to French people for producing some of the nation's finest chocolate and ham.

Inside the **Musée Basque et de l'Histoire de Bayonne** (📞 05 59 59 08

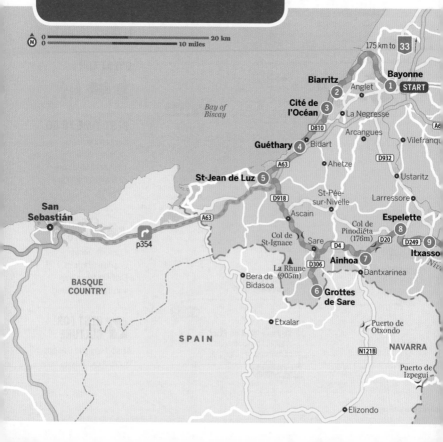

98; www.musee-basque.com;
37 quai des Corsaires; adult/
child €8/free, 1st Sun of month
free; ⊙10am-6pm Tue-Sun)
the seafaring history,
traditions and cultural
identity of the Basque
people are all explored.

Also worth a visit
is Bayonne's Gothic
Cathédrale Ste-Marie
(www.cathedraledebayonne.
com; place Monseigneur
Vansteenberghe; ⊙8am-
6.30pm Mon-Sat, to 8pm
Sun, cloister 9am-12.30pm &
2-6pm summer, to 5pm winter),
whose twin towers soar
elegantly above the old
town.

 p357

The Drive » Bring a towel
because we're taking the 13km
(25 minute) beach-bums'
route to Biarritz. Follow the
Adour River out of Bayonne
down allées Marines and av de
l'Adour. At the big roundabout
turn left onto bd des Plages and
take your pick from any of the
beaches along this stretch. This
road will eventually lead into
Biarritz.

TRIP HIGHLIGHT

2 Biarritz

As ritzy as its name
suggests, this stylish
coastal town took off as
a resort in the mid-19th
century when Napoléon
III and his Spanish-born
wife, Eugénie, visited
regularly. Along its rocky
coastline are architec-
tural hallmarks of this
golden age, and the Belle
Époque and art deco eras
that followed. Although
it retains a high glamour
quotient (and high prices
to match), it's also a
magnet for vanloads of
surfers, with some of
Europe's best waves.

Biarritz's *raison
d'être* is its fashionable
beaches, particularly the
central **Grande Plage** and
Plage Miramar, which
are lined end to end with
sunbathing bodies on hot
summer days.

For a look under the
waves, check out the
**Aquarium de Biar-
ritz** (☎05 59 22 75 40; www.
aquariumbiarritz.com; esplanade du Rocher de la Vierge;
adult/child €15/11, combined
ticket with Cité de l'Océan
€24/16; ⊙9.30am-7pm), rich
in underwater life from
the Bay of Biscay and
beyond.

For life further afield,
have a poke about the
stunning museum
collection of Asian art
at **Asiatica** (Musée d'Art
Asiatique; ☎05 59 22 78 78;
www.museeasiatica.com; 1 rue
Guy Petit; adult/child €10/free;
⊙10.30am-6.30pm Mon-Fri,
2-7pm Sat & Sun Jul, Aug & during school holidays, 2-7pm Sat &
Sun rest of year).

 p357

The Drive » It's a 35-minute,
2.6km walk or a 10-minute drive

 LINK YOUR TRIP

30 Cheat's Compostela
From St-Jean Pied de Port
work your way in reverse
through our cheat's version
of this ancient spiritual
journey.

33 Heritage Wine Country
From Bayonne it's a 192km
pine-tree-scented drive
to the capital of wine,
Bordeaux, and the start of
our wine tour.

south out of Biarritz along rue de Madrid to the Cité de l'Océan. On the way you'll pass some fantastic stretches of sand just calling for you to dip a toe in the sea or hang 10 on a surfboard.

----

⑤ Cité de l'Océan

We don't really know whether it's fair to call Biarritz's showpiece **Cité de l'Océan** (📞05 59 22 75 40; www.citedelocean.com; 1 av de la Plage; adult/child €13/9, combined ticket with Aquarium de Biarritz €24/16; ⏰10am-7pm Apr-Oct & school holidays, 2-7pm rest of year) a mere 'museum'. At heart it's a museum of the ocean, but in reality this is entertainment, cutting-edge technology, theme park and science

museum all rolled into one spectacular attraction. Inside the eye-catching building you'll learn how the ocean was born, surf like a pro, and join an underwater expedition to study Polynesian grey sharks.

The Drive » It's an often painfully congested drive 7km south down the D911 (av de Biarritz) and D810, passing through the village of Bidart, to the ocean views of pretty Guéthary. Traffic is invariably hideous.

----

④ Guéthary

Built onto cliffs overlooking the ocean south of Biarritz, this red-and-white seaside village has gained a reputation as

the Basque Country's chichi resort of choice for the jet set. The pebble beach below the village offers safe bathing for all the family, while the offshore reefs offer some exceptional surf for the brave.

The Drive » It's another seriously traffic-clogged 7km south along the D810 to St-Jean de Luz. This short 6km hop should only take 10 minutes but it rarely does! Sadly, there's no worthwhile alternative route.

TRIP HIGHLIGHT

⑤ St-Jean de Luz

If you're searching for the quintessential Basque seaside town – with atmospheric narrow streets and a lively fishing port pulling in large catches of sardines and anchovies that are cooked up at authentic restaurants – you've found it.

St-Jean de Luz's beautiful banana-shaped sandy **beach** sprouts stripy bathing tents from June to September. The beach is sheltered from Atlantic swells and is among the few child-friendly beaches in the Basque Country.

With plenty of boutique shops, bijou cafes and pretty buildings, walking the streets of the pedestrianised town centre is a real pleasure. Don't miss the town's finest church, **Église St-Jean Baptiste** (www.paroissespo.com/eglise-st-jean-baptiste-st-jean-de-luz;

DETOUR:
SAN SEBASTIÁN, SPAIN

Start: ⑤ St-Jean de Luz

Spain, and the elegant and lively city of San Sebastián, is just a few kilometres along the coast from St-Jean de Luz and put simply, San Sebastián is not a city you want to miss out on visiting. The town is set around two sickle-shaped beaches, at least one of which, **Playa de la Concha** (Paseo de la Concha), is the equal of any city beach in Europe. But there's more to the city than just looks. With more Michelin stars per capita than anywhere else in the world, and arguably the finest tapas in Spain, many a culinary expert has been heard to say that San Sebastián is possibly the world's best food city.

By car from St-Jean de Luz, it's just a short 20-minute motor south along the A63 (and past an awful lot of toll booths!), or you can endure the N10, which has no tolls but gets so clogged up that it will take you a good couple of hours to travel this short distance.

St-Jean de Luz Église St-Jean Baptiste

rue Gambetta; ⏰8.30am-6pm Mon-Sat, 8am-7.30pm Sun), which has a splendid interior with a magnificent baroque altarpiece.

✗ 🛏 p357

The Drive » The 15km, 20-minute drive down the D918 and D4 to Sare is a slow road through the gorgeous gentle hills of the pre-Pyrenees. From the village of Sare, which is well worth a wander, pick up

the D306 for a further 6km (12 minutes) to the Grottes de Sare.

- - - - - - - - - - - - - - - -

❻ Grottes de Sare

Who knows what the first inhabitants of the **Grottes de Sare** (📞05 59 54 21 88; www.grottesdesare. fr; off the D306; adult/child €9/5; ⏰10am-6pm Jun-Sep, to 5pm Oct, reduced hours rest of year) – who lived some 20,000 years ago

– would make of today's whizz-bang technology, including lasers and holograms, during the sound-and-light shows at these caves. Multilingual 45-minute tours take you through a gaping entrance via narrow passages to a huge central cavern adorned with stalagmites and stalactites.

The Drive » To get to the next stop, Ainhoa, 13.5km

northeast, retrace your steps to Sare to pick up the D4. Count 20 minutes for the journey. If you're feeling adventurous, you could weave your way there on any number of minor back roads or even cross briefly into Spain and drive via the lovely village of Zugarrmurdi.

7 Ainhoa

Beautiful Ainhoa's elongated main street is flanked by imposing 17th-century houses, half-timbered and brightly painted. The fortified **church** has the Basque trademarks of an internal gallery and an embellished altarpiece.

The Drive » It's 6km down the D20 to Espelette, the next tasty port of call.

TRIP HIGHLIGHT

8 Espelette

The whitewashed Basque town of Espelette is famous for its dark-red chillies, an integral ingredient in traditional Basque cuisine. In autumn, the walls of the houses are strung with rows of chillies drying in the sun. To learn more about the chillies, and taste and buy chilli products, visit **L'Atelier du Piment** (📞05 59 93 90 21; www.atelier-du-piment-espelette.fr; chemin de l'Église; ⏰9am-noon & 2-6pm) on the edge of town.

The Drive » It's an exceedingly pretty 6km (10 minutes) down the D249 to the cherry capital, Itxassou.

9 Itxassou

Famed for its cherries, as well as the beauty of its surrounds, Itxassou is a classic Basque village that well rewards a bit of exploration. The cherries are used in the region's most famous cake, gateau Basque, which is available pretty much everywhere you look throughout the Basque Country.

The Drive » It's 28km (about 30 minutes) down the D918 and D948 to St-Étienne de Baïgorry. On the way you'll pass the village of Bidarry, renowned for its white-water rafting, and some pretty special mountain scenery.

10 St-Étienne de Baïgorry

The riverside village of St-Étienne de-Baïgorry is tranquillity itself. Like so many Basque settlements, the village has two focal points: the **church** and the **fronton** (court for playing *pelota,* the local ball game). It's the kind of place to while away an afternoon doing nothing very much at all.

The Drive » It's a quiet 11km (20 minute) drive along the rural D15 to our final stop St-Jean

Pied de Port. The thirsty will be interested to know that the hills around the village of Irouléguy, which you pass roughly around the halfway point, are home to the vines that produce the Basque Country's best-known wine.

TRIP HIGHLIGHT

11 St-Jean Pied de Port

At the foot of the Pyrenees, the walled town of St-Jean Pied de Port was for centuries the last stop in France for pilgrims heading south over the Spanish border and on to Santiago de Compostela in western Spain. Today it remains a popular departure point for hikers attempting the same pilgrim trail.

St-Jean Pied de Port isn't just about hiking boots and God, though; its old core, sliced through by the Nive River, is an attractive place of cobbled streets and geranium-covered balconies. Specific sights worth seeking out include the **Église Notre Dame du Bout du Pont**, which was thoroughly rebuilt in the 17th century. Beyond Porte de Notre Dame (the main gate into the old town) is the photogenic **Vieux Pont** (Old Bridge), the town's best-known landmark.

🍴 🛏 p333, p357

Eating & Sleeping

Bayonne ❶

✗ La Table de Sebastien Gravé
French €€

(📞05 59 46 14 94; www.latable-sebastiengrave. fr; 21 quai Amiral Dubourdieu; menu lunch 2-/3-course €21/26, dinner €39, mains €22; ⏲ noon-2pm & 7-10pm Tue-Sat) **Born-and-bred** Bayonnais chef Sebastien Gravé and wife Laure cook traditional Basque flavours in all kinds of innovative ways at their river-facing restaurant in Grand Bayonne. The sleek and minimal interior sports plain wooden tables and pop-art prints on the walls, and the dessert menu is particularly enticing. The chocolate mousse with salted caramel and smoked peanut ice cream is truly sublime. Immediately next at 17 quai Amiral Dubourdieu, the same chef serves a single, fixed, eight-course dinner menu (€60) around a shared table at the more gastronomic **Séquence(s)**.

Biarritz ❷

✗ Le Clos Basque
Basque €€

(📞05 59 24 24 96; 12 rue Louis Barthou; entrées/ mains/desserts €10/17/8; ⏲ noon-1.45pm & 7.30-9.45pm Tue-Sat, noon-1.45pm Sun) One of Biarritz's more traditional tables, with a sweet front patio sheltered by climbing plants and an awning. The menu is proudly Basque, so expect classic dishes such as axoa (mashed veal, onions and tomatoes spiced with red Espelette chilli). It gets very busy, so service can be slow.

🛏 Le Château du Clair de Lune
Hotel €€

(📞05 59 41 53 20; www.hotelclairlune.fr; 48 ave Alan Seeger; d/q from €140/199; 🅿🛜❄) It's only fitting that the 10 rooms at this peaceful countryside chateau are poetically named rather than numbered. Soothing palettes of crisp white and muted pastels in the modern rooms enhance the dreamy theme, and 8 hectares of landscaped grounds provide ample space for meandering at leisure beneath centurion oaks and cedars. Michelin-starred restaurant **L'Atelier Alexandre Bousquet** (📞05 59 41 10 11; 52 rue Alan Seeger; lunch menu €38, 4-/6-course dinner menu €78/98; ⏲ noon-1.30pm & 7.30-9.30pm Tue-Sat; 🅿) –

tucked away in a former 18th-century Basque farm on the estate with sweeping terrace views of the Pyrenees – is an address in its own right.

St-Jean de Luz ❺

✗ Buvette de la Halle
Seafood €

(📞05 59 26 73 59; 18bis bd Victor Hugo; dishes €8-16; ⏲6am-2pm & 7-9pm Sep-Jun, closed Tue) For the full-blown French market experience, this tiny corner restaurant in red-brick Les Halles is a must. Sit at the counter under its collection of vintage teapots, and tuck into hearty plates of Bayonne ham, *piperade maison* (tomato, red pepper and onion stew laced with Espelette chilli pepper), grilled sardines and prawns, oysters, mussels and fries, fish soup and local cheeses. Dining is delightfully al fresco beneath a racing-green awning for much of the year.

🛏 Hôtel Txoko
Boutique Hotel €€

(📞05 59 85 10 45; www.hotel-txoko.com; 20 rue de la République; d €70-190; ❄🛜) There is no escaping the high-season tourist crowd at this nine-room hotel, slap-bang on one of St-Jean's buzziest dining streets and just steps from the beach. Brightly coloured Basque fabrics add a cheery dash to rooms, a courtesy tray with tea and coffee inject a welcome touch of home, and the best doubles have a balcony. Breakfast €12.

St-Jean Pied de Port ⓫

✗ Chez Arrambide
Gastronomy €€€

(📞05 59 37 01 01; www.hotel-les-pyrenees. com; 19 place Charles de Gaulle; menus €42-105, mains €36-52; ⏲12.15-1.45pm & 7.45-9pm Jul & Aug, Wed-Mon Sep-Jun; 🅿❄🛜) Slumbering on the ground floor of four-star Hôtel des Pyrénées, Michelin-starred Chez Arrambide is renowned for miles around. Dining is formal, with white tablecloths amid a classical decor. Chef Philippe Arrambide works wonders with market produce, transforming hare, rabbit, beef and a shoal of fresh seafood into edible works of art. His roast duck fillets served with a sweet potato panna cotta, spiced French toast, mango purée and roasted sesame seeds is sublime.

Heritage Wine Country

This trip venerates the finer things in French life: great wine, fabulous regional cuisine and gentle driving through glorious vine-ribboned countryside studded with grand châteaux.

33

TRIP HIGHLIGHTS

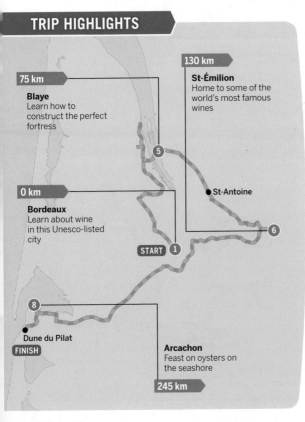

130 km

St-Émilion
Home to some of the world's most famous wines

75 km

Blaye
Learn how to construct the perfect fortress

5

● St-Antoine

0 km

Bordeaux
Learn about wine in this Unesco-listed city

START ① **1**

6

8

Dune du Pilat
FINISH

Arcachon
Feast on oysters on the seashore

245 km

**5 DAYS
257KM / 160 MILES**

GREAT FOR...

BEST TIME TO GO

September and October: the grape harvest takes place, oysters are in season.

ESSENTIAL PHOTO

Red roofs of St-Émilion from place des Créneaux.

BEST FOR FOODIES

Slurping fresh oysters at Bordeaux's Marché des Capucins.

Bordeaux Grape harvest

33 Heritage Wine Country

10am: the southern sun warms your face and you're standing in a field surrounded by vines heavy with ready-to-burst grapes. 1pm: cutlery clinks, tummies sigh in bliss and you're on a gastronomic adventure in a top-class restaurant. 7pm: toes in the sand and Atlantic breezes in the hair and you down an oyster in one. All this and more awaits you on this refined culinary trip.

TRIP HIGHLIGHT

1 Bordeaux

Gourmet Bordeaux is a city of sublime food and long, lazy sun-drenched days. Half the city (18 sq km) is Unesco-listed, making it the largest urban World Heritage Site – and an absolutely delight to wander around. Barista-run coffee shops, on-trend food trucks, an inventive dining scene and more fine wine than you could ever possibly drink make it a city hard to resist.

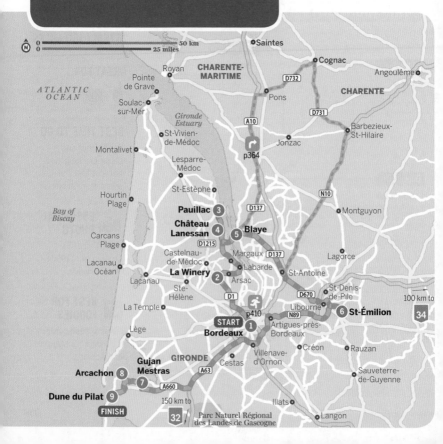

Wine aficionados will adore **La Cité du Vin** (☎05 56 16 20 20; www.laciteduvin.com; 134 quai de Bacalan; adult/child €20/9, priority access €25/14; ⏱10am-7pm May-Aug, shorter hours rest of year), a stunning contemporary building designed to resemble a modern wine decanter on the banks of the River Garonne. The curvaceous gold building glitters in the sun and its 3000 sq metres of exhibits inside, dedicated to immersing visitors in the complex world of wine, are equally sensational. Tours end with a glass of wine in the panoramic Latitude 20 wine bar on the 8th floor.

The **tourist office** (☎05 56 00 66 00; www.bordeaux-tourisme.com; 12 cours du 30 Juillet; ⏱9am-6.30pm

LINK YOUR TRIP

32 **Basque Country**
From Arcachon drive 182km through the forests of Les Landes to Bayonne and our Spanish-flavoured Basque Country tour.

34 **Gourmet Dordogne**
Slip some truffle hunting into your wine tour. From St-Émilion it's a mere 100km to Périgueux and our Gourmet Dordogne drive.

TOP TIP: OYSTERS AT CAPUCINS

A classic Bordeaux experience is a Saturday morning spent slurping oysters and chilled white wine from one of the seafood stands at **Marché des Capucins** (www.marchedescapucins.com; place des Capucins; ⏱6am-1pm Tue-Sun). Afterwards you can peruse the stalls while shopping for the freshest ingredients to take on a picnic.

Mon-Sat, 9.30am-5pm Sun) runs a packed program of city tours in English, including gourmet and wine tours, river cruises in the warmer months, and child-friendly tours. All tours take a limited number of participants; reserve ahead.

 p44, p366

The Drive ›› It's a 24km trip along the D1 from Bordeaux to La Winery in Arsac. Technically this should take around 40 minutes, but traffic around Bordeaux can be dreadful so allow longer.

- - - - - - - - - - - - - - -

❷ La Winery

Part giant wine shop, part wine museum, **La Winery** (☎05 56 69 08 51; www.winery.fr; Rond-point des Vendangeurs, rte du Verdon, Arsac-en-Médoc; ⏱10.30am-7.30pm Mon-Sat, to 6.30pm Sun) is a glass-and-steel wine centre just off the D1215 that mounts concerts and contemporary-art exhibits alongside various fee-based tastings, including innovative ones that determine

your *signe œnologique;* advance reservations are required. The boutique stocks over 1000 different wines.

Should you leave with an urge to taste more fine wine in the company of exceptional food and picture-postcard vineyard views, follow smart local gastronomes to **Nomade** (☎05 56 35 92 38; www.restaurant-nomade.fr; 3 rte des Châteaux, Labarde; 3-course lunch/7-course dinner menu €35/70; ⏱noon-1.30pm & 8pm Tue-Sat), squirrelled away into the teeny former train station building in the village of Labarde. Young Pauillac-born chef Thibault Guiet, with partner Manon Garret, serves a sensational modern cuisine, firmly rooted in local seasonal products.

The Drive ›› It's a 15-minute drive (11km) east from La Winery to Labarde along the rural D208 and D105E1. From here, it's 35 minutes (25km) north along the scenic D2 via Margaux to Pauillac. Bages is 2km south of the latter.

❸ Pauillac

Northwest of Bordeaux, along the western shore of the Gironde Estuary – formed by the confluence of the Garonne and Dordogne Rivers – lie some of Bordeaux's most celebrated vineyards. On the banks of the muddy Gironde, the port town of Pauillac is at the heart of Bordeaux wine country, surrounded by the distinguished Haut-Médoc, Margaux and St-Julien appellations. Extraordinary châteaux pepper these parts, including prestigious Château Margaux, with cellars designed by Lord Norman Foster in 2015; they cannot be visited.

The Pauillac wine appellation encompasses 18 *crus classés* in all, including the world-renowned Mouton Rothschild, Latour and Lafite Rothschild. The town's tourist office houses the **Maison du Tourisme et du Vin** (☏05 56 59 03 08; www.pauillac-medoc.com; La Verrerie, quai Paul Doumer; ◷9.30am-12.30pm & 2-6pm Mon-Fri, 10am-1pm & 2-6pm Sat), with information on châteaux and how to visit them; advance reservations are essential.

Memorable and delicious is lunch at **Café Lavinal** (☏05 57 75 00 09; www.jmcazes.com/en/cafe-lavinal; place Desquet, Bages; menus €29 & €39, mains €22-45; ◷noon-2.30pm & 7-9.15pm; ✵ 🛜 🛖), a 1930s-styled village bistro in Bages with retro red banquet seating, a zinc bar and revisited French classics cooked up by a duo of local Médoc chefs.

The Drive ⟫ Count no more than 15 minutes to cover the 9km between Bages and the next stop. Follow the D2 south out of Pauillac for almost 7km, turn right towards Lachesnaye, and continue for another 1.5km then turn right to Château Lanessan.

ON THE WINE TRAIL

The 1000-sq-km wine-growing area around the city of Bordeaux is, along with Burgundy, France's most important producer of top-quality wines. The Bordeaux region is divided into 57 appellations, grouped in turn into seven families, then subdivided into a hierarchy of designations; *premier grand cru classé* is the most prestigious. Most of the region's reds, rosés, sweet and dry whites and sparkling wines include the abbreviation AOC (Appellation d'Origine Contrôlée) on their labels, indicating that the contents have been grown, fermented and aged according to strict regulations governing viticultural matters.

Bordeaux has more than 5000 châteaux, referring not to palatial residences but rather to the estates where grapes are grown, picked, fermented and matured as wine. A handful are open to visitors, by advance reservation only. Many close during the *vendange* (grape harvest) in October.

Whet your palate with wine-tasting workshops (from €25) organised by the Bordeaux tourist office or an introductory two-hour workshop (€32) at the highly regarded **École du Vin** (Bordeaux Wine School; ☏05 56 00 22 85; www.bordeaux.com; 3 cours du 30 juillet).

❹ Château Lanessan

There are so many châteaux around here with such a confusing web of opening times and visiting regulations that it can be hard to know where to begin. One of the easiest to visit is **Château Lanessan** (☏05 56 58 94 80; www.lanessan.com; Cussac-Fort-Medoc; adult/child tour cellar €8/2, horse museum €8/2, gardens €8/2, cellar & museum €15/2; ◷10am-noon & 2-6pm by advance reservation), a neoclassical castle with English-style gardens and a 19th-century greenhouse. You can tour just the wine cellar (one hour); visit the impressive stables built in the

St-Émilion Village and vineyards

shape of a horseshoe in 1880 with marble feed troughs, a pine-panelled tack room and a museum of 19th-century horse-drawn carriages; or do both (1½ hours). The property also offers vertical wine tastings (€18; 1½ hours) and two-hour wine-blending workshops (€30).

The Drive » Getting to Blaye involves splashing over the Gironde River on a car ferry – how exciting! Return to the D2 and head south to Lamarque where you hop on board the small TransGironde ferry (www.transgironde.fr; per car/adult/child May-Sep €18.50/3.10/1.50, low season Oct-Apr €12/2.30/1) for the short 4.5km, 20-minute crossing to Blaye. It's 11km from the château to the ferry.

TRIP HIGHLIGHT

5 Blaye

If you want a lesson in how to build a protective citadel, then spectacular **Citadelle de Blaye** is about as good an example as you could hope to find. Largely constructed by that master fortress builder Vauban in the

17th century, it was a key line of defence protecting Bordeaux from naval attack. It was inscribed onto the Unesco World Heritage List in 2008.

The Drive » From Blaye to St-Émilion is a 50km drive. From Blaye take the D137 toward St-André de Cubzac, where you join the D670 to Libourne. After a bit of time stuck in traffic you continue down to St-Émilion. It should take an hour but traffic means it will probably take longer!

TRIP HIGHLIGHT

➏ St-Émilion

The medieval village of St-Émilion perches above vineyards renowned for producing full-bodied red wines and is easily the most alluring of all the region's wine towns.

The only way to visit the town's most interesting historical sites is with one of the tourist office's varied **guided tours** (adult/child from €8/free).

The tourist office also organises two-hour afternoon **château visits** (adult/child €12/free), and runs various events throughout the year, such as **Les Samedis de l'Oenologie**, which combines a vineyard visit, lunch, a town tour and a wine-tasting course on Saturdays.

For a fun and informative introduction to wine tasting, get stuck into a themed tasting at the wine school inside the **Maison du Vin** (📞05 57 55 50 55; www.maisonduvin saintemilion.com; place Pierre Meyrat; ⊙9.30am-6.30pm May-Oct, 9.30am-12.30pm & 2-6pm Nov-Apr).

✕ 🛏 p366

The Drive » To get to the next stop you've simply no option but to endure the ring road around Bordeaux – avoid rush hour! Head towards Bordeaux on the N89, then south down the A63 following signs to Arcachon and then Gujan Mestras. It's a 100km journey that should, but probably won't, take an hour.

➐ Gujan Mestras

Take a break from the grape and head to the seaside to eat oysters in the area around Gujan Mestras. Picturesque oyster ports are dotted around the town, but the best one to visit is **Port de Larros**, where locally harvested oysters are sold from wooden shacks. To learn more about these delicious shellfish, the small **Maison de l'Huître** (📞05 56 66 23 71; www.maison-huitre.fr; rue du Port de Larros; adult/child €5.90/3.90; ⊙10am-1pm & 2.30-6.30pm Jul & Aug, 10am-12.30pm & 2.30-6pm Mon-Sat Sep-Jun) has a display on oyster farming, including a short film in English.

The Drive » It's 10 sometimes-traffic-clogged but well-signposted kilometres from Gujan Mestras to Arcachon.

DETOUR: COGNAC

Start: ➎ Blaye

On the banks of the Charente River amid vine-covered countryside, the picturesque town of Cognac, home of the double-distilled spirit that bears its name, proves that there's more to southwest France than just wine.

The best-known Cognac houses are open to the public, running tours of their cellars and production facilities, and ending with a tasting session. The **tourist office** (📞05 45 82 10 71; www.tourism-cognac. com; 16 rue du 14 Juillet; ⊙9.30am-6.30pm Mon-Sat, to 1pm Sun Jul & Aug, shorter hours rest of year) can give advice on current opening hours of each Cognac house.

It's 85km from Blaye to Cognac, much of which is along the A10 highway. From Cognac you can cut down to stop 6, St-Émilion, in two hours on the D731 followed by the busy N10.

TRIP HIGHLIGHT

⑧ Arcachon

The seaside town of Arcachon has lured bourgeois Bordelaises since the end of the 19th century. Its four little quarters are romantically named for each of the seasons, with villas that evoke the town's golden past amid a scattering of 1950s architecture.

Arcachon's sandy beach, **Plage d'Arcachon**, is flanked by two piers. Lively **Jetée Thiers** is at the western end. In front of the eastern pier, **Jetée d'Eyrac**, stands the town's turreted **Casino de la Plage**, built by Adalbert Deganne in 1953 as an exact replica of Château de Boursault in the Marne. Inside, it's a less-grand blinking and bell-ringing riot of poker machines and gaming tables.

On the tree-covered hillside south of the Ville d'Été, the century-old **Ville d'Hiver** (Winter Quarter) has over 300 villas ranging in style from neo-Gothic through to colonial.

For a different view of Arcachon and its coastline, take to the ocean waves on one of the boat cruises organised by **Les Bateliers Arcachonnais**

TOP TIP:
OYSTER TASTE TEST

Oysters from each of the Bassin d'Arcachon's four oyster-breeding zones hint at subtly different flavours. See if you can detect these:
Banc d'Arguin – milk and sugar
Île aux Oiseaux – minerals
Cap Ferret – citrus
Grand Banc – roasted hazelnuts

(UBA; ☎08 25 27 00 27; www.bateliers-arcachon.com; 75 bd de la Plage; 🖬). It offers daily, year-round cruises around **Île aux Oiseaux**, the uninhabited 'bird island' in the middle of Arcachon bay. It's a haven for tern, curlew and redshank, so bring your binoculars. In summer there are day excursions to the **Banc d'Arguin**, the sand bank off the Dune du Pilat.

✕ 🛏 p367

The Drive » Dune du Pilat is 12km south of Arcachon down the D218. There are restrictions on car access in summer for the last part of the route.

⑨ Dune du Pilat

This colossal sand dune (sometimes referred to as the Dune de Pyla because of its location in the resort town of Pyla-sur-Mer) stretches from the mouth of the Bassin d'Arcachon southwards for almost 3km. Already the largest in Europe, it's spreading eastwards at 4.5m a year – it has swallowed trees, a road junction and even a hotel.

The view from the top – approximately 114m above sea level – is magnificent. To the west you can see the sandy shoals at the mouth of the Bassin d'Arcachon, and dense dark-green pine forests stretch from the base of the dune eastwards almost as far as the eye can see. The only address to have a drink or dine afterwards is **La Co(o)rniche** (☎05 56 22 72 11; www.lacoorniche-pyla.com; 46 av Louis Gaume; 2-/3-course lunch menu €63/68, seafood platters €40-85), a 1930s hunting lodge transformed by French designer Philippe Starck into one of France's most stunning seaside restaurants.

Eating & Sleeping

Bordeaux ➊

✖ Le Magasin Général   International €

(☎05 56 77 88 35; www.magasingeneral.
camp; 87 quai des Queyries; mains €10-25;
🕗8am-8pm Mon-Fri, 10am-midnight Sat &
Sun; 🛜 � 👶) Follow the hip crowd across
the river to this huge industrial hangar on the
right bank, France's biggest and best organic
restaurant with a gargantuan terrace complete
with vintage sofa seating, ping-pong table and
table football. Everything here – from vegan
burgers and superfood salads to smoothies,
pizzas, wine and French bistro fare – is *bio*
(organic) and sourced locally. Sunday brunch
(adult/child €26/12) is a bottomless feast.
Find the restaurant in a former military
barracks, abandoned in 2005 and since
transformed into the green creative hub known
as Darwin.

✖ Le Petit Commerce   Seafood €€

(☎05 56 79 76 58; www.facebook.com/
LePetitCommerceBDX; 22 rue du Parlement
Saint-Pierre; mains €17-27; 🕗10am-1am) This
iconic bistro, with dining rooms on both sides of
a narrow pedestrian street and former Michelin-
starred chef Stéphane Carrade in the kitchen, is
the star turn of the trendy St-Pierre quarter. It's
best known for its excellent seafood menu that
embraces everything from Arcachon sole and
oysters (per dozen €22 to €28) to eels, lobsters
and *chipirons* (baby squid) fresh from St-Jean
de Luz.

✖ La Tupina   French €€€

(☎05 56 91 56 37; www.latupina.com; 6 rue
Porte de la Monnaie; lunch menu €18, dinner
menus €64 & €74, mains €20-60; 🕗noon-2pm
& 7-11pm Tue-Sun) Filled with the aroma of soup
simmering inside a *tupina* ('kettle' in Basque)
over an open fire, this iconic bistro is famed
for its hardcore, southwestern French fare:
calf kidneys with fries cooked in goose fat,
milk-fed lamb, tripe and goose wings. Dining
is farmhouse-style, in a maze of small elegant
rooms decorated with vintage photographs,
antique furniture and silver tableware.

🛏 Chez Dupont   B&B €€

(☎05 56 81 49 59; www.chez-dupont.com; 45
rue Notre Dame; s €110-150, d €130-170; 🛜) Ten
impeccably decorated rooms, peppered with
a wonderful collection of vintage curiosities,
inspires love at first sight at this thoroughly
contemporary, design-driven B&B in Bordeaux's
wine-merchant district. Some rooms have
a kitchenette, while the suite is in another
building, a few doors down the street opposite
Chartron's 'village' church. Chez Dupont runs
the bistro of the same name.

🛏 L'Hôtel Particulier   B&B €€€

(☎05 57 88 28 80; www.lhotel-particulier.com;
44 rue Vital-Carles; s €80, d €219-249; 🛜) Step
into this fabulous *chambre d'hôte* and be wowed
by period furnishings mixed with contemporary
design, extravagant decorative touches and an
atmospheric courtyard garden. Five individually
designed rooms match up to expectations
with vintage fireplaces, carved ceilings and
bathtubs; the 12 well-furnished self-catering
apartments, sleeping one to four people, are
exceptional value.

St-Émilion ➏

✖ L'Envers du Décors   French €€

(☎06 57 74 48 31; www.envers-dudecor.com;
9 rue du Clocher; 2-/3-course lunch menu
€26.50/32, mains €25-34.50; 🕗noon-2.30pm
& 7-10.30pm) A few doors from the tourist office,
this legendary wine bar with fire-engine-red
facade is one of the finest places to eat – and
inevitably drink – in this tasteful wine town. Chef
Bertrand Bordenave cooks fabulous market-
driven local classics, including *escargots à la
Bordelaise* (snail stew with tomatoes, white wine
and chilli pepper), veal liver pan-fried in sherry
vinegar, and oysters by the dozen.

✕ La Table de Pavie Gastronomy €€€

(Hôtel de Pavie; 📞05 57 55 07 55; www.
hostelleriedeplaisance.com; 5 place du Clocher;
menu lunch €58, dinner €155 & €205; ⏱noon-
1.15pm & 7.30-9.15pm Tue-Sat) Wine pairings are
in a league of their own at this exquisite Michelin
double-starred restaurant, in the heart of the
village in a luxurious, five-star hotel. Since 2020
multi-starred chef Yannick Alléno has been
the celebrity mastermind behind the sublime
menu that smokes tender milk-fed lamb over
grape vines, marries pigeon with asparagus
lettuce, and serves Breton lobster in a Graves
wine sauce.

🛏 Grand Barrail Historic Hotel €€€

(📞05 57 55 37 00; www.grand-barrail.com;
rte de Libourne, D243; d from €270; ❄🛜⛲)
Grand doesn't even begin to describe this
immense five-star château-hotel, built in 1850,
with its 46 antique-dressed rooms, spa, stone-
flagged heated swimming pool, vast park and
helipad on the front lawn. Undoubtedly the best
seat in its gastronomic **restaurant** (*menus
two-/three-course lunch €29/34, dinner €55
to €90*) is the corner table framed by exquisite
19th-century stained glass. Find the castle 3km
from St-Émilion village, signposted off the D243.

Arcachon 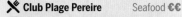 8

✕ Club Plage Pereire Seafood €€

(📞05 57 16 59 13; www.clubplagepereire.com;
12 bd de la Mer; mains €14-30; ⏱restaurant
noon-3pm & 7-10pm, club 10am-midnight Apr-
Sep) Each year this pop-up beach hut on sandy
Plage Pereire is built afresh, much to the joy of
local foodies and bons vivants who flock here
for tasty seafood cuisine, tapas and burgers,
the buzzing beach vibe, drinks on the sand and
stunning sunsets. To get here, follow the coast
west along bd de la Plage and bd de l'Océan
for 2km.

🛏 Hôtel
Villa d'Hiver Boutique Hotel €€

(📞05 56 66 10 36; www.hotelvilledhiver.
com; 20 av Victor Hugo; d/tr from €140/165;
❄@🛜⛲) Secreted away in Arcachon's
1860s Ville d'Hiver district, this chic and
deliciously eclectic, boutique hotel seduces
with 18 rooms in a trio of garden-clad houses.
Pricier rooms with balcony can glimpse the sea,
the atmospheric flora-strewn outdoor pool is in
an upcycled tanker, and the hotel's pop-up Club
Plage Pereire is one of the hottest addresses in
town. Find the hotel a 10-minute walk from the
train station and beach.

Gourmet Dordogne

34

The Dordogne is definitely a place that thinks with its stomach. This foodie tour indulges in the region's gastronomic goodies, from walnuts and truffles to fine wine and foie gras.

TRIP HIGHLIGHTS

95 km

Bergerac
Educate your palate by tasting your way through Bergerac's multifarious wines

Mortemart

Ste-Alvère

START
1

7

● **Monbazillac**
FINISH

2

19 km

Castelnaud-la-Chapelle
Taste freshly pressed walnut oils in the orchard-shadow of a famous fortress

0 km

Sarlat-la-Canéda
Browse the stalls of Sarlat's atmospheric street markets

2 DAYS
113KM / 70 MILES

GREAT FOR...

BEST TIME TO GO

September and October for harvest markets; December and February for truffle season.

ESSENTIAL PHOTO

Monbazillac's conical château turrets rising above endless neat rows of vines.

✓ **BEST FOR FOODIES**

Drooling at the wonderful open-air markets.

34 Gourmet Dordogne

If you enjoy nothing better than soaking up the sights, sounds and smells of a French market, you'll be in seventh heaven in the Dordogne's picturesque villages and history-draped towns. Immersing yourself in this region's culinary culture is one of the best – and tastiest – ways to experience life in rural France. Note that for some of the best tasting experiences, calling ahead is advisable.

TRIP HIGHLIGHT

❶ Sarlat-la-Canéda

Start in the honey-stoned town of Sarlat-la-Canéda, the beautifully preserved medieval town that's the central hub of tourism in the Dordogne. It hosts a busy **outdoor market** on Saturday mornings, with a more subdued version on Wednesdays. Local farm stalls selling seasonal treats such as cèpe mushrooms, duck terrines, foie gras and walnuts fill the central place de la Liberté and

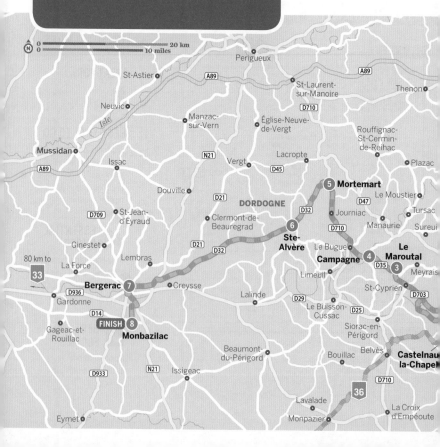

radiate out into virtually every space in the town centre. There's also an atmospheric **night market** (place du 14 Juillet; ◷6-10pm Thu Jul & Aug) .

Even if you're not here on market day, you can shop for fine produce at Sarlat's **Marché Couvert** (Covered Market; place de la Liberté; ◷8.30am-2pm daily mid-Apr–mid-Nov, closed Mon, Thu & Sun rest of year), housed in a former church, imaginatively converted by French star architect Jean Nouvel. A lift takes visitors to the tower-top for panoramic

views across Sarlat's multi-spired slate rooftops.

You might choose to stay two nights in Sarlat and return here after the first day's drive: distances are short.

 p375

The Drive » Though there's a more direct route (13km via Vézac), it's worth taking your time and an extra 6km to admire the Dordogne Valley's signature stretch of majestic castle-crowned scenery. Start by heading south to Vitrac, then turn west, approximately following the river's north bank. You'll drive right through the classic cliff-backed village of La-Roque-Gageac, a picture-perfect place to sip a waterside coffee, and for boating, canoeing or kayaking depending on your energy levels. Continuing, you pass the base of the remarkable topiary gardens of Marqueyssac (www.marqueyssac.com) as an unforgettably impressive trio of castles comes into view. Cross the bridge and climb through Castelnaud, initially following signs to the castle and upper car park, then turning left just after the bus park on a signed lane

to the Eco-Musée de la Noix du Perigord.

TRIP HIGHLIGHT

② Castelnaud-la-Chapelle

The humble *noix* (walnut) has been a prized product of the Dordogne for centuries, and remains widely used in liqueurs and many local recipes, not just the ubiquitous dessert, *gâteau de noix* (walnut cake). Set in a pretty hillside orchard, the **Eco-Musée de la Noix du Perigord** (adult/child €5/4; ◷2pm-6pm Mon-Sat) is part farm shop, part museum at which you can watch fragrant walnut oil being made on an antiquated original mill-contraption. Lots of nut-based goodies are available for sale. Barely 800m away, don't miss also visiting the medieval **Château de Castelnaud** (www.castelnaud.com) with its superb museum of historical weaponry.

ATLANTIC COAST **34** GOURMET DORDOGNE

LINK YOUR TRIP

33 Heritage Wine Country

The hallowed vineyards of Bordeaux lie 96km to the west of Bergerac along the D936.

36 Dordogne's Fortified Villages

At the castle village of Castelnaud-la-Chapelle, this route intersects our trip visiting the Dordogne's best *bastides* (fortified market-towns).

The Drive » The 19km drive northwest from Castelnaud is the same distance via either bank of the Dordogne. The north bank route takes you right past the domineering Château de Beynac (www.chateau-beynac.com), an archetypal medieval fortress crowning the clifftop above delightful Beynac village. The south bank route is partly on tiny country lanes and passes the more homely Château des Milandes (www.milandes.com), once home to 1920s music-hall star and civil-rights activist Josephine Baker (1906–75). The two routes converge as the D703 to St-Cyprien where, opposite the station, you turn right onto the D49. Just 200m after that converges with the D35; veer right following signs to the Domaine de la Voie Blanche.

MARCO MAYER / SHUTTERSTOCK ©

❸ Le Maroutal

This part of the Dordogne isn't generally known for its wines, but **Domaine de la Voie Blanche** (☏06 79 45 82 48; www.domaine-voie-blanche.com; St-Cyprien; tastings €4-7 per person; ⏰1pm-6pm Jul-Aug, by reservation Sep-Jun) is a special case, and a pioneer in using earthenware amphorae instead of barrels to mature its sophisticated all-organic reds. This is a small family operation so it's worth calling ahead, but in summer the farm's tasting room is generally open.

The Drive » Backtrack southwest to the D35, then follow that road to Campagne. In Campagne the postcard-perfect local castle is now an occasional exhibition centre set in a glorious park of lawns, streams and giant mature trees: entrance is free so it's well worth stretching the legs. About 1km further, the D35 crosses the river: after the bridge turn very sharp left and follow the Grolière signs for 700m.

❹ Campagne

Alongside black truffles, the Dordogne is also famous for its foie gras (fattened goose liver). You'll see duck and goose farms dotted all over the countryside, many of which offer tours and a *dégustation* (tasting). A much-lauded producer, **Grolière** (☏05 53 07 22 64; www.foiegras-groliere.com; Malmussou Bas; ⏰9am-12.30pm & 4-6.30pm Mon-Fri, plus Sat mid-Jul–Aug), has shops in several tourist centres but its farm base is in a soothingly rural spot in Malmussou, across the Vézère River from Campagne, with honking geese and an enticing shop. Given a little advance notice, they'll also show you a five-minute film explaining foie gras production and let you visit the cannery.

✕ 🛏 p375

The Drive » Drive the D703 through the bustling town of Le Bugue then follow Périgueux

Campagne Pâté de Campagne

signs onto the D710, continuing 13km north to Mortemart. If you'd rather give the boar farm a miss, an alternative, slightly circuitous route to Ste-Alvère starts off heading southwest from Le Bugue taking in the lovely hilltop village of Limeuil, then swinging northwest via Paunat with its austere abbey church and great restaurant.

---

5 Mortemart

Les Sangliers de Mortemart (☏06 17 74 06 64; www.elevage-sangliers-mortemart.com; adult/child €3/1.50; ☺10am-7pm Jul & Aug, 1-5pm Sep-Jun) is an unsophisticated family farm where, for a token fee, you can see wild boars being raised in the semi-freedom of fenced fields and woodlands. These porky cousins of the modern pig are fed a rich diet of *châtaignes* (chestnuts), which gives the meat a distinctive nutty-gamey flavour. Boar meat is a key ingredient in the hearty stew known as *civet de sanglier,* as well as pâtés and country terrines. The farm's shop sells a range of home-produced boar-themed goodies.

The Drive » From Mortemart, it's a lovely 12km drive through classic Dordogne countryside on the D32 to Ste-Alvère.

---

6 Ste-Alvère

The charming little village of Ste-Alvère has lots of genuine rustic character, and is famed as another centre for truffles. In mid-winter, time your arrival for the brief but much-celebrated Monday morning **truffle market** (www.valdelouyre-et-caudeau. fr/le-marche-aux-truffes-de-sainte-alvere; rue Pasteur; ☺10-11am Mon Dec-Feb). At other times, displays in the little **tourist office** (☺9am-12.30pm Mon-Thu

TRUFFLE SECRETS

Few ingredients command the same culinary cachet as the *truffe noire* (black truffle), variously known as the *diamant noir* (black diamond) or, hereabouts, the *perle noire du Périgord* (black pearl of the Dordogne). The gem references aren't just for show, either: a high-end truffle crop can fetch as much as €1000 per kg.

A subterranean fungus that grows naturally in chalky soils (especially around the roots of oak trees), this mysterious mushroom is notoriously capricious; a good truffle spot one year can be bare the next, which has made farming them practically impossible. The art of truffle-hunting is a closely guarded secret; it's a matter of luck, judgement and experience, with specially trained dogs (and occasionally pigs) to help in the search.

In season (December to February), special truffle markets are held around the Dordogne, notably at Sarlat and Ste-Alvère.

& 2-5pm Tue-Thu Oct-Mar) offer insights into truffle cultivation and there are signposted walks in the nearby truffle woods. The village has two good restaurants, a cafe-bar and a foie-gras merchant.

 p375

The Drive » Continue to Bergerac on the D32. Some 24km from Ste-Alvère, just before you arrive at the N21 junction, a short detour south brings you to the famed Chateau de Tiregand winery (https://chateau-de-tiregand.com), which offers tastings though you can't go into the palacial castle itself. Otherwise continue 6km into Bergerac and park at Le Forail, one of the city's few free car parks. Walk 500m west along rue Junien Rabier to find the old town.

TRIP HIGHLIGHT

⑦ Bergerac

Vineyards carpet the countryside around Bergerac, producing rich reds, fragrant whites, fruity rosés and particularly famous honeyed dessert wines. With 13 Appéllations d'Origines Contrôlées (AOCs), and more than 1200 growers, the choice is bewildering. Thankfully, the **Quai Cyrano** (www.vins-bergerac-duras.fr; quai Salvette; ⏱bar 9am-1am Tue-Sat, 11am-11pm Sun & Mon) knows all the best vintages, offers free tastings and can help you target vineyards to visit. You could happily spend at least another couple of days touring the local

wineries using Bergerac as a base.

 p375

The Drive » Monbazillac is 8km south of Bergerac via the D936E then the D13.

---

⑧ Monbazillac

Of all the wines produced around Bergerac, none is more instantly recognisable than the sweet, liquid sunshine of Monbazillac. The name is also synonymous with the iconic **Château de Monbazillac** (☎05 53 63 65 00; www.chateau-monbazillac.com; D13; tour & tasting adult/child €7.80/3.90; ⏱10am-7pm daily Jun-Sep, 10am-noon & 2-5pm Oct-May, closed Jan), a grand 16th-century château that surveys row after row of nearly planted vines on a steep slope south of Bergerac. However, the tour-bus crowds can be oppressive here and there are plenty of alternatives nearby to taste not just dessert wines but also Bergerac AOC dry whites and structured Pécharmant reds (from north of Bergerac). Family-run **Château Montdoyen** (☎05 53 58 85 85; www.chateau-montdoyen.com; Le Puch; ⏱9am-6pm Jun-Sep, 8am-5pm Mon-Fri Oct-May) is a good, offbeat choice whose wines take curious catch-phrase names.

 p375

Eating & Sleeping

Sarlat-la-Canéda ❶

✖ Le Grand Bleu — Gastronomy €€€

(📞05 53 31 08 48; www.legrandbleu.eu; 43 av de la Gare; menus €58-130; ⏱7.30-9.30pm Tue & Wed, 12.30-2pm & 7.30-9.30pm Thu-Sat, 12.30-2pm Sun; 🅿) Chef Maxime Lebrun's creative cuisine has won a Michelin star, with elaborate *menus* using plenty of luxury ingredients from sturgeon to truffles to sweetbreads. It's near the train station, 1.5km south of the town centre.

🛏 La Maison des Peyrat — Hotel €€

(📞05 53 59 00 32; www.maisondespeyrat.com; Le Lac de la Plane; d/tr/q from €72/112/130; ⏱Apr–mid-Nov) This beautifully renovated 14th- to 17th-century house was once a nuns' hospital and later an aristocratic hunting lodge. It's set in a garden just 800m east of Sarlat's inner ring road, with a large pool and easy parking. The 10 rooms vary greatly in size, but each is carefully described on the website and many come with exposed stone walls.

Campagne ❹

✖ Chez Julien — French €€

(Le Restaurant de l'Abbatiale; 📞05 53 63 21 08; Paunat; mains from €17; ⏱Thu-Sun) Impeccable traditional food – escargot, scrumptious scallops – is created by a master chef and served in the idyllic setting of a presbytery with its terrace facing the grand old abbey church at Paunat (aka Paunac), a stone hamlet 6km northwest of Limeuil.

🛏 Le Moulin du Porteuil — B&B €€

(📞05 53 54 48 73; www.moulin-du-porteil.com; rte de La Bugue, Campagne; d €80-100; 🅿 ❄ 🛜 🏊) Jessica and Stéphane have created a perfect blend of comfortable, family-friendly B&B and well-priced yet artistically imaginative regional restaurant (lunch/dinner *menus* €18/26.50). It's between Campagne and Le Bugue, in an expansive garden with adults' and kids' pools.

Ste-Alvère ❻

✖ Dix — French €€

(📞05 53 61 78 83; www.dixdordogne.com; 10 rue du Pré St Jean; mains €18-41, lunch menu €21-25; ⏱noon-2pm Mon & Tue, noon-2pm & 7.30-9pm Thu & Fri, 7.30-9pm Sat & Sun) Run by a young Anglo-French couple, this picture-perfect little restaurant has rough wooden tables set with fresh-picked flowers and is dominated by a big window into the show kitchen. The regularly changing menu includes a veggie option, and yes, you can have truffles on your meal (in season, €8 extra).

Bergerac ❼

🛏 Château les Merles — Boutique Hotel €€€

(📞05 53 63 13 42; www.lesmerles.com; Tuilières; d/ste €190/250, apt €350; 🅿 🛜 🏊) Behind 17th-century cream stone, this very attractive little wine château 15km east of Bergerac has 14 guest rooms that counterpoint modish monochrome colour schemes with artfully chosen antiques. There's a whole series of delightful lounges, a ravishing restaurant (dinner *menus* from €29.50), and a bistro offering international flavours plus barista coffees. Did we mention the nine-hole golf course?!

Monbazillac ❽

✖ La Tour des Vents — Gastronomy €€€

(📞05 53 58 30 10; www.tourdesvents.com; Le Moulin de Malfourat; menus €51-72; ⏱7.30-9.15pm Wed-Sun; 🖈) Chef Damien Fagette's Michelin-starred restaurant is the Bergerac area's gourmet grail, overlooking a panoramic sweep of view from beside a disused windmill tower. To get the same view you could have lunch at the cohabiting bistro, where prices are far more modest.

Cave Art of the Vézère Valley

The limestone caves of southwest France contain some of Europe's finest examples of prehistoric art, along with some truly lovely festivals of geological wonder.

35

TRIP HIGHLIGHTS

18 km

Grotte de Rouffignac
A web of prehistoric caves that you visit by subterranean train

50 km

Le Thot
Get up close to some of the wildlife depicted by prehistoric painters

Rouffignac

Plazac

⑤

⑦

⑧ **FINISH**

59 km

Grotte de Lascaux
Marvel at the modern-day replica of France's finest ancient artwork

① ②

START

Les Eyzies
Explore a treasure trove of prehistoric artefacts

0 km

Grotte de Font de Gaume
A multicoloured menagerie of ancient animals adorns this memorable cave

1 km

**3 DAYS
79KM / 50 MILES**

GREAT FOR...

BEST TIME TO GO

April to June, when most sites are open, but the summer crowds haven't arrived.

 ESSENTIAL PHOTO

A fortified mansion squeezed into the cliff-overhang at Reignac.

 BEST FOR FAMILIES

Le Thot's 'prehistoric' zoo hosts bison, reindeer and ibex.

35 Cave Art of the Vézère Valley

This trip feels like opening a time capsule into the prehistoric past. Hidden deep underground in murky caves around the Vézère Valley, Cro-Magnon people left behind a remarkable legacy of ancient artworks, ranging from rock sculptures to multicoloured murals – and this is one of the few places in the world where it's possible to see their work up close. Best of all, the caves are set in beautiful rural countryside that makes for lovely driving.

TRIP HIGHLIGHT

1 Les Eyzies

Hugging an overhanging curl of cliff, this attractive little tourist village, 20km northwest of Sarlat-la-Canéda, is the ideal starting point for exploring the Vézère Valley. Most major caves are within half-an-hour's drive, but tickets for some are in short supply so both timing and planning are important. Think ahead by prebooking online for Lascaux (day 3). Then on day 1, dash

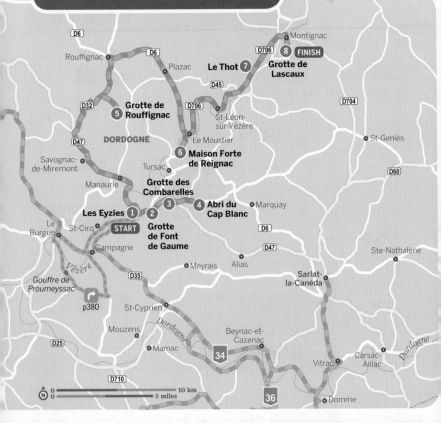

straight for the ticket booth at Fond de Gaume, joining the early morning queue. Hopefully you'll be able to score tickets to Comberelles as well as Font de Gaume; both have extremely limited availability, online booking is impossible. and tickets must be bought on the day of your visit and in person (so you can't send just one of your group to buy for everyone). While you're here, why not also buy the Cap Blanc ticket to get a reduced combo-price for the three entrances. If you've started late and no tickets remain, consider rerouting your driving trip and then trying again early next morning. Once your tickets are arranged, you'll probably

LINK YOUR TRIP

34 **Gourmet Dordogne**

Lascaux IV is 27km north of Sarlat-la-Canéda, the start of our Gourmet tour, which also passes through Campagne, just 6km southwest of Les Eyzies.

37 **The Lot Valley**

From Sarlat-la-Canéda, it's another 10km's drive to either Beynac or Domme, both on our Fortified Villages route.

have some time before (or between) your visiting slots. So head back into Les Eyzies and aquaint yourself with the cultures of the prehistoric human cave-artists through brief film-presentations at **PIP** (Pôle Internationale de la Prehistoire; www.pole-prehistoire. com; ☺9.30am-5.30pm Mon-Fri, 10.30am-5.30pm Sat Sep-Jun, 9.30am-6.30pm daily Jul & Aug), a free, modernist exhibition centre. To learn a whole lot more, walk 400m west from PIP along a pretty, pedestrian lane to the **Musée National de Préhistoire** (☎05 53 06 45 65; www. musee-prehistoire-eyzies.fr; 1 rue du Musée; adult/child €6/free; ☺9.30am-5.45pm daily Jul & Aug, to 4.45pm Wed-Mon Sep-Jun), home to France's most comprehensive collection of prehistoric artefacts from Stone Age tools and jewellery to animal skeletons and original rock friezes taken from the caves. Allow an hour or two to do it justice.

 p383

The Drive » Font de Gaume is barely 1km from Les Eyzies, east along the D47.

- - - - - - - - - - - - - - - - - - -

TRIP HIGHLIGHT

❷ Grotte de Font de Gaume

Now you've got the background, it's time to see some real cave art. **Font de Gaume** (☎05 53 06 86 00; www.sites-les-eyzies. fr; 4 av des Grottes; adult/

child €11.50/free; ☺guided tours 9.30am-4pm Sun-Fri) is a particularly celebrated underground cavern as it contains the only original multicoloured cave paintings that are still open to public view in their original state. Its full 'gallery' contains over 230 animal images and includes reindeer, horses, mammoths, bisons and bears, though only limited sections are visited, illuminated solely by the guide's torch. Of the six daily tours (each maximum 13 people) just the 11.15am and/or 4pm tours are usually in English.

The Drive » Continue along the D47 for 1km from Font de Gaume and turn off at the brown sign for the Grotte de Combarelles. Be sure to arrive at least 10 minutes before the time slot on the ticket, which you'll need to have prepurchased at Font de Gaume earlier that day.

- - - - - - - - - - - - - - - - - - -

❸ Grotte des Combarelles

This narrow, very long **cave** (www.sites-les-eyzies.fr; adult/child €10/free; ☺guided tours 9.30am-5.30pm Sun-Fri) is renowned for animal designs that are engraved rather than painted. Squint in the guide's lamp-light to make out scratched forms of mammoths, horses, reindeer and human figures, as well as a fantastic mountain lion that seems to leap from the rock face. Claustrophobes beware.

The Drive » Travel 1km further east of Combarelles, then turn left onto the twisty D48 into a pleasant wooded valley. Continue for 7km, following the road up the hillside towards the Cap Blanc car park. The museum entrance is a short walk downhill along a rough track.

---

④ Abri du Cap Blanc

This ancient **sculpture gallery** (📞05 53 59 60 30; www.sites-les-eyzies.fr; adult/child €8/free; ⏰guided tours 10am-4pm, to 4.30pm mid-May–mid-Sep) makes a fascinating comparison with Combarelles. It's a cliff-overhang that was used as a natural shelter 14,000 years ago by Cro-Magnon people, who left behind an amazing 40m-long frieze of

horses and bison, carved directly into the rear wall of the site using flint tools. Originally the cave would have been open to the elements, but it's now fronted by a modern museum.

The Drive » Backtrack to Les Eyzies (10km) and stay overnight. Next morning start early, cross the river and follow the pleasant but busy D47 northwest. Initially the route is squeezed between cliffs and the Vézère as you pass the Grotte de Grand Roc cave entrance. Then it climbs the Manaurie Valley, paralleling the railway. Around 11km from Les Eyzies, 250m after you pass the big viaduct beside the farmstead of La Loulie, fork right onto the narrower D32. That road climbs through woodlands onto an agricultural plateau, where after 5km you'll need to turn right. A brown sign says 'Grotte

Préhistorique de Rouffignac 2km' but it's easy to miss.

TRIP HIGHLIGHT

⑤ Grotte de Rouffignac

The astonishing **Grotte de Rouffignac** (📞05 53 05 41 71; www.grottederouffignac. fr; adult/child €7.90/5.20; ⏰9-11.30am & 2-6pm Jul & Aug, 10-11.30am & 2-5pm Apr-Jun, Sep & Oct, closed Nov-Mar) is often known as the 'Cave of 1000 Mammoths' thanks to its plethora of painted pachyderms. The paintings are spread along the walls of a subterranean cavern system that stretches over 8km in total, though you won't see all of that and the visit is made easier thanks to a rickety electric train: no chance of getting lost. Along the way, a highlight is a frieze of 10 mammoths in procession. You'll also see many hollows in the cave floor, scratched out by long-extinct cave bears. Tickets are sold at the cave entrance.

The Drive » From the Grotte de Rouffignac, retrace your route 2km north then turn right taking the D32 to the roundabout in Rouffignac, a large village whose lack of old buildings is a result of WWII destruction – German reprisals for the daring of the French Resistance. Take the D6, curving back south on a pretty route that descends a ridge through Plazac to rejoin the Vézère Valley at Le Moustier (15km total). Neanderthal bones have been found near here. As

DETOUR:
GOUFFRE DE PROUMEYSSAC

Start: ① Les Eyzies

If you find you've got to wait a day for another shot at getting Font de Gaume tickets, why not visit a very different type of cave that's attractive for its sheer beauty rather than its ancient art? The **Gouffre de Proumeyssac** (📞05 53 07 27 47; www. gouffre-proumeyssac.com; Audrix, Le Bugue; adult/child €10.90/7.60, incl basket ride €19.40/13.10; ⏰hours vary, closed Jan), 22km southwest of Les Eyzies, displays its magnificent 'cathedral' of stalactites through a very professional sound-and-light show and offers the unique opportunity (extra fee) of descending into the gaping space on an 11-person dangling basket. Booking an arrival slot is wise, online in July-August, or by phone at other times. The audioguide is a very worthwhile extra.

Grotte de Rouffignac Cave painting

you cross the river, a cliff rising to the left is incised with a very long *abri* (cliff-overhang shelter) known as La Roque Saint-Cristophe. Keep ahead, however, and head 2.5km south (towards Les Eyzies) for the Maison Forte de Reignac.

- - - - - - - - - - - - - - - - - -

⑥ Maison Forte de Reignac

This three-storey medieval **mansion** (☏05 53 50 69 54; www.maison-forte-reignac.com; adult/child €8.20/4; ☺10am-8pm Jul & Aug, reduced hours rest of year, closed Dec–mid-Feb) was built straight into the cliff-face using *abri*-caves that once sheltered prehistoric humans. Now it's kitted out with period furnishing and displays of everything from prehistoric finds to medieval weaponry.

Even if you don't go in, it's photogenic when seen from outside.

The Drive » If you missed out on Font de Gaume earlier, you could nip back from here to Les Eyzies and try again for a ticket tomorrow. Otherwise, head northwest towards Montignac through the pretty village of St-Léon-sur-Vézère with its dainty mini-castle in a walled, riverside garden. Le Thot is 1.8km off the main D706

PREHISTORY 101

The earliest cave art around the Vézère dates from approximately 20,000 BCE, during the last ice age. The artists were early modern humans known to history as Cro-Magnon people after the cave where their first remains were discovered. They lived a hunter-gatherer lifestyle using the mouths of caves as temporary hunting shelters, though why they ventured much deeper inside to paint the walls remains a mystery: it's assumed that the images held some kind of magical, religious or shamanic significance. Designs range from geometric forms and occasional stylised humans to depictions of the various animals that the artists hunted, notably mammoths, woolly rhinoceros, reindeer and aurochs – ancestors of the modern cow. Some were scratched, a few chipped as sculptures and many more painted using mineral pigments, including charcoal (black), ochre (red/yellow) and iron-ore (red). The painting seems to have ceased around 11,000 BCE, about the same time that temperatures rose, many predators became extinct, and humans settled down to a more fixed lifestyle of farming and agriculture.

TRIP HIGHLIGHT

❼ Le Thot

Le Thot (☎05 53 50 70 44; www.parc-thot.fr; Thonac; adult/child €10/6.50, joint ticket with Lascaux €24/15.60; ◷10am-6pm Jul & Aug, to 4pm or later Sep-Dec & early Feb-Jun, closed Jan) introduces in 3D beasts that were depicted by prehistoric artists. Some, including reindeer, stags, horses, ibex and European bison, live in the park. Others – like woolly mammoths – have fibreglass stand-ins since the real animals are long extinct. Combo tickets including Lascaux IV can save a little money.

The Drive » Get back onto the D706 and head for Montignac (7km), an attractive riverside town to explore, dine and sleep. Next morning, head to the hilltop 1km south of town where you'll find the entrance to Lascaux IV.

TRIP HIGHLIGHT

❽ Grotte de Lascaux

Sometimes nicknamed the Sistine Chapel of cave art, the Lascaux caves are home to France's most famous – and finest – prehistoric paintings. Though the original cave has been closed for its protection since 1963, **Lascaux IV** (International Centre for Cave Art; ☎05 53 50 99 10; www.lascaux.fr; Montignac; adult/child €20/12.90; ◷8.30am-6pm Jul & Aug, 9am-5pm Apr-Jun, Sep & Oct, 10am-4pm Nov-Mar, closed Jan) is a cutting-edge copy. Using laser technology and 3D printing, the exact contours, engravings and nearly 600 paintings have been reproduced to the millimetre, and the result feels remarkably like a real cave – it's damp, dark and chilly, and the whole experience can be spine-tingling.

After the hour-long cave visit, you're turned loose with a tablet to explore the excellent Lascaux Studio, where life-size renderings of all the major scenes are given context with superimposed images, there's a multimedia show, a 3D film and an interactive gallery examining relationships between prehistoric and modern art.

Online reservations (advisable) can be made up to two days ahead. A certain number of same-day tickets are sold on-site, so if you show up bright and early you might still get in without prebooking.

✕ ⯎ p383

Eating & Sleeping

Les Eyzies ❶

✖ Au Vieux Moulin   French €€

(📞05 53 06 94 33; www.moulindelabeune.com; 2 rue du Moulin Bas; menus €29-39; ⏱7-8.30pm Mon-Sat Apr-Oct) Reserve ahead for a dinner spot at this renovated water mill where French classic cuisine includes truffle- and foie-gras-based dishes and beef Rossini. It's part of the stream-side Moulin de la Beaune, a **hotel** (d €76-96) tucked into a quiet garden area between the main road and Les Eyzies' cliffside village lanes.

🛏 Hôtel des Glycines   Hotel €€

(📞05 53 06 97 07; www.les-glycines-dordogne. com; 4 av de Laugerie; d from €145; ⏱Jan–mid-Nov; ❄🖥🌊) Les Eyzies' poshest pad has contemporary-meets-antique styling, a beautifully manicured park and both a gastronomic restaurant and a bistro, the latter serving *bib-gourmand* lunches. The on-site spa costs extra. It's beside the main road, close to the train station.

🛏 Hôtel Le Cro-Magnon   Hotel €

(📞05 53 06 97 06; www.hotel-cromagnon.com; 54 av de la Préhistoire; d €70-90; 🅿🖥🌊) Behind a pretty wisteria-clad façade, this old-world hotel has a beamed restaurant, comfy sitting areas and a tree-shaded garden but is most unusual for the upper corridors built straight into the rock face. Decent-sized rooms are comfortable if unsophisticated, with pastel decor in varying states of renovation. A building on this site was once the ferryman's cottage in whose foundations the region's first Cro-Magnon artefacts were discovered. It's been a hotel since 1868. Its latest owners, Flemish-born Jan and Ruud, reopened the place in 2020 just before the Covid-19 virus shut down tourism across France, their unlucky adventure featuring on a Belgian reality TV show.

Montignac ❽

✖ La Chaumière   French €

(📞05 53 50 14 24; 53 rue du 4 Septembre; menu €21; ⏱noon-2pm Sun-Fri, 7-9pm Thu-Mon, closed Wed) Squeeze into this attractively rustic-styled little restaurant, dangling with assorted knick-knacks, for generous portions of hearty dishes both regional (*cassoulet*, duck confit) and Alpine *(raclette)*.

✖ UniVert   Vegetarian €

(📞06 33 22 20 68; 7 place Carnot; mains €8-14; ⏱9.30am-3pm Mon-Fri Sep-Jun, to 6pm or later Jul & Aug;📵) This simple little *salon de thé* (tea room) serves meat-free plates, including well-garnished quiches, and makes a pleasant choice for a terrace coffee facing the church.

✖ Le Triskell   Cafe €

(📞05 53 50 15 85; 1 rue du 4 septembre; galette/menu from €8/16; ⏱noon-3pm & 7-10pm Thu-Tue) This popular little crêperie offers not just delicious savoury-filled pancakes and generously loaded salads but also fine-weather rooftop seating with views out across the river... once you've handled the spiral stairs to get up there.

🛏 Hôtel de Bouilhac   Historic Hotel €€

(📞05 53 51 21 46; www.hoteldebouilhac-montignaclascaux.fr; ave du Prof Faurel; d from €110) Once the home of Louis XV's personal doctor, this splendidly restored four-storey stone mansion has retained original details from the parquet floors to a priceless Aubusson tapestry while lavishing rooms with top-quality bedding and toiletries.

🛏 Hostellerie La Roseraie   Hotel €€

(📞05 53 50 53 92; www.laroseraie-hotel.com; 11 place d'Armes; d €90-197, tr/q from €120/176; ⏱Apr-late Oct; 🖥🌊) This mansion boasts its own gorgeous rose garden, set around a palm-fringed pool, and the terrace is a delight. Room decor veers towards a hearts-and-flowers feel.

Dordogne's Fortified Villages

36

The Dordogne spoils for choice with its hilltop history. This trip links some of the region's distinctive fortified villages and medieval castles, and takes in holy Rocamadour.

TRIP HIGHLIGHTS

125 km

Rocamadour
Follow in the footsteps of countless pilgrims at this holy town

230 km

Najac
Stand on the battlements of a storybook castle

Gourdon

Monpazier

Monflanquin
START

Figeac

Beynac & Castelnaud
The Dordogne's two classic castles face off across a dreamily photogenic stretch of riverscape

65 km

FINISH

**5 DAYS
230KM / 143 MILES**

GREAT FOR...

BEST TIME TO GO

April or October; restaurants are open, but the tourist numbers remain manageable.

ESSENTIAL PHOTO

Rocamadour at dusk seen across the valley.

BEST FOR HISTORY

The superb museum of medieval armour within the classic castle at Castelnaud.

36 Dordogne's Fortified Villages

The Dordogne Valley may be a picture of tranquillity now, but during the Hundred Years War it often marked the military frontier between antagonistic English and French forces. The area's many châteaux and fortified villages are a reminder of this war-torn past and especially distinctive features are bastides (fortified towns) whose square-grid street plans are focussed on a central market place, originally encircled by defensive walls and ramparts.

1 Monflanquin

Founded in 1256, beautifully preserved Monflanquin crowns a hilltop, its roads forming the gridlike street layout of a classic *bastide* but with an unusual slope to its market square, the **place des Arcades**. That's lined by impressive *couverts* and buildings in a picturesque mixture of architectural styles. Here you'll find a **tourist office** (www.coeurdebastides. com) that doubles as a museum about *bastides,* and four very tempt-

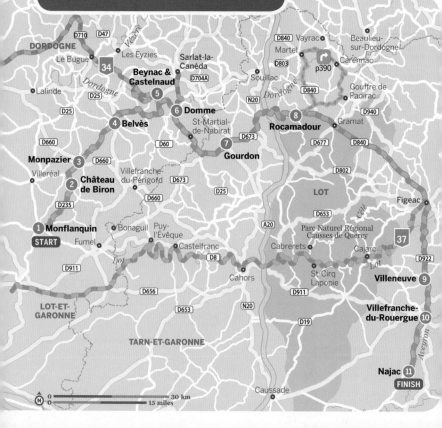

ing dining options in differing price ranges. Thursday is market day year-round plus in July and August there's a musical night market

 p391

The Drive ›› Start east along the D150 signed to Salles. After 4km turn north on the narrow D235 via Paulhiac. Much is through forest but after 11km you'll spot the impressive castle ahead across fields. Turn left at the D53 crossroads.

---

❷ Château de Biron

Looming agressively on a prominent hilltop, this much-filmed **château** (📞05 53 63 13 39; www. semitour.com; D53; adult/child €8.80/5.90; ⏰10am-12.30pm & 2-5pm or later, 10am-7.30pm Jul & Aug, closed Jan) is one of the most formidable fortresses in the region. It's a glorious mishmash of styles, having been fiddled with by eight cen-

LINK YOUR TRIP

34 Gourmet Dordogne

In Beynac you can link up with our gastronomic road trip around the Dordogne.

37 The Lot Valley

This trip meets our route along the Lot Valley at the enchanting medieval town of Figeac.

turies of successive heirs. You'll get a pretty good idea of the place from walking round the photogenic hamlet outside, but paying for an entry ticket allows you inside to see regularly changing exhibitions of contemporary art along with some grand fireplaces and a double loggia staircase supposedly modelled on one at Versailles. Ticket sales end one hour before closing.

The Drive ›› Montpazier is around 8km from Biron, head north then northeast.

---

❸ Monpazier

Monpazier is perhaps the best example of *bastide* architecture in southwest France. It's crisscrossed by arrow-straight streets, some barely a shoulder's width, and retains gateway towers from the fortifications that would once have surrounded it. The arcaded **place Centrale** is a gem with an ancient-timbered market hall in one corner complete with a trio of original grain measures.

Despite its small size, Monpazier has several restaurants, pottery workshops, a glass-blowing studio, a (not-quite mad) hatter, an unexpectedly contemporary barista coffee shop and a superb British-run microbrewery... all within a couple of minutes' walk.

 p391

The Drive ›› Take the D53 northeast from Monpazier, and follow it for 16km, much of the route through lichen-bearded woodlands.

---

❹ Belvès

Another of the Dordogne's great hilltop fortress-towns, Belvès is an atmospheric hodgepodge of medieval towerhouses and fine viewpoints with a reasonable assortment of eating and drinking options.

The beautiful oldwooden **market hall** remains almost intact, just a few 'golden' beams replacing a small area of fire damage. A neck-ring from a former pillory is still attached to one upright. Half a dozen subterranean former **cave dwellings** can be visited by arrangement with the tourist office: see www. perigordnoir-valleedor dogne.com for timings.

The Drive ›› The most direct route to Beynac (22km) is north up the D710, then along the Dordogne Valley on the D703. For confident drivers, a lovely alternative uses much smaller (indeed at times minuscule) back lanes wiggling northeast across country to the garden-set Château de Milandes (16km), a castle most famously owned by glamourous 1920s music-hall star and US civil-rights activist Josephine Baker. Further tiny lanes cross the ridge to the Château de Castelnaud (5km). Beneath Castelnaud village you can cross the river and backtrack another 5km to Beynac.

TRIP HIGHLIGHT

⑤ Beynac & Castelnaud

The **Château de Beynac**
(☏05 53 29 50 40; www.cha
teau-beynac.com; adult/child
€9.50/7; ⊙10am-7pm) is
surely the most dramatic
of all the medieval for-
tresses that guard the
Dordogne's cliff-edged
banks. Mostly built dur-
ing the 12th and 13th
centuries, it is perched
above a picture-perfect
village that featured
in the Lasse Hallström
movie *Chocolat* (2000),
starring Johnny Depp
and Juliette Binoche.
From the ramparts you
gaze upriver across one
of France's most magical
landscapes, pimpled
with several other cas-
tles. The most notable
(4.5km southwest) is the
Château de Castelnaud
(☏05 53 31 30 00; www.
castelnaud.com; Castelnaud-
la-Chapelle; adult/child
€10.90/5.50; ⊙9am-8pm Jul
& Aug, 10am-7pm Apr-Jun &
Sep, shorter hours rest of year)
hosting a particularly
impressive museum of
medieval warfare. Facing
that across the river, the
Jardins de Marqueyssac
(☏05 53 31 36 36; www.mar
queyssac.com; Vézac; adult/
child €9.90/5; ⊙9am-8pm Jul
& Aug, 10am-6pm Feb-Jun &
Sep–mid-Nov, 2-5pm mid-Nov–
Jan) are superb topiary
gardens high atop a
river-view promenade.

✕ ⏤ p391

The Drive ≫ The route from
Beynac to Domme follows the
meandering Dordogne through
its most classic castle-dotted
section and past the ultra-
photogenic village of La Roque
Gageac, pressed magically into
the cliffside by the river: a fine
place for boat rides or kayaking.
Cross the river to Cenac and
wind steeply up to Domme. In
summer you'll generally need
to park outside the walls and
walk in.

⑥ Domme

Combining pano-
ramic views across the
Dordogne Valley with
13th-century ram-
parts, original fortified
gateways and plentiful
cafes and souvenir shops,
Domme is a well-pre-
served *bastide* village
high on a prominent
outcrop. While deserv-
edly popular, the tourist
crowds can get oppres-
sive in summer.

The Drive ≫ The D46 heads
southeast through St-Martial-
de-Nabirat to Gourdon (25km).

⑦ Gourdon

Bigger, less complete,
but far less visited than
Domme, Gourdon has a
compact medieval core
that slopes up steeply
from a ring avenue of
cafes. Follow charm-
ing rue de Majou past
tall, old buildings to the
sturdy central church,
then take the stairway
up to an esplanade with
a 360-degree panorama
of vast proportions.

This was once the site
of one of the region's
great hilltop castles,
but that was completely
dismantled after 1619
as a punishment for
the lord of Gourdon's
disobedience towards
French king Louis XIII.
Nothing remains but the
viewpoint.

The Drive ≫ Pick up the
twisty D673, which crosses
underneath the A20 motorway,
winding on with fine views
across the Ouysse River and the
cliffs around Rocamadour after
30km. There are car parks at the
top and bottom of Rocamadour
and several more in L'Hospitalet,
around 1km beyond, but the
village itself is pedestrianised.

Castelnaud-la-Chapelle Château de Castelnaud

TRIP HIGHLIGHT

8 Rocamadour

Clinging precariously to a rocky cliffside, the holy town of Rocamadour looks like something out of *Lord of the Rings*. It's been an important pilgrimage destination since the Middle Ages thanks to the supposedly miraculous powers of its Vierge Noire (Black Madonna), which is now housed in the Chapelle de Notre Dame, one of several chapels that make up the town's holy hub, the **Sanctuaires** (Sanctuaries).

These are accessed up a long stairway (or lift) from the one commercial street that overflows (just as in the pilgrims' day) with souvenir shops and touristy restaurants. One of the medieval gateways is still standing at the end of this 'Grande Rue'.

Alternatively from the Sanctuaires you can climb to the clifftop via a switchback footpath/stairway following the Stations of the Cross and emerging next to Rocamadour's dinky little 14th-century **château** (€2; ⏰8am-8pm). During the Middle Ages, pilgrims would have climbed the route on their knees as a demonstration of piety. These days you can cheat by catching a funicular.

🛏 p391

The Drive » A 45km drive southeast brings you to historic Figeac, which is well worth stopping to explore, have lunch and consider an overnight stay. From there, head due south on the D822: it's an attractive 23km run once you're clear of the industrial zone on Figeac's upper southern edge.

9 Villeneuve

Worth a 10-minute stop as you whizz by, Villeneuve is an oval lozenge of historical fortified

389

DETOUR:
MARTEL & CARANNAC

Start: ⑧ **Rocamadour**

Historic **Martel**, 22km north of Rocamadour, was the ancient capital of the Vicomte de Turenne. It's locally famed for its seven (fairly modest) towers, including Tour Tournemire (once a prison) and Tour des Cordeliers (the last remnant of a 13th-century Franciscan monastery). Most memorable is the central square with its covered market hall (active Wednesday and Saturday), within a stone's throw of which are several great place to drink and eat: don't miss the wonderfully rustic farm shop-restaurant **Au Hasard Balthazar** (📞05 65 37 42 01; www. auhasardbalthazar.fr; rue Tournemire; lunch/dinner menus from €19/29.50; ⏱noon-1.30pm & 7.30-9.30pm Tue-Sat, noon-1.30pm Sun, closed Oct–mid-Apr).

From Martel, follow the D43 18km east along the Dordogne to idyllic **Carannac**, a tiny riverside village that wraps stone buildings so tightly around its former castle that the latter is virtually invisible. It contains a church with a magnificent tympanum and cloister plus a small museum section. With a minor detour you can loop back to Rocamadour (26km) via the **Gouffre de Padirac** (📞05 65 33 64 56; www.gouffre-de-padirac.com; Padirac; adult/child €15/10.50; ⏱hours vary, closed mid-Nov–Mar), a mineral-spangled cave system with an underground lake that you visit by boat.

village complete with two portcullis gates.

The Drive » Villefranche is 11km south of Villeneuve. Driving into the heart of the old centre is impractical, but several metered car parks are well placed along the diamond-shaped inner ring road (the first hour is free).

- - - - - - - - - - - - - - - - - -

⑩ Villefranche-de-Rouergue

Once you get through its sprawling outskirts, Villefranche's mostly pedestrianised centre reveals itself as a beautifully pre-

served *bastide* grid. At its centre is the **place Notre Dame**, host to one of the region's most authentic weekly markets (Thursdays). The square's wide stone arcades are broken in the northeast corner by the arch-base tower of the city's main church, the **Collégiale Notre Dame**. Inside, the wooden choir stalls are ornamented with a menagerie of comical and cheeky figures. Two blocks southwest via rue du Sergent Bories, place Grifol (place de la

Fontaine) is a sunken square centred upon an octagonal 1336 fountain that was once the city's public laundry.

The Drive » The D922 continues south towards Najac, 23km south of Villefranche.

- - - - - - - - - - - - - - - - - -

TRIP HIGHLIGHT

⑪ Najac

If you were searching for a film set for Camelot, you've found it. Najac's long, wide village square is memorable enough for its medieval cottages. But what's so special is the photo-perfect view from its western end where the cascade of descending antique buildings perfectly frames a medieval **castle** (📞05 65 29 71 65; adult/child €6/4.50; ⏱10.30am-7pm Jul-Aug, 10.30am-1pm & 3-5.30pm or later Apr-Jun, Sep & Oct) that tops the next hillock along. Straight from the pages of a fairy tale, the austere tower flutters with flags and pennants, while on either side dizzyingly steep slopes plunge into the Aveyron River far below.

The main access footpath (unsuitable for those with limited mobility) passes the Maison du Gouverneur, a powerfully built 13th-century stone mansion with exhibits about local history.

In winter, most dining options close but a cafe-bar and a *boulangerie* (bakery) open year-round.

✕ ⌂ p391

Eating & Sleeping

Montflanquin ❶

🛏 La Bastide des Oliviers   Hotel €

(📞05 33 36 40 01; www.labastidedesoliviers.fr; 1 Tour de Ville; d €70-90, q €80-100) **Far more attractive inside than you'd guess from the traditional exterior, this decently refurbished eight-bed hotel sits above a quirky, good-value cafe-restaurant, open daily.**

Monpazier ❸

✖ Bistrot 2   Bistro €€

(📞05 53 22 60 64; www.bistrot2.fr; Foirail Nord; lunch/dinner menus from €19.50/24.50; 🕐 noon-2pm & 6.30-8.15pm Sat-Thu, noon-2pm Sun, to 10pm summer, closed Jan & Feb) **Great local French food (duck, foie gras, walnut tart) is beautifully presented on sheets of slate at a lovely wisteria-covered terrace facing the town's pair of gateway towers. Excellent *cabécou* (hot goat-cheese salad).**

Beynac & Castelnaud ❺

✖ La Cantine   French €€

(📞05 53 30 34 54; www.fabricelechef.fr; Daglan; lunch/dinner menu €15/27; 🕐 noon-2pm & 7-9.30pm Wed-Mon, lunch only Oct-Mar except weekends) **This relaxed bistro-style restaurant hits the sweet spot between locally inspired quality ingredients and imaginative, full-flavoured creativity at a very fair price that warrants the drive to little Daglan village, 8km south of Castelnaud. The slow-cooked lamb shank on seasonal vegetables is a weekend favourite and the house malbec-merlot red wine is far better than most Dordogne restaurant plonk.**

🛏 La Tour de Cause   B&B €€

(📞05 53 30 30 51; https://latourdecause.com; Pont de la Cause; d €100-123; 🕐 closed Dec-Feb;

(P ❄ 🛜 🏊) **Oozing with gentrified country class, this impeccable B&B is a seductive five-room getaway around 2.5km south of Castelnaud. Hammocks are strung in the truffle oaks behind the pool, and shared social spaces including the extensive apero-garden help guests to become 'family'.**

Rocamadour ❽

🛏 Château de la Treyne   Castle €€€

(📞05 65 27 60 60; www.chateaudelatreyne. com; Lacave; r €320-1300; 🕐 Apr-early Nov; P 🛜 🏊) **As you drive across the single-lane D43 bridge between Souillac and Rocamadour you might spot a turret of this dream-hotel peeping through riverside woodland. It boasts 17 indulgent rooms, many with four-poster beds. The Michelin-starred cuisine is served in a stunning Louis XIII dining room or on a candlelit terrace teetering on the clifftop, high above the Dordogne. It's near Pinsac village.**

Najac ⓫

✖ Oustal del Barry   French €€

(📞05 65 29 74 32; www.oustaldelbarry.com; place du Faubourg; menu €30; 🕐 closed Nov-Mar; ❄ 🛜) **Part of a classic 17-room hotel (refurbished in 2020) at the top of the main square, Najac's best restaurant serves artistically refined modern cuisine created by master chef Remy Simon, based around fresh, locally sourced ingredients.**

🛏 Elelta   B&B €

(📞09 66 90 21 26; www.elelta.com; 14 place du Faubourg; d/tr from €62/77; 🛜) **In a medieval house above their delightful craft shop, jeweller Tsedey and weaver Gareth operate three great-value B&B rooms with sparkling new showers. One overlooks the main square, the others a sweep of valley. Kettles are provided and there's a shared dining-room-library to unwind in.**

The Lot Valley

Descend from magical Figeac, then follow the snaking valley of the Lot River, first hugging a cliffside, then roller-coastering between vineyards and hilltop villages.

37

TRIP HIGHLIGHTS

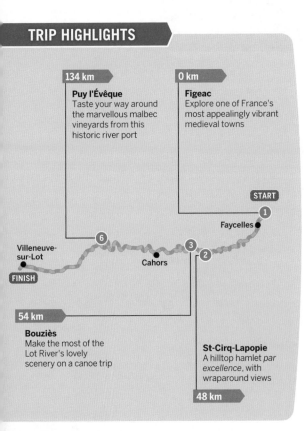

134 km

Puy l'Évêque
Taste your way around the marvellous malbec vineyards from this historic river port

0 km

Figeac
Explore one of France's most appealingly vibrant medieval towns

START

Faycelles

Villeneuve-sur-Lot

FINISH

Cahors

54 km

Bouziès
Make the most of the Lot River's lovely scenery on a canoe trip

St-Cirq-Lapopie
A hilltop hamlet *par excellence*, with wraparound views

48 km

3 DAYS
176KM / 109 MILES

GREAT FOR...

BEST TIME TO GO
March to May, when the valley's at its most tranquil.

ESSENTIAL PHOTO

Standing on top of St-Cirq-Lapopie's ruined sky-top château.

BEST FOR FAMILIES

Paddling down the Lot River in a canoe from Bouziès.

37 | The Lot Valley

For river scenery, the Lot is right up there alongside the Loire and the Seine. Over countless millennia, it's carved its way through the area's soft lemon-yellow limestone, creating a landscape of canyons, ravines and cliffs, best seen on the zigzagging 80km-odd section between Faycelles and Cahors. It's a journey to savour: take your time, pack a picnic and soak up the vistas.

TRIP HIGHLIGHT

❶ Figeac

Riverside Figeac is packed with gems of medieval and Renaissance architecture, yet has a lived-in authenticity trumping that of many more tourist-centric places. Founded by Benedictine monks, the town was later an important medieval trading post, a leather-making centre and a pilgrim stopover.

Figeac is also famous as the birthplace of François Champollion

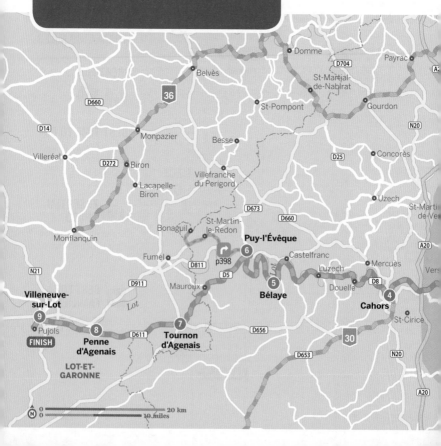

(1790–1832), the Egyptologist and linguist whose efforts in deciphering the Rosetta Stone provided the key for cracking hieroglyphics. Explore his story at the engrossing **Musée Champollion** (☎05 65 50 31 08; www.musee-champollion.fr; place Champollion; adult/child €5/free; ⏰10.30am-6.30pm daily Jul & Aug, shorter hours rest of year) in the heart of the old town.

🛏 p399

**The Drive ›› ** The corkscrew drive west of Figeac along the D662 is a classic, descending steeply from the pretty hamlet of Faycelles then tracking the course of the Lot River all the way to Cahors. The 48km stretch of road to St-Cirq-Lapopie is particularly scenic, at some points cut directly into the cliffside, at others snaking along the peaceful riverbanks. Take it slowly and enjoy the drive, making regular stops at a whole series of delightful villages en route. Don't miss a brief glimpse of the cliffside castle in Larroque-Toriac, consider a meal stop in Cajarc and admire the serrated village silhouette of Calvignac topping a ridge across the river – especially dramatic at sunset. At Tour de Faure cross the bridge and climb 3km west to St-Cirq.

TRIP HIGHLIGHT

2 St-Cirq-Lapopie

This famously photogenic hilltop village teeters at the crest of a sheer cliff, high above the Lot. It's a delightful tangle of red-roofed houses, cobbled streets and medieval buildings, many of which now house potters' and artists' studios. The village is essentially one long, steep main street; at the top is the ruined **château**, which has a magnificent viewing terrace that overlooks the whole Lot Valley. It's a magical setting, but be warned: if it's peace and tranquillity you're looking for, you won't find it in high summer when the access lanes can get jammed with visitors. Car parks ring

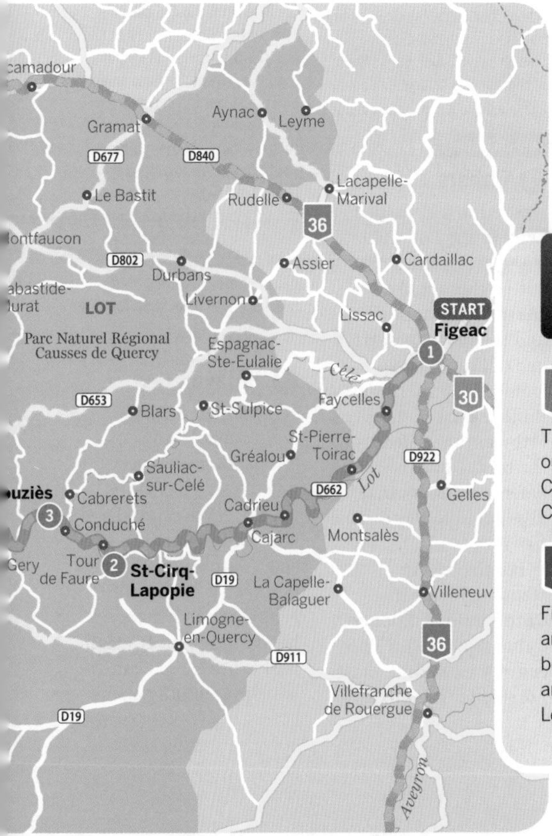

LINK YOUR TRIP

30 Cheat's Compostela

This route intersects with our road-trip version of the Chemin de St-Jacques at Cahors and Figeac.

36 Dordogne's Fortified Villages

Figeac is also on our *bastide* and fortress tour, which begins at Monflanquin around 20km north of the Lot Valley.

the village at a discreet distance (per day €4, free after 7pm).

📖 p399

The Drive >> Leave St-Cirq heading east, being careful not to miss a poorly signed right-hand turn after 1.1km. Descend steeply for 5km and you'll reach the river at Bouziès.

- - - - - - - - - - - - - - - -

TRIP HIGHLIGHT

❸ Bouziès

In front of Bouziès' very functional Hotel Les Fallaises, **Les Croisères de St-Cirq-Lapopie** (🎵05 65 31 72 25; www.croisieres-saint-cirq-lapopie.com; 1hr tour adult/child €12.50/8.50; ⊙Apr-Oct) runs regular river cruises on its small fleet of boats, including aboard an open-topped *gabarre*, a traditional flat-bottomed barge. A narrow suspension bridge crosses the Lot from Bouziès village, joining the main D662 beneath a curious cliff-side. Closer inspection shows that that is riddled with little caves which had once been fortified into ancient little retreat-shelters. Around 1km east, **Kalapca** (🎵05 65 24 21 01; www.kalapca.com; D41, Conduché; canoe rental half/full day €20/24; ⊙Apr-Sep) hires out kayaks and canoes, perfect for experiencing the gorgeous river scenery at your own pace. It also has a zip-line right across the valley to experience the

scene from the air. Some 6.5km north of here via Cabarets is the entrance to the 1200m-long **Grotte du Pech Merle** (🎵05 65 31 27 05; www.pechmerle. com; adult/child €14/8.50; ⊙9.30am-5pm Apr-Oct) with prehistoric art from painted mammoths to hand tracings. Booking ahead online is recommended year-round and essential on summer weekends.

The Drive >> The twisty 28km riverside route to Cahors is a gently appealing drive. En route, tiny Laroque-des-Arcs is worth a brief stop to photograph its small chapel on a rock pillar. In Cahors there is free parking on place Charles de Gaulle, or a free half-hour by meter close to Pont Valentré if you just want snaps of the famous bridge.

- - - - - - - - - - - - - - - -

TRIP HIGHLIGHT

❹ Cahors

Nestled in a U-shaped bend in the Lot, Cahors is the area's main city with a thoroughly charming historic core and the **Pont Valentré**, one of France's most iconic medieval bridges. Built as part of the city's 14th-century defences, the bridge has three tall defensive towers that give it a uniquely distinctive form.

It's also worth stepping inside the **Cathédrale St-Étienne**, Cahors's beautiful 12th-century cathedral, most notable for the mixture

of swooning saints and barbaric stabbings on its sculpted north portal.

Cahors brands itself the Capital of Malbec: don't miss sampling a selection of the region's splendidly rich reds at the **Malbec Lounge** attached to the city centre tourist office. If these appeal, there are plenty of wineries to visit, especially once you reach Puy l'Évêque.

📖 p399

The Drive >> Head west of town via the D8, following signs to Luzech. A short detour into Parnac, on a peninsula of the Lot, reveals a dazzling wealth of vines from the Cahors AOC. The route crosses a neck of the Lot at Luzech, with its single medieval street, fortress tower and riverfront tea shop-lunch stop, Quai No5. The road roughly parallels the river's south bank passing close to Castelfranc where, just across the suspension bridge, there's a delightfully 'real' cafe-bar. As the road swings south again, a 2km hairpin detour zigzags up to Bélaye, 35km total from Cahors.

- - - - - - - - - - - - - - - -

❺ Bélaye

The hamlet of Bélaye is tiny and its ancient fortifications are very much a series of ruins, partly recycled into local houses. It's worth the short detour for the viewpoint with its magnificent panorama across a bend in the Lot. It's right beside a seasonal cafe, which essentially opens

Cahors Pont Valentré

on holidays and whenever the sun shines.

The Drive » The drive to Puy l'Évêque via Grézels is just 10km, but wine buffs might consider adding an extra 13km loop via Floressas to take in two very different malbec wine-tasting experiences. In a lovely hilltop setting 1km east of the village, Château Chambert (www.chateaudechambert.com) is easy as a drop-in site with a impressive welcome room that becomes a bistro in summer. Right in Floressas, Château Laur (https://vignobles-laur.fr/en/) is a smaller outfit that's unique in using its deeply coloured malbec grapes not just for full-bodied reds but also to make sparkling and dry white wines. Floresss to Puy l'Évêque is 9km.

TRIP HIGHLIGHT

6 Puy l'Évêque

On a rocky hillside above the northern bank of the Lot, Puy l'Évêque was once one of the most important medieval ports in the Lot Valley. The former quays are lined with once-grand merchants' houses and the old town climbs a steep, deep-cleft valley topped with a fortress tower (now the town hall) and many medieval stone mansions, mostly tumbledown and decaying. The scene is best appreciated from the main road bridge that spans the Lot. For touring the Cahors wineries, Puy l'Évêque is an ideal base. Around 4km southwest at Bru near Vire-sur-Lot, try comparing the malbecs at suave **Clos Triguedina** (☎05 65 21 30 81; www.jlbaldes.com; Bru; 30min tour & tasting €5; ◷9am-noon & 2-6pm Mon-Sat), where there's a museum and guided-tour option with those at next-door **Château Nozières** (☎05 65 36 52 73; www.chateaunozieres.com; Bru; ◷9am-noon & 2-7pm Mon-Sat), a merrily unpretentious family place

DETOUR:
BONAGUIL

Start: **6** Puy l'Évêque

If you have some extra time, or don't fancy touring the wineries, an easy detour from Puy l'Évêque takes you on narrow back lanes to the tiny hamlet of **St-Martin-Le-Redon** with its impressive midsized Romanesque church. Continuing northwest, the road reveals the first breathtaking view of the **Château de Bonaguil** between trees. It's a fine example of late-15th-century military architecture, incorporating towers, bastions, loopholes, machicolations and crenellations. Although ruined, the powerful walls that remain are extremely impressive. There's a couple of places to eat at the base of the castle and just down the lane is a historic *lavoir* (village washing point).

offering free tasters, some dispensed directly from the inox tanks to your glass via petrol-style pumps.

 p399

The Drive >> Head southwest through classic river-valley wine country then climb into the hills on the D5 via Mauroux to Tournon (18km).

---

7 Tournon d'Agenais

The region is pimpled with impressive hilltop *bastides* (fortified towns), but unlike many, Tournon is a little off the tourist trail so you're likely to get the sweeping rampart views pretty much to yourself. The cosy central square has a hotel, a small restaurant and a *brocante*-cafe but facilities are otherwise limited.

The Drive >> Driving west to Penne d'Agenais (16km) you're fired down a series of long straight roads through undulating fields and classic French countryside.

---

8 Penne d'Agenais

The old core of Penne crowns a high, steep ridge looking down on the Lot. The town's most visible landmark is the silvered dome of a 19th-century neo-Byzantine

pilgrims' church, and there's plenty of charm in the climb that takes you there from the main square up a doglegged lane past several older buildings.

 p399

The Drive >> Villeneuve is a straight run 11km west on the D661.

---

9 Villeneuve-sur-Lot

Villeneuve should be a great discovery – a 1253 *bastide* retaining two prominent gatehouse towers and a gridlike city plan curiously cut in half by the river. There's a 13th-century bridge, a market square and a soaring brick church (1930s), but sadly the overall feel is slightly downtrodden and you'd do best to hurry 3km south through the sprawling suburbs to contrastingly charming **Pujols**. In a cute medieval hamlet on a ridgetop with extensive views, here you'll find a free museum-shop of handmade wooden toys, a bell tower/gateway, several arts studios and a couple of restaurants.

 p399

Eating & Sleeping

Figeac ❶

🛏 Château de Viguier du Roi　　Hotel €€

(Mercure Figeac; ☎05 65 50 05 05; www.
mercure.com; 52 rue Émile Zola; summer/
winter r from €169/99; ❇🛜💺) Bringing
a stylishly inventive mixture of modern and
period design to one of Figeac's most beautiful
historic palaces, this stunning city-centre
hotel is like a museum, complete with picture-
perfect courtyard garden, library and four
sitting-room salons. Rooms range from big
(33 sq metres) to vast (101 sq metres). Chef
Anthony Carballo brings a gastronomic twist
to Quercy-style cuisine in the hotel's revered
in-house restaurant, **La Dinée du Viguier**
(www.ladineeduviguier.fr; 4 rue Boutaric; mains
€23-36, 3/5-course menu €37/57; ☉noon-2pm
Sun-Fri & 7-9pm daily).

St-Cirq-Lapopie ❷

🛏 Hôtel Le Saint Cirq　　Hotel €€

(☎05 65 30 30 30; www.hotel-lesaintcirq.com;
Tour-de-Faure; r €90-198; 🛜💺) In a vineyard
facing St-Cirq across the river valley, this
stylishly luxurious hotel is designed like a series
of farmhouses, with terracotta-tiled floors and
French windows, many with fine views. Use of
the indoor pool and spa costs an extra €18 per
person. Staff can be brusque.

Cahors ❹

🛏 Hôtel Divona　　Hotel €€

(☎05 65 21 18 39; www.hoteldivona.fr; 113 av
André Breton; d €109-222; 🅿❇🛜💺) Built in
2016 with a classy yet pared-back vibe and hints
of 1970s retro styling, this highly comfortable
hotel's biggest appeal lies in the river-facing
balconies. Each room has one, along with a
coffee maker, a kettle, and use of the sauna
and indoor pool. However, it's worth upgrading
to much bigger 'superior' or 'privilege' rooms,
notably 207, which surveys Pont Valentré.

Puy-l'Évêque ❻

🍴 Le Dodus en Ville　　French €

(☎05 65 22 91 82; http://auxdodus.free.fr; rue
Ernest-Marcouly; 2-/3-course menus €12.50/15;
☉noon-2.30pm & 7-9pm Tue-Fri, 7-9pm Sat) For
older travellers, this superb-value one-woman
restaurant might be the kind of place that brings
back memories of the France of your childhood:
tasteful simplicity, great food and remarkably
drinkable *pichets* (jugs) of rosé for a song. What's
decidedly more modern: you'll be offered at least
one vegetarian option daily.

🛏 Le Presbytère　　B&B €

(☎06 45 45 97 41; www.lepresbyterefr.com;
5 place du Rampeau; d incl breakfast €62-72)
This hard-to-leave British-run B&B goes the
extra mile with a welcome drink, an excellent
breakfast, body-pampering memory-foam
mattresses and a well-judged mix of antique
furniture and quality modern fittings. All three
rooms have wonderful views, as do the lounge
and terrace.

Penne d'Agenais ❽

🍴 Le Peyragude　　French €

(☎05 53 41 22 17; 7 place Gambetta; menus from
€9.50) Le Peyragude is an archetype of a local
bar-restaurant serving great southwestern-
French food in unfussy surroundings to a
constant flow of hungry locals. The quality is
vastly better than you'd expect for a €9.50
lunchtime *plat du jour* (dish of the day).

Villeneuve-sur-Lot ❾

🍴 Les Allées Gourmandes　　Brasserie €

(☎05 53 36 21 79; www.lesalleesgourmandes.
fr; rue Lakanal; dishes/menu from €3.50/12.50;
☉9am-1pm & 4-7pm Tue-Fri, 8am-1.30pm &
2.30-7pm Sat, 9am-2pm Sun, bar from 7am)
Villeneuve's large, historic wrought-iron *halles*
were upgraded and relaunched in 2019 as a
stylish indoor market with a hipster-worthy yet
inexpensive brasserie.

Classic Trip

Atlantic to Med

38

Atlantic ports, pristine mountain vistas, the bouquet of fine wine, reminders of Rome and Hollywood glam: this sea-to-sea trip takes you through the best of southern France.

TRIP HIGHLIGHTS

0 km

La Rochelle
Made for waterfront mooching, lunching and sunset drinks

175 km

St-Émilion
Wine tasting and shopping for some of the world's finest drops

1 START

2 St-Émilion

FINISH
Nice

Montpellier

Bayonne

6

8

Narbonne

Carcassonne
Walk the ramparts of France's most magnificent fortress city

863 km

Marseille
Visit MuCEM, icon of modern Marseille, with stunning views to boot

1158 km

**10 DAYS
1498KM / 931
MILES**

GREAT FOR...

BEST TIME TO GO

Spring or autumn, for warm weather sans the crowds.

 ESSENTIAL PHOTO

Pose like a film star on the steps of Cannes's Palais des Festivals et des Congrès.

 BEST FOR FAMILIES

La Rochelle, with child-friendly attractions and boats.

Classic Trip

38 Atlantic to Med

In May the film starlets of the world pour into Cannes to celebrate a year of movie-making. Let them have their moment of glam — by the time you've finished scaling Pyrenean highs, chewing Basque tapas, acting like a medieval knight in a turreted castle and riding to the moon in a spaceship, you too will have the makings of a prize-winning film.

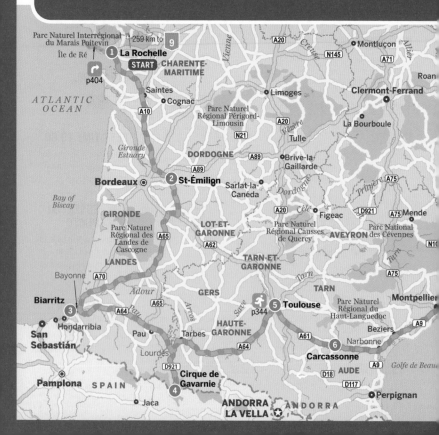

TRIP HIGHLIGHT

❶ La Rochelle

Known as La Ville Blanche (the White City), La Rochelle is home to luminous limestone façades, arcaded walkways, half-timbered houses and gargoyles glowing in the coastal sunlight. A prominent French seaport from the 14th to the 17th centuries, it remains one of France's most attractive seafaring cities.

There are several defensive towers around the **Vieux Port** (Old Port), including the lacy **Tour de la Lanterne** (www.tours-la-rochelle.fr; rue sur les Murs; 3 towers adult/child €9.50/free; ⏱10am-6.30pm Jul & Aug, 10am-1pm & 2.15-6.30pm Apr, Jun & Sep, 10am-1pm & 2.15-5.30pm Oct-Mar), that once served to protect the town at night in times of war. Scale their sturdy stone heights for fabulous city and coastal views.

La Rochelle's number-one tourist attraction is its state-of-the-art **aquarium** (☎05 46 34 00 00; www.aquarium-larochelle.com; quai Louis Prunier; adult/child €16.50/12, online €14.50/10; ⏱9am-11pm Jul & Aug, to 8pm Apr-Jun & Sep, 10am-8pm Oct-Mar). Equally fun for families is the **Musée Maritime** (Maritime Museum; ☎05 46 28 03 00; www.museemaritimelarochelle.fr; place Bernard Moitessier; adult/child €9/6.50; ⏱10am-6.30pm Apr-Oct, 2-5.30pm Mon-Fri, 10am-5.30pm Sat & Sun Nov-Mar), with its fleet of boats to explore; and a trip out to sea with **Croisières Inter-Îles** (☎08 25 13 55 00; www.inter-iles.com; cours des Dames) to admire the unusual iceberg of an island fortress, Fort Boyard.

🛏 p409

The Drive » Using the main A10 toll road it's 187km (about 2½ hours) to St-Émilion. Turn off the A10 at exit 39a, signed for Libourne. Skirt this industrial town and follow the D243 into St-Émilion.

LINK YOUR TRIP

9 **Breton Coast**
The wind-swept coast of Brittany is a wild tonic to the south's refined atmosphere. Drive three hours north of La Rochelle to start the trip in Vannes.

23 **Riviera Crossing**
Starting in Nice, this drive takes you through the glitzy, glam French Riviera.

TRIP HIGHLIGHT

❷ St-Émilion

Built of soft honey-coloured rock, medieval St-Émilion produces some of the world's finest red wines. Visiting this pretty town, and partaking in some of the tours and activities on offer, is the easiest way to get under the (grape) skin of Bordeaux wine production. The **Maison du Vin de St-Émilion** (📞05 57 55 50 55; www.maisonduvinsaintemilion.com; place Pierre Meyrat; ⏰9.30am-6.30pm May-Oct, 9.30am-12.30pm & 2-6pm Nov-Apr) runs wine-tasting classes and has a superb exhibition covering wine essentials.

Guided tours of the town (adult/child from €9/free) and surrounding châteaux are run by the **tourist office** (📞05 57 55 28 28; www.saint-emilion-tourisme.com; place des Créneaux; ⏰9.30am-7.30pm Jul & Aug, shorter hours rest of year); reserve ahead in season. Several tours include tastings and vineyard visits.

✗ p409

The Drive » Leave St-Émilion on the D243 to Libourne, cross the town, then pick up the D1089 signposted 'Agen, Bergerac, Bordeaux'. Continue on the N89 towards Bordeaux until you see signs for the A630 toll road – at which point sit back and hit cruise control for the remaining 226km to Biarritz. Count 240km and about 2½ hours in all.

❸ Biarritz

This coastal town is as ritzy as its name makes out. Biarritz boomed as a resort in the mid-19th century due to the regular visits by Napoléon III and his Spanish-born wife, Eugénie. Along its rocky coastline are architectural hallmarks of this golden age, and the Belle-Époque and art-deco eras that followed.

DETOUR:
ILE DE RE

Start: ❶ La Rochelle

Bathed in the southern sun, drenched in a languid atmosphere and scattered with villages of green-shuttered, whitewashed buildings with red Spanish-tile roofs, Île de Ré is one of the most delightful places on the west coast of France. The island spans just 30km from its most easterly and westerly points, and just 5km at its widest section. But take note: the secret's out and in high season it can be almost impossible to move around and even harder to find a place to stay.

On the northern coast, about 12km from the toll bridge that links the island to La Rochelle, is the quaint fishing port of **St-Martin-de-Ré**, the island's main town. Surrounded by 17th-century fortifications (you can stroll along most of the ramparts) constructed by Vauban, the port town is a mesh of streets filled with craft shops, art galleries and sea-spray ocean views.

The island's best beaches are along the southern edge – including unofficial naturist beaches at **Rivedoux Plage** and **La Couarde-sur-Mer** – and around the western tip (northeast and southeast of Phare-des-Baleines). Many beaches are bordered by dunes that have been fenced off to protect the vegetation.

From La Rochelle it's 24km and a half-hour drive to St-Martin-de-Ré via the toll bridge **Pont de l'Île de Ré** (www.pont-ile-de-re.com; return ticket €16 mid-June to mid-September, €8 rest of the year).

Biarritz is all about its fashionable beaches, especially the central **Grande Plage** and **Plage Miramar**. In the heat of summer you'll find them packed end to end with sun-loving bathers.

The Drive » It's 208km (2¾ hours) to the village of Gavarnie. Take the A63 and A64 toll roads to exit 11, then the D940 to Lourdes (worth a look for its religious Disneyland feel). Continue south along the D913 and D921.

❹ Cirque de Gavarnie

The Pyrenees doesn't lack impressive scenery, but your first sight of the Cirque de Gavarnie is guaranteed to raise a gasp. This breathtaking mountain amphitheatre is one of the region's most famous sights, sliced by thunderous waterfalls and ringed by sawtooth peaks, many of which top out at over 3000m.

There are a couple of large car parks in the village of Gavarnie, from where it's about a two-hour walk to the amphitheatre. Wear proper shoes, as snow lingers along the trail into early summer.

The Drive » Retrace your steps to Lourdes, then take the N21 towards Tarbes and veer onto the A64 to reach Toulouse. It takes nearly three hours to cover the 228km.

❺ Toulouse

The vibrant southern city of Toulouse is dubbed 'La Ville Rose', a reference to the distinctive blushing-pink brickwork of its classic architecture. Its city centre is tough to navigate by car, but there's a paying car park right beneath Toulouse's magnificent central square, **place du Capitole**, the city's literal and metaphorical heart. South of the square, walk the tangle of lanes in the historic **Vieux Quartier** (Old Town). Then, of course, there are the soothing twists and turns of the nearby Garonne River and mighty Canal du Midi – laced with footpaths to stretch your legs.

Having a car is handy for visiting two out-of-town sights celebrating modern Toulouse's role as an aerospace hub: the gigantic museum of Airbus, **Aeroscopia** (☎05 34 39 42 00; www.musee -aeroscopia.fr; allée André Turcat; adult/child €14/11; ☻9.30am-6pm, closed early Jan; P; 🚌T1 to Beauzelle), just north of the airport; and, across town, **Cite de l'Espace** (☎05 67 22 23 24; www.cite-espace.com; av Jean Gonord; adult €21-26, child €16-19.50; ☻10am-7pm daily Jul & Aug, to 5pm or 6pm rest of year, closed Mon in Feb, Mar & Sep-Dec, closed Jan; P 🚼), which brings this interstellar industry vividly

to life through a shuttle simulator, a planetarium, a 3D cinema, a simulated observatory and so on. Both have free parking.

🍴 🛏 p409

The Drive » It's an easy 95km (one hour) down the fast A61 to Carcassonne. Notice how the vegetation becomes suddenly much more Mediterranean about 15 minutes out of Toulouse.

TRIP HIGHLIGHT

❻ Carcassonne

Perched on a rocky hilltop and bristling with zigzagging battlements, stout walls and spiky turrets, from afar the fortified city of Carcassonne is most people's perfect idea of a medieval castle. Four million tourists a year stream through its city gates to explore La Cité, visit its **keep** (www.remparts-carcas sonne.fr; 1 rue Viollet le Duc, Cité Médiévale; adult/child €9.50/ free; ☻10am-6.30pm Apr-Sep, 9.30am-5pm Oct-Mar) and ogle at stunning views along the city's ancient ramparts.

The Drive » Continue down the A61 to the Catalan-flavoured town of Narbonne, where you join the A9 (very busy in summer) and head east to Nîmes. From there the A54 will take you into Arles. Allow just over two hours to cover the 223km and expect lots of toll booths.

❼ Arles

Arles' poster boy is the celebrated impressionist painter Vincent van

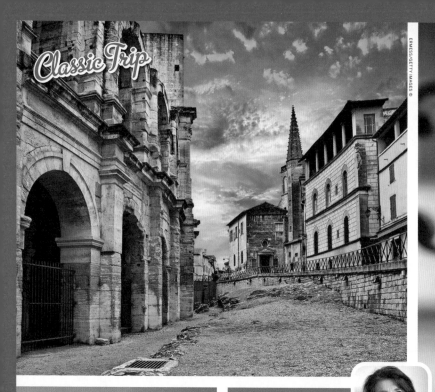

WHY THIS IS A CLASSIC TRIP
NICOLA WILLIAMS, WRITER

I simply cannot resist the big blue or fine wine, so this tasty seafaring trip is right up my alley. Feasting on fresh oysters on the seashore aside, I strongly advise a long lazy lunch at La Terrasse Rouge (p409) near St-Émilion. This spectacular vineyard restaurant was borne out of Jean Nouvel's designer revamp of Château La Dominique's wine cellars: dining on its uber-chic terrace overlooking a field of dark-red glass pebbles is the ultimate French road-trip reward.

Above: Les Arènes, Arles
Left: Cirque de Gavarnie
Right: Wine, St-Émilion

Gogh. If you're familiar with his work, you'll be familiar with Arles: the light, the colours, the landmarks and the atmosphere, all faithfully captured. But long before Van Gogh rendered this grand Rhône River locale on canvas, the Romans valued its worth. Today it's the reminders of Rome that are probably the town's most memorable attractions. At **Les Arènes** (Amphithéâtre; ☎08 91 70 03 70; www.arenes-arles. com; Rond-Point des Arènes; adult/child incl Théâtre Antique €9/free; ⏰9am-8pm Jul & Aug, to 7pm May, Jun & Sep, shorter hours Oct-Apr) slaves, criminals and wild animals (including giraffes) met their dramatic demise before a jubilant 20,000-strong crowd during Roman gladiatorial displays.

📖 p244, p303, p409

The Drive » From Arles take the scenic N568 and A55 route into Marseille. It's 88km (an hour's drive) away.

TRIP HIGHLIGHT

❽ Marseille

With its history, fusion of cultures, *souq*-like markets, millennia-old port and *corniches* (coastal roads) along rocky inlets and sun-baked beaches, Marseille is a captivating and exotic city. Ships have docked for more than 26 centuries at the colourful **Vieux Port** (Old Port) and it remains a

DETOUR:
AIX-EN-PROVENCE

Start: **7** Arles

Aix-en-Provence is to Provence what the Left Bank is to Paris: an enclave of bourgeois-bohemian chic. Art, culture and architecture abound here. A stroller's paradise, the highlight is the mostly pedestrian old city, **Vieil Aix**. South of cours Mirabeau, **Quartier Mazarin** was laid out in the 17th century, and is home to some of Aix's finest buildings. Central Place des Quatre Dauphins, with its fish-spouting fountain (1667), is particularly enchanting. Further south locals play *pétanque* beneath plane trees in peaceful **Parc Jourdan** (av Anatole France; ⏱9am-sunset). From Arles it's a 77km (one-hour) drive down the A54 toll road to Aix-en-Provence. To rejoin the main route take the A51 and A7 for 32km (30 minutes) to Marseille.

thriving harbour. Guarding the harbour are **Bas Fort St-Nicolas** and **Fort St-Jean**, founded in the 13th century by the Knights Hospitaller of St John of Jerusalem. A vertigo-inducing footbridge links the latter with the stunning **Musée des Civilisations de l'Europe et de la Méditerranée** (MuCEM, Museum of European & Mediterranean Civilisations; ☎04 84 35 13 13; www.mucem.org; 7 promenade Robert Laffont; adult/child incl exhibitions €11/free; ⏱11am-6pm Nov-Apr, to 7pm May, Jun & Oct, 10am-8pm Jul-Sep, closed Tue year-round; 🚻; Ⓜ Vieux Port, Joliette), the icon of modern Marseille.

From the Vieux Port, hike up to the fantastic history-woven quarter of **Le Panier**, a mishmash of steep lanes hiding *ateliers* (workshops) and terraced houses strung with drying washing.

The Drive » To get from Marseille to Cannes, take the northbound A52 and join the A8 toll road just east of Aix-en-Provence. It's 181km and takes just under two hours.

- - - - - - - - - - - - - - -

9 Cannes

The eponymous film festival only lasts for two weeks in May, but thanks to regular visits from celebrities the buzz and glitz are in Cannes year-round. The imposing

Palais des Festivals (Festival & Congress Palace; www.palaisdesfestivals.com; 1 bd de la Croisette; guided tour adult/child €6/free) is the centre of the glamour. Climb the red carpet, walk down the auditorium, tread the stage and learn about cinema's most prestigious event on a 1½-hour guided tour run by the **tourist office** (☎info 08 26 50 05 00, tour booking 04 91 13 89 16; www.marseille-tourisme.com; 11 La Canebière; ⏱10am-5pm; Ⓜ Vieux Port).

The Drive » Leave the motorways behind and weave along the D6007 to Nice, taking in cliffs framing turquoise Mediterranean waters and the yachties' town of Antibes. It's 31km and, on a good day, takes 45 minutes.

- - - - - - - - - - - - - - -

10 Nice

You don't need to be a painter or an artist to appreciate the extraordinary light in Nice. Matisse, Chagall et al spent years lapping up the city's startling luminosity, and for most visitors to Nice, it is this magical light that seduces. The city has several world-class sights, but the star attraction is the seafront **Promenade des Anglais**. Stroll and watch the world go by.

🍴 🛏 p264, p409

Eating & Sleeping

La Rochelle ❶

🛏 La Fabrique   Design Hotel €€

(📞05 46 41 45 00; www.hotellafabrique.com;
7-11 rue de la Fabrique; d €58-160; ❄ @ 🛜) At
home in a former rope factory, design-driven La
Fabrique sports 58 rooms arranged in a quad,
above a vast open-plan lounge with Chesterfield
sofas and an aerial art installation. Serene,
almost-all-white rooms enjoy walk-in Italian
showers, and summertime breakfasts (€12) are
served on a peaceful patio.

St-Émilion ❷

🍴 La Terrasse Rouge   French €€

(📞05 57 24 47 05; www.laterrasserouge.com;
1 Château La Dominique; 3-course menu €39,
mains €21-32; 🕐 noon-2.30pm Sun & Mon,
noon-2.30pm & 7.30-9.30pm Thu-Sat; P 🛜 🚻)
Foodies in the know adore this spectacular
vineyard restaurant, born out of Jean Nouvel's
designer revamp of Château La Dominique's
wine cellars, 5km north of St-Émilion. Chefs
work with small local producers to source the
seasonal produce used in their creative cuisine.
Oysters are fresh from Cap Ferret, caviar comes
from Neuvic in the Dordogne, and the wine list is
naturally extraordinary.

Toulouse ❺

🍴 Une Table à Deux   French €€

(📞06 50 06 00 34; www.unetableadeux.fr; 10
rue de la Pléau; lunch/dinner menus from €17/35;
🕐 noon-1.30pm & 7.30-9.30pm Mon-Fri, closed
lunch Wed) It takes some searching to find
this exciting little gem, whose talented, well-
travelled chefs turn super-fresh locally sourced
produce into short but wonderfully inspired,
regularly changing menus. Veggie option
usually available.

🛏 Villa du Taur   Boutique Hotel €€

(📞05 34 25 28 82; www.villadutaur.com; 62 rue
du Taur; d €89-159; P ❄ 🛜) This hip yet super-
friendly hotel has stylishly comfortable guest

rooms that double as mini galleries, with the
artworks available for sale – even the Banksy
vinyls. Showers are fashioned like luxury cages
and you get an in-room Illy coffee maker.

Arles ❼

🛏 Le Cloître   Design Hotel €€

(📞04 88 09 10 00; www.hotelducloitre.com; 18
rue du Cloître; r €185; ❄ @ 🛜) The traditional
Mediterranean courtyard that greets you on
arrival at 'The Cloister' is charming enough, but
doesn't betray the inventiveness of the warm,
colourful design within. Le Cloître's 19 rooms
are all distinct, with Italian showers and unusual
furniture that sacrifices no comfort. There's a
panoramic rooftop terrace and excellent meals
are available from the neighbouring Épicerie
du Cloître.

Nice ❿

🍴 Bar des Oiseaux   French €€

(📞04 93 80 27 33; 5 rue St-Vincent; 3-course
lunch menu €20, dinner menus from €30;
🕐10am-10pm Tue-Sat) Hidden down a narrow
backstreet, this old-town classic has been
in business since 1961, serving as a popular
nightclub before reincarnating itself as a
restaurant (some of its original saucy murals
have survived the transition). Nowadays it's a
lively bistro serving superb traditional French
cuisine spiced up with modern twists. The
weekday lunch special offers phenomenal value.
Book ahead.

🛏 Hôtel Villa Rivoli   Boutique Hotel €€

(📞04 93 88 80 25; www.villa-rivoli.com; 10
rue de Rivoli; d €89-215; ❄ 🛜; 🚌7, 9, 22, 27,
59, 70 to Rivoli) This charming but strangely
shaped villa dates back to 1890, and it's packed
with period detail – gilded mirrors, fireplaces,
cast-iron balconies and old-world wallpapers,
as well as little conifer trees on the balconies
and a sweeping marble staircase. Rooms are on
the small side, with the least expensive on the
ground floor, and service is excellent. There's a
small garden and a car park beside the hotel.

STRETCH
YOUR LEGS
BORDEAUX

Start/Finish Cathédrale St-André

Distance 5km

Duration 1½ hours

An intoxicating cocktail of 18th-century savoir faire, millennial hi-tech and urban street life, France's sixth-largest city is a Unesco World Heritage Site and one of the country's most exciting urban destinations to explore. The pedestrian-friendly streets, stately architecture and silky-smooth riverside promenades in downtown Bordeaux are made for walking.

Take this walk on Trip

Cathédrale St-André

Lording over the city, the **cathedral** (☏05 56 44 67 29; www.cathedrale-bordeaux.fr; place Pey Berland; treasury adult/child €2/free; ☺2-7pm Mon, 10am-noon & 2-6pm Tue-Sat, 9.30am-noon & 2-6pm Sun, treasury 2.30-5.30pm Wed, Sat & Sun) dates from 1096, but most of what you see today was built in the 13th and 14th centuries. Next door is the gargoyled, 50m-high Gothic belfry, **Tour Pey Berland** (☏05 56 81 26 25; www.pey-berland.fr; place Pey Berland; adult/child €6/free; ☺10am-6pm Jun-Sep, 10am-12.30pm & 2-5.30pm Oct-May), erected between 1440 and 1466.

The Walk » Head up rue Elisée Reclus and turn right to find the small but elegant Jardin de la Mairie and Musée des Beaux-Arts.

Musée des Beaux-Arts

The evolution of occidental art from the Renaissance to the mid-20th century is on view at this fine arts **museum** (☏05 56 10 20 56; www.musba-bordeaux.fr; 20 cours d'Albret; adult/child €5/free; ☺11am-6pm Wed-Mon), occupying two wings of the 1770s-built Hôtel de Ville.

The Walk » Continue down cours d'Albret, across place Gambetta and onto cours Georges Clemenceau. At place Tourny turn left onto rue Fondaudège, then take the second right.

Jardin Public

Stroll through landscaped **gardens** (cours de Verdun; ☺7am-8pm Jul & Aug, shorter hours rest year) where Bordelais feed ducks on sunny days.

The Walk » Exit the park via cours de Verdun, then head down cours du Maréchal Foch, turn left onto rue Ferrére and continue to CAPC.

Musée d'Art Contemporain (CAPC)

Built in 1824 as a warehouse for French colonial produce such as coffee, cocoa, peanuts and vanilla, this cavernous building creates a dramatic backdrop for contemporary art at the **CAPC** (CAPC; ☏05 56 00 81 50; www.capc-bordeaux.fr; 7 rue Ferrère; adult/child €5/free, free 1st Sun

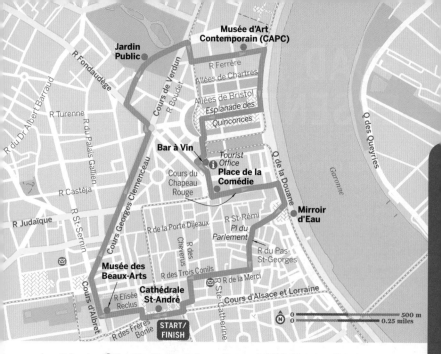

The Walk » Follow the river along quai des Chartrons to esplanade des Quinconces. Cross the square, past the Girondins monument, and continue down cours du 30 Juillet.

Bar à Vin

Time for a drink? The holy of holies **Bar à Vin** (📞05 56 00 43 47; http://baravin. bordeaux.com; 3 cours du 30 Juillet; ⏱11am–10pm Mon–Sat), inside the hallowed **Maison du Vin de Bordeaux**, is the hot spot for a tipple with people who know their wine.

The Walk » Continue 150m down Bordeaux's swankiest street to people-watching place de la Comédie.

Place de la Comédie

The city's grandest square is dominated by Bordeaux's 18th-century opera house, the **Grand Théâtre** and legendary **Le Grand Hôtel**, with fashionable summertime rooftop bar and Gordon Ramsay's Michelin-starred restaurant and brasserie. Don't miss **Sanna** (2013), a sculpture by Spanish artist Jaume Plensa.

The Walk » Turn left behind the theatre and walk down the attractive cours du Chapeau Rouge. Turn right and walk along the waterfront to place de la Bourse.

Miroir d'Eau

Surrounded by magisterial public buildings attesting to Bordeaux's 18th-century wealth is vast place de la Bourse. Its highlight is the world's largest reflecting pool, the **Miroir d'Eau** (Water Mirror; place de la Bourse; ⏱10am–10pm summer). Every 23 minutes a fog-like vapor is ejected over the thin slick of water for three minutes to add to the fun.

The Walk » Head up rue Fernand Philippart to place du Parlement with its numerous cafes, then weave along rue du Pas-St-Georges, rue St-Siméon and rue de la Merci to turn left onto rue de Cheverus and back to the cathedral.

ROAD TRIP ESSENTIALS

France Driving Guide

With stunning landscapes, superb highways and one of the world's most scenic and comprehensive rural road networks, France is a road-tripper's dream come true.

DRIVING LICENCE & DOCUMENTS

Drivers must carry the following at all times:

➡ passport or an EU national ID card

➡ valid driving licence (*permis de conduire;* most foreign licences can be used in France for up to a year)

➡ car-ownership papers, known as a *carte grise* (grey card)

➡ proof of third-party liability insurance (*assurance au tiers*)

An International Driving Permit (IDP), issued by your home country's automobile association, translates and vouches for the authenticity of your driver's licence. It is not required when renting a car but can be useful in the event of an accident or police stop.

INSURANCE

Third-party liability insurance (*assurance au tiers*) is compulsory for all vehicles in France, including cars brought from abroad. Normally, cars registered and insured in other European countries can circulate freely. Contact your insurance company before leaving home to make sure you're covered, and to verify whom to call in case of a breakdown or accident.

In a minor accident with no injuries, the easiest way for drivers to sort things out with their insurance companies is to fill out a *constat amiable d'accident automobile* (accident report), a standardised way of recording important details about what

happened. In rental cars it's usually in the packet of documents in the glove compartment. Make sure the report includes any proof that the accident was not your fault. If it *was* your fault, you may be liable for a hefty insurance deductible/excess. Don't sign anything you don't fully understand. If necessary, contact the police (☑17).

French-registered cars have their insurance-company details printed on a little green square affixed to the windscreen (windshield).

HIRING A CAR

To hire a car in France, you'll generally need to be over 21 years old, have had a driving licence for at least a year, and have an international credit card. Drivers under 25 usually have to pay a surcharge (*frais jeune conducteur*) of €25 to €35 per day.

Car-hire companies provide mandatory third-party liability insurance, but things such as collision-damage waivers (CDW, or *assurance tous risques*) vary greatly from company to company. When comparing rates and conditions (ie the fine print), the most important thing to check is the *franchise* (deductible/excess), which for a small car is usually around €600 for damage and €800 for theft. With many companies, you can reduce the excess by half, and perhaps to zero, by paying a daily insurance supplement of up to €20. Your credit card may cover CDW if you use it to pay for the rental, but the car-hire company won't know anything about this – verify conditions and details with your credit-card issuer to be sure.

Arranging your car hire or fly/drive package before you leave home is usually considerably cheaper than a walk-in rental, but beware of website offers that don't include a CDW or you may be liable for up to 100% of the car's value.

International car-hire companies include the following:

Avis (www.avis.com)

Budget (www.budget.com)

EasyCar (www.easycar.com)

Europcar (www.europcar.com)

Hertz (www.hertz.com)

Sixt (www.sixt.com)

French car-hire companies:

ADA (www.ada.fr)

DLM (www.dlm.fr)

France Cars (www.francecars.fr)

Renault Rent (www.renault-rent.com)

Rent a Car (www.rentacar.fr)

Deals can be found on the internet and through companies such as:

Auto Europe (www.autoeurope.com)

DriveAway Holidays (www.driveaway.com.au)

Holiday Autos (www.holidayautos.co.uk)

Rental cars with automatic transmissions are the exception in France, though less so than a few years back. They may need to be ordered in advance and are more expensive than manual cars.

For insurance reasons, it is usually forbidden to take rental cars on ferries, eg to Corsica.

Never leave anything of value in a parked car, even in the boot (trunk).

BRINGING YOUR OWN VEHICLE

Any foreign motor vehicle entering France must display a sticker or licence plate identifying its country of registration. Right-hand-drive vehicles brought from the UK or Ireland must have deflectors affixed to the headlights to avoid dazzling oncoming traffic.

MAPS

Smartphone GPS apps have greatly improved their France coverage in recent years but old-fashioned paper road maps are still valuable as a planning tool and driving companion, and they're especially useful for navigating back roads and exploring alternative routes. Buy them from

Priority to the Right

Under France's venerable *priorité à droite* ('priority to the right') rule, any car entering an intersection (including a T-junction) from a road (including a tiny village backstreet) on your right has the right of way unless street signs indicate otherwise. Locals assume every driver knows this, so don't be surprised if they courteously cede the right of way when you're about to turn from an alley onto a highway – and boldly assert their rights when you're the one zipping down a main road.

Priorité à droite is suspended (eg on arterial roads) when you pass a sign showing an upended yellow square with an upended black square in the middle. The same sign with a horizontal bar through the square lozenge reinstates the *priorité à droite* rule.

When you arrive at a roundabout (traffic circle), cars already in the roundabout, not you, have the right of way. You'll often see signs reading *vous n'avez pas la priorité* (you do not have right of way) or *cédez le passage* (give way).

Road Distances (KM)

	Bayonne	Bordeaux	Brest	Caen	Cahors	Calais	Chambéry	Cherbourg	Clermont-Ferrand	Dijon	Grenoble	Lille	Lyon	Marseille	Nantes	Nice	Paris	Perpignan	Strasbourg	Toulouse
Bordeaux	184																			
Brest	811	623																		
Caen	764	568	376																	
Cahors	307	218	788	661																
Calais	164	876	710	339	875															
Chambéry	860	651	120	800	523	834														
Cherbourg	835	647	399	124	743	461	923													
Clermont-Ferrand	564	358	805	566	269	717	295	689												
Dijon	807	619	867	548	378	572	273	671	279											
Grenoble	827	657	1126	806	501	863	56	929	300	302										
Lille	997	809	725	353	808	112	767	476	650	505	798									
Lyon	831	528	1018	698	439	755	103	820	171	194	110	687								
Marseille	700	651	1271	1010	521	1067	344	1132	477	506	273	999	314							
Nantes	513	326	298	292	491	593	780	317	462	656	787	609	618	975						
Nice	858	810	1429	1168	679	1225	410	1291	636	664	337	1157	473	190	1131					
Paris	771	583	596	232	582	289	565	355	424	313	571	222	462	775	384	932				
Perpignan	499	451	1070	998	320	1149	478	1094	441	640	445	1081	448	319	773	476	857			
Strasbourg	1254	1066	1079	730	847	621	496	853	584	335	551	522	488	803	867	804	490	935		
Toulouse	300	247	866	865	116	991	565	890	890	727	533	923	536	407	568	564	699	205	1022	
Tours	536	348	490	246	413	531	611	369	369	418	618	463	449	795	197	952	238	795	721	593

Amazon (the surest way to find exactly what you need) or look for them at bookshops, newsagents, airports, hypermarkets, tourist offices and service stations along the autoroutes.

Michelin (https://boutique.voyages.michelin.fr) Publishes excellent, tear-proof yellow-orange 1:200,000-scale regional maps with precise coverage of smaller back roads.

Institut Géographique National (IGN; www.ign.fr) Publishes regional fold-out maps for driving as well as hiking maps.

ROADS & CONDITIONS

France has one of Europe's densest highway networks. There are four types of intercity roads:

Autoroutes (highway names beginning with A) Multilane divided highways, usually (except around Calais and Lille) with tolls (*péages*). Generously outfitted with rest stops.

Routes Nationales (N, RN) National highways. Some sections have divider strips.

Routes Départementales (D) Local highways and roads.

Routes Communales (C, V) Minor rural roads.

The latter two categories, while slower, offer some of France's most enjoyable driving experiences, though many lack verges/shoulders.

Motorcyclists will find France great for touring, with high-quality roads and stunning scenery. Just make sure your wet-weather gear is up to scratch.

Note that high mountain passes, especially in the Alps, may be closed from as early as September to as late as June. Conditions are posted at the foot of each pass ('*ouvert*' on a green background means open, '*ferme*' on a red background

Road Trip Websites

AUTOMOBILE ASSOCIATIONS
RAC (www.rac.co.uk/driving-abroad/france) Info for British drivers on driving in France – on the right, of course.

CONDITIONS & TRAFFIC
Bison Futé (www.bison-fute.gouv.fr)

Les Sociétés d'Autoroutes (www.autoroutes.fr)

ROUTE MAPPING
Mappy (https://fr.mappy.com)

Via Michelin (www.viamichelin.com)

means closed). Snow chains or studded tyres are required in wintry weather.

ROAD RULES

Enforcement of French traffic laws (see www.securite-routiere.gouv.fr), including speed limits, has been stepped up considerably in recent years, a major reason why France's traffic fatality rate is now less than half that of the US. Speed cameras are common (if you see a flash you've probably just been caught), as are radar traps and unmarked police vehicles. Fines for many infractions are given on the spot (serious violations can lead to the confiscation of your driving licence and car) or may be sent to your home address (provided by your car-rental company, for which they'll charge your credit card €25) months after your trip ends. Savvy French drivers avoid exceeding the speed limit by using cruise control.

Speed Limits
Speed limits outside built-up areas (unless signposted otherwise):
Undivided highways 80km/h (reduced from 90km/h in 2018)
Undivided highways with at least two lanes in each direction 90km/h (80km/h when raining)
Non-autoroute divided highways 110km/h (100km/h when raining)
Autoroutes 130km/h (110km/h when raining)

Unless otherwise signposted, a limit of 50km/h applies in all areas designated as built up, no matter how rural they may appear. You must slow to 50km/h the moment you come to a white sign with a red border and a place name written on it; the speed limit applies until you pass an identical sign with a horizontal bar through it. In recent years more and more cities, towns and villages have lowered local speed limits to 30km/h – keep an eye out for signs.

You're expected to already know the speed limit for various types of roads; that's why most speed-limit signs begin with the word *rappel* (reminder). You can be fined for going as little as 10km over the speed limit.

Alcohol
➡ The blood-alcohol limit is 0.05% (0.5g per litre of blood) – the equivalent of two glasses of wine for a 75kg adult.

➡ Police often conduct random breathalyser tests. Penalties can be severe, including imprisonment.

Motorcycles
➡ Riders of any two-wheeled motorised vehicle must wear a helmet.

➡ No special licence is required to ride a motorbike whose engine is smaller than 50cc, which is why rental scooters are often rated at 49.9cc.

Child Seats
➡ A baby weighing under 13kg must travel in a backward-facing child seat.

➡ Up to age 10, children must use a size-appropriate type of front-facing child seat or booster.

➡ Children under 10 are not permitted to ride in the front seat (unless the back is already occupied by other children under 10).

Other Rules
➡ All passengers, including those in the back seat, must wear seat belts.

➡ Mobile phones may be used only if equipped with a hands-free kit or speakerphone.

➡ Turning right on a red light is always illegal.

➡ All vehicles driven in France must carry a high-visibility reflective safety vest (stored inside the vehicle, not in the trunk/boot), a reflective triangle, and a portable, single-use breathalyser kit.

PARKING

Parking in French city centres, especially Paris, is a nightmare and an expensive one at that.

In city centres, most on-street parking places are *payant* (metered) from about 9am to 7pm (sometimes with a break from noon to 2pm) Monday to Saturday, except public holidays. *Stationnement* (parking), also known in French as *parking*, is often limited to two hours. Pay at a *horodateur* (parking meter) and place the printed ticket on your dashboard on the side nearest the sidewalk.

Many medium-sized towns have concentric parking zones, with the highest per-hour fees and shortest time limits in the city centre and cheaper, less restricted parking a bit further out. For details (generally in French) on zones, *tarifs* (rates), underground lots in the centre, free (*gratuit*) parking further out and seasonal regulations (eg in ski resorts), including maps, search online for the name of the town plus the French words *parking* or *stationnement*. Watch out for market days, when a spacious public car park can turn into a sea of food stalls – any cars not moved before the posted time (look for signs) will be towed away. Urban hotels

Driving Problem-Buster

I can't speak French. Will that be a problem? While it's preferable to learn some French before travelling, French road signs are mostly of the 'international symbol' variety, and English is increasingly spoken among the younger generation.

What should I do if my car breaks down? Safety first: turn on your flashers, put on a safety vest (legally required, and provided in rental-car glove compartments) and place a reflective triangle (also legally required) 30m to 100m behind your car to warn approaching motorists. Call for emergency assistance (☑112) or walk to the nearest orange roadside call box (placed every 2km along French autoroutes). If renting a vehicle, your car-hire company's service number may help expedite matters. If travelling in your own car, verify before leaving home whether your local auto club has reciprocal roadside-assistance arrangements in France.

What if I have an accident? For minor accidents you'll need to fill out a *constat amiable d'accident* (accident statement, typically provided in rental-car glove compartments) and report the accident to your insurance and/or rental-car company. If necessary, contact the police (☑17).

What should I do if I get stopped by the police? Show your passport (or EU national ID card), licence and proof of insurance.

How do I know the speed limit in France and how is it enforced? Speed limits (indicated by a black-on-white number inside a red circle) range from 30km/h in some built-up areas to 130km/h on the fastest autoroutes. If the motorcycle police pull you over, they'll fine you on the spot or direct you to the nearest gendarmerie to pay. If you're caught by a speed camera (placed at random intervals along French roads and highways), the ticket will be sent to your rental-car agency, which will charge you something like €25 to provide the French government with your home address – also the destination of tickets incurred when you're driving your own vehicle. Fines depend on how much you're over the limit.

How do French tolls work? Almost all French autoroutes charge tolls except right around cities. Take a ticket from the machine upon entering the highway and pay as you exit. Some exit booths are staffed by people; others are automated and will accept only credit cards (possibly only chip-equipped credit cards) or coins.

France Playlist

Bonjour Rachid Taha and Gaëtan Roussel

Coeur Vagabond Gus Viseur

La Vie en Rose Édith Piaf

Minor Swing Django Reinhardt

L'Americano Akhenaton

Flower Duet from Lakmé Léo Delibes

De Bonnes Raisons Alex Beaupain

often offer reduced-price parking in nearby underground garages.

In some town centres, parking in a *zone bleue* (blue zone) – marked with blue lines on the pavement – is free but time-limited so drivers place a blue *disque de stationnement* (parking disk) indicating the *heure d'arrivée* (time of arrival) on the dashboard. These are available, often for free, at supermarkets and car-accessory shops.

FUEL

Essence (petrol), also known as *carburant* (fuel), costs between €1.30 and €1.67 per litre for 95 unleaded (Sans Plomb 95 or SP95, usually available from a green pump) – that's about US$5.85 to US$7.52 per US gallon – and €1.17 to €1.57 for diesel (*diesel, gazole* or *gasoil*, usually available from a yellow pump). Check and compare current prices countrywide at www.prix-carburants.gouv.fr.

Filling up *(faire le plein)* is most expensive at autoroute rest stops, and usually cheapest at super- and hypermarkets such as Carrefour, Intermarché, Leclerc and Super U.

Many small petrol stations close on Sunday afternoons and, even in cities, it can be hard to find a staffed station open late at night. In general, after-hours purchases (eg at hypermarkets' fully automatic, 24-hour stations) can only be made with a credit card that has an embedded PIN chip and/or was issued in France (or the EU), so if all you have is cash or a foreign credit card you could be stuck.

SATELLITE NAVIGATION SYSTEMS

GPS devices are available from car-rental agencies, usually for an extra per-day fee, but if you've got a French SIM card with plenty of gigs you're probably better off using your smartphone. (Do not use your smartphone from home without verifying the cost of data, which can be ruinous if you don't have a roaming plan.) If your gadget leads you astray, don't hesitate to fall back on common sense, France's excellent road signs – among the world's most logical and easy to follow – and an old-fashioned printed Michelin map.

SAFETY

Never leave anything valuable inside your car, even in the boot (trunk); theft is especially prevalent in the south. In cities like Marseille and Nice, aggressive theft from cars stopped at red lights is also occasionally an issue.

RADIO

For news, tune in to the French-language France Info (105.5MHz or thereabouts; www.francetvinfo.fr), multilanguage RFI (89MHz in Paris; www.rfi.fr) or, in northern France, BBC Radio 4 (198kHz). Popular national FM music stations include NRJ (www.nrj.fr), Virgin (www.virginradio.fr), La Radio Plus (www.laradioplus.com) and Nostalgie (www.nostalgie.fr).

In many areas, Autoroute Info (107.7MHz) has round-the-clock traffic information.

France Travel Guide

GETTING THERE & AWAY

AIR

Air France (www.airfrance.com) is the national carrier, with plenty of domestic and international flights in and out of major French airports, including Charles de Gaulle and Orly near Paris, Lyon St-Exupéry, Marseille Provence and Nice Côte d'Azur.

International flights, mainly from the UK, continental Europe and North Africa, serve two dozen regional French airports. Many are run by low-cost carriers.

CAR & MOTORCYCLE

Entering France from nearby countries is usually a breeze – no border checkpoints and no customs – thanks to the Schengen Agreement, signed by all of France's neighbours except the UK, the Channel Islands and Andorra.

Eurotunnel

The Channel Tunnel (Chunnel), inaugurated in 1994, is the first dry-land link between England and France since the last ice age.

High-speed **Eurotunnel Le Shuttle** (☑France 08 10 63 03 04, UK 03443 35 35 35; www.eurotunnel.com) trains whisk bicycles, motorcycles, cars and coaches in 35

International Ferry Companies

Company	Connection	Website
Brittany Ferries	England-Normandy, England-Brittany, Ireland-Brittany, Ireland-Normandy	www.brittany-ferries.co.uk; www.brittany-ferries.ie
Condor Ferries	England-Brittany, Channel Islands-Brittany	www.condorferries.co.uk
Corsica Linea	Algeria-France, Tunisia-France, Sardinia-France	www.corsicalinea.com
CTN	Tunisia-France	www.ctn.com.tn
DFDS Seaways	England-Channel Ports, England-Normandy	www.dfdsseaways.co.uk
Irish Ferries	Ireland-Normandy	www.irishferries.com
Manche Îles Express	Channel Islands-Normandy	www.manche-iles.com
P&O Ferries	England-Channel Ports	www.poferries.com
Stena Line Ferries	Ireland-Normandy	www.stenaline.ie

minutes from Folkestone through the Channel Tunnel to Coquelles, 5km southwest of Calais. Shuttles run 24 hours a day, with up to three departures an hour during peak periods. LPG and CNG tanks are not permitted, meaning gas-powered cars and many campers/caravans must travel by ferry.

Eurotunnel sets its fares the way budget airlines do: the further in advance you book and the lower the demand for a particular crossing, the less you pay. Unrestricted fares can cost a small fortune (up to £229/€320 one-way). For very short-term return travel, fares for a car, including up to nine passengers, start at just £31/€43 each way.

SEA

To get the best fares, check **Ferry Savers** (www.ferrysavers.com).

TRAIN

Rail services link France with virtually every country in Europe. The **Eurostar** (www.eurostar.com) whisks passengers from London (St Pancras International) to Paris (Gare du Nord) in 2¼ hours.

You can book tickets and get train information from **Rail Europe** (www.raileurope.com).

High-speed train travel between France and the UK, Belgium, the Netherlands, Germany and Austria is covered by **Railteam** (www.railteam.co.uk).

DIRECTORY A–Z

ACCESSIBLE TRAVEL

While France presents constant challenges for *visiteurs à mobilité réduite* (visitors with reduced mobility) and *visiteurs handi-capés* (visitors with disabilities) – cobblestones, sidewalks crowded with cafe tables, a lack of kerb ramps, budget hotels without lifts – but don't let that deter you from visiting. The French government is making significant strides in improving the situation and, with a little careful planning, an accessible stay is eminently possible. Download Lonely Planet's free Accessible

Travel guide from https://shop.lonelyplanet.com/categories/accessible-travel.

➡ Paris' tourist office provides ample information for travellers with disabilities – see www.parisinfo.com (click on the UK flag, then 'Practical Paris' and finally 'Visiting Paris with a Disability').

➡ The Paris metro, most of which was built decades ago (and some of it more than a century ago), is hopeless. Line 14 was built to be wheelchair-accessible, although in reality it remains challenging to navigate in a wheelchair – unlike Paris buses, which are 100% accessible.

➡ The Parisian taxi company Taxis G7 (☑01 47 39 00 91 for travellers with disabilities; www.g7.fr/en/discover-our-services/g7-access-taxi) has vehicles especially adapted to carry wheelchairs and drivers trained in helping passengers with disabilities.

➡ Countrywide, many SNCF train carriages are accessible to people with disabilities. If you use a wheelchair, you and a person accompanying you may qualify for discounts. For information in English, see www.sncf.com/en/passenger-offer/travel-for-everyone/accessibility.

Accès Plus (☑36 35, 09 69 32 26 26; www.accessibilite.sncf.com; ☉phone staffed 7am-10pm) The SNCF assistance service for rail travellers with disabilities (the website is in French). Can advise on station accessibility and arrange a wheelchair or help getting on or off a train.

Île de France Mobilités (☑09 70 81 83 85; www.iledefrance-mobilites.fr/le-reseau/transports-faciles-d-acces; ☉phone staffed 7am-10pm) Has comprehensive information on

---

Practicalities

➡ **Time** France uses the 24-hour clock and is on Central European Time, which is one hour ahead of GMT/UTC. During daylight saving time, which runs from the last Sunday in March to the last Sunday in October, France is two hours ahead of GMT/UTC.

➡ **Weights & Measures** France uses the metric system.

accessible travel in Paris and the surrounding Île de France area.

Mobile en Ville (☏06 52 76 62 49; www.mobileenville.org; 8 rue des Mariniers, 14e) Association that works to make independent travel within Paris easier for people in wheelchairs. Among other things it organises some great *randonnées* (walks) in and around Paris.

Tourisme et Handicaps (☏01 44 11 10 41; www.tourisme-handicaps.org; 15 av Carnot, 17e, Paris) Issues the blue 'Tourisme et Handicap' label to tourist sites, restaurants and hotels that comply with strict accessibility and usability standards. Different symbols indicate the sort of access afforded to people with physical, mental, hearing and/or visual disabilities.

Access Travel (☏UK 07973 114 365; www.access-travel.co.uk) Specialised UK-based agency for accessible travel.

ACCOMMODATION

Be it a fairy-tale château, a boutique hideaway or floating pod on a lake, France has accommodation to suit every taste and pocket. If you're visiting in high season (especially July and August), reserve ahead – the best addresses, especially on the coast, fill up months in advance.

Categories

As a rule of thumb, budget covers everything from basic hostels to small family-run places; midrange means a few extra creature comforts, generally including a lift; and top-end places stretch from luxury five-star palaces with air-conditioning, swimming pools and restaurants to boutique-chic alpine chalets.

Costs

Accommodation costs vary wildly between seasons and regions. Summer (July and August) is the most expensive time of year in many areas, especially along the coasts and near bodies of water (but *not* in inland cities).

Reservations

Virtually all French hotels, hostels, B&Bs etc have websites that allow you to reserve a room and can also be booked through online services such as Booking.com (www.booking.com). Small family-run hotels, especially, appreciate reservations

Sleeping Price Ranges

The following price ranges refer to a double room in high season, with private bathroom (any combination of toilet, bathtub, shower and washbasin), excluding breakfast unless otherwise noted. Breakfast is assumed to be included at a B&B. Where half board (breakfast and dinner) and full board (breakfast, lunch and dinner) is included, this is mentioned with the price.

€ less than €90 (€130 in Paris)

€€ €90–190 (€130–250 in Paris)

€€€ more than €190 (€250 in Paris)

made directly as this saves them the significant fees they must pay to booking sites.

Some tourist offices, if you drop by, can help find same-day accommodation in their area. In the Alps, ski-resort tourist offices run central reservation services for booking accommodation.

Seasons

➡ In ski resorts, high season is Christmas, New Year and the February–March school holidays.

➡ On the coast, high season is summer, particularly July and August.

➡ Hotels in inland cities often charge low-season rates in summer.

➡ Rates often drop significantly outside the high season – in some cases by as much as 50%.

➡ In business-oriented hotels in cities, rooms are most expensive from Monday to Thursday and cheaper over the weekend.

➡ In the Alps, hotels usually close between seasons, from around May to mid-June and from mid-September to early December; many addresses in Corsica only open Easter to October.

B&Bs

For charm, a heartfelt *bienvenue* (welcome) and solid home cooking, it's hard to beat France's privately run *chambres d'hôte* (B&Bs) – rare in cities but as common as mistletoe in rural areas. By law a *chambre d'hôte* must have no more than five rooms and breakfast must be included in the price; some hosts prepare an evening meal (table d'hôte) for an extra charge of around €30, including wine. Pick up lists of chambres d'hôte at tourist offices, or find one to suit online.

Bienvenue à la Ferme (www.bienvenue-a-la-ferme.com)

Chambres d'Hôtes France (www.chambresdhotesfrance.com)

Fleurs de Soleil (www.fleursdesoleil.fr) Selective collection of stylish maisons d'hôte, mainly in rural France.

Gîtes de France (www.gites-de-france.com) France's primary umbrella organisation for B&Bs and self-catering properties (gîtes); search by region, theme (charm, children, by the sea, on the farm, gourmet, great garden etc), activity (fishing, wine tasting, cycling, skiing etc) or facilities (pool, fireplace, baby equipment etc).

iGuide (www.iguide-hotels.com) Gorgeous presentation of France's most charming and often-times most upmarket B&Bs, organised by region and/or theme (romantic, gastronomic, seaside, mountains, sports and so forth).

Samedi Midi Éditions (www.samedimidi.com) Country, mountain, seaside...choose your chambre d'hôte by location, theme or activities.

Camping

Camping is hugely popular in France so thousands of well-equipped campgrounds dot the country, many near rivers, lakes and the sea.

➡ Most campgrounds open from March or April to late September or October; popular spots fill up fast in summer so it is wise to book ahead.

➡ The price of an emplacement (site) includes lodging for two people, including space for a tent and a car. Otherwise the price is broken down per adult/tent/car. Factor in a few extra euros per night for taxe de séjour (holiday tax) and electricity.

➡ Euro-economisers should look out for no-frills campings municipaux (municipal campgrounds).

➡ Many campgrounds rent mobile homes with mod cons like heating, fitted kitchen and TV.

➡ Pitching your tent in nondesignated spots (camping sauvage) is illegal in France.

➡ Campground offices often close during the day.

➡ Accessing many campgrounds without your own transport can be slow and costly, or simply impossible.

Hostels

Traditional hostels in France range from spartan to funky, although with a wave of design-driven, uber-hip hostels opening in Paris, Marseille and other cities, hip hangouts with perks aplenty seem to be the trend of the future.

➡ In university towns, foyers d'étudiant (student dormitories) are sometimes converted for use by travellers during summer.

➡ A dorm bed in an auberge de jeunesse (youth hostel) costs €20 to €50 in Paris, and anything from €15 to €40 in the provinces, depending on location, amenities and facilities; sheets are always included, breakfast more often than not.

➡ To prevent outbreaks of bed bugs, sleeping bags are not permitted.

➡ Hostels by the sea or in the mountains sometimes offer seasonal outdoor activities.

➡ French hostels are 100% nonsmoking.

Hotels

Hotels in France are rated with one to five stars, although the ratings are based on strictly objective criteria (eg the size of the entry hall), not the quality of the service, the decor or cleanliness.

➡ French hotels almost never include breakfast in their rates. Unless specified otherwise, prices quoted don't include breakfast, which costs around €8/12/25 in a budget/midrange/top-end hotel.

➡ When you book, hotels usually ask for a credit card number; some require a deposit.

➡ A double room generally has one double bed (sometimes two singles pushed together!); a room with twin beds (deux lits) is usually a bit

Book Your Stay Online

For more accommodation reviews by Lonely Planet authors, check out http://hotels.lonelyplanet.com. You'll find independent reviews, as well as recommendations on the best places to stay.

more expensive, as is a room with a bathtub instead of a shower.

➡ Feather pillows are practically nonexistent in France, even in top-end hotels.

➡ Smoking is permitted on hotel restaurant terraces; if you are sensitive to smoke, you may need to sit inside.

ELECTRICITY

230V/50Hz

FOOD

The French table waltzes taste buds through a dizzying array of dishes sourced from aromatic street markets, seaside oyster farms, sun-baked olive groves and ancient vineyards, mirroring the beauty of each season. Discovering regional cuisines – made using the freshest ingredients and a phenomenal variety of cooking methods – is a hugely rewarding experience.

Restaurants and bistros Range from unchanged for a century to contemporary minimalist; urban dining is international, rural dining staunchly French.

Brasseries Open from dawn until late, these casual eateries are great for dining in between standard meal times.

Cafes Ideal for breakfast and a light lunch; many morph into bars after dark.

Eating Price Ranges

Price indicators refer to the average cost of a two-course meal, be it an *entrée* (starter) and *plat* (main course) or main and dessert, or a two- or three-course *menu* (pre-set meal at a fixed price).

€ less than €20

€€ €20–40

€€€ more than €40

INTERNET ACCESS

➡ Wi-fi (pronounced 'wee-fee' in French) is available at airports, hotels, cafes, restaurants, museums and tourist offices.

➡ Free public wi-fi hotspots are available in cities and many towns; Paris alone has 250 different locations city-wide (www.paris.fr/pages/paris-wi-fi-152), including parks, libraries and municipal buildings. In parks look for a purple 'Zone Wi-Fi' sign near the entrance; select the 'Paris Wi-Fi' network.

➡ To search for free wi-fi hot spots in France, visit www.wifimap.io.

➡ Tourist offices in some larger cities, including Lyon and Bordeaux, rent out pocket-sized mobile wi-fi modems that you carry around with you, ensuring a fast wi-fi connection while roaming the city.

➡ Alternatively, rent a mobile wi-fi device online before leaving home and arrange for it to be delivered by post to your hotel in France through HipPocketWifi (http://hippocketwifi.com), Travel WiFi (https://travelwifi.com) or My Webspot (www.my-webspot.com).

➡ Internet cafes are increasingly rare, though most cities still have a handful whose main business is providing immigrants with cheap international phone calls.

LGBTIQ+ TRAVELLERS

The rainbow flag flies high in France, a country that allowed its LGBTIQ+ citizens out of the closet long before many of its European neighbours. *Laissez-faire* perfectly sums up France's liberal attitude towards homosexuality and people's private lives in general, in part because of a long tradition of public tolerance towards unconventional lifestyles.

➡ Paris has been a thriving gay and lesbian centre since the late 1970s, and most major organisations are based there today.

➡ Bordeaux, Lille, Lyon, Montpellier, Toulouse and many other towns also have an active queer scene.

➡ Attitudes towards homosexuality tend to be more conservative in the countryside and villages.

➡ France's lesbian scene is less public than its gay male counterpart and is centred mainly on women's cafes and bars.

➡ Same-sex marriage has been legal in France since 2013.

➡ Gay Pride marches are held in major French cities mid-May to early July.

MONEY

ATMs

Automated teller machines (ATMs) – known as *distributeurs automatiques de billets* (DAB) or *points d'argent* in French – connected to international networks are situated in all cities and towns.

Cash

You always get a better exchange rate in-country, but it is a good idea to arrive in France with enough euros to take a taxi to a hotel if you have to.

Credit & Debit Cards

➡ Credit and debit cards, accepted almost everywhere in France, are convenient, relatively secure and almost always offer a better exchange rate than travellers cheques or cash exchanges.

➡ Visa, MasterCard and (usually) American Express can be used in shops and supermarkets and for train travel, car hire and – usually – motorway tolls.

➡ Don't assume that you can pay for a meal or a budget hotel with a credit card – enquire first.

➡ Cash advances are a supremely convenient and inexpensive way to stay stocked up with euros, but getting cash with a credit card involves both bank fees (sometimes US$10 or more) and interest – ask your credit-card

issuer for details. Debit-card fees are usually much less.

Moneychangers

➡ Commercial banks charge up to €5 per foreign-currency transaction – if they even bother to offer exchange services any more.

➡ In Paris and major cities, *bureaux de change* (exchange bureaus) are faster and easier, and have longer hours and better rates, than banks.

➡ Some post-office branches exchange travellers cheques and banknotes in a variety of currencies but charge a commission; most won't take US$100 bills.

Tipping

By law, restaurant and bar prices are *service compris* (ie they include a 15% service charge), so leaving a *pourboire* (tip) is not mandatory. If you were extremely satisfied with the service, however, you can – as many locals do – show your appreciation by leaving a small 'extra' tip for your waiter or waitress.

Where/Who	Customary Tip
bar	No tips for drinks served at bar; round to nearest euro for drinks served at table
cafe	5-10%
hotel porter	€1-2 per bag
restaurant	10% for excellent service
taxi	10-15%
toilet attendant	€0.50
tour guide	€1-2 per person

OPENING HOURS

Opening hours vary throughout the year. We list high-season opening hours and, where possible, hours in the shoulder and low seasons.

Banks 9am–noon and 2pm–5pm Monday to Friday or Tuesday to Saturday

Restaurants noon–1.30pm, 2pm or 2.30pm and 7pm–9pm or 10pm six days a week

Cafes 7am–11pm

Bars 7pm–1am

Clubs 10pm or later–3am, 4am or 5am Thursday to Saturday

Shops 10am–noon and 2pm–7pm Monday to Saturday

PUBLIC HOLIDAYS

The following *jours fériés* (public holidays) are observed in France:

New Year's Day (Jour de l'An) 1 January

Easter Sunday & Monday (Pâques & Lundi de Pâques) Late March/April

May Day (Fête du Travail) 1 May

Victoire 1945 8 May

Ascension Thursday (Ascension) May; on the 40th day after Easter

Pentecost/Whit Sunday & Whit Monday (Pentecôte & Lundi de Pentecôte) Mid-May to mid-June; on the seventh Sunday after Easter

Bastille Day/National Day (Fête Nationale) 14 July

Assumption Day (Assomption) 15 August

All Saints' Day (Toussaint) 1 November

Remembrance Day (Onze Novembre) 11 November

Christmas (Noël) 25 December

The following are *not* public holidays in France: Shrove Tuesday (Mardi Gras; the first day of Lent); Maundy (or Holy) Thursday and Good Friday, just before Easter; and Boxing Day (26 December).

Note: Good Friday and Boxing Day *are* public holidays in Alsace.

SAFE TRAVEL

France is generally a safe place in which to live and travel despite crime and terrorism rates having risen in the last few years. Although property crime is a problem, it is extremely unlikely that you will be physically assaulted while walking down the street. Always check your government's travel advisory warnings.

Because of the threat of terrorism, French police are very strict about security. Do not leave baggage unattended, especially at airports or train stations: suspicious objects may be summarily blown up. In large museums and monu-ments, it is routine for bags to be checked upon entering.

Hunting season runs from September to February. If you see signs reading '*chasseurs*' or '*chasse gardée*' strung up or tacked to trees, think twice about wandering into the area. As well as millions of wild animals, some 25 French hunters die each year after being shot by other hunters. Hunting is traditional and commonplace in all rural areas in France, especially the Vosges, the Sologne, the southwest and the Baie de Somme.

Natural Dangers

➡ There are powerful tides and strong undertows at many places along the Atlantic Coast, from the Spanish border north to Brittany and Normandy.

➡ Only swim in *zones de baignade surveillée* (beaches monitored by life guards).

➡ Be aware of tide times and the high-tide mark if walking or sleeping on a beach.

➡ Thunderstorms in the mountains and the hot southern plains can be extremely sudden and violent.

➡ Check the weather report before setting out on a long walk and be prepared for sudden storms and temperature drops if you are heading into the high country of the Alps or Pyrenees.

➡ Avalanches pose a significant danger in the French Alps.

Theft

Pickpocketing and bag/phone snatching (eg in dense crowds and public places) are as prevalent in big French cities – Paris, Marseille and Nice in particular – as in other big cities in Europe. There's no need whatsoever to travel in fear. A few simple precautions will minimise your chances of being ripped off.

➡ On trains, avoid leaving smartphones and tablets lying casually on the table in front of you and keep bags as close to you as possible: luggage racks at the ends of carriages are easy prey for thieves; in sleeping compartments, lock the door carefully at night.

➡ Be especially vigilant for bag/phone snatchers at train stations, airports, fast-food outlets, outdoor cafes, beaches and on public transport.

→ Break-ins to parked cars are a widespread problem. Never, ever leave anything valuable – or not valuable – inside your car, even in the boot (trunk).

→ Aggressive theft from cars stopped at red lights is occasionally a problem, especially in Marseille and Nice. As a precaution, lock your car doors and roll up the windows.

TELEPHONE

→ French mobile phone numbers begin with 06 or 07.

→ France's mobile phone networks use 900/1800MHz, which means that standard North American cellphones won't work here unless they have tri-band or other international capabilities.

→ Check with your service provider about roaming charges – using a North American cellphone in France without a special roaming plan can be incredibly expensive (around US$2 for one minute or 1MB of data).

→ For reasonable rates and maximal flexibility, buy a local prepaid SIM card from a French provider such as Lebara or Orange. For about €20, you get a local phone number, a generous allocation of domestic calls and texts/SMSs, free international calls to certain countries (including the US and Canada), and oodles of data – more than enough to drive around with your phone's GPS app running. Prepaid SIM cards are usually available at major airports, either at desks run by providers or from newsagents such as Relay. Make sure that your phone is unlocked and compatible with French mobile frequencies – or purchase a cheap local smartphone.

→ Recharge cards are sold at most *tabacs* (tobacconists/newsagents), supermarkets and online through websites such as Topengo (www.topengo.fr).

TOURIST INFORMATION

Almost every city, town and village has an *office de tourisme* (a tourist office run by some unit of local government) or *syndicat d'initiative* (a tourist office run by an organisation of local merchants). Both are excellent resources and can supply you with local maps as well as details on accommodation, restaurants and activities. If you have a special interest such as walking, cycling, architecture or wine sampling, ask about it.

→ Many tourist offices help with local hotel and B&B reservations, sometimes for a nominal fee.

→ *Comités régionaux de tourisme* (CRTs; regional tourist boards), their *départemental* analogues (CDTs) and their websites are a superb source of information and hyperlinks. Useful websites include:

Explore France (www.france.fr) This French government website gives you the lowdown on sights, activities, cultural events and festivals in all of France's regions. Offers brochures for downloading.

French Tourist Offices (www.tourisme.fr) Offers mountains of inspirational information organised by theme and region.

VISAS

→ For up-to-date details on visa requirements, see the website of the **Ministère des Affaires Étrangères** (Ministry of Foreign Affairs; www.diplomatie.gouv.fr; 37 quai d'Orsay, 7e; M Assemblée Nationale) and click 'Coming to France'.

→ Visitors with passports from 62 countries, including almost all of North and South America, Australia and New Zealand, do not require visas for tourist stays of up to 90 days.

→ Starting sometime in 2022, visitors to France (or any other Schengen Zone country) from visa-exempt countries, including the UK, will need to obtain travel authorisation (€7) online in advance through the European Travel Information and Authorisation System (ETIAS).

Language

The sounds used in spoken French can almost all be found in English. There are a couple of exceptions: nasal vowels (represented in our pronunciation guides by o or u followed by an almost inaudible nasal consonant sound m, n or ng), the 'funny' u (ew in our guides) and the deep-in-the-throat r. Bearing these few points in mind and reading our pronunciation guides below as if they were English, you'll be understood just fine.

BASICS

Hello.	*Bonjour.*	bon·zhoor
Goodbye.	*Au revoir.*	o·rer·vwa
Yes./No.	*Oui./Non.*	wee/non
Excuse me.	*Excusez-moi.*	ek·skew·zay·mwa
Sorry.	*Pardon.*	par·don
Please.	*S'il vous plaît.*	seel voo play
Thank you.	*Merci.*	mair·see

You're welcome.
De rien. der ree·en

Do you speak English?
Parlez-vous anglais? par·lay·voo ong·glay

I don't understand.
Je ne comprends pas. zher ner kom·pron pa

How much is this?
C'est combien? say kom·byun

ACCOMMODATION

Do you have any rooms available?
Est-ce que vous avez es·ker voo za·vay
des chambres libres? day shom·brer lee·brer

How much is it per night/person?
Quel est le prix kel ay ler pree
par nuit/personne? par nwee/per·son

DIRECTIONS

Can you show me (on the map)?
Pouvez-vous m'indiquer poo·vay·voo mun·dee·kay
(sur la carte)? (sewr la kart)

Where's ...?
Où est ...? oo ay ...

EATING & DRINKING

What would you recommend?
Qu'est-ce que vous kes·ker voo
conseillez? kon·say·yay

I'd like ..., please.
Je voudrais ..., zher voo·dray ...
s'il vous plaît. seel voo play

I'm a vegetarian.
Je suis végétarien/ zher swee vay·zhay·ta·ryun/
végétarienne. vay·zhay·ta·ryen (m/f)

Please bring the bill.
Apportez-moi a·por·tay·mwa
l'addition, la·dee·syon
s'il vous plaît. seel voo play

EMERGENCIES

Help!
Au secours! o skoor

I'm lost.
Je suis perdu/perdue. zhe swee·pair·dew (m/f)

Want More?

For in-depth language information and handy phrases, check out Lonely Planet's *French Phrasebook*. You'll find it at **shop.lonelyplanet.com**

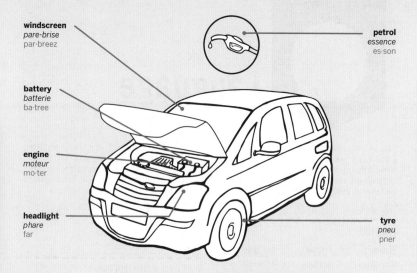

windscreen
pare-brise
par-breez

battery
batterie
ba-tree

engine
moteur
mo-ter

headlight
phare
far

petrol
essence
es-son

tyre
pneu
pner

Signs

Cédez la Priorité	Give Way
Sens Interdit	No Entry
Entrée	Entrance
Péage	Toll
Sens Unique	One Way
Sortie	Exit

I'm ill.
Je suis malade.　　zher swee ma·lad

Call the police!
Appelez la police!　　a·play la po·lees

Call a doctor!
Appelez un médecin!　　a·play un mayd·sun

ON THE ROAD

I'd like to hire a/an ...	*Je voudrais louer ...*	zher voo·dray loo·way ...
4WD	*un quatre-quatre*	un kat·kat
automatic/ manual	*une automatique/ manuel*	ewn o·toma·teek/ ma·nwel
motorbike	*une moto*	ewn mo·to

How much is it daily/weekly?
Quel est le tarif par jour/semaine?　　kel ay ler ta·reef par zhoor/ser·men

Does that include insurance?
Est-ce que l'assurance est comprise?　　es·ker la·sew·rons ay kom·preez

Does that include mileage?
Est-ce que le kilométrage est compris?　　es·ker ler kee·lo·may·trazh ay kom·pree

What's the speed limit?
Quelle est la vitesse maximale permise?　　kel ay la vee·tes mak·see·mal per·meez

Is this the road to ...?
C'est la route pour ...?　　say la root poor ...

Can I park here?
Est-ce que je peux stationner ici?　　es·ker zher per sta·syo·nay ee·see

Where's a service station?
Où est-ce qu'il y a une station-service?　　oo es·keel ya ewn sta·syon·ser·vees

Please fill it up.
Le plein, s'il vous plaît.　　ler plun seel voo play

I'd like (20) litres.
Je voudrais (vingt) litres.　　zher voo·dray (vung) lee·trer

Please check the oil/water.
Contrôlez l'huile/l'eau, s'il vous plaît.　　kon·tro·lay lweel/lo seel voo play

I need a mechanic.
J'ai besoin d'un mécanicien.　　zhay ber·zwun dun may·ka·nee·syun

The car/motorbike has broken down.
La voiture/moto est tombée en panne.　　la vwa·tewr/mo·to ay tom·bay on pan

I had an accident.
J'ai eu un accident.　　zhay ew un ak·see·don

BEHIND THE SCENES

SEND US YOUR FEEDBACK

We love to hear from travellers – your comments help make our books better. We read every word, and we guarantee that your feedback goes straight to the authors. Visit **lonelyplanet. com/contact** to submit your updates and suggestions.

Note: We may edit, reproduce and incorporate your comments in Lonely Planet products such as guidebooks, websites and digital products, so let us know if you are happy to have your name acknowledged. For a copy of our privacy policy visit **lonelyplanet.com/legal**.

WRITER THANKS

ALEXIS AVERBUCK

Ideal travel companion Ryan Ver Berkmoes and I headed out for one of our peachy favourites: research in France. And just as we arrived, the COVID-19 restrictions rolled out. Many thanks due to intrepid editor Daniel Bolger and Team France for all of their generous help navigating these extraordinary conditions with aplomb!

JOEL BALSAM

A big thank you to editor Dan Bolger for pushing forward with this book. Stéphanie Engelvin in Lyon was a big help. Thanks to my sister-in-law Bérengère for sharing her excitement about the region with me. And thanks to my loving partner Stephanie for her neverending support.

OLIVER BERRY

A big thank you to everyone who helped me with my research this time round, including Fabien Latour, Yves Martigny, Agnès Caron, Sophie Dupont, Jean Robarte and Aurelie Martin. Back home, thanks to Rosie Hillier for putting up with all those long days and nights of write-up, and to everyone in the LP team putting the project together, especially commissioning editor

Dan Bolger. Un grand merci à tous!

CELESTE BRASH

Thanks to Margaret for being an excellent research partner, Kimberly Lovato for tips and kindness, the Verducci sisters, Vero in Antibes, Gilles and Angela in Cannes, Todd and Sonia in Nice, previous author Gregor Clark and my family Josh, Jasmine and Tevai for holding down the fort.

STUART BUTLER

Thanks to COVID-19 this was the most complicated book I have ever worked on and I would like to thank my fellow writers

THIS BOOK

This 3rd edition of Lonely Planet's *France's Best Road Trips* guidebook was researched and written by Alexis Averbuck, Joel Balsam, Oliver Berry, Celeste Brash, Stuart Butler, Jean Bernard Carillet, Gregor Clark, Mark Elliot, Steve Fallon, Anita Isalska, Catherine Le Nevez, Christopher Pitts, Daniel Robinson, Regis St Louis, Ryan Ver Berkmoes and Nicola Williams. The previous edition was written by Alexis Averbuck,

Oliver Berry, Jean Bernard Carillet, Kerry Christiani, Gregor Clark, Anita Isalska, Catherine Le Nevez, Hugh McNaughtan, Daniel Robinson, Regis St Louis and Nicola Williams. This guidebook was produced by the following:

Commissioning Editors Daniel Bolger, Kirsten Rawlings

Senior Cartographer Mark Griffiths

Product Editor Kate James

Coordinating Editor Bridget Blair

Book Designer Virginia Moreno

Assisting Editors Imogen Bannister, Monique Choy, Anne Mulvaney, Kristin Odijk, Charlotte Orr

Assisting Cartographer Corey Hutchison

Cover Researcher Fergal Condon

Thanks to Karen Henderson, Sonia Kapoor, Genna Patterson, Angela Tinson and everyone in-house at LP – especially Darren O'Connell and Daniel Bolger – for keeping the project afloat despite the hurdles. But, what pleasure it was to be out walking when the world was collapsing. For joining me on so many of my walks thank you to my wife, Heather, and children Jake and Grace. I would also like to thank Simon Mahomo and Oliver Fitzjones for their companionship on many a trail.

JEAN BERNARD CARILLET

A huge thanks to everyone who helped me during these weird circumstances when travelling around Lorraine. Thanks to Didier and Clémence for their patience, as well as Francesca and Sabrina in Strasbourg. At Lonely Planet, a huge thanks to Daniel for his trust and understanding.

GREGOR CLARK

Thanks to all my contacts in Corsica and my colleagues at Lonely Planet, who helped make this new edition possible despite incredible obstacles in the age of COVID-19. Here's wishing for happier days ahead. May we all return sooner than later to explore the eternal wonders of l'Île de Beauté!

MARK ELLIOT

A very special thank you to the wonderful Sally Cobham for so much love and insight: it's hard to imagine a more delightful travel companion in France or in life. Many thanks also to Nicola Williams for her kind suggestions and to a huge list of helpful folk in France including Eric, Ilse, Sally & Paul, Amanda & Derek, Thierry, Mirelle, Pamela, Trevor and the mysterious Mr Guppy.

STEVE FALLON

A number of people helped me in the updating of my bits of this book, including staff at both Brittany and Normandy Tourism, in particular London-based Fran Lambert. Thanks to friends and contacts for assistance, ideas, hospitality and/or a few laughs along the way, including Brenda Turnnidge, Olivier Cirendini, Caroline Guilleminot and Chew Terrière. As always, I'd like to dedicate my share of the book to my husband Michael Rothschild, a veritable walking *Larousse Gastronomique.*

ANITA ISALSKA

Whole-hearted thanks to Vanessa Michy, Laure Chapuis, Janet Darne, Magali Garreau and Sylvain Pasdeloup for sharing their local knowledge. *Bisous* to my champion and cheerleader Normal Matt, who kept my spirits up while writing and flew to my rescue during the lockdown. *Je t'aime.*

CATHERINE LE NEVEZ

Merci mille fois first and foremost to Julian, and to all of the locals in and around Paris who provided insights, information and inspiration during this project and always. Huge thanks too to Dan Bolger and everyone at LP. As ever, *merci* encore to my parents, brother, *belle-sœur, neveu* and *nièce.*

CHRISTOPHER PITTS

Special thanks to all the crew at LP who have put so much hard work into making this book what it is. *Bises* as always to the Pavillard clan, and my dearest partners in crime: Perrine, Elliot and Céleste.

DANIEL ROBINSON

Special thanks to Mary and Conor (Château de Beaulieu, Saumur), Cédric (Musée du Compagnonnage, Tours), Mark Lelandais and Sophie (Château Gaillard, Amboise), Gloria Belknap and her late husband Bob – may his memory be a blessing (Le Vieux Manoir, Amboise), Emmanuel (Blois tourist office), Mathilde (Orléans tourist office) and Kingdao (Musée des Beaux-Arts, Orléans). My old friends Anny Monet and Patrick and Annick Rivière once again contributed invaluable insights in the Loire Valley. And the entire project would not have been possible without the extraordinary support (and patience) of my wife Rachel and our children Yair, Sasson and Talya.

REGIS ST LOUIS

Countless chefs, winemakers, baristas, innkeepers, guides and others helped along the way – and I am deeply grateful to the warmhearted people in the south of France. Special thanks to Daniel Bolger for bringing me on board, and my fellow co-authors for a much-needed morale boost during a difficult research period. Thanks especially to the support of Cassandra and daughters Magdalena and Genevieve, who share my deep love for this extraordinary country.

RYAN VER BERKMOES

Many thanks to Dan Bolger at LP who kept us on course with kindness and understanding throughout a project that fully reflected the turbulent times during which it was completed. And thanks to all the rest of the people at LP, especially those that have moved on, for their collective centuries of experience and remarkable passion for producing the world's best guidebooks. And nothing but love for Alexis Averbuck, the best reward I could imagine after 23 years and 133 books for LP.

NICOLA WILLIAMS

Heartfelt *bisous* to the many friends and professionals who aided and abetted in tracking down the very best in and around Bordeaux, on the Atlantic Coast and in French Basque Country, including Basque-born Paris-based photographer Puxan Chawla-Bhowmick (@ puxanphoto), Tristane de La Presle (Pauillac), Claire Payen (St-Émilion), Stuart Butler (Pyrenees), Ann Menschel (Villa Anvers in Guéthary), Sylvia Sabes (Biarritz) and chef Dominic Quirke (Pickles, Nantes). Kudos to my always-fabulous co-writers and trilingual 'France-en-famille' research team, Matthias, Niko, Mischa and Kaya Luefkens.

ACKNOWLEDGE-MENTS

Climate map data adapted from Peel MC, Finlayson BL & McMahon TA (2007) 'Updated World Map of the Köppen-Geiger Climate Classification', *Hydrology and Earth System Sciences*, 11, 1633–44.

Cover image: Hunawihr, Alsace, Rasto SK/Shutterstock ©

INDEX

N

O

P

RYAN VER BERKMOES

Ryan has written more than 110 guidebooks for Lonely Planet. He grew up in Santa Cruz, California, which he left at age 17 for college in the Midwest, where he first discovered snow. All joy of this novelty soon wore off. Since then he has been travelling the world, both for pleasure and for work, which are often indistinguishable. He has covered everything from wars to bars – though he definitely prefers the latter. Ryan calls New York City home. Read more at ryanverberkmoes.com and at @ryanvb. His byline has appeared in scores of publications, and he's talked travel on the radio and TV.

NICOLA WILLIAMS

Border-hopping is a way of life for British writer, runner, foodie, art aficionado and mum-of-three Nicola Williams who has lived in a French village on the southern side of Lake Geneva for more than a decade. Nicola has authored more than 50 guidebooks on Paris, Provence, Rome, Tuscany, France, Italy and Switzerland for Lonely Planet and covers France as a destination expert for the *Telegraph*. She also writes for the *Independent*, *Guardian*, lonelyplanet.com, *French Magazine*, *Cool Camping France* and others. Catch her on the road on Twitter and Instagram at @tripalong.

CATHERINE LE NEVEZ

Catherine's wanderlust kicked in when she roadtripped across Europe from her Parisian base aged four, and she's been hitting the road at every opportunity since, travelling to some 60 countries and completing her Doctorate of Creative Arts in Writing, Masters in Professional Writing, and postgrad qualifications in Editing and Publishing along the way. Over the past decade-and-a-half she's written scores of Lonely Planet guides and articles covering Paris, France, Europe and far beyond. Her work has also appeared in numerous online and print publications. Topping Catherine's list of travel tips is to travel without any expectations.

CHRISTOPHER PITTS

Born in the year of the Tiger, Chris's first expedition in life ended in failure when he tried to dig from Pennsylvania to China at the age of six. Hardened by reality but still infinitely curious about the other side of the world, he went on to study Chinese in university, living for several years in Kunming and Shanghai. A chance encounter in an elevator led to a Paris relocation, where he lived with his wife and two children for over a decade before the lure of Colorado's sunny skies and outdoor adventure proved too great to resist.

DANIEL ROBINSON

Over the past three decades, Daniel has worked on scores of Lonely Planet projects, including the first editions of *Vietnam*, *Cambodia* and *Paris* (the latter two co-authored with Tony Wheeler) and 13 of the 14 editions of France, researched in rain, sleet, snow and – when he's lucky – the kind of luminous sunlight that inspired the post-Impressionists. Daniel's travel writing has appeared in *National Geographic Traveler*, the *New York Times* and the *Los Angeles Times* and has been translated into 10 foreign languages. His twitter handle is @RobinsonEnRoute.

REGIS ST LOUIS

Regis grew up in a small town in the American Midwest – the kind of place that fuels big dreams of travel – and he developed an early fascination with foreign dialects and world cultures. He spent his formative years learning Russian and a handful of Romance languages, which served him well on journeys across much of the globe. Regis has contributed to more than 50 Lonely Planet titles, covering destinations across six continents. His travels have taken him from the mountains of Kamchatka to remote island villages in Melanesia, and to many grand urban landscapes. When not on the road, he lives in New Orleans.

GREGOR CLARK

Gregor Clark is a US-based writer whose love of foreign languages and curiosity about what's around the next bend have taken him to dozens of countries on five continents. Chronic wanderlust has also led him to visit all 50 states and most Canadian provinces on countless road trips through his native North America.

MARK ELLIOT

Mark Elliott had already lived and worked on five continents when, in the pre-Internet dark ages, he started writing travel guides. He has since authored (or co-authored) around 70 books including dozens for Lonely Planet. He also acts as a travel consultant, occasional tour leader, video presenter, public speaker, art critic, wine taster, interviewer and blues harmonicist.

STEVE FALLON

Steve, who worked on the first nine editions of Lonely Planet's *France,* returned to the 'the Hexagon' for this guidebook to update the Brittany section, where he drank copious amounts of *sistr* (cider), ate lots of *kouign-amann* (calorific 'butter cake') and added basic *brezhoneg* (Breton) to his list of languages.

ANITA ISALSKA

Anita Isalska is a travel journalist and digital content strategist. After several merry years as a staff writer and editor – a few of them in Lonely Planet's London office – Anita now works freelance between California, the UK, and any French mountain lodge with wi-fi. Anita specialises in Eastern and Central Europe, Australia, France, and her adopted home, San Francisco. Read her stuff on www.anitaisalska.com.

OLIVER BERRY

Oliver Berry is a writer and photographer from Cornwall. He has worked for Lonely Planet for more than a decade and has worked on more than 30 guidebooks. He is also a regular contributor to many newspapers and magazines and his writing has won several awards, including the Guardian Young Travel Writer of the Year and the *TNT Magazine* People's Choice Award. His latest work is published at www.oliverberry.com.

CELESTE BRASH

Like many California natives, Celeste now lives in Portland, Oregon. She arrived however after 15 years in French Polynesia, a year and a half in Southeast Asia and a stint teaching English as a second language (in an American accent) in Brighton, England – among other things. She's been writing guidebooks for Lonely Planet since 2005 and her travel articles have appeared in publications from *BBC Travel* to *National Geographic*. She's writing a book about her five years on a remote pearl farm in the Tuamotu Atolls and is represented by the Donald Maass Agency, New York.

STUART BUTLER

Stuart has been writing for Lonely Planet for a decade and during this time he's come eye to eye with gorillas in the Congolese jungles, met a man with horns on his head who could lie in fire, huffed and puffed over snowbound Himalayan mountain passes, interviewed a king who could turn into a tree, and had his fortune told by a parrot. Oh, and he's met more than his fair share of self-proclaimed gods. When not on the road for Lonely Planet he lives on the beautiful beaches of Southwest France with his wife and two young children.

JEAN-BERNARD CARILLET

Jean-Bernard is a Paris-based freelance writer and photographer who specialises in Africa, France, Turkey, the Indian Ocean, the Caribbean and the Pacific. He loves adventure, remote places, islands, outdoors, archaeological sites, food and, of course Paris, his home. His insatiable wanderlust has taken him to 119 countries across six continents, and it shows no sign of waning. It has inspired many articles and photos for travel magazines and some 100 Lonely Planet guidebooks, both in English and in French.

OUR WRITERS

OUR STORY

A beat-up old car, a few dollars in the pocket and a sense of adventure. In 1972 that's all Tony and Maureen Wheeler needed for the trip of a lifetime – across Europe and Asia overland to Australia. It took several months, and at the end – broke but inspired – they sat at their kitchen table writing and stapling together their first travel guide, *Across Asia on the Cheap*. Within a week they'd sold 1500 copies. Lonely Planet was born.

Today, Lonely Planet has offices in the US, Ireland and China, with a network of more than 2000 contributors in every corner of the globe. We share Tony's belief that 'a great guidebook should do three things: inform, educate and amuse'.

ALEXIS AVERBUCK

Alexis Averbuck has travelled and lived all over the world, from Sri Lanka to Ecuador, Zanzibar and Antarctica. In recent years she's lived on the Greek island of Hydra, in the wilds of NYC, and on the California coast. For Lonely Planet she explores the cobbled lanes of Rome and the azure seas of Sardinia, samples oysters in Brittany and careens through hill-top villages in Provence; and adventures along Iceland's surreal lava fields, sparkling fjords and glacier tongues. She's also a painter – visit www. alexisaverbuck.com – and promotes travel and adventure on video and television.

JOE BALSAM

Joel Balsam is a Montreal-based freelance journalist and travel guidebook writer who has spent years living and working remotely across the globe (51 countries and counting). For Lonely Planet, he has worked on guidebooks for *France, Armenia* and *Morocco*. He has also written for *National Geographic, TIME, the Guardian, BBC Travel, Travel + Leisure, Thrillist* and more. When in Canada and the US, Joel and his partner, photographer Stephanie Foden, love road tripping in their 1987 Chevy RV and exploring lesser-known places.

 MORE WRITERS

Published by Lonely Planet Global Limited
CRN 554153
3rd edition – Oct 2022
ISBN 978 1 7865 762 5 5
© Lonely Planet 2022 Photographs © as indicated 2022
10 9 8 7 6 5 4 3 2 1
Printed in China